The Good, The Bad, and THE CRAZY

(NO ONE'S EVER CALLED ME BORING)

ABOUT THE AUTHOR

The author entered a 6-year-accelerated BS/MD program (Bachelor of Science and Medical School degrees) with Rensselaer Polytechnic Institute (R.P.I.) and Albany Medical College.

(Dr. Duke operating on a cataract patient)

The author became a medical doctor at the age of twenty-three.

Dr. Mary Ann Duke originally is from Johnson City, N.Y. where she was the valedictorian of both her junior and senior high school classes. Additionally, President of the National Honor Society; President of the Key Club; Most valuable player (M.V.P.) of Track and Tennis; and winner of the first Army R.O.T.C. 10 K at Rensselaer Polytechnic Institute.

Throughout her education, the author was well-rounded and played the piano, tenor sax and sang in her church and school select choirs. The author was always very highly regarded by her teachers and peers. (The boys even let "Dukie" quarterback their touch football team!)

Upon graduation from Albany Medical College, she was awarded the coveted Dean's Senior Research Award and the only recipient of the Sandoz Award for Excellence in Ophthalmology.

By the age of thirty, she became a board-certified ophthalmologist and started her solo private practice in Potomac, MD, a beautiful and prestigious suburb of Washington, D.C. She was granted privileges at the world-renowned Johns Hopkins' Wilmer Eye Institute and operated on many difficult eye surgeries from cataracts, retinal tears and diabetic retinopathy to LASIK. Her patients were Who's Who of the Washington Metropolitan social register of important persons.

In almost fifteen years of solo private practice, Dr. Duke never hurt any patients' sight nor ever came close to a lawsuit. (The average physician is sued every seven years in America.)

Small town Czechoslovakian girl, first doctor in her family and only one, still, moved to the big city and did just fine…until…

Baba and I on my medical school graduation day

The Good, The Bad, and THE CRAZY

(NO ONE'S EVER CALLED ME BORING)

Mary Ann Duke, M.D.

Duke, M.D. Literary Enterprises, L.L.C.

Copyright © 2006, 2008 and 2009 by
Mary Ann Duke, M.D.
President, Duke, M.D. Literary Enterprises, L.L.C.

First Edition

Duke, M.D. Literary Enterprises, L.L.C.

www.thegoodthebadandthecrazy.com

Cover designed by Sarena Norton Design, L.L.C.

All rights reserved. No part of this publication may be reproduced, stored in retrieval system, or transmitted, in any form or by any means, electronic, mechanical, photocopying, recording, or otherwise, without the written prior permission of the author.

ISBN - 978-0-6152701-6-6

Library of Congress Control Number: 2009900931

Printed in the United States of America

DEDICATION

This book is dedicated to my angels from heaven, my children, and my dear grandmother I called Baba.

Also, I dedicate this book to my heroic and sensitive friend Dr. Amy Castillo, M.D., who has endured the unendurable.

MARY ANN DUKE, M.D.
EYE PHYSICIAN AND SURGEON

EDUCATION

Bachelor of Science, Biology, Rensselaer Polytechnic Institute (Six-year accelerated Biomedical Program)	1979-1983
Doctor of Medicine, Albany Medical College	1981-1985

MEDICAL TRAINING

Transitional Medical Internship Hackensack Medical Center, Hackensack, New Jersey	1985-1986
Ophthalmology Residency Albany Medical College, Department of Ophthalmology Albany, New York	1986-1989

HONORS

Dean's Senior Research Award	1985
Sandoz Award for Excellence in Ophthalmology	1985

BOARD CERTIFICATION

American Academy of Ophthalmology	1991

PAST PROFESSIONAL AFFILIATIONS

American Academy of Ophthalmology
Maryland Society of Eye Physicians and Surgeons
Sigma Xi Research Foundation
Montgomery County Medical Society
Medical and Chirurgical Faculty of Maryland
(Representative of Med Chi to Maryland State Legislature)

PAST HOSPITAL STAFF PRIVILEGES

Johns Hopkins University Hospital, The Wilmer Eye Center
Suburban Hospital
Shady Grove Adventist Hospital
George Washington University Hospital
Holy Cross Hospital
Washington Adventist Hospital

PROFESSIONAL SPECIALITIES

Refractive Eye Surgery, Excimer Laser including LASIK
Cataracts and Implants
Glaucoma Treatment
Eyelid Surgeries including Cosmetic Blepharoplasty
All laser Surgeries for Diabetic Retinopathy, Retinal Tears, Glaucoma, and S/P Cataract Surgery
Retinal Pathology
Children's Eye Problems
Complete Contact Lens Service
All Routine General Ophthalmology

PUBLICATIONS

Duke, M.A., R.M. Webb, and R.A. Catalano: "A New Rapid Immunoperoxidase Diagnostic Staining of herpes Simplex Virus I Indolent Corneal Ulcer." Cornea, Vol. 3, No. 2 (1984), pp. 115-118.

Catalano, R.A., R.M. Webb, R.S. Smith, and M.A. Duke: "Immunoperoxidase Method for Rapid Diagnosis of Herpes Simplex I Ocular Investigations." Investigative Ophthalmology and Visual Science, Vol. 25 No. 3 (May 1984) p.26.

Webb, R.M., and M.A. Duke: "Bacterial Infection of a Neurotrophic Cornea in An Immunocompromised Subject." Cornea, Vol. No. 1 (1985-1986). Pp. 14-18. Presented at the Albany ophthalmology Update (August 1984).

Catalano, R.A., R.M. Webb, M.A. Duke, And R.S. Smith: "A Modified Immunoperoxidase Method for Rapid Diagnosis of Herpes Simplex Keratitis." American Journal of Clinical Pathology, Vol. 86 (July 1986), pp. 102-104.

Duke, M.A., R.M. Webb, and R.A. Catalano: "A New Rapid Immunoperoxidase Diagnostic Staining of herpes Simplex Virus I Indolent Corneal Ulcer.: Yearbook of Ophthalmology, (1986) pp. 93-94

Krohel, G.B., M.A. Duke, and M. Mehu: Bloody Tears Associated with Familial Telangiectasis." Archives of Ophthalmology, Vol. 105 (1987) p. 1489.

Duke, M.A. "An Unusual Presentation of Epithelial Ingrowth." Presented at the Albany Ophthalmology Update (May 1987).

AUTHOR'S NOTE

Some of the names have been changed to protect the innocent.

Some of the names have been changed to protect the guilty, but *you know who you are.*

The Appendix and Documentation sections are both all real people with real names.

TABLE OF CONTENTS

Chapter 1
My Ninth Life   1

Chapter 2
Dear Baba   21

Chapter 3
My Angels from Heaven   29

Chapter 4
Magnificent Martyrdom   43

Chapter 5
Forward to After Court in the Small Gray Cell   71

Chapter 6
My Roommates   83

Chapter 7
Growing Up a "Good Girl"   93

Chapter 8
Becoming a Doctor   105

Chapter 9
What Next?   123

Chapter 10
Forward to Seven Locks Jail and the Alleged "Killer"   139

Chapter 11
MORE COURT   153

Chapter 12
Dreams, Back to the Spring Before the Separation
And Divorce (4 years Before Jail)   163

Chapter 13
Mother's Day and Turning FORTY   175

Chapter 14
Just the Facts, Ma'am   191

Chapter 15
911 and Baby Bliss   213

Chapter 16
More Reports   229

Chapter 17
My Children, My Life   241

Chapter 18
My Major Medical Mistake   261

Chapter 19
WHY?   273

Chapter 20
Persevering Can Be Painful   283

Chapter 21
Out of Control   297

Chapter 22
The Maryland Medical Board   307

Chapter 23
Papers, Cars and Candy (Six weeks after the
Board hearing, May, 2005)   313

Chapter 24
The Few Months Before Jail — 323

Chapter 25
"Real" Jail, Seven Locks and on to Clarksburg — 337

Chapter 26
HELP! — 351

Chapter 27
Gray to Tan to Yellow...and I like RED — 367

Chapter 28
Nice Inmates and Those Not So Nice and...Napoleon — 377

Chapter 29
Breaking Every Rule For My Children Risking "Hell/Cell" — 395

Chapter 30
"Real" Work — 409

Chapter 31
WILD AND CRAZY — 415

Epilogue — 423

Appendix A — 443

Appendix B-H — 449

Documentation — 463

Chapter 1

My Ninth Life

My attorney looks like the "Wizard of Oz", thus I nicknamed him the "Wizard". It's an apropos nickname too, because he's a self-proclaimed magician in court. But the movie's wizard was taller and thinner than my wizard attorney, didn't sport copious hair plugs, or wear suspenders that pulled taut across a huge gut. I view all of this now as my friend Jane and I approach him. I'm late again for court, of course my fault.

It's not like I'm arriving to the operating room a few minutes late. The eye surgery can't begin without the eye surgeon, right? Appearing in court late is different; a late defendant angers the Judge, not to mention one's Wizard even though he can simply bill more. Late for court is "ka-ka", an old Upstate New York term, especially for an educated doctor. Doctors are expected to know better, and are held to that higher standard.

I dread going to court. I always seem to lose, *by a lot*.

Entering a courtroom to me is like trying to win a track race on a pair of poorly fitted crutches, one big crutch for being a doctor and the other for being a strong woman. By the time *I* get passed the baton, it's a tremendous haul to catch up and win against whomever the plaintiff.

Life has been quite the hard race. Sometimes I think I must be part feline; I've run through at least eight lives and should have been a corpse many moons ago. Instead I luckily land on my feet, no matter how badly wounded and keep persevering relentlessly. Anyone who knows me knows I never give up. Bring it on!

This morning, however, on my way to defend myself from going to jail, I'm feeling a little down on my luck, tired and very afraid. (Did I just think "Bring it on"? Yikes!) Calm down, stay "cool", c'mon Mary Ann, I encourage myself as I push my shoulders back and walk into the stuffy vestibule outside of the courtroom as proudly as I can.

I introduce the Wizard to Jane and they shake hands. Jane is my born again Christian girlfriend who never swears, doesn't have sex and never even drinks real coffee. Jane offered to drive me to court after Edward, my soon-to-be-*ex*-boyfriend told me he couldn't, because he had an "important meeting at work". I wanted to punch him last night for picking a fight with me and leaving me alone just before the hearing. Luckily for Edward, he laid rubber on my driveway before getting mangled. Such a great guy. Most likely he was craving a scotch, but I certainly could have used a good dose of multiple orgasmic therapy, no doubt, especially if I get locked up for a while. Oh well, to hell with him. I should have known better about him a long time ago.

My luck with men thus far has not been good; maybe it will be in my next life. Ah, Jane can handle court better than "Prince" Edward (I call him behind his British back), anyway. Her husband hung himself while she was trying to have his baby. She was hoping to be pregnant even after his suicide but remains childless. If Jane could handle that, she can handle anything.

"You look just right," the Wizard compliments me.

"Thanks, wish I felt it. I hate this boring brown suit. My pumps already hurt and I didn't wear any makeup."

"You're fine." (I *hate* that word. The acronym for F.I.N.E. from rehab is "fucking insecure, neurotic, and emotional".)

"Oh, really? Then why did your secretary call me yesterday to tell me to be sure to refill any medications I might be on?" I fire back.

I know the Wizard thinks I talk too fast so he always pauses, but this pause I don't like. Jane and I exchange a quick look. Oh God, her pupils are dilated. She's anxious, too; that's a sure sign.

"Just a precaution. Listen, I've struck a great deal with the State's Attorney. They are going to 'Nolle Prosequi' most of your charges."

I can hear people walking and talking around us but all I can do is stare down my Wizard's hair and fire back, "What's 'Nolle Prosequi'?"

"They aren't going to prosecute you for them."

"Why not? How'd you pull *that* off?"

"I just did. But you do have to plead guilty to a few charges, because you *are* guilty, you do understand me?" All of a sudden I feel very hot and I'm usually cold. I'd rather be operating on my ten most difficult cases than standing in this stuffy basement of a courthouse waiting to see a Judge. Or maybe I just want to go back outside, breathe the biting November air and feel free.

I am still in complete shock that me, a respected ophthalmologist and a good, God-fearing small town girl is in so much trouble. But I am, and I shouldn't be, not *this* much, after so much hard work. I had to pull the Wizard's measly fee, $15,000.00, off the trees in my yard. It was back-breaking work all by myself, but there's nothing green in the bank. All my savings are gone and only a few credit cards with space left. I abused alcohol during my divorce and lost my life's work along with custody of my precious children! For God's sake, why do I have to plead guilty to anything except "temporary insanity", which is exactly what it was?!

"You have three DUIs and three DWIs, and several other charges, remember?" the Wizard states. I barely nod and look toward my friend. Jane's eyes are as wide as saucers; they show real concern.

He now boasts, "I got the State's Attorney to agree to drop two of the DUIs, if you plead guilty to one of them, and the other two will be reduced to DWIs." I am confused and blankly stare at my attorney. It's too noisy in this hallway. What did he just say? What kind of options are those, I ask myself. I hired the Wizard because he told me his record for "NO Jail Time" was defending a man with *seven* DUIs, and the Wizard helped write the traffic laws for the State of Maryland. (So who better knows how to defend them *or navigate* around them?)

The Wizard runs an impatient hand through his hair probably to refrain from chastising me with a squeeze on the cheek. "I know I've already explained this to you. The meaning of DUI is different now. A DUI is 'driving under the influence', and a DWI is not 'driving while intoxicated', but 'driving while impaired.' A DUI is a much harsher charge than a DWI." (In reality, the blood alcohol level for DUI is .1 and for DWI .08.)

"I'm sure you told me, but that was before I went away to rehab for four months, remember? I've only been home two weeks. I can't keep your legal mumbo jumbo straight! Medical jargon is enough for me, and anyway, I've been trusting your negotiating skills to get me off, because I *did* do that jail-like rehab for so long." The Wizard is a wee bit annoyed with me, but hides it well, as he should for $15,000 dollars. "Okay," I say to him, "please, go on."

"A first DUI can mean up to a year in jail, two more DUIs with all of your other charges could be much longer... years." The Wizard has totally stunned me now, and I can feel my heart beating hard in my chest. "I got the two other DUIs reduced to DWIs, and the sentences to run concurrent."

"Sentences can run concurrently?!" I'm lost again and Jane looks at me bewildered.

"*Concurrent*" the Wizard retorts. "All three sentences run at the same time, instead of one after the other, so time is served for all of them at once. We (meaning the judicial system, I presume) do this all the time." That makes *no* sense to me whatsoever, overlapping jail time for different arrests? But I'll take it, no argument here.

"The State's Attorney will 'Nolle Prosequi' everything else, and she is recommending suspending six months of your sentence, so the most you will serve is six months, and I'm trying to get you home confinement."

"*Trying* to get me home confinement? I thought that was a given. I'll stay locked in my bedroom for decades, but could I still go to jail for a whole year?"

"Honey, I told you I'm trying to keep you out of jail."

The Wizard didn't answered my question.

"You are going to stress... that four month, thirty thousand dollars plus jail-like rehab time I spent?"

"Of course."

"Is my judge a woman?"

"No."

"Damn. Do you know him?"

"Yes."

"Is he nice?"

"It's Judge Collins. He's retired, but they call him in when they get really busy." That wasn't the answer to my question either, but at this point I finally realize that the show must go on.

"Great, listen, I won't talk back. You just keep me out of jail."

"That's what I'm trying to do, honey, but remember, when you're asked if you plead guilty to one DUI and two DWIs, the answer is 'yes.' We're not coming back to court, because we'll never get such a good deal on an appeal. An appeal could get you *several* years. Now c'mon, we've got to go in."

I look at Jane. She read my mind. The Wizard did not answer my most important questions and scared the hell out of me with that "several years" comment. Jane looks freaked out. It's the "fight or flight" response, a rush of adrenaline causing dilated pupils, increased heart rate and more blood flow to the muscles, readying one to flee from danger. I want to sprint home in my stockings but no such luck. I slowly follow the Wizard into the oppressive courtroom, as noisy and crowded as the hallway.

Dear God, I think for the zillionth time; how could I let such a horrible thing happen to get me into so much trouble?

*   *   *

It is a full house, just before 1:00 p.m. Terrific, I didn't want a front row seat anyway.

Geez, what a zoo this is. It's not like in the movies where everyone is sitting straight in their chairs, looking perfectly starched and powdered. This courtroom seems *un*orderly to me. People talking, slouching, not too well-dressed, and others scurrying around like they had ants in their pants. I figure the "ants-in-pantsers" are the attorneys, still striking deals, as the Wizard calls it.

Everything seems so surreal, but it isn't. It's REAL. I really *am* in court, really charged with three DUIs, three DWIs, and three times three, nine other charges that my wizard attorney somehow made disappear up and away, like a balloon from Oz. I wish I was anywhere else but in this room. I let my mind wander for a minute. It's certainly not like the disciplined, organized, sterile perfection of the operating room in here, not one little bit. But who expects organized, disciplined perfection from lawyers anyway? *Only doctors are expected to be perfect.*

Lawyers have the luxury of not having to be perfect. They lose cases all the time and still get paid in full, or they sue you for it. So you can pay another attorney to represent yourself against the attorney who's suing you. What a racket! And if you're *my* Wizard, you get paid up front. I asked him in his office if I could pay a percentage, with the rest to follow after the case, and he bluntly stated, "No. We take Visa and MasterCard." One hundred and eighty degrees different from medicine, where a surgeon has to wait at least thirty days to get paid after the operation. Then, if the surgery doesn't go well, an attorney's letter arrives causing chest pain. Mine's feeling tight right now for the first time in my life.

I look up as his Honor enters the courtroom, "All Rise." *Uh, oh*, honorable Judge Collins doesn't look like he's in a very good mood. I whisper to Jane, "He looks grumpy and stern."

"Shhh, he's a Judge."

We were supposed to be in court at one o'clock, but I guess so was everyone else. Something makes me turn my head. There's Alma, my 72-year-old AA sponsor, with her Amish-looking boyfriend Henry and his scraggly beard. She smiles at me. God bless Alma, she did come, after all, to support me like she said she would. She also brought a girlfriend of hers who had been through this before. I smile gratefully at all of them. Three other people here to support me besides Jane and the Wizard, who was paid to show up, but no boyfriend because he had an "important" meeting. Damn it. Why didn't I call all my grateful patients to come and pack this place with fans? Too late now, Mary Ann, they probably wouldn't have believed it was true anyway. Plus I couldn't ask the big Duke family to drive down, because there aren't enough people in this room who know CPR if I *do* go to jail.

I should have taken a second 800 mg of ibuprofen for my pounding head if not my heart.

Judge Collins bangs his gavel, "Order in the Court!" Everyone grabs a seat but still do not shut up. This is "order"? I think again about the organized clean and quiet of the operating room and really miss it.

My daydreaming is being crushed by the insanity around me. Judge Collins, I'm sure, didn't have sex last night either, or last week. Perhaps, not even in the last six years. Everyone seems to be leaving in handcuffs! But the other people ahead of me have done *very* bad things. Yeah right, Mary Ann, like it's okay to drink and drive. Stupid ass. I certainly wouldn't have done it if I was in my right mind, or even if I was *in* my mind at all… Three blackouts. I don't remember a single minute of any one of them. I just remember waking up in a hospital with horrendously tight bed ties on all four limbs. They were the same type of restraints that I've helped put on "difficult" patients, who were combative and wild from drugs or just plain old craziness while in med school. I never thought I'd have the "pleasure" of experiencing such humiliating torture firsthand.

Oh my God, I could have died in any one of those wrecks or killed someone else. God spared me. (I think He really wants me to write about all of this since He knows what a great challenge it will be.)

"Let's go!" the Wizard nudges me. I didn't hear my name called at all. Shit, this is it!

I turn to Jane and give her my purse with my medication in it. She gives me a weak smile and hands me the speech the Wizard had me prepare. It's a heartfelt monologue about being an upstanding citizen of the community, very regretful, a good mother, eye surgeon and extensive rehab. I am chagrined that my life had taken such a turn.

The State's Attorney and my Wizard exchange banter with Judge Collins. The Wizard introduces me to the Judge and he replies, "Yes, I *know* Dr. Duke."

What? I think. I've never seen him before; how does he think he knows me? How does he know me? Damn. I've been in this Montgomery County court system for *way* too long and must be becoming famous or infamous, neither by choice.

I hate courtrooms with a passion. I always seem to lose to the "good ole' boys" sitting on the bench. So many multiple court appearances for my divorce and custody battles that probably every judge in Montgomery County knows Dr. Duke in Potomac. (The "Beverly Hills of

Washington, D.C." as I call it, certainly a lot different than where I grew up in Upstate NY.)

Still, I am amazed that even a semi-retired judge like Judge Collins has heard of me since this is the first time I am in his courtroom because I broke the law. Immediately, a feeling of cold doom surrounds me, and I stand shivering slightly as I break a sweat. Why am I not just a Susie Homemaker right now? Why do I always stand out a little? Just because Dad taught me to march to my own beat and people don't like that? Is it better to meander with the herd like most?

The Wizard nudges me hard in the ribs. Ow! Oh, it must be his signal to read my speech along with a sideway's glance. I hold my speech up and read it proudly and loudly, like I always speak. "I am a respectable member of the community, a caring physician and mother…" Glancing up, I see Judge Collins looking down, but not at me. I think, damn... he's not listening to a single word.

The drivers of the two cars I sideswiped before totaling my 750iL BMW, at least 50 miles per hour into a tree in my third and final DUI, now have their turn to speak. The first woman appears in her seventies and speaks softly: "She crossed over the line and hit my car near the front." The woman is not speaking in an angry tone at all. I look at both women with great compassion and remorse.

The second woman is something more.

"I didn't get hurt, but she crossed over into my lane so fast, and if she had hit me just a little further back, *she would have KILLED me!* I don't care about jail, but *I never want her to drive AGAIN!"*… For the first time all afternoon, the courtroom went dead silent.

The Wizard turns his face up to mine with now a twist in his hair plugs and rolls his eyes. Honorable Judge Collins' face muscles tightened. Everyone in this courtroom can easily see his wrath and I am only a few feet away. My vision is great, even though my hearing is going a little in my 40's, but *this* lady, I'm quite sure, was heard outside the building and well across the street. (I have to agree with her, though, I'll *never drive again,* just don't make me go to jail!)

I look down. Oh Sweet Jesus, the Wizard looks none too pleased either. His Honor barks at the State's Attorney for her recommendation. She recites, "The State wants to impose a one year sentence for DUI with six months suspended, and sixty days for each DWI to run concurrent, and for the plea bargain to be binding." As always, I can't follow the legal mumbo jumbo. There are many 'Nolle Prosecuis', but my adrenal glands squeeze tightly yet again at that "one year sentence" part; it makes my ears start ringing deafeningly loud.

My low blood pressure has just skyrocketed.

Judge Collins turns his seems to me angry face to the Wizard and I. The Wizard is a smooth talker, as he should be. "Dr. Duke has taken tremendous strides, your Honor. She understands the seriousness of her offenses. These offenses occurred, however, during a blackout period... Her use of alcohol was greatly exacerbated...", and the Wizard winds on doing a decent job, I think.

"We would appreciate credit for the four months she has undergone rehabilitation at the renowned Talbott Recovery Center, in Atlanta. Dr. Duke paid for her treatment at great expense. I have here the records of her successful recovery from her doctor including all negative random urine alcohol and drug screens...", and the Wizard is still speaking, but the ringing in my ears is so loud, as I watch Judge Collins' increasing scowl, that I can't understand him anymore.

His Honor does not hesitate with his reply, but I can't hear it! I can only hear bits and pieces. Judge Collins is seemingly tongue thrashing the State's Attorney and the Wizard and me all at once. That's all I can tell. OhMyGOD! It sounds like he's going along with the State's Attorney's recommendations! He's not going to credit me the four months of rehab? Why not? *It* was like jail! Six months? Six months with possibly six more and probation for three years??? Yes, that's what he said.

I poke the Wizard in *his* ribs and hiss "What about home confinement?" The Wizard requests, "Would your Honor consider home confinement?" Before I could begin to hope for it, His Honor belched a resounding "NO!" and he finishes his tongue thrashing with: "Don't you ever bring another case like this into my courtroom again!"

I hear that last part, along with the loud "NO!" But now I'm totally numb and lightheaded. I feel like I might pass out. I've never fainted over anything. All of a sudden I'm pissed off too, and I complain to the Wizard, "Is *this* what I paid you fifteen thousand dollars for!?" He doesn't even look up at me.

Some "Magician", huh?

*   *   *

The State's Attorney is trying to get my attention. I can't hear her. I can't hear again! "What?!" I yell. She asks me something about my "free and voluntary plea of guilty" to something or other. I glance at the Wizard who mouths "yes." It seems like she's asking me the same thing over and over again. She is…Oh my God, I'm doing it, I'm pleading guilty to three drunk driving charges and waiving my right to an appeal. Oh my dear God, I'm really going to jail!!...And I can't hear anything! Why can't I hear?!

Someone else is behind me, talking to me. I can't comprehend a word. Now they are roughly grabbing my arms from my sides and pulling them behind my back. I'm being handcuffed with a guard on either side!

The room is spinning. I can't hear a damned thing, and everyone's face is getting blurry. I stand proud, though, and turn around as I'm being led out of the courtroom to look at Jane one last time. There's Edward sitting next to her. He came. He *came after all.* I've always been a sucker for a broad-shouldered, good-looking man, but his big green eyes look so sad. His whole face looks terrible. It's too long and so very sad. I've never seen him look that way, not even at his mother's funeral. Jane looks like she's about to cry.

I'm being led away very fast.

But my brain feels like it's in slow motion. Like in a movie scene where the sound goes out and the camera slows everything down for emphasis. I see Alma. She looks terrible too. I've never seen faces look like hers and Edward's. I mouth, "I'm sorry" to her. I don't know why I do it, I just do. Maybe I'm really saying I'm sorry to Baba, my dear grandmother. Dear Baba, dear Baba help me. Pray for me up there. Pray for my babies. Please. I'm sorry!

I can't cry. I usually cry at the drop of a hat, but somehow I do not cry. "I need my medication," I tell the guards, as one is gripping either arm. They ignore me. "No, I *need* my medication." Since I am going to go jail, I am not going without my sleeping pills. Well, Mary Ann, looks like you are going to be sleep deprived yet another six months...dear God, in jail.

* * *

My vision is still blurry as I walk down a narrow hallway with my hands cuffed behind my back and a guard clutches either arm tightly. They lead me into a small elevator with them. It has two doors, and can barely hold a fourth person but a third guard squeezes in. WTF, I'm in a small cage. This is terrible. A cockatoo gets a bigger cage than this closet. My claustrophobia kicks in big time and I feel my throat tighten. We are going down, far down. To hell, I think, and this is my cagey casket of an elevator.

Damn, my blood pressure *must* be soaring with this pounding headache! But at least I'm getting some hearing back and my sight. And these damned tight pumps are going straight in the garbage when I get home. Yeah, right, *when* I get home. Oh fuck, these handcuffs hurt! They're way too tight! Why did they have to handcuff me anyway? I would have gone with them peaceably. I'm a well-respected doctor in the community, not some crazy criminal. I think, "This, Dr. Duke, is by far the most humiliating and disgusting day of your life. Grin and fucking bear it".

"This is Miss Duke." That's all the guard says. I'm dropped off, after finally getting out of that birdcage of an elevator, to face three different guards and a desk with monitors on it. It's like a nurses' station in a coronary care unit where the nurses watch patients' EKGs and vital signs; however, *these* monitors are watching caged humans.

One of the guards is a woman in a dark uniform, pants and shirt, same as the men. I don't see their weapons, but getting shot does not scare me now as much as going without sleep does. I know sleep deprivation from residency and having children and how horribly miserable it feels, and I'm going to need sleep to cope. "I need my medication that is back in the courtroom. Can someone please get it for me?" I ask her quietly. She doesn't even look up; she totally ignores me too. I'm not used to being ignored.

"Are you all deaf"?! I bitch to myself. And by the way, I'm *Dr.* Duke, not *Miss* Duke. Thinking too much Mary Ann, rein those thoughts in. Super, at least *my* brain is working again. Geez, I haven't been called Miss in over twenty years since graduating medical school. No, don't correct them on that, Mary Ann. Better to be a "Miss" in jail. Don't let anyone know that I am a doctor, or everyone will probably treat me harsher, make sure I get put down even harder. (At least that's been the Montgomery County Courts' M.O. for me.) Be a Miss for once. I usually correct people to call me Doctor because I earned it, but not today.

The sitting female guard looks up while the bigger of the two male guards produces a huge set of keys and takes my arm. Still no one speaks to me. I am led through a thick metal door into a small hallway, all gray. Gray cement floor with gray cement walls with no windows, and three cells with gray bars, much darker and mustier than any courtroom. Two women are sitting in each of the first two cells on a gray metal bench that is attached to the wall. They both are sitting on their own benches staring at the floor. One is in street clothes and the other in an ugly tan jumpsuit. Neither woman bothers to look up at me, as I stare in at them.

The guard opens the third cell door and pushes me in. "Turn around!" he barks. I turn around. He takes off my handcuffs, doesn't say another word to me, leaves, locks my cell, walks the short hallway, opens the big metal door, then slams and locks it again on the other side. I'm left standing there, just standing in a totally gray, ugly cell that's smaller than my bathroom at home. Immediately, I feel the worst claustrophobia ever.

I look at my bleak surroundings. I'm staring at a dinky gray metal sink, and a gray metal toilet jutting out of the gray cinderblock wall, with no cover and even no seat. "Good thing Mom taught me to always squat in public places", I think to myself.

I walk over to the tiny sink to get a sip of water. I'm so thirsty. Since I had sweated hard on the bike this morning, in a vain attempt to calm my nerves, I'm totally parched. The faucet, opened full bore, only lets out a trickle of lukewarm water. There are no paper cups in sight, not even a bar of soap. The trickle is so slight that I would have to touch the metal back of the sink if I wanted to cup some water in my hand. "Jesus Christ", I bitch to myself yet again (and I *always* hate myself for taking the Lord's name in vain), if the last person in here had A.I.D.S., that damned HIV virus can live for up to twenty-four hours on a moist surface, so don't touch that metal! Give it up, Mary Ann. They must bring you something to drink in this place and not expect you to put your mouth on that gross metal to reach that stupid trickle of a faucet.

At least I don't have to use the disgusting toilet right now because I'm dehydrated. I turn around and through the bars see the little red light of a camera. That's right. *Beautiful.* They're watching me on a monitor. Do they even watch me squat and pee? Oh God, they must! How fucking rude.

It really did happen. I am in jail. For six long months. *Oh... my... God!*

I sit on the cold, hard metal bench with no cushion whatsoever and put my head in my hands. I am going to go crazy in here. There isn't even enough *air* in here. One could probably lose their mind in six months.

I try to give myself a pep talk like I did before a track race in high school. You know, Mary Ann, it's not like you haven't been in a real jam before. But this is different; jail is not the real world. I can fight and stick up for myself in the real world, and that's enough of a bitch. In this shit-hole I've lost my freedom. I will have to be submissive and not talk back. Oh sweet Jesus, you know that's impossible for me.

My thoughts are everywhere at once. I tell myself, I can do it. I am Dr. Mary Ann Duke. Oh NO, my poor babies! *My poor babies!* They are going to be so unhappy. They don't deserve *any* of this!! My eyes well up with tears. I have to persevere. I have to, for them, and for me. Even if I go a little insane from claustrophobia, I have to get through this for them. Six months, six months, I can do *anything* for six months. Sure you can, Mary Ann, keep thinking that way. Look at what you've done before, and still come out smelling like a rose. Thank God it isn't a whole year and could have been. But look at this bloody awful cell. Even a God damned gerbil has a treadmill in his little cage.

Who is going to pay my bills while I'm in jail? Who is going to watch over my home? Edward moved out for good two years ago and went back to his Dad's home after his mom died to help his father. We have been fighting so much about his drinking, that I wouldn't dare trust him with power of attorney, even though he keeps nagging me for it. I'm almost out of credit card room, been putting the more than $8,000 grand mortgage, and every other bill on them, for months. My house didn't sell while I was in rehab, so I took it off the market two weeks ago to spend the holidays at home with my children and now this. How am I supposed to keep from losing the one thing I have left, my home?

Dear God, when am I going to see my babies again?! My poor, sweet children. Dear James only turned ten and is already acting like a little man, not like the little boy without troubles he should enjoy being. He's protective of his three little sisters. My dear baby girl Marika is only eight and looks the most like my side of the family with brown hair, big brown eyes and big smile. Marika is very positive and strong, but no little girl should have to endure this. Nadia is only six and a beauty, fair and blue eyed like her father, my ex-husband. But like me, marches firmly to her own beat already. Luckily she has Marika and James to watch over her.

But then there is three-year-old little Eloise, and she is all alone without siblings under the same roof to play with. Eloise is Edward's child, the soon-to-be-ex-boyfriend, not my ex-husband's child. (Just think of them like Dr. Seuss's "Thing 1" and "Thing 2"; they *cleaned me out* financially and emotionally.) They don't deserve the outstanding children I bore them, when all they did was annihilate my hard-earned financial resources and devastate all my dreams.

My eyes well up with tears again. I am going to miss each of my children desperately, my little angels from heaven. I hope some day they will understand more and forgive me. I certainly never meant to hurt them at all. I would give my life for any one of my little angels. I wipe my eyes with my sleeve. Those damned tight-lipped guards. I'm not going to give them the satisfaction of watching me cry!

I've not been in this cell ten minutes and I'm already starting to go out of my mind. So I start to pray, but not on my knees, not on this dirty gray floor, and not with those guards watching me.

Please, God, watch over my children. Give them strength, and please, help me to persevere, too.

Dear Baba, how did your little darling get to this point? We were always so positive, and strong and happy with our lives. *What the hell happened to mine?*

Chapter 2

Dear Baba

Baba was the kind of Grandmother that every little boy or girl should have. She was the perfect Baba. Everyone who knew her loved her. She spoiled her grandchildren absolutely rotten and always was ready with a joke and a huge smile. One of those smiles where her upper gums all showed over her perfect false teeth. Big dimples too, on beautiful wide Czechoslovakian cheekbones, so her whole face lit up when she smiled, and her dark brown eyes twinkled. She glowed with so much goodness, and wore such bright outfits, that you needed sunglasses 24/7 around her.

Three years before Baba died, we were drinking coffee in her cheery, red and white, crochet-laden kitchen, just talking. I could talk to her about anything. Men, sex, being a doctor, having babies, growing flowers, anything. Medka, she called me. That means "little Mary" in Slovak. She was Mary, my Mother was Mary, so I guess I was "little Mary", even though I'm much taller than either one. I do look like them though, with my brown hair, brown eyes and big smile.

"Medka, come here."

"What?"

"Come here, Honey, I want to give you something." Baba was hunched over, bending at the waist but not bending her knees at all, with her flat feet spread wide, furiously digging into some boxes in the bottom of her bedroom closet (a.k.a. "the vault").

She always bent over funny like that in her garden, too, for hours on end. I never could figure out how she stood up straight again, with no pain and not needing an emergency chiropractic adjustment. Baba was as round as she was tall at 4'9" and always dressed to the nines for church every Sunday, color coordinated from head to toe. Red was her favorite color. If she wore a red polyester dress to church, she accessorized with a red hat, stiletto red pointy pumps (which I don't know *how* she walked in), a red coat, and topped it all off by carrying a red patent leather purse. Baba even had long cotton white gloves, which she dyed herself in every color Ritz dye had to offer. I never saw her without matching gloves for church.

The finishing touch for Baba's ensemble was matching costume jewelry. *Loads* of it, fake ruby drop earrings, a crimson broach on her coat, red necklaces, many large, tacky rings (worn *over* her gloves) and even a fake ruby hat pin. Baba was poor but to her rich. She didn't have hardly any real jewelry but she certainly had tons of costume!

The only real jewelry she had were her beautiful garnets from Czechoslovakia. There were several pairs of gorgeous, dangling clip earrings with at least thirty garnets each, all magnificently hand-crafted in the age of the "flappers", and two necklaces suffused with stones like a princess would wear, along with a huge broach and three fabulous cocktail rings. I *loved* playing with Baba's jewelry and she knew it. She knew I loved jewelry just as much as she did.

"Baba, what are you doing? What have you got hiding in there *now*?"

"Just a minute, just a minute, I'll find it. Oh, here it is. Take it. I want you to have it."

It was the old red velvet box I always played with. Inside were all of Baba's precious garnets.

"Oh, Baba, they are so beautiful, but you can't give me *all* of them!"

"I want you to have them." Her smile was beaming from ear to ear.

"But Baba, you have three other granddaughters."

"I want you to have them. Just take them. I know you'll wear them." Her dark brown eyes were twinkling at me like they always did.

"But Baba..."

"Just take them and enjoy them, Medka."

"Thank you, Baba." I kissed her and hugged her for a long time. "Thank you very much." I felt all warm inside. Baba loved me. Baba loved me very much. I was her favorite. She was the one person in my life that loved me unconditionally, the one person in my life for whom I could do no wrong. I hope and pray to be just like her when I grow old.

Baba would have been so proud of my *real* jewelry collection. Being able to afford real gems would have meant success to her. It did to me, too, however, I shopped at estate sales instead of Tiffany's and bargain hunted. Baba would have loved both, the jewelry and been gleeful that "You found a great bargain, Medka!" I smile every time I think of her. *She* was a very rare gem. Wish I still had all of her precious garnets. Damn those thieves.

Later one spring, a few months before she died, Baba came to visit me when the cherry blossoms are blooming, the amazing azalea bushes are peaking, and the Washington, D.C. area is at its best. "Baba?"

"Yes Medka?"

"I'm over thirty now, and if I don't get married before I'm thirty-five, I'm going to go to Johns Hopkins Hospital's sperm bank and pick the best medical student's sperm I can find and have a baby."

Baba wasn't shocked. She just clasped her hands together, bowed her head, and shook it a little.

"It's okay, Baba. I want to be a perfect grandmother to my grandchild some day just like you are to me."

Baba had to look up and smile at *that* compliment.

Baba and Popsi were my Mother's parents. Baba was actually born here in Pennsylvania in 1910 and her sister in 1912, but my great-grandfather was involved in some kind of duel or bar-room brawl up in Canada (some imbibing was involved, I'm sure) and people got hurt including himself. The destitute and scared Maharovich (Baba's maiden name) family, with the patriarch suffering a knife wound, all high-tailed it back home to the Carpathian Mountains in Czechoslovakia or "Slovakia", as it is now split from the Czech Republic, when Baba was only two years old. Baba returned to America on a boat to Ellis Island from the "old country" when she was a teenager, an immigrant going back to her birthplace to claim her citizenship.

My father's family is from the same place. Talk about *in*breeding! Close breeding like that can be excellent or dangerous. It's bad because it is easier for the often disastrous, recessive genes to pair up and then be expressed. But inbreeding can be good, one can get a double-strong dose of a desired gene. The British believe in it. I don't know a pure-bred Brit that doesn't like to tell you about his "pedigree", I mean family tree. Certainly it's worked for all of the great racehorses. I sometimes think of myself as a "thoroughbred", albeit "Eastern Bloc". No wonder I've always been a little skittish.

Anyway, I was very happy when I found out my family name on my father's side was anglicized to Duke from Djubyk when they hit Ellis Island. How would anyone have even pronounced it, "Die, *byuck*"?! Yes, the "Dukes'" have come a long way. Most of my family is still in Slovakia, probably still picking potatoes for all I know. Thank God my grandparents left.

In 1928, when Baba was 18, the Russians came in and told her and her younger sister, "If you want to claim your U. S. citizenship, you have to leave now", so they did.

Wilkes Barre, Pennsylvania was where Baba's godmother lived, and godparents are important in the Russian Orthodox religion that we were all brought up in. One is supposed to help one's godchild. Well, sure, this distant relative took them in, *but* she also took over half of their salaries for room and board. Despite that, my Baba still sent money back to help her mother. Baba's father had died young from complications related to the stabbing, and she never saw him again.

"I was very poor, Medka. I wore the same black-laced shoes for seven years. I just kept getting them resoled," she confessed to me during one of our wonderfully intimate talks. "And my only pair of shoes often got soaked at work, so my feet were cold and wet for most of the day. I worked in the basement of a hospital laundering pukey, poopy, bloody hospital sheets and ironing doctors' lab coats." She continued telling me about her youth, having seen that I was fascinated with her story.

"One day I was delivering a doctor's lab coats to his room. I knocked and no one answered. I knocked again, but even if he had called out, I didn't know English. I opened the door and there was the doctor, 'hola hola' ('naked' in Slovak), on top of a young nurse." (A classic scenario and one of the perks of nursing school, if one wishes to partake.)

"Before I could leave," she told me, "he kicked the door so fast and so hard that it caught my right arm, my good arm. I had to iron lefty for months. It hurt so bad but I never saw a doctor for it. We didn't have the money." No x-ray. No pain pills. "Twenty years later," Baba said, "I had an x-ray of that arm for something else, and the doctor told me that my arm had been broken in two places!"

Baba was strong, *very* strong, both physically and in spirit. She had to be, just to leave her family and try to make it in America, taking care of her little sister without ever seeing her parents again. Even her parents returned to their homeland, having given up on the so-called "good life" in America.

It must have been working in that hospital, seeing the doctors strutting around in her perfectly starched lab coats, giving orders, helping people, saving lives, doing the most important thing anyone can do for another person, that inspired her conviction I should be a doctor.

"Be a doctor. Be a doctor, Medka, and you'll have a good life," she used to say. I heard that from as far back as I can remember. Over and over, "Be a doctor and you'll have a good life. It's a good thing to be a doctor. You'll get respect, and you'll make a good living. You're smart. You can do it. You will have a good life."

What would she say now? What the hell would she say now? Is it *still* a "good life"? And how did she know that I could even get into medical school? She finished sixth grade, and my parents finished high school, but no one had ever received a college degree in my family. Who said I could even get in?

Besides, I wanted to get married and have babies. Doesn't every little girl, at least once, think that it would be nice to have a child, even if they never want to be pregnant and go through giving birth? Even if they are gay? Even if they didn't like their mothers? I definitely wanted to get married and have children. *I wanted to get married and have babies more than I wanted to be a doctor.* Don't most women doctors feel like as I feel? Am I really so different? Do female physicians *really* want to be doctors and "save lives" *more* than they want to be a mother? Aren't they torn, if they do have a baby, and want to be a Mommy more than a doctor after the baby is born? Or do female physicians sacrifice being a mother, because it's so grueling and grinding to become a doctor, and the reality of the job is so demanding that they feel deep-down inside, that they wouldn't be able to handle it all? I think that's the answer for most.

Plus, it takes so damned long to become a doctor. Most students are at least twenty-six years old when they finish medical school, and the rest of their twenties and even half of their thirties can be flushed right down the toilet in a three to seven year residency. Add on one or two years for a fellowship to become a *real* specialist, and at least another five to ten years to get a good practice going, that a female physician can easily be forty by the time she can take a breath and *think* about having a baby, and now the poor gal's gettin' too old!

I wanted it all. Baba said I could have it all.

Baba said I would get "R.E.S.P.E.C.T." if I became a doctor and have a "GOOD LIFE".

Baba was wrong. Baba was very, very wrong.

I still don't know for sure, though, if she was so very wrong, wish I did.

Chapter 3

(10 years before court appearance for drunk driving arrest)

My Angels from Heaven

"Okay, push hard!" Nurse Christy encourages me for the hundredth time. Christ, I think, I *am*! (And I *really do* hate when the Lord's name in vain pops into my head.) I'm pushing so hard my fucking freckles are popping off! Oh dear God, there I go thinking in obscenities again. Do other women do it as often as me, or just men? Oh hell, I learned how to swear well in medical school.

I'm thirty-four-plus years old and have been pushing so hard for the last two hours and twelve minutes that, along with a clear complexion, there'll probably be thirty hemorrhoids hanging off my ass like a cluster of grapes when this is over.

In great physical shape from my running and lifting program, which I put on hold my last trimester, I certainly know what the word "PUSH" means. I've been pushing myself since I started varsity girls' track as the only eighth grader ever on the team, lucky number 13 at thirteen years of age. I was so good they retired my number when I graduated from high school. See, some things do last forever. I *definitely* know how to *push.*

But third trimester pregnant women shouldn't be running five miles or bench pressing their own weight, especially when it has recently shot up by thirty-five pounds, so I quit exercising at the seven month mark.

(How some women can run marathons pregnant is beyond me. Pregnancy is enough of a marathon all by itself.) Only two months before this pregnancy I spontaneously miscarried at only six weeks, so I've been good and paranoid the last nine months and eight days of this wonderfully overdue baby.

    My first delivery could easily be a skit on "Saturday Night Live". Picture Gilda Radner, God rest her soul, with a giant basketball strapped to her skinny body, and Jane Curtin in fake boobs, to make her waist look even smaller, as her nurse. Nurse Good Body/Jane Curtin reaches behind the baby monitoring machine to sip vodka out of a paper bag, in sync with Gilda's contractions, and screams at her to "PUSH!" after Jane swallows a shot. Gilda, sweating and salivating, screams back at her, "What do you think I'm doing, you lush bitch… *pulling*"?

    I grin briefly at my thoughts and then wince as another contraction takes over. This baby boy has baked enough, but he sure is taking his sweet old time coming out! The contractions started Friday evening, while my husband Dieter and I were watching an action movie in bed, over thirty-six hours ago.

    *   *   *

    "Ow! What was that?!"

    Dieter, engrossed in the movie, mumbles, "What?"

    I'm wincing and holding my huge belly, which really looks big on my size 4-6 body. All thirty-five pounds right in front. Everyone's been telling me I don't even look pregnant from the back, but the side shot is a real winner. "I think I'm having a contraction!"

    "Really?" Dieter asks, without turning his gaze from the TV.

Now the pain is going away. Was it gas? No, no way. "I definitely had some kind of contraction."

"Do you want to call Dr. Belizan?" as Dieter turns and looks at my belly.

"No, not yet!" I blurt to my tall, handsome German husband. Dieter is a not too successful traveling I.T. consultant who knows nothing about medicine, except that doctors make a lot of money. I was very much in love with him and thought he loved me. If I had any doubts, I'd push them to the back of my mind every time he flashed his big baby blues. I was a sucker for his good looks and European good manners from the get-go, definitely love at first sight.

"Dr. Belizan said to call him if I break my water or start having contractions *often.* That was only *one*! *One* isn't *often* and this bed isn't floating in water or you'd have complained by now!" (Nine months' plus pregnant women are allowed to be short-tempered.)

We finish the movie. Twenty minutes later I yell, "Ow!" again. My belly feels like it is being stuffed into my Baba's old-fashioned wringer. So it goes, all night. Every twenty minutes. Every time I start to nod off, I can't, because I'm getting wrung out, while Dieter snores on.

The next day, Saturday morning, I'm sleepless and exhausted, but don't think I should have any coffee as the contractions are increasing. Torture. No coffee. Who gets up and just starts the day chirping like a bloody robin without any caffeine? Maybe the Mormons, but I still think they like a good cappuccino, if incognito. The phone rings. It's Dieter's best buddy, Klaus. He thinks he's got something in his eye and it is very painful. I agree to see him in an hour, the ever-on-the-go-ophthalmologist, but expecting my husband to drive me to the office, even though it's only a mile away turns out to be a mistake.

"Why can't you drive yourself?" he asks, annoyed to have to shut off the football game.

"If I get one of these belly twisters in the car, I'm gonna go off the road!" I yell at him. Dieter jumps off of the couch after that comment.

Klaus has a corneal abrasion, the easiest diagnosis for an ophthalmologist to make, bar none. The anesthetic drop that I give him is like manna from heaven to my grateful now pain free patient. I wish there was some kind of moisturizer I could rub on my belly and get the same instant pain relief those damned drops give.

In the middle of his brief eye exam, I have a strong contraction and almost fall off my wheeled exam stool. Klaus tries to lean past the slit lamp to grab me and yells, "Are you okay?!"

I can't respond for a second catching my breath, then squeak, "Sure, just a little contraction." They are definitely getting more intense, definitely more annoying and frequent. "I can't believe you saw me in this condition," Klaus exclaims, "you should be worrying about yourself!"

Dear God, even in labor, I'm still seeing patients.

"Thanks" I say, as I hobble over to the copier with his insurance card. He has good insurance and while I agreed to see him out of sympathy, the truth is that we need the money.

I've just paid over a million dollars for a new home/office three months ago, an absolute fortune to me. I always wanted to be a millionaire some day, but *not* a million in debt. My more-than-a-dream home is in Potomac, Maryland, where all the big-shot D.C. lawyers live, where everything's over-sized and over-priced. The manicured lawns and magnificent landscaping get regularly tended by in ground sprinklers and there's no worry of massive dogs biting while out jogging because Fido has his own electric fence to keep him in line. People own so much land here, less than twenty minutes outside our nation's capitol, that some can stable and ride their own horses on their property.

I'm probably the only person in the history of Potomac who bought a million dollar home without rich parents and only forty thousand dollars cash of my own. Somehow I still came up with 20% down to avoid having to shell out for private mortgage insurance. (Or PMI, as it's referred to.)

Talk about creative financing! Dieter's meager earnings barely cover his car loan and debts. As it turns out, there's quite a bit of "Dieter Debt", something I found out about three months *after* we were married, while meeting his family in Europe on our honeymoon. *How romantic.* I should have seen the writing on the wall about his deceit even way back then but I was willfully naive. How does a husband not tell their future spouse that they have almost $150,000 dollars huge debt from school? That was twice my school loans, and I had four years more education than him with medical school.

Flying Lufthansa on the way home from Europe, I was so upset at these revelations that the contemplation of divorce first reared its ugly head. My Baba had married Popsi in six weeks and their marriage lasted almost fifty years. I thought I knew Dieter better in six months of dating than Baba could have possibly known Popsi in six weeks so I wasn't afraid of marrying him.

"Why didn't you tell me?" I remember asking him tearfully on the plane.

"I was hoping the bank would burn down" was Dieter's feeble response.

"Did you ever hear of computers between bank branches?!" I yelled out loud not caring I was in a plane.

No response from Dieter except downcast big blue eyes. But I already knew I was going to forgive him anyway. Since what can a thirty-three-year-old from a strict religious background, with a loudly ticking biological clock possibly do, especially if she's madly in love? Get a divorce in three months and stroke out both of my parents? Nope. Not an option.

So I forgave him and did some of that creative financing I was becoming an expert at, begging the bank to wipe out all of the late penalties, getting a home equity loan on my townhouse, asking my sister for help, you name it. Probably just like my strong relatives back in Czechoslovakia did in their own way, just give birth in a field and keep on pickin' those potatoes! Yep, "100% wild and crazy Slovak, in love and wanting children, will handle all problems".

I also didn't believe in divorce so that's what this ever-the-over-achiever did, bailed him out in the name of love. I'm overworking to pay the fat mortgage, loans from my parents and sister (not to mention a grateful and trusting patient), a small $67,000.00 second trust from the builder, the office expenses, credit cards, and every other shitty bill, all while happily, exhaustingly pregnant.

*　　　　　*　　　　　*

Later that Saturday afternoon after taking care of Dieter's friend, I call Dr. Luciano Belizan, my wonderful, swarthy, sexily- *Thick-accented* Obstetrician and exclaim to him, "I've had contractions every ten minutes for the last eighteen hours, haven't slept a wink and they hurt a lot!"

Dr. Belizan's voice is comforting, but not comforting enough. "You ressst, Marry Annn, you ressst.

You have a big day ahead of you. Call me if you brreak your water or your contrrractions are five to seeex minutes aparrt, okay?"

I love Dr. Belizan. He's so nice. His amniocentesis let me know the baby was a healthy boy, which made Dieter ecstatic and relieved us both.

No rest for the weary, pregnant women or their OBs.

A few hours later, over twenty-four hours into labor, I'm still in too much pain to sleep. I call Dr. Belizan, probably right as he's about to have a great dream. "Yes, Marrry Annn?" he asks groggily and I blurt, "I haven't broken my water and my contractions are still 8-10 minutes apart but I'm *in pain* and want some morphine!"

I have never experienced morphine, but I've given it I.V. I know it works and it works *fast*. Dr. Belizan sighs. "We don't give prrregnant women morrpheene. But I will give you something to be comforrtable. I will meet you at the hospital."

God bless him, just his luck to have *me* as a neurotic first-time-in-labor-eight-day-overdue-doctors-make-the-worst-patients delivery, late on a Saturday night. I can't wait to see my baby boy! Oh my God, I'm going to realize my greatest dream and have a child. I nudge Dieter awake. He looks a little dazed.

"Let's go!" I pipe, "We're going to have a baby!" Yeah, right. *I'm* going to have a baby, and Dieter's going to watch.

We never did that Lamaze/breathing/natural childbirth classes' crap. As a doctor I helped deliver several babies in medical school by assisting in C-sections. I even injected a woman with Lidocaine, did her episiotomy, then caught her newborn and handed it to her.

Fuck that natural shit, Cindy Crawford can keep it. I want all the drugs, epidural/underdural/make-it-plural, this is the nineties, not the Wild West, and I don't like pain!

We reach the hospital in record speed and Dr. Belizan doesn't make me wait, giving me a small shot of Nubane, a narcotic that won't suppress the baby's breathing.

Relief.

Not complete comfort, but definitely the best I've felt in a long time. Then the anesthesiologist on call starts my epidural. Now I'm going numb from the waist down but more so on the left side, so I'm told to lie on my right. When I lay on my right, my baby's heartbeat slows. Something about that position isn't working, so the only option is flat on my back. My left leg is a dead log but I can still feel a semi-contraction on the right side, all the way down to my big toe. This anesthesia is definitely whacky.

I'm obviously doing better, however, than the lady I hear screaming in Spanish on a gurney getting wheeled down the hallway past my room. Nurse Christy says, "She's Dr. Belizan's patient as well."

"Great. I'm glad he didn't get out of bed just for me."

Dr. Belizan breaks my water with a sort of hook-like probe and I wet the whole bed. I exclaimed to him, "So *that's* what breaking your water is like!" Dr. Belizan smiles wearily. "I have to go check on my other patient. You starrt to dilate now, okay?"

By the time he returns to check on my progress, Dr. Belizan has already delivered the Spanish lady's baby. The new mother is wheeled back out of the "Labor and Delivery" suite, now happily cooing in Spanish instead of screaming, and I still haven't dilated past two centimeters. What's taking so long?

Up goes the Pitocin drip at 4:25 a.m., the "natural" hormone that is supposed to make a pregnant woman dilate. Where the hell is my uterus when I need it, on a Starbuck's break? Pitocin usually works within a couple of hours, dilating the cervix in preparation for the delivery.

But not on Mary Ann, no, not for me! Nothing has ever been easy for me. I should have been a marathon runner for this baby boy, not just a high school track star. My long distance records are forever from 1979, because the next year everything went metric. Once again, I think, some things *do* last forever...just like this labor. Thank God for the stamina I gained from running track.

Dieter looks like he needs something stiffer to drink than coffee. So do I.

*   *   *

By Sunday morning (time to go to church and pray!), I'm finally fully dilated and I dutifully push for over two hours for my way-too-energetic, new morning-shift nurse. After no sleep in two days, I feel like crap. Where is my baby, already?

I have not been allowed to eat or drink for the past eight hours since I may need a C-section. Exhaustion is too weak a word. Spent. That's it. Totally SPENT. But now I'm asked to be a semi-paraplegic acrobat, due to my uneven anesthesia, and push in the "opposite direction". WTF? I don't remember this from medical school, seems like I'm a crazy American driving down the wrong side of the road in England but do as I'm told.

The nurse helps me hoist myself up on my unevenly numb haunches. Now I'm facing where my head used to lie, holding on to the rails of the bed, pushing so hard in a squat position I'm sure even Arnold Schwarzenegger would be impressed.

At that very moment, in full straining splendor with my ass in full view from the gape in my hospital gown, the male anesthesiologist with whom I've done cataract surgery before walks in to check my epidural. Fuck Me! This is insane! "Come back later!!" I scream at him. Open mouthed and speechless, he does an abrupt about face and exits.

That's it! I'm cooked, overdone, just like this baby! "You want to take the baton?" I whimper at Dieter, who's been up all night as well and looks numb *without* having had any anesthesia. He reaches down and hugs me, but I am 1,110% out of patience and not comforted by his embrace. Not very gracefully, I flip myself onto my back and scream, "Get Dr. Belizan, NOW!!!"

It wasn't Dr. Belizan's fault. He'd warned me several times that first labors can be very difficult, and also my baby boy was going to be a big one, especially after baking an extra eight days. It doesn't help either that I'm built like my mother's younger brother: wiry and lean with broad shoulders, and no God-damned-hips.

Dr. Belizan examines me, "Your baby is sunny-side up."

"Sunny-side up?" I didn't learn *that* "medical term" during eight weeks of Ob/Gyn in medical school. "What's that mean?!"

"Your baby is 180 degrees turned. His face is facing up instead of down so his head won't fit out of your pelvis that way."

I close my eyes wanting to sob. "I don't need a C-section after all this, do I?"

Dear God, if I knew I was going to need a C-section anyway, I wouldn't have been torturing myself for the last two days. I could already be holding and nursing my little baby. I would have just scheduled the C-section and called it a day, like picking up a cantaloupe instead of a watermelon at the store. But I never wanted to be cut open and Dr. Belizan knows it.

"I can try a forrceps or suction deliverry."

"No suction!" I yell. I remember one baby in medical school that came out like a cone head from a suction delivery and even needed brain surgery. But in ophthalmology, I also saw forceps' babies with corneal scarring from getting their eyes scraped over by the big metal tools the obstetricians' use, and they then needed corneal transplants or they'd develop permanent sight loss.

Dieter is staring at me. He's not saying anything. He knows it's my body and my decision. I turn back to the doctor.

"Are you good at forceps deliveries?"

"Yes, I have a lot of experrience with them."

"Okay, Dr. B., do your thing."

"Marry Annn, if I cannot get the baby out with forrceps, we will have to do a C-section."

"I know," I answer him, and close my eyes again, dreading the thought.

"We have to shut off your epidural now to take you to the operating room and then you will receive pain medication there."

"Okay." I look at Dieter and hold out my hand. He takes it. He looks worried. So am I…

* * *

"My back hurts! My back is killing me!" Now *I'm* the patient screaming on the gurney in the hallway. The worst back pain in my life is on the way to the O.R. This pain is worse than when I broke my neck two years ago in a car accident and almost died! The epidural wore off just enough, and I want to explode! Instead, I start sobbing very hard. It's like someone opened the floodgates. I'm crying out of control now, totally exhausted mentally and physically.

Beautiful, just perfect. I'm going to have a huge episiotomy in order for those damned big forceps to fit in, and will probably need hemorrhoid surgery from pushing so hard, *and* I may end up getting cut open after all! You win the trifecta, Mary Ann, outrageously, with only one horse. Please God, please let my baby be healthy.

The tears just keep flowing and Dr. Belizan is an incredibly swift saint. Those forceps flip my baby's head and he's out in two pushes. All the eyes in the O.R., peering over their masks, look happy, relieved and surprised at how fast he propelled out.

The joy of seeing my blue little boy is overwhelming. *I have never felt so high in my life.* "He's a gift from God, my little angel from heaven!" I'm still crying uncontrollably, but now with elation. Dieter is mesmerized, watching while the pediatrician checks him over. I strain to see my baby from my stirrups, even though Dr. Belizan wants me to hold still and then I shout, "Is he *all right*?! He's too damned blue!"

"They're giving him oxygen" Dieter says without turning, still rapt. My baby's color is slowly changing from blue to a healthy pink. The pediatrician, who Dr. Belizan had called in, finishes his exam and says, "He's a big, healthy boy, eight pounds, eleven ounces."

I can't believe it. I almost had a nine-pounder the "old-fashioned" way (yeah, right, probably we both wouldn't have made it back in the Wild West). Thank you, dear God, for modern medicine and my healthy baby boy.

"Thank you Dr. Belizan." He looks up over his mask as he's sewing me up. The good Doctor's eyes have a relieved look in them as well. "You're a miracle worker Dr. Belizan. By the way, how many hemorrhoids are down there?"

"I donn't see annny." Another damned miracle.

The nurse hands me my baby boy, all cleaned off and wrapped snuggly in a hospital baby blanket. He feels lighter than the dolls I remember playing with as a child, but he's so much softer and warmer. I gently touch his cheek with my finger and blessedly know for sure he is really here. His hair is wispy and so light and his eyes so blue, neither from my side of the family. Oh my God, you gave me a blonde, blue-eyed baby boy! And he's got full pink lips too! What a doll!

His left eye is totally bruised in a big circle, so is the right side of his head. I peer at his left cornea. It looks fine; the forceps must have just circled the orbital bones and thankfully just missed his eye. He is so amazing and adorable, even if he looks like he's been in a fight. Why not? He was. He's been fighting to get out. His Mom is a real fighter, why shouldn't he be, too?

*   *   *

<u>The greatest moment of my life.</u> Nothing will ever come close to the feeling I had when holding my angel from heaven for the first time. Three more times I feel that God-given joy with the birth of my three daughters. James is my only son: he's the king. He and my three little princesses need me to teach them and protect them and, most of all,

love them unconditionally, like my grandmother, my Baba, loved me.

I really never wanted to be anything but a great Mom. When growing up all I ever wanted was to get married and have babies. This whole "Doctor thing" was a giant detour. A decade of baby making put on hold during my most fertile years, just flushing my twenties down the toilet to become a physician, to "be a doctor, help people, and have a good life" like my dear, very poor Baba wanted for me. My mom's mom, "Baba", the strongest, sweetest, most important person in my whole life told me, over and over for as long as I can remember: "Be a doctor and you'll have a good life".

Being a great doctor and surgeon does not give me nearly the satisfaction of an "I love you, Mom" or a hug from one of my children. Dear God, thank you for my angels from heaven. They are the reason I live on.

*   *   *

I am discharged the next day. Welcome to managed care. One overnight for a "normal" vaginal delivery. (Only thirty-eight hours of pain.) Two weeks from the Monday I am discharged, my five year office lease is up, and I'm seeing patients full time in my new home/office, needing a few Percocet now and then for episiotomy pain. Sure. No problem. Especially hard, too, with Dieter gone and travelling, even more for his job.

I can have a baby, breastfeed every two hours, skip sleep, move my entire practice, charts, furniture and tons of ophthalmology equipment, when I'm not supposed to be lifting, and start back to work full time, all within two weeks post-partum, to support the family. Doesn't everyone? Not quite… Or am I just another working mom, a magnificent martyr?

Chapter 4

Magnificent Martyrdom

My favorite name is Mommy. I love being called Mommy. I love being called Mommy much more than "Sweetheart", "Love of my Life", *any* endearment really. And certainly a lot more than "Doctor". My Dad's cherished name for my Mom is "Zen". "Zen" is actually a very sweet Slovak endearment for "wife", but at the risk of sounding cynical, wife to me now is a four-letter word. I can't come up with an excellent acronym for wife that defines its meaning to me, but maybe "Woman In Forced Enlistment" is appropriate. For Mommy, however, an easy acronym pops right to mind, "Martyr Over Many, Many Years".

My dear Mom always called herself a martyr. I should have looked martyrdom up in *Webster*'s years ago, as I always thought martyrdom had the religious connotation of sacrifice. Aren't almost all of the patron saints men? Yes, of course, they are. But my Mom, bless her, was using the word correctly, whether she knew it or not.

The definition of martyrdom is: *n* 1. the suffering of death on account of adherence to one's religious faith or to *any cause;* 2. AFFLICTION, TORTURE. That is *exactly* how the definition reads in my over forty year old *Webster's*. (It must be correct being over forty like me, ha!) We all know what torture means, but affliction is interesting also, as its definition reads "the cause of continued pain or distress".

I'll be damned. That's it! The one learning experience ingrained in me from childhood that most definitely was severely detrimental in my adult years was watching my Mom and Baba be *martyrs*. They would run circles around their husbands as self-sacrificing worker bees for their families, even if it caused them "continued pain or distress", practicing not "medicine", but something *much* more intense… (drum roll, please)… *magnificent martyrdom*.

I thought that was the only way to live one's life as a wife. I firmly believed I had to put my husband, and of course, my children first, always before myself… so I did!! Work also had to come before my own needs, because Mommy needs to make a hell of a lot of money so we can all keep on living the way we live!

In doing so, I lost everything I ever loved. I almost even lost my own life.

It is only by God's grace that I am here to tell the story, and hopefully some women and some men will learn from my tragic mistakes before they have to learn it the hard way like I did. Or then it's too late, and they die.

*   *   *

I'll never forget sitting as a young girl in Baba's eighty degree kitchen (she had a coal furnace) during the dead of winter, the ironing board folded down from the wall near the back door (a total safety hazard if one had to hurdle over it to get out of the kitchen door in case of a fire), and watching her iron… *everything*. She ironed sheets, pillowcases, handkerchiefs, every article of clothing imaginable all while barefoot and after cooking and washing the dishes from dinner. Meanwhile, my grandfather Popsi, we called him, sat in the living room with his feet up watching TV and drinking beer. (No chauvinism in our family, huh?)

Popsi *and* Baba worked full time in the same shoe factory during the day, but only Baba also worked second shift. Second shift was harder than her day job, because it included not only evenings but all weekends. Baba was chief cook and bottle washer, "canner" of everything from peaches and plums to pickles and sauerkraut, an on-the-knees-type of cleaning lady, the grocery shopper, gardener, general housekeeper and, of course, laundry scrub woman complete with old-fashioned wringer. Small joke... Popsi was a great deer hunter and coal shoveler so Baba's feet could be warm, while she stood barefoot in the kitchen cooking venison or ironing.

"Baba, what *are* you ironing? Those aren't Popsi's boxer shorts, are they?!"

"Yes, Honey." I just couldn't believe it; Baba was ironing Popsi's underwear.

"Why are you doing that?! Nobody is going to see them, Baba! And the first time he sits down, they're going to get wrinkled anyway! Baba, ironing underwear *is crazy*!!"

Baba was unaffected by my comments and simply responded, "It's okay, Medka. Popsi likes his shorts neat."

I think that is, indeed, above and beyond the call of duty even for an Eastern-bloc wife. I was totally shocked, way back then in the sixties. Baba didn't even have a dryer. After the laundry got wrung out, she hoisted it all upstairs and hung it out, summer and winter alike. It's exhausting just to *imagine* her toiling up and down the stairs with heavy wet laundry. Today, I want to do a stand up comic routine about the sheer insanity of it all, all the martyrdom, including my own.

My Mom was almost as crazy. Short and slightly built, her facial features made her look like a sibling to my

Dad, which makes sense as their ancestors came from neighboring villages in the Carpathian Russian Mountains of Czechoslovakia. Dad was taller, broader and physically stronger, *but* the kind of strength that sustains a martyr is not physical.

The good news for Mom was that Dad wore briefs. They got Clorox and extra soaks to make sure the "nicotine stains", as he called them, got out so thankfully, no ironing. I can't remember the last time I ironed a damned thing. Thank God for polyester.

My Mom worked her ass off raising four kids while working full time most of my years growing up. She kept such an immaculate house that one could eat off her kitchen floor (still can), and also did all of the laundry and ironing (for six), and had a hot meal and one of his favorite homemade desserts ready for Dad when he walked in from work, after *her* hard day in the office. No hired help whatsoever. It wasn't an option, no extra money.

Mom practiced magnificent martyrdom in every way imaginable (except ironing Dad's briefs) and probably in some ways wealthy Potomac women can't even *possibly* imagine. Many of them marrying for money, like women everywhere still do, they don't dare demand such sacrifice even from their well paid hired help!

Mom also sacrificed her career for her family. She was always the one who would be late for work if we missed the bus by accident and she had to drive us to school. She was the one who had to leave early if one of us got sick. She shouldered the lion's share of the responsibility of raising us and never complained. Liking it, loving it, accepting her round the clock schedule even if it caused her "continued pain and distress", because she was "M.O.M.M.Y".

Baba and Mom were my role models. I wanted to get married and have babies and be as great as them. Always the over-achiever, I was going to go to medical school and make a good living, too. Baba said I was smart enough to be a doctor, but how did she know I could make it? She just finished sixth grade and my parents completed high school, but *Baba always had undying confidence in me.*

*   *   *

The only thing I couldn't ever possibly emulate was their manic coupon cutting. They both were furious couponaholics out of necessity, because money was so tight and being frugal was the way of life. My Mom had an extra, empty checkbook alphabetized just for her precious coupons.

To this day, I hate grocery shopping; the reason being that Mom would take me to three stores on one Saturday afternoon. One store had milk and eggs for sale. The second store had double coupons and the third store had a few items for triple coupons. For a bag of cheese curls, it just didn't seem worth my time. I loved being with Mom and her frugality taught me to love a good buy but after waiting in *one* checkout line, I was ready to go home and watch *Star Trek* reruns on our black and white TV with my bag of junk food, no contest.

But, without a doubt, I unconsciously aspired to magnificent martyrdom status and wouldn't stop until I attained it. Like a fool, I wouldn't allow myself to relax and read a magazine unless I was on the "john". Nor would I allow myself to go window shopping or get my nails done with my friends, because I never saw Baba or Mom take a break or spend money on something as frivolous as a manicure. Even when they finally sat down in the evening to watch a TV show, they really weren't watching it because they were crocheting doilies for someone or mending some clothes.

So "Little Miss Overachiever" tried to do it all and do it 110% and love every minute of it, because I had finally aspired to "Magnificent Martyrdom Status". I had it all with my handsome young trophy husband, or so everyone thought. I was also drawn to Dieter's sophistication, gained from his extensive travels and wide reading. Being a Mommy, wife, solo practicing ophthalmologist, wet nurse, nanny, general manager of you-name-it-whatever all on my own, kept me insulated in constant activity around the home.

A repeated comment from my patients, especially when my small children would get away from the nanny and run screaming, "Mommy! Mommy!" into the office from the house was: "Dr. Duke, how do you do it all"? My answer should have been: "I don't know", but instead I would just smile, introduce my little toddlers, and then carry little blonde James or brunette Marika, both still in diapers, back inside. It got to be so disruptive that I eventually put a deadbolt between my home and office. But that still didn't stop me from bringing patients right into my home to see one of my beautiful, sleeping children.

If I was into control, this would have been a great scenario, but actually I'm not a control freak and was in desperate need of some help. But everyone, including my husband and myself, thought (wrongly) that I could handle it all. Truthfully, the answer is simply *"One can't"*. No one can be that on-the-ever-go phenomenal. It's an impossible feat, especially with a husband who travels extensively for work. Everyone needs a break, and I never took one. I kept persevering, and barely hung onto my life. Raising babies was far more demanding than residency.

* * *

A typical day in the married life of Dr. Duke:

1. Wake up 7:30. If pregnant first trimester, nausea and vomiting until eleven. If not pregnant, breastfeed and change diapers before nanny arrives at 8:00 and/or get older children ready for pre-school. Dieter, of course, usually not home, traveling too much for work. If home, not one to volunteer with the children and usually busy with his own chores, i.e. keeping track of the money.

2. Patients all day starting at nine, or surgery which usually started earlier. Always tried to eat something before surgery, but usually only time for coffee before office hours, unless of course pregnant and coffee vomitus not a great option. Luckily only a two step commute from house to office as I'm not the best morning person, especially uncaffeinated. Surgery, however, requires leaving home and dealing with hideous D.C. traffic so was usually a little late, if not a little lot late.

3. Nanny opens door between house and office as necessary. "James is hungry" or sixteen months later when my first daughter was born, "Marika is hungry" or two years later, "Nadia is hungry". There my baby would be crying inside the living room and I could hear the hungry yells from the office. Usually, I drop everything and make excuses: "Oh, you aren't quite dilated yet", "Why don't you try putting the contacts in by yourself now?", "I just need to run to the ladies' room", or simply tell the truth, "I'll be right back. I have to go breastfeed my baby". Then I ran into the house, peeling off my white coat on the way in, hoist my shirt over my head and flung off my bra.

My babies and I had breastfeeding down to a science. It's like somehow they knew Mommy had to get back to work so they latched on hard for six minutes per booby and seemed to be basically satisfied while I was drained. My poor nanny had a free show every couple of hours. If I couldn't break away from the office or my breasts were engorged when my baby was sleeping, I just repeated the above exercise and had a double breast pump so everything took only six minutes instead of twelve. It's a wonder I even had any milk at all because I often worked right through lunch, didn't eat, and my morning just blurred right into my afternoon.

4. I always tried to finish by five. Have to, or that meant paying overtime to my office manager, my only employee. I never had an ophthalmic tech to help me. I was a one-woman-band because another employee meant more overhead and working past five meant overtime for my nanny, too. I can't work more hours to pay more than the $75,000 in salaries to my nanny and office manager on top of the $100,000 a year in mortgage or there won't be enough *time* to eat! (What is eating for anyway? Can't I just slap on a new battery pack?)

Dieter's average gross salary the first four years we were married was under $40,000 a year and that barely covered his school loans, car loan and a few of his polo shirts. I paid the $8,000 plus a month mortgage, $2,000 a month plus nanny, $4,000 plus a month office manager, all of the household bills, insurances (except health insurance by Dieter's firm minus co-pays and deductibles), extra car payment, food bills, etc…

I was the breadwinner, penis-less Daddy (because Dieter was away), W.I.F.E. (when Dieter was not away) and M.O.M.M.Y. At five p.m. I performed another strip tease, this time into sweats, to be comfortable for an evening of feedings and diaper changing, playing with the babies, baths, homework and story telling. Dieter might roll around on the floor with our kids if he was in the mood to play with them, but was often too tired for them *and* for me.

The biggest regret of my life was never having live in help. But I didn't grow up with it, so I just kept pushing on myself even if I was totally exhausted, or even sick with the flu.

5. Second shift goes right into third with feedings, diaper changing, consoling a child after a nightmare and broken sleep. I had three children in four years and also supported the family, only taking a yearly one week vacation with points earned on my credit cards from all the contact lens buying and ordering of office supplies.

Those one-week vacations with the children, of course and not alone together, were not enough to stop our marriage from slowly losing its intimacy. The arguments over money and expenses were exhausting our relationship, and making it harder to remember what we felt for each other to begin with.

*   *   *

Dear God, I was so exhausted seven months after having my first child, James, and my milk was drying up, I thought I might have something really wrong with me. "Dieter, I'm so tired," I tell him one night. "My milk is drying up and I'm so exhausted."

Dieter just looked at me, scared.

"I think I better go see Dr. Belizan."

Dieter was enjoying James, really enjoying being a father for the first time, and there I was with all the warning signs of another pregnancy, or a malignancy; I was *so* exhausted. I was overjoyed by the possibility of another baby, though, because I was getting older, but Dieter was overwhelmed and asks, "Why did you get pregnant so soon?"

I look at him wide eyed in shock, as if *I* was the only one involved. Our sex life was scarce, what with

Dieter's job and my work plus little James' demanding schedule, and I'm not supposed to be on the pill and breast-feeding. Who says I'm always in charge of the birth control anyway?!

Without ever having one period after James, I was pregnant again. The skinny little Czech girl, who worried for so many years that she was waiting too long to have babies and might have infertility problems (especially after a disappointing miscarriage preceding James), was pregnant again at thirty-six.

Little James was such a comfort to me. Heavily pregnant, we danced to *These Are The Days* by 10,000 Maniacs, me holding him close and slowly waltzing in circles until he fell fast asleep, his soft breathing on my shoulder. Often I fell asleep for a few minutes myself, still holding him when the music stopped. Just flopping on the couch, I'd briefly close my eyes and startle myself awake after a few moments and realize I had dozed off, too exhausted to yet carry James up to bed. My baby boy would only sigh but never be disturbed to the point of opening his eyes. Those *were* special days of bonding with James I pray he subconsciously still feels.

I easily could have used a trimester off just to lie in bed reading *People Magazine* between trips to the bathroom to vomit. But no such frivolousness even crossed my mind. I needed to work to pay the bills, must generate at least 30K a month just to stay afloat. So patients simply had to wait while I went into the house to vomit now instead of breast-feed.

Marika finally came out, 8 lbs. 2oz., so dark, furry and soft. My little brunette with big brown eyes, just like her mom. I remember Dieter looking at me in the delivery room and jokingly saying, "Is she *mine?*" She was full of dark brown hair, *everywhere,* it seemed, like a furry little teddy bear! I thought, "I'm going to hold her next to me and have her for lunch after she has me". Incredible. Unbelievable. My little girl. Marika was fun to dance with naked except for a diaper in the heat of summer, because she had so much fine baby hair all over her making her extra soft.

So in no time I had two in diapers, breast feeding all over again, and Dieter started a new job that took him away from home even more often, two children probably making him even more aware of the tender years he was missing. The first thing he would do when he came in from a business trip was scoop them both up into his arms and bury his head next to theirs. I know he missed us and had to work, but it still left me being Doctor Duke by day, Mommy by evening, wet nurse for one and diaper changer for two by night... by myself.

Just do it! Just do it, and do it well and like it, no... *love it.* I had finally arrived and become a magnificent martyr, to be just like Mom and Baba. But Mom and Baba had one little advantage. They got married in the era when there wasn't a fifty-five percent divorce rate. People stuck it out back then whether they loved each other or not or they grew to love each other again after first loving each other, than hating each other, then somehow were blessed with loving each other again. Granted, now women and men have many more pressures on them with both working, but it seems that when the going gets tough couples just don't work as hard at making their marriages last, and they should, especially when they have children.

*   *   *

Did Dieter marry me to get his U.S. citizenship? Did he marry me to get out of debt? Or did he marry me for my future earning potential as a doctor? I think the answer might be "all of the above". But did Dieter *ever* love me?

When we met my practice was young, and I wasn't making much more than him. Dieter was a man who really courted me, who took me to see *Cats* in New York City, never argued with me (*before* we got married) and often cooked for me. Here was a man who knew how to dance and looked magnificent in a tuxedo, who even flew his parents over to meet me before he proposed. I even loved his accent. I married for love, but did Dieter… *really?*

Only God knows for sure. Anyone who has ever gotten a divorce knows marriages don't die overnight, most of the time it takes years. A slow death is always more painful than a quick death. It's not like one morning the bride or groom wakes up to some alarm that rings and chimes, "Today is a new day. I think I'm going to have some hot cocoa this morning instead of hot coffee and not be married anymore!" Gees, if it only were so easy, all of the divorce lawyers would be panhandling!

You know the penny in the jar story? Put a penny in a (hopefully) *large* jar every time you make love before you get married. Take one out each time you make love after you are married… you'll never get to the bottom of the jar. (I didn't, and remember it was only a six-month courtship, talk about starvation.) Once, my electrician told me, "My wife has become a fixture". Oh my God, how sad for both of them.

Maybe that's what I became to Dieter. Just some money-making tree… no, *cactus,* that he rarely needed to water. During the worst of it I even called Nadine, my best friend growing up back in Binghamton, and asked her how often she and her husband were intimate, and her response made me feel even more unloved. Not enough tenderness, not enough laughter, not enough of anything except babies and bottles.

I never could seem to make Dieter truly happy. There was never enough, especially not enough money nor lovemaking.

"Our bills are more than we earned this month," Dieter blandly informs me one evening. "So what else is new"? I think.

"So we have *more* credit card debt?" I ask.

"Yes."

Dieter started doing the billing in my office, and took charge of paying the office and the household bills, but still kept his paychecks going to his company's credit union. I was naïve and probably stupid, too, looking back. I never knew how much was going in or out, I just saw more and more patients as Medicare and every insurance company's reimbursements kept going down every year. I had to work harder and harder to maintain the same income, but the spending never stopped. I was too overwhelmed with doctor and M.O.M.M.Y. duties to pay good attention.

"Please," I beg Dieter, shouting into the study where he often was on the computer, from the living room where I was watching the children "No more debt!"

"Well, you wanted the hot tub too!" is his response, and I spat back "Yeah, but not the most expensive one, like you did"!

I begged and pleaded with Dieter to stop spending money. We started to argue *way* too much. The worst arguments were always after I had a couple glasses of wine and Dieter had a few beers. I even toyed with the idea of buying him a $27,000 hand-made Patec Phillipe watch when we were on one of our yearly free airline/hotel point vacations in St. Thomas. You can't buy love though, maybe some sex, but not love.

I, unknowingly at the time, tried. We bought the hot tub. Anyone who's anyone has a hot tub. And, of course, the $2,000 hot tub wasn't good enough for us. We had to have the Mercedes Benz of hot tubs, the $6,000 plus one. Had to get the $18,000 B.M.W. motorcycle for Dieter (I never once rode on) because a Harley wasn't good enough, plus $1,000 worth of gear, boots, leather jacket, etc. A shirt had to have a little horse on it or it wasn't good enough. Even Dieter's socks had to have little horses on them. And they shrunk in the wash just like the un-horsed ones do. Who cares that everything has to have a designer label?

Dieter did. Joneses-keeper-uppers do. People who always "want" and are never happy in this life unless they think they are better or have more than the next guy. I'm too tired to argue and just take a sip of my wine. Maybe it was because Dieter is basically an atheist and has a defeatist attitude. I think it's good to believe in something. For me it's God, but really any "higher power" as AA calls it, so one isn't just bitter about life and thinks: "We are all going to grow old, get uglier, and die anyway and rot in a hole or incinerate into dirty ashes, so why not play as hard as we can while we're alive? Have as much fun and buy as many 'toys' as we can and just party until we drop? Because there is no afterlife to be 'good' for, so who cares who we take advantage of in the meantime because it's all about me"?!

Not my mindset at all. I believe in being a good person, a giving person. Who gives a shit about "keeping up with the Joneses"? It's better to give than to receive, ignorant idiots, in my book. Too bad there are so many of them.

Thank God Baba taught me to be happy without always wanting to have more.

*　　　　　*　　　　　*

Four years into a marriage I hoped would last forever, Dieter's and my arguing escalated to domestic violence. It was a hot August night, a Friday after a hard work week for both of us, but as was the case the lion's share of the time, I put James and Marika to bed then walked into our master bedroom and decided to pick a fight when I saw Dieter already sprawled in bed with the television on.

"You don't help me enough with the children!" I scream at him.

"You've had too much to drink!"

"No, I haven't. I've had two glasses. I did surgery and killed myself in the office and *you're* the one who is already in bed!"

"Oh, go have another drink and leave me alone" and Dieter gets up and walks towards the bathroom.

"No. You're not getting off that easy this time. Why don't you help me more?!" and I stomp right after Dieter into the bathroom.

"Get out of here."

I don't remember who hit who first, and the police reports are conflicting, but it was one hell of a fight. A phone was thrown and there's still a dent in the bathroom wall. A hair dryer, cup and can of shaving cream went flying, too. That fight was definitely the turning point for our marriage into its final descent. I accused Dieter of throwing me to the ground and he accused me of hitting him first. Never before had our verbal arguments turned to physically hurting one another.

I ran downstairs to my office and accidentally set the house alarm off by opening the office door before disarming the alarm, so the police came because of that, not because one of us called them. Dear God, I hope the alarm and yelling didn't wake the babies. Gratefully, I didn't hear any crying from their rooms.

"Who started this?" the officers ask us.

"He did!"

"She did!"

"Are either of you hurt? Do you want to go to the hospital?"

"No," I said.

"No," Dieter mimed.

The police completed two conflicting domestic violence supplements because they could not decide who indeed the aggressor was.

"Do you own any guns?" one policeman asks.

Dieter liked guns and kept a shotgun under our bed. I don't *think* it was loaded. The police left with the shotgun, a 357 Magnum and a semi-automatic Glock. Dieter agreed to spend the night at a friend's. Looking back, how frightening that evening was and how quickly it became violent. We had never laid a hand on one another before, but we could have killed each other that night with two babies less than three years of age in the house. Within a couple months Dieter retrieved his guns from the police station, and they were back in the house under lock and key. I would have been happier with them in the trash.

Nonetheless, Dieter and I must have made up in the next two weeks because nine months later beautiful, fair haired, blue eyed, pink cheeked, 8lb. 13oz. Nadia was born, and I don't recall taking a penny out of the jar. The rhythm method was pretty much unnecessary as there was no rhythm in my life to anything except my job. I'll never forget my one surgeon buddy's comment: "Jesus, Duke, you can't sit in the same chair with a man without getting pregnant"!

I knew in my heart that my marriage was in a dangerous skid, but I was so happy and grateful that I was pregnant with another little girl. Not just for me, but for Marika. Marika was just over two when Nadia was born, and she was thrilled to have a baby sister. I remember thinking, "Marika is a lot like me, very nurturing, and if Dieter and I ever really do get a divorce, Marika will have a little sister to nurture and play dolls with, in addition to her strong big brother James who will protect her".

M.O.M.M.Y. had established herself well now with three children in less than four years. Life was very full with my beloved babies and magnificent martyrdom was in full bloom.

*   *   *

The years 2000 and 2001 were my best in the office, ever. Grossed, *not netted,* just over half a million a year. Good thing our stocks were so lucrative with all of the outrageous spending going on. Remember "Spyglass" on the NASDAQ? What a nutty stock. We made over $8,000 in 24 hours day-trading it. Dieter was in hog heaven. Meanwhile, I toiled and saved 30K a year, like my accountant told me to do, then stupidly let Dieter blow almost all of it, buying worthless penny stocks on bullshit "tips" from the no-minds he worked with, because we were going to "get rich quick and be multi-multi-millionaires".

So then my poor retirement account fell to barely over 30K, after working as a doctor for twenty years. That's insane! We just atomic bombed $200,000 and couldn't even write the losses off, because they were in those retirement accounts that one can't claim the losses on one's tax returns.

I think even my dear accountant had a good cry for me.

*   *   *

Hey, what about me? What about us? What about our three beautiful children?! Aren't we priceless?!

Guess not. Money fucks up priorities. Keeping up with the "Joneses" is for fucked up people.

Lasik was $5,000 a patient in 2000 and 2001. Now I see it advertised for $299 an eye. I had privileges and operated at the Johns Hopkins' Wilmer Eye Institute Greenspring Station facility. Their facility fee was $700 an eye. How could I possibly compete with that $299 fee when just using Johns Hopkins' laser was over twice that per eye? Luckily for me, in Potomac there are some big shots, with big money, to operate on. People who can pay $250,000 for *N'Sync* to play at their daughter's bat mitzvah. That tidbit even made the list of wildest events for *People Magazine* that year. Hearing about it on the radio while I was out running, I immediately recognized that it was one of my patients. I guess I should have charged more than 5K for her daddy's Lasik. Great eyesight for the rest of your life is worth at least 50K if you can pay five times that for a party band, don't you think?! The next daughter only got the Dave Matthews Band. (Guess The Rolling Stones were booked.)

Good thing LASIK was a financial bonanza because cataract surgery reimbursements from Medicare were cascading from the $2,800 in 1988 to a dismissive $563.27 in 2008. One can balance bill $140.82 for a monumental $704.09. I don't care what anyone says about cataract surgery being "routine" now, and with all of the sophisticated equipment, it may only take fifteen minutes. The Medicare fee includes 90 days of post-operative care. All of those visits are demanding and energy draining to a conscientious physician, and the average doctor, the average surgeon does not have the balls to cut open an eyeball; more margin for error cutting open a belly. The Medicare reimbursement for cataract surgery including the post-operative care, in all fairness, should have never gone below $1,200. It is light years easier for an ophthalmologist to become a glorified optometrist (never operate or pay high malpractice) and hawk designer frames.

    Anyway, everything was just fine. Super. Everything was okay because M.O.M.M.Y. made a lot of money so everything was just F.I.N.E. I hadn't learned that acronym yet, but I always told my parents on the phone that "Everything is just *fine.*" F.I.N.E., my ass. (Fucked up, Insecure, Neurotic and Emotional was more perceptive.)

    Obtaining my dreams of having my own practice and having babies and taking care of everything was definitely starting to take its toll. It was unfortunate, so unfortunate that working so incredibly hard to have the dreams be reality was so exhausting and stressful, especially with a traveling husband and a dying marriage, that the exhaustion to maintain the dreams was eating away at the happiness of even fulfilling the dreams. Does that make sense? It was sad to have pushed so hard for so long that I forgot how to smell the roses; I only knew how to plant them.

    It was like a giant pac-man was eating me alive, and it wasn't a game I could just stop playing. Always so stressed out about working hard enough to pay the bills took away my happiness. I hated myself, for the first time in my life, for being jealous of women who were stay-at-home moms. Those moms had *free time,* free time to have perfect French-tipped acrylics, and I was biting mine.

*   *   *

One perfectly beautiful summer Saturday afternoon, one of those rare D.C. summer days without 95% humidity, I was on the deck in my yellow, high school bikini. (My closet spans three to four decades. Why not? Baba's closet was *much* more impressive! 'Cause everything comes back in style anyway, at ten times the price, like my bell bottom, hip hugger jeans from seventh grade. Dieter called me his "vintage" wife, because I still liked to play my record player, ha!) I was sunbathing with my first two babies in six inches of water in a small, plastic, green baby pool that a sweet patient had bought me. She brought it over in her van, slide and all.

I'm watching James and Marika, remember only sixteen months apart, screeching and happily splashing around naked, fighting to be the next one to go down the slide. Water toys everywhere, total sun and fun. (Nadia was not born yet.) Dieter is away on business, and I think this should be one of the happiest moments in my life, despite his absence. Instead, a crazy thought goes through my mind... I think of the title of Erma Bombeck's book, *If Life Is a Bowl of Cherries, What Am I Doing in The Pits?* I will never forget that thought at that moment.

I hate that it crossed my mind and was so real.

My stress level was off the charts. I had postpartum depression with every baby and was given Prozac or Celexa or Paxil. (The popular serotonin-reuptake inhibitors used for depression.) Nothing helped. My sleep patterns were worse. I felt horrible, when I should have been joyous with my beautiful babies. Instead, I was just a totally stressed out M.O.M.M.Y.

So I started to drink a glass of wine after work. I think it's making me feel better, helping me cope. Chardonnay became my "Mother's Little Helper". I so looked forward to that drink of cold Chardonnay at the end of the day. One glass became two, two might become two and a half, but I always tried to cork the bottle and save some in case I didn't get a chance to buy some more the next day. I never bought a case at a time to make it cheaper, because I didn't want to look like a lush at any liquor store, especially the ones in Potomac, where my practice was located. I tried to only have one glass before getting the kids to bed, but wasn't always successful. Then I would crash, forget TV or reading an ophthalmology journal or even a magazine, wake up and do my day all over again.

I was making a ton of money, but I just could not seem to make Dieter happy enough. Something came over me in my ninth month with Nadia. One Saturday morning, I rolled my biggest belly yet out of bed and went downstairs to the exercise bike. James and Marika were still sleeping. Dieter had awakened with a hard on, but I was in no mood whatsoever for a "quickie". I was so unhappy; I just didn't want to make love.

I started to sweat a little on the bike. I desperately tried to exercise more than drink while pregnant with Nadia, and I certainly am not proud that I drank *at all* with her, even though I limited it to one glass of wine, two at the most, and not every night.

Surprised by hearing a cough, I look up from the bike's monitor to see Dieter plopped into my Baba's well-worn barkal lounger. (I had insisted it shouldn't go to *Good Will* and hauled it down from Johnson City.) Dieter obviously got out of bed and followed me downstairs to watch me exercise, which was a first.

"What's the matter with you?!" Dieter asks sounding frustrated, probably because I said no to sex.

"I've been thinking. I want this baby's last name to be 'Duke.'"

"You can't do that."

"Yes I can."

I *finally* had figured out what made Dieter tick. "I'll buy you the SUV of your choice if you hyphenate the children's names. I found out it costs $90 each to change James' and Marika's last names at the courthouse, but this baby will be free, because we'll do it in the hospital."

Pause. *Not a long one.* Dieter's wheels were turning fast. I plunge on, "I don't care if you put your name first or last; I've pictured it okay both ways on a jersey. Whichever way you want it, but I want to give my children my last name. When they are eighteen, they can change it to Smith if they want!"

Dieter asks, "*Any* SUV?" I nod. No pause whatsoever. "Okay, we'll do it."

Dieter, however, made a big boo-boo. Maybe because he's European he didn't know which way to do it, that the man's surname is supposed to be last. He wanted his last name first, so Duke is my children's last name. Within two weeks, we bought a $60,000 plus Lexus 470, top of the line SUV. Best money I ever spent.

I'm sure he hates me for it, but… oh well, all's fair in love and war. And anyway, it's the *least* I deserve after what he put me through.

My marriage was dying and no one knew it but me. My family, my patients, my friends thought I had it all. I did have it all, a thriving practice, babies… but I was unloved, sexually frustrated, and plain old exhausted and depressed.

*   *   *

(December, 2003, four and a half years later)

I sit next to my female attorney in court waiting for the male judge's decision. I have just survived a "War of the Roses" divorce.

Why am I always the defendant? My Godfather taught me the best defense is a strong offense when I was only a toddler. I know football better than most from his tutelage. So why am I never the plaintiff? Just too nice, too damned nice, and too damned busy to plan an attack. A mother who loves *and supports* her children as much as I do cannot possibly lose custody of them, can she?

But as I sit there, I think that *stress* is my silent but italicized middle name.

The male judge looks imposing high on his throne, I mean bench, really what's the difference? I think about Dieter. I don't think he even wants more physical custody. Dieter only has our children now for the minimum State required days to pay the minimum child support, and he's getting remarried in a few weeks. Jeepers, his fiancé has no children of her own. I'm sure she wasn't counting on all of mine moving in before she even gets hitched!

Still waiting for his Honor, my brain returns to my most important thought: I'll never lose custody of my children. Never. All I ever wanted to be is a mom. I love being a mom more than anything on this earth. Everyone knows how much I love my children. I have never hurt or abused them. The court isn't going to take them from me, right? *I'll die.* How could they give them to a father who's never home, a traveling consultant who's never there! C'mon God, I'll do whatever the judge wants me to do, go to rehab, hire twenty-four hour help, *anything*, just please, God, don't take my babies from me!

The gavel raps. It sounds like gunshots. "Will the defendant please rise?"

And here's how it comes, in slow, even tones:

His Honor states, "Now this hearing is on the plaintiff's motion for temporary custody right? And that is what this hearing is; all right…

She (meaning me, the defendant) has also indicated that she has abused alcohol. I don't think it is clear from the record that she, by any means, is an alcoholic but clearly in the past she has overused alcohol. …There is a lot of smoke in this case… Now she clearly has been under a lot of stress. (*no kidding*) … I thought the testimony, frankly, from her boyfriend was simply untrue. I give him absolutely no credence. (*Wow. The judge just slam-dunked Edward. Called him a liar.*) With respect to her ex-husband's motivations, I am not sure what his motivations are. He may be like a lot of men – and I use this advisedly, because it would appear to happen more to men than women that they would rather have the mother take care of the children and they exercise their visitation and so be it. That may have been his motivation at the time. Eleven days may well have been a motivation to reduce child support." (Duh, it indeed was.)

Certainly it wouldn't be the first case, but I think that he is doing what he had to do under the circumstances, here and now." (*Of course he is. Dieter screamed at me on the phone that if he "didn't go for full custody, the county was going to split the children up and put them in foster care". Of course Dieter has to step up to the plate; I was on the verge of a total physical collapse. Only the devil himself wouldn't pick up a bat and pinch-hit.*)

On and on the judge drones, in this big, stuffy courtroom, and finally gives "temporary physical custody" to Dieter, but we still share legal custody. I am allowed to see my little children only every other weekend and every other Wednesday.

I feel like some maniac took a giant hook, a filthy, huge barb like on Captain Hook, and shoved it in my gut, twisted it upwards, and ripped my heart right out of my chest.

I'm in severe pain, dying and incredulous.

How could this happen? How could this be? How could Dr. Mary Ann Duke lose custody of her children? I plop down into my chair and just stare at my attorney. Time is slowing down and speeding up all simultaneously.

"Every *other* Wednesday," his Honor is saying. My mind starts to race. Dear God, if I didn't see them *every* Wednesday, I would have to go a whole week and a half without seeing my babies!

"Every Wednesday," I make deals in the courtroom, even as my mind can't deal at all. *What the hell is going on?!* "We *have* to appeal this!" I swear to my attorney and she can only nod. She looks crestfallen too. I lean back. Just like that it's over. The thousand-year split second. The courtroom is emptying out, but I cannot think of moving.

How can I possibly move my body when my heart's been ripped out of my chest?

I close my eyes, hoping when I open them I will wake up from this nightmare. I can hear people talking and leaving, but I cannot bear to open my eyes... because then it will be *real*.

Why did the judge do this? Why didn't he give me a second chance? Why didn't he just give the children to my ex-husband for two or six months or something, so I can rest and recover, and get my strength back? Why didn't he mandate me to rehab and let the children stay in their same schools, at home with their nanny they adore?! Dieter's never home anyway; he's always gone for work! Two large tears fall from my jaw. I don't bother to wipe them.

Why did he have to take them away from me at all?! Why couldn't he have just made me get 24 hour live in help if I need "constant supervision"? As it is, within a day of knowing I had to go to court to fight for custody of my children, I had already set up a plan with my present nanny. She would work more hours and stay until her sister, a full-blown nurse, could get off work and relieve her at night. On weekends they would be like a tag team. These two Filipino women are God-fearing, non-drinking, excellent caretakers. My children love them. Why couldn't the judge just let me keep my angels with help from them?!

For God's sake, my *poor babies,* doesn't the damned judge know how much *they* are going to *miss Mommy?!*

*   *   *

I lost. I lost my children. All I ever wanted was to get married and have children and now I lost both of my dreams. I want to die so my heartache will be gone, but I can't. I have to appeal and get them back.

One month later I lose the appeal. My faithful nanny of three years waited for the appeal hearing before finding a new job. To this day she still helps me and remembers my children's birthdays. She told me she will come back to work for me full time in a heartbeat. And it's not because I ever overpaid her. It's because she loves us; we're family.

Wide-awake, I am living my worst nightmare. I lost physical custody of my precious children and was given minimal visitation.

The utter despair, mental and emotional exhaustion *and* loneliness, I felt when there were no children to see after a long day at work, is a feeling I don't wish on my worst enemy. I was totally defeated after the appeal. Dieter was remarried by then, had the American dream/fake nuclear family thing going on, and all I had was alcohol.

(Appendix A)

Chapter 5

Forward to After Court in the Small Gray Cell

(Not even two full years after losing primary custody of my children)

No water. Not in jail. I can't even get water when I need it? Am I not still in America, or has Scottie really beamed me to another planet? For the fourth time in four hours, I yell (this time much louder) at the thick gray door from my third cell down the line, "Guard, may I *please* have some water?!" Keys, I hear keys in the lock. Hurrah! I'm dying of thirst. Someone is finally going to bring me some water from the water cooler I saw on the way into this awful, gray cage. My butt is sore as hell from sitting on the hard, cold metal bench. For the one and only time in my life, I grumble, "If I had a fat ass, it wouldn't be so sore." At least being so thirsty the whole time, means I didn't have to smile and go pee for the camera.

The female guard is looking in at me. "Hi," I say brightly, even though I feel anything but bright. "I rode the exercise bike this morning and sweated a lot. I'm absolutely parched. May I, please, have some water?" (Last bike ride for a long time, says her stare.)

"There's a sink behind you."

"I know, but the water just trickles out of it and there aren't any paper cups."

"I can't give you a cup."

Pause. Why not, I think, because I'm going to wad it up and try to choke myself? No chance, honey. "Could you please bring me a drink of water from the cooler outside?"

"No, I can't. It's only for us."

Now I *am* confused. "Well, how am I supposed to get a drink?"

"There's water behind you," she repeats in a deadpan voice.

I'm pissed, but desperately try not to show it. This guard obviously doesn't know what AIDS is or just doesn't care, probably the latter. She then abruptly turns and walks away from my dungeon door.

Oh shit. This is crazy. Time to sit and wait again, because I have to get my poor feet back out of these damned tight shoes! They've swollen since being out of them. But I don't want to pace anyway. I don't want to give the guards the satisfaction, watching me on their monitors. My cell is so cold and gray it isn't worth keeping my eyes open. I guess that is what the other two girls in their cells are doing as well, trying to escape simply by sleeping.

* * *

A half an hour more goes by and then there's the sound of keys again. I don't bother to get up. But the opened outside door is for me and the Wizard appears. *Finally.* I'm surprised to see him, but don't bother to put my shoes on my aching feet. My feet hurt more than my ass. So I just sit there and look up at him expectantly through my bars. "What's taking so long? I don't have to *sleep* here, do I?!"

I can not even imagine trying to sleep on that narrow metal bench. I'd already tried to lie down three or four times, to give my butt a break, and had to brace myself from falling off. It wasn't worth lying down if I had to steady myself with one hand on my shoe the whole time. Can't touch the floor... no soap!

"No. I was told that you will be transferred to Seven Locks Jail very soon." Seven Locks is a street very close to my home. It intersects Democracy Boulevard only about a mile from my home. Great. I'm going to jail right around the corner from home. Woe is me.

The Wizard, however, looks pleased with himself, almost smiling. Why, I think, you failed me.

"They made some mistakes on your paperwork. They didn't make your sentences run concurrent." He runs his hand through his hair plugs, a habit I always find annoying. "Actually Edward noticed the error even before me," (yeah Prince Edward, you get *one* kudo for the day) "so they had to redo them." I'm still not sure what's going on and look at him questioningly. "Concurrent" the Wizard explains, "you are serving six months for the DUI, and sixty days each for the two DWIs, but since the sentences are to run concurrent, time served will be at the end of six months. And then you'll get 'good time', so you probably won't be in more than four and a half."

"*Good* time?!"

"They give you five days per month, I think it is, off, so you never serve your whole sentence." I truthfully have no clue what the hell he's talking about, but four and a half months certainly sounds better than six, and I do plan on being "good".

"Okay" is all I can answer, but then ask the big question, "Why didn't *I* get home confinement?"

"The judge just wouldn't go for it."

"Why not?!"

"He just wouldn't," the Wizard says with a blank look. I hear two loud coughs from my fellow inmates in their adjacent cells. "Listen, we're lucky we got what we did! I struck a great deal with the State's Attorney. If you had been prosecuted for three DUIs, *and* three DWIs and every other charge you had, you could easily be serving five to seven years." My mouth is dry but I try to swallow anyway, quickly thinking again about my four little children.

I can't imagine missing all those years of them growing up. I can't fathom how horrible that would be. I've cried twice already thinking about them while sitting in my cage for the last four hours. Not the full mascara dripping down the chin sobs I usually have when I miss them, because I'm on camera now and am not wearing any mascara anyway, but my heart has been wrenching over them the whole time.

My poor babies. I won't get to see them, and they won't get to see Mommy. It's going to be brutal, but I did it for four months of rehab, just two one-day visits, back and forth from Atlanta to D.C., so I can handle four and a half more in jail. But the poor things… will they feel so very ashamed to know Mommy's in jail? Will they tell their friends?

"Mary Ann?" The Wizard knows he blew my mind with that worse case scenario.

"Yes? I'm just living with the thought that I can make it six months, four and a half, whatever, doing anything, anywhere, but what about my medications?"

"They have them. They should give them to you."

"Should?"

"Yes, they should."

"I should have been an attorney" is my retort. "Attorneys make a lot more money than doctors and have a hell of a lot less stress. You're smarter than me probably, because you became a lawyer instead of a doctor."

"That's why I'm out here and you're in there."

I look right into the Wizard's eyes and don't need to speak. There is nothing to say to that. Maybe "Fuck you", but it's just not worth it. Men have been putting me down for years. Most men just can't handle me, are intimidated by me. And screw him anyway. Everyone knows being a doctor is better than being a lawyer any day of the week, any second of the day. Our training is much more grueling both intellectually and physically.

Doctors save people's entire bodies, and not just their *asses!* The Wizard may be a J.D. (Juris Doctor), but M, as in M.D., comes after J in the alphabet and doctors always have and always will be many notches higher on the food chain, no matter *who* is counting. Period. And every attorney knows it and hates it, that's why doctors have to carry so much malpractice insurance. Not so much for the fact that a patient can't forgive us for not being perfect, but because the lawyers *won't let them!* Why should they when they take at least a third?

The Wizard attempts a bit of bravado. "We really did well today. It could have gone much worse." *Well,* I think, wish I was near a well with a bucket right now. "Thank you for everything" is all I can muster.

I also could have killed someone and lived with that ultimate guilt the rest of my life, so I should be F.I.N.E., with six months. The Wizard says, "Call me if you need me, and remember we have Dieter's spiteful theft charge next week."

Oh my God. That's right! I have to go to court again for "stealing" back my own grandmother's candy dish. Damn Dieter should never have taken it out of my home in the first place. He was nothing if not vindictive in his pettiness when I reclaimed it from his home one day when I came to pick up the children. I saw it on the middle of his living room coffee table, put it under my coat and walked it out to my car, while he and the children were upstairs getting dressed. Dieter called the police over a glass candy dish and would have had me hand-cuffed for a twenty dollar candy dish in front of my own children if I hadn't taken off on a run yelling "Sorry, angels, but sometimes Daddy isn't so good to me and now I have to go!" I was stopped by the police on a side street away from Dieter's house (which I gave him the down payment for, only a measly $235,000), so my children didn't see anything when the police came, thank God.

I push the Wizard. "I thought you got that thrown out of court already."

"I can't. Your ex is still prosecuting. You can get additional jail time for that theft charge." Oh, Jesus Christ, I think, I've asked Dieter at least six times to drop it, but he wouldn't.

"Can't you get him to drop it *now?*" For Christ's sake, I think again, isn't this punishment enough?! Should I suffer even more for Baba's candy dish?

"I'll try. I have to go. Call me if you need me."

"Yeah, sure." And the Wizard vanishes.

Without intention, the thought pops into my head: *I could really go for a drink!*

An ice cold Chardonnay… Mary Ann, you stupid ass! How could you let that thought get into your head?! But I didn't let it. The devil just reared its ugly head by itself. Jesus, Joseph, and Mary, here I am in a claustrophobic cage for six months because of alcohol, and it rears its ugly head still. Forgive yourself, Mary Ann, remember you are thirsty and stuck in a cell with only a dripping tap. Okay, okay, calm down. Like Jane had said before court, "It's going to be okay, you're strong". I *am* strong. Baba was strong. Baba would want me to be strong now. Okay, persevere…yet again.

Keys, sound in a lock. Now keys are in my lock. I force my poor feet into my tight pumps and stand. "Turn around," the male guard says gruffly. I turn. See one, do one, teach one, the old motto from medical school. I know the drill now, after one example. I'm being handcuffed. "Ow! That's tight!" The guard says nothing except, "You're going to Seven Locks now."

* * *

The ride to the Seven Locks Jail (which is the holding tank before you go to *real* jail) is *un*real. In pitch black in the paddy wagon, sitting on yet another, even colder, hard metal bench, I realize on the first turn that you get tossed back and forth unless you hold onto the cloth strap behind you, easily accessible to handcuffed prisoners. (Not!) It is imperative that one holds that strap tightly to avoid brain damage from hitting the top of the damned paddy wagon driving over a speed bump! Bumping my sore butt up and down is inevitable, though. I never remember seeing one of these shockless little trucks in the movies, but here it is. The women sit facing the men, separated by a metal partition, enduring snide comments like "What's your name, Sweetie?", "How is you feelin' tonight?" and "Yous smells fine!" most of the way from the courthouse, until the passenger guard in the front finally barks, "Shut up back there!"

I'm thinking emphatically and want to scream: Hey driver, drop these losers off! Then just keep going straight and turn right on Democracy Boulevard and take me home! *Fat chance.* Wow, I'm really cold. I should have worn a coat this morning instead of Chanel #19. This morning. "This morning" feels like eons ago.

The paddy wagon finally stops and I almost trip and fall in my high heels on the two narrow steps down, easy to lose your balance with your hands behind your back. I never could ice skate. I'm certainly the best dressed of all of us, now that I can see exactly who I was riding with. They're a sorry looking lot, disheveled attire, bad haircuts and bad grammar. I am shivering now, standing outside on this damp November night.

November, for the rest of my life, will be *the* dreaded month. Something horrendous always happens to me in November. To name a few: my miscarriage, divorce, breaking my neck, a C1 C2 Hangman's fracture that I suffered in a car accident two months after Baba died. I should not have survived, or at the very least have been a quadriplegic like Superman, but my neck fracture was a rare non-displaced one so I am perfectly fine after thirteen weeks in a metal halo of screws stuck right into my skull. I even saw patients in it, looking like something close to Frankenstein. Just another cat's life gone. God wasn't ready for me yet I guess, just not my time. And now going to jail. Damned month only has one good day in it, but this year's Thanksgiving will be a record low.

*   *   *

First, I'm signed in. This gray concrete building looks exactly like where I came from. Boring and cold. They take my name and address, but you don't need a credit card to register for this hellhole of a hotel/jail. I don't even want to give my address in front of the others, so I whisper it. They take my picture for my future badge. I don't smile. No fingerprints. I, apparently, already had been fingerprinted. I don't remember being fingerprinted before. Oh, that must have happened during my first arrest, last November, when I was in a total blackout. Guess so. Hurry up and wait. Now, I'm sitting in a room four times the size of my cell. At least it's not so claustrophobic. And I have company, one attractive, 60-ish, African American woman with a tight, graying ponytail.

I speak first. "Hi, I'm Mary Ann. I'm in here for DUI. What are you in here for?" She gives me one of those looks like I'm from another planet, a truly weird alien, and I should mind my own business. But with my pug nose, freckles and attempt at a smile, she decides to answer me. "I'm Glenda, drugs." That's it. That's all she says.

Well, that says it all.

Another hour later, Glenda and I are led, one at a time, to a gray concrete bathroom to change. They had already taken my only gold watch and ring at the front desk. Probably won't see them again. Why, in God's name, did I wear any jewelry to court?! Because, you really were hoping *not* to go to jail, Mary Ann. This certainly wasn't a planned event, like everything else I've ever accomplished.

The single, female guard is watching me undress. "Is that an underwire bra?"

"I don't know. I think so."

She feels it. "Yes, it is. You have to give it to me."

"Why?"

"The underwire" is all she responds.

I hand her my bra. Now I'm taking off my pantyhose. Oh Christ, I think, yet again, I don't have any underwear on or socks. Perfect. I'm totally naked and barefoot on the dirty floor hoisting on a rough, tan jumpsuit. Jeepers, this jumpsuit's crotch is almost to my knees, and (shit!) my nipples show, especially in the cold! The guard hands me some over-sized, black flip flops, like my dad used to wear to the public pool. Now my feet are not only sore, but cold, too. I have to spread my legs for her, but she doesn't do a cavity search. Luckily, I guess, somehow I didn't require a vaginal exam for smuggled drugs. Who knows why? I thought they always did *that* in the movies.

"I have to go to the bathroom."

"Go ahead," and she points to a stall. At least she isn't watching me. After an unsurveilled, long overdue potty, I am extremely grateful to have a sink with a strong flow. I let it run for awhile, and then cup my hand and drink from it fifty times. Then it's back to the gray sitting room, waiting with Glenda for another hour at least. I find out Glenda just came from court, too. She is a drug dealer, has been her whole life. "Never did 'em, though" is her claim to fame. "One last run, I was doing, one last run. I was coming back from Mexico and the bastards caught me." She says it like she didn't deserve to be caught. She says she just should have "retired in Mexico" and not been "greedy to do one last run".

My first encounter with a real life drug dealer. Glenda doesn't fit the mold of a drug dealer. I've always pictured a drug dealer as a seedy looking character, someone with slicked-back hair, in need of a good shave and wearing a zoot suit. Glenda just looks like a grandma, with her hair in such a small ponytail that it looks like a bun. Turns out, Glenda *is* a grandmother, but obviously a far cry from my grandmother, my beloved Baba.

Finally, we are escorted to a large gray cement room, the "holding tank".

The tank is approximately 20' by 50', a simple rectangle that could hold at least sixteen women, because there are over eight bunk beds, with only one toilet and one shower. The metal toilet has no seat, just a metal bowl behind a short blue plastic shower curtain, so everyone can hear every fart of every woman just fine. I had no idea what that orchestral sound was at first, upon entering, and then realized it was someone behind the drape doing a loud "number two". So much for modesty, might as well let 'em rip right at the dinner table, which sits right in front of our dubious, just behind a blue curtain, "bathroom".

To the left of the bathroom there's one pay phone in this ugly gray musty room, with a television screwed into the cinderblock wall right above it. Most of the women seem mesmerized by the dinky, decrepit TV, despite the bad sound and snowy picture. A very large woman is yelling into the phone. You can hear every word of her conversation in this reverberating, high ceilinged, absolute shit hole of a room. At least, the tall ceiling means less claustrophobia and more air. Forget privacy, just forget about it Mary Ann.

I've been given some bedding, if you can call it that, some flat sheets, a hard plastic pillow and a burlap bag of a blanket. Actually, my blanket is worse than burlap. This whatever-it-is-made-out-of-blanket is more like the steel wool Baba washed pots and pans with. Except, "Mr. Burlap" seemed to be constantly mutating into something else and shedding, because there are little balls of blanket "tumors" metastasized all over the cement floor. The entire room is painted; you guessed it, gray from floor to ceiling. Dear Lord, this is so depressing. This is so fucking disgusting.

I'm freezing, hungry, exhausted, totally depressed and paranoid. I choose the bed in the corner just in case someone wants to attack me in the middle of the night. The corner turns out to be a good and bad choice. Good, because of reason number one. Bad, because it's near the cinderblock wall and small window; therefore, it's the draftiest and coldest spot in the house. Also bad, because it's right next to the box that the guard comes in and registers to every half an hour, twenty-four hours a day. I soon find out the box is some kind of state requirement that proves the guards are checking on us. Their noisy key check-ins and heavy booted strutting jolt me awake numerous times that night. Did I actually sleep?

My "bed" was definitely not purchased at Sears; I think it was special ordered directly from hell for my personal designated name of the holding tank at Seven Locks Jail, *Hotel Hell*. My God, this bed is barely better than the cold metal benches I've been on all day. My bed is simply a metal slab with a mattress on top that is a single piece of plastic, the exact consistency of a grade school gym mat but even thinner. I try to not let my brain even begin to recall my beautiful, mahogany, king-sized bed and down comforter that I usually don't even share now. I manage a smile to the girl lying on her own slab next to me. She's a "Mick" if there ever was one, with her black hair and white skin and Irish looking face. She smiles back, even looks happy to see me, as there is only one other white woman in the room.

Chapter 6

My Roommates

I sit on my gym mat holding my bedding, completely stunned. Just in shock. If it hadn't sunk in already; it certainly sank in right now. I'm horrendously humiliated, naked in a rough jumpsuit, locked up for six months with a bunch of drug dealers and Lord only knows what else. The "Mick" is watching me. "You better make your bed before they yell at you." I look at her blankly. *What bed,* I think. You call this metal slab and gym mat a bed? So I get up and make a vain attempt. There's really nothing to make but tuck the flat sheet between the metal and the gym mat. I sit down, wrap the shitty blanket around me to stop shivering and introduce myself to the brunette, "Hi, I'm Mary Ann."

"Hi, I'm Peggy."

Nice to meet you would be the usual next line, but not today. My hushed response is instead, "This is pretty nasty, isn't it?"

"Yep, fucking sucks."

I look around the room from my corner vantage point and really begin to assess the situation. I need to call my children, but a new woman is yelling into the phone over the blaring television now. I want to cry thinking about them again. What am I going to say? "Hi kids, everything's okay, Mommy's just in jail for *six months.* Sorry I can't have you over for Thanksgiving on Thursday". I bow my head for a minute. Oh my God, it's my year to have them for Thanksgiving. Guess no one is going to pick up my order from Giant. My poor babies, my dear sweet little angels. They don't deserve this. Truthfully, God, neither do I.

The bunk above me is empty, another reason I immediately gravitated to this corner. Peggy next door looks harmless, and so does the girl above her, but who knows what they did to join this harrowing club.

On the far opposite side of the room is an extremely slight, African American woman. She can't be a pound over eighty, if that, and spends all day in bed huddled under two blankets, her cheekbones popping out of her gaunt face. They gave her two blankets because she's sick, coughing this horrendously loud, mucous producing cough, and every so often spitting into her Styrofoam cup. They do have an old brown cooler for us in the corner with water in it but, according to Peggy, never enough cups.

I hoard mine like its gold on the tiny shelf of my window. My cup sits next to my one inch toothbrush, miniscule tube of toothpaste and little comb that came in my "vanity pack" when I was checked in to Hotel Hell. From the top bunk one can see out of the narrow window, but the lower half is covered for some reason. Maybe so that one can't see the outside world. Who cares, there's nothing to see but a tiny cement, walled in yard of brown grass and weeds. A far cry from the magnificent two acre, backyard view I have at home with its blue spruces, crepe myrtles and of course, beautiful flowers of all kinds I transplanted from Baba's garden.

The sickly girl coughs again. Peggy whispers, "She's our age, only 42, and she has AIDS. She says she got it from a rape." My eyes widen. 42? She looks 72! I've been to rehab and she looks exactly like a heroin addict to me, but who am I to judge?

I'm a nobody in here just like everyone else. Next to "Coughing Cathy", I definitely have the lowest body fat in the room and shivering, I asked for two blankets. The guard gave me a resounding, "No"! I look at my spare jumpsuit and the damned thing is a large, instead of a medium, so I just put it on over my medium. I could have easily fit into a small and thus look like I'm ready for Halloween, but Halloween isn't celebrated in jail. (But probably should be. We're all costumed ready jail bait characters!)

"Why is she here?" I whisper back to Peggy. It is impossible to not hear the loud coughing and gagging from across the room.

"BWI."

"What?" I thought I didn't hear her correctly, but then she stumps me completely.

"Biking while intoxicated."

"You've *got* to be kidding, right?"

"Nope. That's what she said. She was given a $500 fine and can't pay it so she's staying here until her court date, January 8th." Now I'm really over the top. I have never, ever heard of "*Biking* While Intoxicated"; something's fishy about that. And the poor thing can't come up with $500 to get out? So she'll be spending *all* of the holidays, Thanksgiving, Christmas, and New Year's in jail? In this shithole? Jesus, I'm ready to offer her $500 to leave, just to get rid of her coughing whatever bactcriae and viri (plural in Latin) all over our enclosed space.

"That's insane!" I hiss to Peggy, "She sounds like she has pneumonia!"

Peggy nods. I'm preaching to the choir, though, because Peggy can't afford to get out on her bond either.

Wish I had the option of bond. I'd top out my platinum card in a heartbeat. How the fuck am I going to pay my bills from here? Or pay them at all? But I can't worry about how to pay over twelve grand of bills a month right now. I have to spend all my energy on keeping warm and not getting sick.

Peggy says she's in for credit card fraud. Her own cousin turned her in for using her credit card unauthorized. But Peggy insists her cousin said she could use it. She says, "I only used $1,000 and she said I could." Whatever. In the same breath she also admits, "I'm a crack cocaine addict and I have depression too. But I haven't taken any meds in awhile because they're so expensive." I bet Peggy spends a hell of a lot more on her crack than the $3.50 a day I do for an antidepressant, but I say nothing. So far, she's the one person I've had over a one sentence conversation with, and I don't want to piss her off, or anyone else for that matter. I haven't even gotten a chance to use the phone yet and speak to anyone in the real world. The phone can only be used during certain hours and is always busy. Only collect calls can be made, so I have to time it to when I think Edward or Dieter will be home.

"I have three children with my ex-husband," Peggy continues in a very hushed tone. "He has custody. I can't even afford an apartment right now. I live with my boyfriend in the back of his van. It's been getting cold at night."

I stare at her. "I'm sorry," is all I can think to say.

"Where do you live?" Peggy asks.

I change the subject and simply respond, "Well, I'm in jail for the next six months!"

Drug dealing Glenda snatches the one *Washington Post,* they give us in the morning and reads all day, handing off sections to others as she finishes them like she owns the joint. Maybe she could afford to buy Hotel Hell having sold drugs her whole life. The younger, drug dealing women treat her with respect, like she's some kind of guru. She commands this reverence because it took the Feds forty-some years to catch her, and most of the other women are in their twenties and thirties and not even close to Glenda's wealthy retirement.

There are two Hispanic women bunking next to each other. I say "Hello" to the short, pretty one and get no response. Her Hispanic neighbor informs me, "She doesn't speak English." Two days later, I find out she's part of a prostitution ring that was busted in Gaithersburg, Maryland where I used to live. She's a Mexican woman who was promised a "good job" when she got to America, so she could send money back home to her mom to feed her two-year-old daughter. She's waiting to be deported. Good for her, I think. She's better off in poverty with her baby back home, than *holding up playing cards* to gringos in America to ask what sexual act they want her to perform. Playing cards. That's how she communicates. Certain cards for certain sex. So humiliating and so dangerous. Just take one look at the lady with AIDS. In contrast to "Coughing Cathy", there's one very obese woman serving thirty days for failure to pay a fine. All she does is ask everyone for their food.

The majority of the people incarcerated in this room are addicts. The percentage, race-wise, is well over two-thirds African American. Do African Americans, who account for 13% of the population, *really* commit well over 67% of the crimes? Or do the old boy white judges just let the white women off with PB&J's (Probation Before Judgment, which equals No Jail Time) and punish the minorities more harshly, most especially the African American women, by incarcerating them for longer sentences than white women for the same crime? I mentally start to keep track. It already seems, though, that the only thing worse than being a white woman in this racist, prejudiced world of ours is to be a black woman. Except in jail. In jail, it's better to be African American. What a horrible thing to say, however true.

There's one African American girl from Chicago who I befriended playing cards. She's a great gin rummy player, doesn't use slang and eventually admits to me, on our third day of rummy, that she's an engineer with a bad crack cocaine habit. I admit I was an abuser of alcohol. Her name is Yvonne and besides me, she is by far the most educated woman in the room. Peggy and I both enjoy her savvy card playing and normal conversation, if anything's close to "normal" in jail.

"See the African American girl by the water cooler?" asks Peggy.

"Yes?"

"Well, she and her husband are a black Bonnie and Clyde!"

"What?"

"They rob banks! They got caught just outside of a bank with only $1,604. Her husband is down the hall. She was supposed to be the getaway driver and her husband wanted her to flee, but the police were yelling they were going to shoot so she never left the parking lot."

"Oh my God!"

"Ya. Nuts, huh? She's got a three-year-old son and thinks she's pregnant right now. Her bond is $25,000."

"Wow." Pregnant in jail. What a total bummer, especially with the over-cooked, starchy crap they feed us along with the mystery meat. The only meal halfway decent is breakfast. But then again, how can one screw up cold toast, milk and powdered juice? The hot (well, lukewarm) cereal, however, is unusual. Unlike anything I've ever eaten before.

"Duke! Miss Duke, come here!"

I jump up. "Yes?"

"Come with me!" the guard barks.

"Coming!" I didn't even hear the solid metal door to the room open.

I get ready to be handcuffed but surprisingly am not cuffed. Guess you don't always get handcuffed when leaving the holding tank. Why should they? Nowhere to run, already in jail. For a fleeting moment, I think about sprinting down the hall as fast as I can. My God, I've been locked up for less than twenty-four hours and I want to break out. No wonder inmates go crazy and futilely make a break for it and fight guards, just to get put in solitary confinement and suffer harder. It's a natural reflex to want to flee out an open door! For some paranoid reason I think, I'm in trouble because I've been talking too much to Peggy.

Stupid thought. Every other woman in the room is jabbering too. They kept me up over half of the first night. Two women knew each other, were actually happy to see each other, and chatted across their upper bunks about their drug highs and lows and deals into the wee hours of the morning. Then, of course, some of the other women chimed in to share their stories. I was too scared to tell them to shut the hell up so I could get some sleep. The only time everyone went silent was when they heard the guard's keys in the lock checking in on us every half hour.

I'm led down two long bare hallways. Gray appears to be the only color in here except for the tan jumpsuits.

"Sit here and wait for your name to be called" is all I'm told. I sit staring at all the desks and people. Dear God, what are they going to do to me now?

A few minutes later a very pretty blonde, blue eyed woman calls, "Miss Duke?" I'm still not used to being called "Miss". Just doesn't sound right. I've been "Dr." Duke for almost twenty-five years. I earned it, to be called "Dr." But in here, fuck it. I'm just glad this lady looks pleasant and isn't going to reprimand me.

"I'm here to do your intake," she says.

"Oh." I thought I had already checked in to Hotel Hell last night at the front desk. She's reading through my paperwork for some time. There's a lot to read. She finally looks up at me. In a quiet monotone she says, "You don't belong here. You are an alcoholic, not a criminal."

I'm dead silent, staring into her big blue eyes, thankful. Thankful that *someone* in this chaotic mess that I can't believe is still my life, understands. I'm not a criminal. I'm a woman who abused alcohol and unfortunately and unwisely broke the law during her blackouts. If I was in my right mind, I certainly wouldn't be trying to break laws and earn myself jail time. Who does? Desperate people. Greedy people. Mentally ill people. Lunatics and addicts. Not necessarily in that order.

I'm still staring at the pretty woman as she looks down again. All at once I'm grateful and hateful of her comment. *Perfect.* Just what I need to hear, sixteen hours into a six month vacation in hell, that I was put on the wrong flight and I can't get off.

*   *   *

My dear Baba was right about one thing, though. I am blessed with "some" smarts, if not enough brains to take care of my own personal well being.

Being a person who doesn't like to throw things out (basically a pack rat) I found this letter from high school. I am still in shock that I found it at all, yellow and faded from almost thirty years ago. Most shocking is that it is from Mr. Kapp, the Chairman of the English Department, my absolute *least* favorite subject of all time. I do not recall at all asking Mr. Kapp for a letter. I only remember him being mad at me for not taking his favorite class senior year, British Literature. "To be or not to be"? Who cares about Shakespeare? Not me, anyway. I prefer Mozart and Vivaldi. So the letter is doubly surprising:

"February 27th, 1979

To Whom It May Concern:

With no reservations whatsoever do I write this letter of recommendation for Mary Ann Duke. Her character is exemplary of what every American parent, teacher, school or citizen might wish.

Mary Ann's scholastic achievements and attitude illustrate not only her scholarship but also her character. Mary Ann possesses the leadership qualities that America needs. She has been actively involved with her fellow classmates since she entered school. Her peers not only admire her but also welcome her participation and leadership in both scholastic and extra-curricular programs. She is co-captain of the Girl's Varsity Basketball team, voted the Most Valuable Player of the Tennis Team, (*He forgot I was MVP of my favorite sport of all, Track.*), not to mention that she was elected President of the National Honor Society, President of the Key Club and is a member of the Senior Class Steering Committee. Her leadership qualities are enhanced by her always pleasant, well-mannered personality and her immaculate appearance.

If any organization has an opportunity to extend itself to a deserving student, indeed Mary Ann Duke is the epitome of just such a student. Whichever college she might attend will certainly be proud to have Mary Ann and will benefit from her attending that university.

To be sure, Mary Ann Duke is the kind of student and person who personifies what every American should strive to become. It is with great pleasure that I write this letter of recommendation; for Mary Ann is a deserving student and will be a definite contribution to any college, but more importantly to America.

Very truly yours,

Paul Kapp, Coordinator of English"

Gees, when I finished reading that letter, I cried. I always thought until that moment that Mr. Kapp resented me for not taking his precious Shakespeare class.

There are six things that keep me alive. I like sixes. I was born on 6/6/61. The six things that keep me going are my four children; I still care for myself, despite some setbacks, and the last paragraph of Paul Kapp's letter.

Chapter 7

Growing Up a "Good Girl"

I unlock my dorm room door in a hurry because my arms were killing me from all the heavy textbooks I was hauling back from class. "Betty!" I scream as I dropped my books on the floor. There was Betty, my farm girl roommate, stark naked and riding high on the guy from across the hall. She twirls her head around but certainly didn't get off. Not then, at least. Below her, the man on deck pays no attention to me.

I left all my homework sprawling on the floor and swiftly back peddle out. "I'll be back in an hour; I have a big test tomorrow!" I yell through the now locked door.

Jeepers Betty, I think, I didn't know you were even *dating* him! Just three weeks into my first semester in college, was this what my roommate was going to be doing every afternoon? I need to study! She didn't even look upset. (Why should she, in the middle of having sex?) Couldn't she have at least left me a note? Thank God I had my sneakers on and shorts so I went for my four mile run then, instead of later.

An hour later, sweaty and spent (so was Betty), I knock before entering my own room. "Come in." I open the door and there's my earth mother roommate clad only in a towel.

"Sorry" was all she says. I pick up my pile of books and scattered notes. I really don't know what to say.

I am embarrassed for both of us. Being a virgin, of course, I'd never seen anyone quite like that before, in the flesh, not even in the movies. So I blurt out, "Could you *please* leave me a note next time?"

"Sure."

God only knows how many notes I pulled off my door after that *and* how many times she still forgot to leave one. I saw it all and in various positions, but now I consistently start going to class in running gear. Couldn't they have just walked two steps across the hall to his room? Nope. His roommate didn't run.

I am in such great shape by spring that I won the first annual Army R.O.T.C. 10K, the first woman to finish, and I beat a lot of the guys as well. It was the first and last 10K I've ever run. I got a great trophy. Quit while I'm ahead, I say.

Betty and I lived in the only coed dorm on campus. And I was being a "good girl," a frustrated good girl, saving myself for marriage. Instead, my knees took a beating from all that running.

*   *   *

I grew up in the Binghamton area, alias "Bingotown", New York. Binghamton, when I grew up in the mid 60's, was barely on the map and couldn't even keep a farm team. Rock concerts were few and far between and a good time was riding my bike to "Polacks' Park" with friends or playing cards with Baba and church events. In hindsight, I love my hometown except it suffers from a lack of sunshine, thus making me suffer from year round "seasonal affective disorder". I think the weather is a little better back home now with global warming.

Back then it was important to be a virgin when you married. Or at the very least, it was important to hurry up and get married before you got pregnant. My parents instilled in me, *branded* in me, the idea that one of the most important things in life was to be a virgin when you got married. Not that they talked to me or my two older sisters about sex. Why should they? No need to. We were smart girls and would remain virgins until our wedding nights when we would assuredly figure it out.

Sex was bad, anyway. Sex was *bad*. Only bad girls had sex before marriage. "Why buy the cow when the milk's for free" was the old saying we heard over and over. No one would want to marry you if you weren't a virgin, and I definitely wanted to get married and have babies more than anything.

The Bible taught, or so we were told, that sex is for procreation, not recreation. The Virgin Mary gave birth to the Son of God after the Immaculate Conception. She didn't even lose her virginity to God Almighty in order to have his son. She was a very good girl. I was going to be a very good girl, too.

I was afraid to be otherwise. My younger brother and sisters and I were brought up in a very strict household. My father, Michael, called himself a benevolent monarch, and so we grew up in a benevolent monarchy. What my father said ruled. He was tall, dark and handsome, with big brown eyes and stood proud. And he should be proud, all four of his children finished college and have grown to be happy, strong, God fearing adults. I'm sure he's very disappointed in me right now but, "c'est la vie" (that's life), no one can be perfect all the time. Shit happens.

Now my mom, she is very sad and more than a little mortified with my present jail scenario. She doesn't want anyone at the church to find out. She didn't even tell my oldest sister, Marta, who's the treasurer at St. Michael's, because she was afraid Marta would talk. Oh well, she means well. She's a good mother and becomes more like Baba as she gets older, but she still worries too much. She's worrying now.

The worst memories from my childhood were of being disciplined with my father's belt. I can't fathom doing that to a child, especially a little girl. After having two daughters I think, like most couples, my parents were hoping for a boy. My brother was born later, after an almost decade gap, and by then my father had given up on corporal punishment. So my little brother Joseph never ran, locking himself in the bathroom to hide or cower in fear as Dad forced the door open. Good for Joseph, no welts for his behind. I broke the mold. We girls were raised in the late 50's and early 60's when I think everyone more or less hit their kids. Joseph was born in 1969. Twenty years later, when I was at the Wilmer Eye Institute at the Johns Hopkins Hospital in Baltimore, I examined a little African American boy who had been blinded by his father's belt. The child must have turned his head right at the wrong time, and the buckle hit him smack in the eye giving him a huge, painful corneal abrasion and the densest retinal hemorrhage. His whole retina was a deep, thick red. I have never seen a nastier, more horrible hemorrhage even in the worst cases of macular degeneration to this day. I doubted this little boy was ever going to see anything but light out of that eye again. The beating had blinded him.

Mine was a strict childhood but a happy one. Even though now I know it wasn't the real world; it was the only world I knew. My years growing up in Johnson City, New York, the even tinier town bordering Binghamton, were very sheltered. The whole area in the mid 60's was not what one would call racially diverse. Everyone went to church on Sunday. Everyone was white, of European descent, and Christian. Now, my hometown is as much of a melting pot as the rest of the nation, but not when I grew up there.

Going to church (Russian Orthodox) was a big deal, a very big deal. The Saturday night ritual was to bathe and get our hair washed before putting our hair up in little spit curls held with toilet paper and bobby pins. We all had to have curly hair and perfect outfits for church. We were three little angels, my sisters and I.

In the early 70's, I rebelled and stayed up watching a new show, *Saturday Night Live*, with the original "Not Ready for Prime Time Players". I loved them. I'd lie on the couch with the black and white television and the family room all to myself, laughing hysterically until the bellow came from Dad and Mom's bedroom: "You have to get up for church!" I'd respond with an "I know Dad, I know" before returning to Steve, Dan, Chevy, Bill, Dennis, Gilda, John, Jane and all the rest.

In the Russian Orthodox Church the norm is to go to confession at least twice a year, Easter and Christmas. We receive communion less frequently than other faiths as you're only supposed to get communion if you have no sins and you only have no sins after going to confession. I used to dread it. In the Orthodox faith one cannot hide in a closet behind a dark screen like the Catholics; we get down on our knees right in front of the priest. He puts a part of his robe on the top of our heads and then his two hands on top of that. The priest's hands are touching our heads the whole time so he can actually feel if we squirm. No way out. Let it out. Speak the truth, tell your sins, ask forgiveness and then go kneel in front of the iconostas and say three Our Father's and three Hail Mary's. The next day on Sunday receive Holy Communion from a spoon shared by the whole church, a piece of bread soaked in wine. (Hopefully, no one had a bad virus that day.) Manishevitz, I think it was.

While growing up I firmly believed I wouldn't go to heaven if I had any sins in me whatsoever. There was always a sense of relief after communion on Sunday because for the moment, I was "sin free". It was safe to die now. Short term gratification because then, usually within 24-48 hours, I would sin and blow it. I would swear by accident and then I had to go to confession all over again in order to feel that "safe to die" feeling... How guilt-tripping insane, and the Catholics and the Jewish faith think *they* have it tough?

Thinking in profanities didn't count as a full-blown sin but was still bad. I hardly ever swore, but it seemed like I would always do it within 48 hours of a confession. Crazy. Like the stress of keeping sin free was too much for me. I didn't even *think* in profanities back then. Now I do it all the time. Not good. Why do I do that? Is my vocabulary so poor? (Nah) Or is it just easier for the human brain to come up with a swear word than an adjective? Less neurons to fire, less energy spent? Answer must be the latter.

Seriously, I know when I started thinking in profanities, R.P.I. Definitely at Rensselaer Polytechnic Institute and then cursing mushroomed in medical school. Everything was profane then. It was the f'ing question on the f'ing test with the f'ing wrong answer. That was the best adjective there was. It got your point across. Even Diz, my devout, chaste Catholic roommate in medical school, who followed the redoubtable Betty at R.P.I. and was "holier than thou", muttered an occasional "Fuck!" At least the F-Bomb was not using the Lord's name in vain.

*   *   *

Rensselaer Polytechnic Institute. R.P.I. <u>R</u>eally <u>P</u>retty <u>I</u>ncredible (Definitely *not* R.I.P., "Rest in Peace.") I was accepted out of high school, with a scholarship, into a

6-year, accelerated B.S. / M.D. program where you're a doctor in six years instead of the usual eight. This is achieved by cramming three years of summer school in between the normally intensive twelve semesters. The first two years at Rensselaer Polytechnic Institute were Intense, with a capital I. R.P.I. was harder for me than medical school. In fact, it was relentless. There were exhausting, enormous amounts of new, difficult concepts to retain and master. I had to do well, needed a 3.2 Science cuum, and not just a 3.2 overall, to go on to Albany Medical College.

The ratio of men to women on campus was at least 10:1, since R.P.I. used to be an all male college for over a hundred years. But hell's bells, I found out right away that the nerd/geek to yummy guy ratio was at least 100:1, so the pickings were still slim, to put it mildly. Maybe Betty was using a different calculator than me.

Anyway, marriage was not in the immediate future, medical school was, so Mary Ann studied her ass off! First semester: Calculus I, Physics I, Chemistry I, and two humanities, German I, and Psych 101. I picked German as a language, instead of the more useful Spanish. Big mistake. Huge! I spent more time memorizing what needed to be das, die or der than I studied for some of my science classes. One would figure a country that thought they could take over the world would have a way of communicating a basic "the" without needing three forms of it. The Germans are still having a hard time figuring out what is indeed male (der), female (die) or neuter (das). "Die cravat" is "The tie". Aren't ties male? "Die" is the female form of "the", shouldn't it be "der cravat"? Just dump the differences and use "duh"! My frustration obviously abounded.

Semester two: (Even more brutal) Calc. II, Chem. II, Physics II, German II (idiot me went back for more punishment), and an easy humanity, "Joyce's Ulysses".

Then summer school: Organic Chemistry I (with a lab), Embryology, Organic Chemistry II (with a lab) and Alcohol & Drug Abuse. (A warning from the future? Not that it did me much good…)

The incredible brainiacs I took Organic with over the summer out voted me to have the weekly tests on Mondays instead of Fridays, so they could have the weekend to study. Freaking maniacs! My protestation that "If we have the tests on Fridays, guys, we'll have the weekend off!" fell on mute ears. Can you believe that? I still can't. Well, thanks to that vote, on a Sunday afternoon I was studying in my dorm room for my Organic Chemistry II test the next day, when there was a knock at the door.

I opened it and was happy to see my older sis, Elena. I immediately hugged her but she had a serious look on her face, so I pulled back but still holding her shoulders said, "What's wrong"?!

Elena was too choked up to speak and somehow I knew immediately, "Did Popsi die"?

"Yes". I knew my grandfather had health problems from his drinking, but he was still only sixty-six.

"When?"

"This morning, while we were all in church. Baba found him on the bathroom floor when she got home. She called Mom and Dad and an ambulance immediately but he was already gone." Tears were pouring down my face. My dear family knew how upset I would be, so my sister drove three hours to get me instead of telling me over the phone.

"Poor Baba! Let's go! I have to see her!" Crazy, I was going to miss Popsi, but all I could think was that my dear Baba was going to be alone now.

We drove straight to Baba's house and I ran in crying. I wanted to see her and hug her and try to console her. And there was dear, strong Baba, all 4'9" of her, looking puffy and cried out, and I just sobbed into her shoulder. Then she is consoling *me!* "It's okay Medka, Popsi is in heaven now." The strong, indelible memories of my Baba's faith and love still never cease to amaze me. She was a widow for twelve of the thirty-one years I knew her, but she remained happy and more giving than anyone I've ever known. Thank God for her example. When Baba left me, she left me with a lot.

I missed almost a whole week of summer school. Somehow, some way, I still pulled out a B in Organic II. I sat in lab crying one afternoon mourning Popsi and feeling bad for Baba. I obviously was not 100% and I ruined my entire lab project. Poof! Up in smoke! There was nothing left in my test tube to hand in! Not a speck! Oh my God! I was going to get an F!

The guy who had been across from me in lab for the last six weeks was watching. The professor was on the other side of the room, so the young man walked around the table, picked up my empty test tube and tapped some of his finished product into it. I was so grateful, yet afraid; I just thanked him with my eyes. It was the first and only time I ever cheated, but I needed a C in that one credit hour lab, because a D means death. D's are *not* allowed. None, whatsoever. One D and you are kicked out of the program. No going on to medical school. One D, or F, as a final grade and *it's over.*

Fifty-eight credit hours in one calendar year, over half of the way to a four-year degree in *one* calendar year and, of course, the Dean's list.

*   *   *

David Jaffe was my best friend at Rensselaer, a tall, dark and handsome Israeli. Perfect, exactly *not* the man my Russian Orthodox parents wanted me to meet. "Yaffay", I endearingly called him, because that's how his last name was pronounced. So he called me "Dukie". Everyone thought we are dating, but actually I was in his all male dorm room every night getting tutored in Physics I and II. Yaffay was brilliant. He really helped me, and somehow I managed Bs. It hurt a lot when he had to leave after one year, because he had turned eighteen and had to go back to Israel to serve his required three years in the military. He really didn't want to leave, but also didn't want to disappoint his father, a Vice President for then Israeli Airlines.

I was walking to class with Yaffay when we saw a huge, purple neon sign in the top window of the boy's biggest dorm, blinking on and off, "NUKE IRAN, NUKE IRAN".

"Why is that sign up there?" I innocently ask Yaffay.

I had been studying so incredibly hard, always buried in books, I didn't even know there were hostages being held in Iran for the past six weeks. Yaffay absolutely could not believe that I was that unaware. "What is vvrrrong with you? Can't you read? It's been all over the papers for weeks!" He yells at me in his thick, Israeli accent, "There are American hostages in Iran! Don't you ever listen to the radio? MY GODT! I don't beleeeve you! I vvvrrreally don't beleeevvve you!"

Yep, R.P.I. is an amazingly diverse and challenging school. It demanded my full attention and kept me oblivious to the outside world, except for the occasional sex scenes from Betty. For God's sake, it seemed like every other student was the valedictorian of *their* high school. I was a little fish in a big pond.

      *   *   *

Year II was more of the same (and, very unfortunately, without Yaffay): Calc III, Physics III and my absolute *favorite*, Physical Chemistry I and II. (Who really cares how a refrigerator works? *I* certainly didn't. If it doesn't stay cold, you call Sears. C'mon!)

Dr. Butz was the Physical Chemistry professor, a truly great man. We all called him "Fat and Fuzzy", because he had a big gut and a perfect, gray crew cut. A more fitting endearment could have been "The Fat and Fuzzy Inferno" since he chain-smoked the entire lecture hour, lighting his next cigarette from the one he was putting out. Sweating profusely, the "Inferno" attempted to occasionally wipe his brow, but he didn't have a free hand. His right wielded a magic marker and the left held a Camel, thus the transparencies he worked on were barely legible and always smeared with sweat. Topping that, every illegible page of formula and related gibberish was swiftly rolled up on completion, to the loud protestations of the class. None of us, not one of us, could come close to taking down all of his notes. Fueled by his nicotine high, he was by far the fastest, sweatiest, most frustrating lecturer I have ever experienced.

So, I gave up taking notes. It was no use, couldn't read my *own* handwriting anyway. I was totally paranoid about getting a D. I needed help; P.Chem. was deadly. "Professor", I went up to him after my last test score was a 26 (which was actually a C-, still passing). "I'm having a very hard time. Could you please give me some pointers?" "Of course, come to my office at four p.m." I was so relieved.

*   *   *

"Dr. Butz, I still don't understand" I coughed, following his patient hour of tutoring and puffing. The air in his small office was extremely thick with smoke.

Luckily my lungs were conditioned by eighteen years of church incense and running.

"Just remember how to apply these forty formulas, Dear, for the exam, and you'll do fine."

"Sure, no problem, thank you very much, Professor," cough. "Can I come back tomorrow please?"

An A and two Bs, an A and two Bs, that was the grade to make. One C in a science class and it got very tough, because then you'd have to get two As to bring it up. Stress. Stress all of the time. Nonstop stress, couldn't get one D! My father comforted me by saying he got a D in Physics when he attended Union College. Great, just *not* what I needed to hear. And remember Baba only finished sixth grade.

*   *   *

Over one-third of the six-year program students usually don't advance to medical school. One third do not make the grade and drop out or are kicked out. I think that most kids still go away to college with the idea that it's going to be one big party, away from their parent's rules and curfews, and for some it is. Not so for me. R.P.I. was no party. If I didn't advance on to Albany Medical College, than those dreams of Baba's and mine to "be a doctor" wouldn't come true, much less the "have a good life" part.

I left R.P.I. with a bang. I took Mammalian Anatomy over the summer. It should have been called "Feline Filleting". Three afternoons a week, in a very hot room with no air circulation, we dissected dead (and very stinky) cats. It's not easy and, moreover, I *like* pussycats. You'd think with the tuition increase at Albany Med from $7,400 to $14,200 in one year (which just about gave my dad a stroke), we'd have been cutting up Rhesus monkeys.

Makes sense, they're a hell of a lot more like humans than some alley cat. Plus, I don't particularly like monkeys. But no, "Fluffy" and "Mittens" were on the dissecting table. I hated it, so I didn't study. At all. Nada. I got the first F of my life on that midterm. I wasn't depressed as much as in shock. I thought I could get away without studying and at least pull a C. Not at R.P.I..

I was called into the Dean's office at Albany Medical College the very next day. I felt claustrophobic in his puffy, leather-couched, thoroughly mahogany office. My heart had been in my throat all day since his call.

"Miss Duke! *Miss* Duke, you are not passing Mammalian Anatomy, and a D is *not* good enough!" he announces, leaning into me. I could tell he was angry from his red face and furrowed brow. "If you proceed to get a D in the course, you will *not* be matriculating on to medical school in the fall. Do I make myself clear... *Doctor?*"

"Yes, sir, I mean, *doctor*. Of course," I jump up and sputte, "Is that all?"

"Yes. Go study."

It was do or die then, down to my last final whether I was going on to medical school or not, whether I really was going to be able to "be a doctor and...".

I was certifiably crazy the days before that exam. I had to study six weeks worth of summer school material, the equivalent of an entire semester during a regular school year, in a week. I had never saved it all to the very end before. I needed God to help me. He did. I pulled a B on the final and a C out of my ass, for that stinky Cat Class.

Chapter 8

Becoming a Doctor

I started medical school at age twenty and was on crutches for the first two months, after annihilating my knee playing frisbee. I was supposed to have major knee surgery over Thanksgiving but by November 1st I was jogging again. Never did have surgery, but my most recent MRI reveals my knee cartilage is all gone, along with my ACL (anterior cruciate ligament) and I can still run. That defies logic but so does much of my life. I finished my ophthalmology residency three weeks after I turned twenty-eight, the youngest one could be, unless, of course, one is a child prodigy who begins college before starting puberty.

Unfortunately (or fortunately, who knows), I came out the same nice and naïve, small town, altruistic, good girl. I was, however, no longer white. I was purple. Bruised from all of the abuse I took, just for being me. Essentially I never learned how to "kiss ass" and still don't know how. Screw it. Even if I learned the proper technique, my personality is such that I refuse to play those games, even if it would greatly help me to get ahead.

Most people think that's a stupid attitude, but that's the only way I know how to be. I know how to be only myself, and I can't pretend to be an ass-kisser just because someone in a position of authority thinks their ass should be kissed.

In the early eighties women in medicine were still supposed to be wearing tight little white dresses, not slacks and long white coats. And women were supposed to be taking orders, not giving them. At the most, female doctors were supposed to be only pediatricians or family practitioners. There was very much chauvinism by the "Good Ole Boys" against women becoming surgeons.

I did, however, do well in medical school and was granted the Dean's Senior Research Award and also the highly esteemed Sandoz Award for Ophthalmology. I won the ophthalmology award over several male medical students, one in particular whose ophthalmologist father expected his son to win.

Here's one tiny, but perfect, example of the chauvinism and my character. Just a few weeks into my ophthalmology residency, I'm summoned to the Chairman of the Ophthalmology Department's office. At twenty-five, I'm in the prime of my youth, working extremely hard and not sleeping enough because I'm on call every three to four nights.

The summons seems ominous, yet I know I haven't done anything wrong. What does he want to see me for? I'm a little scared because in the very first week, the first year residents learned that if one is called into the Chairman's office alone, one is in for a serious reprimand.

I politely knock on the Chairman's door before entering. "Come in!" he barks.

With my racing mind, I can still not think of any reason why he asked to see me and am truly baffled as I open the door.

I enter his over-sized, bookshelf-laden, masculinely decorated office with over-sized desk and couch and remain standing by the door. Dr. Richard, "Dick", as he's known, is busy lighting his pipe. You betcha! It *really* was the "good ole days" of medicine when "the good ole boys" still smoked in their offices and there was even a smoking room outside of the operating room in some hospitals for everyone. I decide to speak first and simply enquire, "You asked to see me?"

Puff, puff. "Yes." Puff...

He doesn't ask me to sit. He takes his sweet old time with his pipe then commands, "I do not want you to wear eye make-up anymore. It is inappropriate for an ophthalmologist."

I'm taken aback. Is that all he pulled me out of lecture for? I glance down at my shirt and see it is brown, so that means my eyeliner is brown. I owned every color Maybelline had to offer and brown is definitely my most conservative Maybelline of all. There is an awkward silence.

Puff, puff. "That is all." Puff. "You may go back to work."

I turn and leave without a word.

After lecture my fellow residents were curious and asked me, "What did Dick say to you"? I told them the truth. "He told me to stop wearing eye-liner". I think even the most ass-kissing conservative of them all thought it was a weird thing to get called in for, but everyone was afraid of the Chairman's power and not a single one of them gave me any support.

The only make-up I ever wore was lipstick and eyeliner, which I put on in the car at the last red light before the hospital, because I slept until the final minute before I had to get ready to drive to work. I would simply grab the Maybelline out of my purse that matched the color top I was wearing, to try not let my tired brown eyes look how they felt. Then I enhanced my pale face by a little lipstick. Why not? I'm single and twenty-five. However, I was definitely in the minority and I stood out. Most of the female residents wore not a stitch of make-up because it was better to look like a young man than a young woman. And... how *dare* you not look exhausted!

That night at home I went over the brief exchange with the Chairman several times in my mind without wanting to. The last time it flipped through my head, I thought, "Gee, well what is *'appropriate'* for an ophthalmologist, to be a pompous ass"?

The next day I wore a purple shirt to the hospital with matching purple eyeliner, and the following day turquoise with turquoise. No one is going to tell me how to wear my eyeliner. And anyway, my patients always complimented me on it, and they are the ones who *really* count.

To this day, however, I hate the word inappropriate. *Webster's* definition of inappropriate is: not appropriate, unsuitable. The definition for unsuitable is: unbecoming, inappropriate. I thought my eyeliner was *very* becoming, most fetching!

This led to Dick demanding that I have a complete psychiatric evaluation. (Can you *believe* this shit? Sometimes even I can't and I lived it). I think Dick, *le Chairman,* thought I must be crazy since I ignored his dogma. (Twenty years later I would have told him to go get shrunk himself. *You need it more than I do.* Good thing I went through residency before my chutzpah tumor metastasized.) The school shrink gave me a clean bill of mental health and literally laughed about the whole incident. He told me to "wear your make-up the way you want, Honey". Thank God he was fair (and not just another "good ole boy"), just as a good shrink should be, especially one raising eight children, several of them girls. But, best of all, guess whose portrait is the only picture, *eye liner and all*, as the ophthalmology centerfold in the Albany Medical Center Residency Program book that only comes out every several years. How *in*appropriate! (Back cover)

*   *   *

More *ap*propriate was my first encounter with the Vice Chairman of the Ophthalmology Department and head of pediatric ophthalmology. On the very first day of my pediatric ophthalmology rotation I heard a loud wheeze (3 out of 4 plus, *very* significant) on an infant. Never had I ever heard such a loud wheeze on a baby. But I learned from Diz, (my medical school roommate who training in pediatrics at Children's Hospital in Boston at the same time I was training in ophthalmology in Albany and we kept in touch), that a loud wheeze on a baby was much more life threatening than a loud wheeze on an adult. I wrote I "recommended a chest x-ray and pediatric consult to rule out asthma before general anesthesia", and "I discussed my findings with the Vice Chairman". It was the first day, Monday, of this new rotation and this little baby with asthma was *elective* surgery for strabismus, the term for "lazy eye". The baby's surgery was scheduled for Thursday, January 7th. (Orthodox Christmas in my faith but I didn't once consider asking for the day off to go to church.)

I kept the mother and baby waiting in their exam room as I knocked on the Vice Chairman's exam room door and poked my head in stating, "Excuse me, Doctor, for interrupting but may I tell you something very important?"

The Vice Chairman looked annoyed at me for interrupting his exam of another child. I apologized for him and me to the child's parents "I am *so sorry* for barging in on your child's exam". I smiled at them and went on, "I am a resident-in-training and truly need to speak to the pediatric chairman just for a moment. I don't want to miss something important"! I smiled again. The patient's parents smiled back at me and nodded, but the Vice Chairman didn't smile at all. He just wheeled back his stool, stood up and said, "Excuse me for a brief minute" and followed me into the hallway with a glare.

I rushed out, "The baby I am examining has an extremely loud, ¾ plus inspiratory wheeze and I believe this baby has untreated asthma and should not have general anesthesia until a complete workup is done". I thrust my required cursory history and physical at him. (Truly, I was amazed when I found out before the rotation started that *we,* the ophthalmology residents, did the brief history and physicals pre-operatively, and not the pediatric residents, because we only get eight weeks of exposure to pediatrics in medical school.) The Vice Chairman read my brief notes and stated, "Her mother cancelled on me five months ago and I plan on going ahead with her daughter's strabismus surgery".

"But, Doctor, I *do hear* a very loud wheeze and I think that a full workup for asthma is necessary before general anesthesia." I look up at him expectantly.

The Vice Chairman dismisses me with, "*Fine.* I'll take care of it."

I don't think my recommendations were completely followed. Three days later the baby girl was a full code blue at the induction of anesthesia ("Code Blue" meaning her heart stopped circulating blood/a full cardiopulmonary arrest which makes one's skin turn blue from lack of oxygen) and she woke up blind and brain dead. I wasn't present for the surgery because Dick asked me to go to the cornea conference and skip my first day operating in pediatric ophthalmology.

Who is it more important to keep happy, the Chairman or the Vice Chairman? A no brainer, of course Dick, so I was at the cornea conference and didn't know what happened. The tragedy in the operating room, however, was all over the six and eleven p.m. news. Oh my dearest God, I remember thinking as I sat staring at my little TV, this rotation is going to be more than interesting, having started out with a full code blue!

Almost every day for the next three weeks every resident asked me, "Duke, did you get a subpoena? Duke! Did you get a subpoena"?! My response was always the same, "No". And I thought why should I be in any trouble? I was right.

Three weeks after that operating room tragedy, I was called into a beautifully furnished boardroom full of suits (must be attorneys) and the Vice Chairman. Multiple attorneys asked me over and over, "Is this your handwriting, Dr. Duke"? My repeated response was, "Yes, of course".

"Are these your recommendations to rule out asthma"?

"Yes. I wrote I recommended a CXR, that means chest x-ray and a full pediatric evaluation before surgery and that I discussed it with the head of pediatric ophthalmology".

"And did you discuss this with the Vice-Chairman"?

"Yes, of course. He told me he would take care of it as he knew I was to be attending the cornea conference".

"You're *sure* that you spoke to him"?

"Yes, I'm confident, plus he could easily see my note to remind him on the top of the chart on that page you are showing to me".

"Is this your signature"? for the third time.

"Yes. I always sign my charts M. Duke, MD".

"You may go now". As I got up to leave, I glanced at the Vice Chairman and I thought his red face and entire head was going to explode and splatter on the ceiling. I never did get a subpoena. The news on the television and radio died down very fast, and truthfully, I thought that the little girl had died, too.

     *   *   *

Twenty years later, after deciding to write the new genre "creative non-fiction" for my book, I called several news channels in Albany and I was told "they couldn't find the record". I called the *Albany Times Union* newspaper and they couldn't help me either. I didn't bother to call Albany Medical Center. I could only remember the number "9". I just remember the number 9. I thought the parents received 9 million dollars for the lawsuit that ensued, but how could I find out the truth? I called my old attorney buddy in Albany. His partner told me my buddy died of pancreatic cancer and he "was sorry", but he didn't remember the case. I called the Attorney General's office and asked for the State Health Commissioner of Albany who was in power in 1988. David Axelrod was his real name and he was dead, too.

Pulling my hair out but persevering, I decided to call the Albany Public Library. A very nice lady there sent me three articles and my hair grew back and curled without a perm, especially after I finally had the *19-month-old's name* and was able to reach her father by phone. (That is where I had that "9" number in my brain, because she was 19-months-old and not for a 9 million dollar settlement, which is what I think the family deserved for their little girl's death.)

One of the three *Albany Times Union* articles was titled: "ALBANY MED BLAMED FOR CHILD'S LAPSE. 'As far as I'm concerned, there was a heavy responsibility on the part of the medical center,' Axelrod said last week". The article continued: "Albany Medical Center in 1985 entered an agreement with Child's Hospital (the hospital near Albany Med where the little girl coded) that sent the medical center's routine out patient surgery (approximately 2,400 surgeries annually) to Child's...During the meeting Axelrod expressed 'concern for the extent of oversight by the medical center' and the 'quality of surveillance' at Child's, he said".

Axelrod quoted verbatim: "I think that the assurances provided to me with respect to Child's Hospital were not fulfilled, and I don't take lightly to failures of that sort. All the concerns that I had were not addressed because, if they were addressed, what happened would not have happened," Axelrod said of the Umstadter incident. "My distress was very much heightened by the fact that we had discussed effectively the very issues which resulted, I think, in a problem of quality at Child's Hospital."

"Dr. Anthony Tartaglia, vice president for patient care at Albany Medical Center, responded to Axelrod's statement: "Quality assurance at Child's Hospital has always remained the responsibility of Child's even under terms of the joint agreement between AMC (Albany Medical Center) and Child's for the ambulatory surgery program there. The medical center has never been given the authority or the responsibility for the management of Child's Hospital's quality assurance program. Although we have the opportunity to provide input into Child's quality assurance program, no one at any time asked us to develop or implement our institution's very stringent quality assurance program at Child's." Personally, I think

Dr. Tartaglia would have been an awesome tap dancer or maybe an attorney.

"The agreement, on file at the State (New York) Health Department, says that the ambulatory surgery medical director 'shall report administratively' to Albany Medical Center and 'shall be responsible for the quality and integrity of the (ambulatory surgery program's) professional activities on a day-to-day basis.' The medical director also was to report to the Child's board and the steering committee of the ambulatory surgery center, according to the agreement. Axelrod said Child's Hospital would ultimately be permitted to continue its ambulatory surgery program. He said the hospital and the department have been *working* out a plan to correct its deficiencies."

The above article's quotes were in the newspaper over *6 ½ months after* Sarra Umstadter's code blue. I would hope by *that amount of time* a *"plan to correct deficiencies "* would have been *worked* out and *completed!*

After I read the second two articles from the *Albany Times Union* dated April 19th and April 20th, 1988 I had a good cry, wiped my eyes, grabbed my phone and called information. I had to know the truth about Sarra because her poor mother was quoted as saying, "You try to move her and she screams. I don't know if she'll be with us for a year, two years or until she's 45. They took her away from me. I have a totally absent baby." Sarra could not move on her own or talk and needed to be fed through a tube. Tragically, her eyes were straight and blind because she was now brain dead except for her brainstem, which kept her breathing on her own. The articles said nothing about whether Sarra was dead or alive or anything about a lawsuit settlement. No wonder I needed to know the truth.

"Hello?" a man answers.

"Hello, Sir. This is Dr. Mary Ann Duke. Is this Mr. Umstadter?"

"Yes, it is." I didn't quite know how to approach the subject without causing the man heartache. There isn't any way. How do you call someone and ask them about their suffering baby girl? But I needed closure and somehow I felt in my heart that he did, too, so I forge on.

"I am very sorry to bother you, but I need some closure on something very important to me. I am the ophthalmology resident from Albany Medical Center Hospital that saw a little girl named Sarra Umstadter before her strabismus surgery many years ago. I heard her wheezing. I wrote it down. Are you her father?" Slight pause.

"Yes."

No other words from him. I continue.

"I have the number nine in my head. Did you get nine million dollars when your daughter died? Please tell me you received nine million dollars." Pause.

"Who did you say you were again?"

"I was the resident twenty years ago that heard your daughter's asthma, Dr. Mary Ann Duke. I live in Maryland now and again, I am sorry to bother you. I called your attorney first, but he said he didn't know anything about the case. If you do not want to speak to me, that's okay, but I was just hoping that you and your wife won a lot of money." No pause whatsoever.

"My wife and I divorced before that case was even settled. It took 3 ½ years! I can't believe that lawyer said that to you! My wife and I split $150,000! *I told that lawyer that he got more money to put my daughter's case off than my wife and I got to watch her die*!!!" I'm shocked by his outburst and my jaw drops.

"Only $150,000?" I repeat in disbelief.

"That is right! $75,000 each!" Mr. Umstadter shouts. Oh my God, that's all? I feel my old adrenaline surge kicking in and my heart starts pounding in indignation.

"Sir, I obtained copies of the *Albany Times Union* newspaper articles and they said that there were "a list of 22 medical violations in the Umstadter case. Among them were failure of the eye surgeon to cancel the operation after abnormal…" Mr. Umstadter interrupts me and raises his angry voice even louder.

"That's right! *Everything* went wrong! I knew my baby girl shouldn't have had that surgery that week! My wife and I were already going to get a divorce before it happened, but Sarra was my baby girl! I have two older boys but she was my baby girl!!"

I start to cry again. My voice is hushed. "I am so sorry. I thought my brief history and physical that I did on your daughter was going to win you a lot of money. I am so sorry. I never got a subpoena" and my voice trails off.

"Nothing would have helped my little girl! My wife and I planned her funeral before they took that tube out of her throat! Then she lived. No one expected her to live, and we planned her funeral, but she lived." Now it's his turn to stop talking.

"The paper said that. It said she 'was left unable to eat, talk or move on her own after her heart stopped. She is fed through a tube.' The paper also said that 'The doctors were not identified by the Health Department and the hospital declined to reveal their names.'"

"That's right!" Mr. Umstadter says again angrily. "It was a big cover up! I watched my daughter suffer in bed for three and a half years! They kept putting off her case! They used every single excuse they could come up with! We should have had a trial by jury. Instead, everyone involved kept putting it off until she died! She didn't die until she was almost five; she would be twenty-one now."

Total shock. I am in complete shock. I decide Mr. Umstadter has probably had enough, too. "Sir, may I call you again? If you don't want me to, I won't. I am so sorry for you and your family. I just remembered the number nine and I was hoping…well, I had no idea what the truth really was. Thank you for talking to me. I am so sorry."

"You can call me whenever you want. I know that it wasn't your fault."

"Thank you very much. May I ask you just one more question?"

"Go ahead."

"Do you have a good job, Mr. Umstadter? Are you making ends meet okay?"

"I'm a stone mason. I work very hard. I never went to college."

Dear God, I think, if Sarra had been my baby girl, I would have known more about "the system" and sued for every last cent, but they were taken advantage of because they didn't know better and probably were trusting their attorney.

It was as if Mr. Umstadter read my mind and he said, "Yep, my buddy lost a finger cutting meat at his work and got $110,000. I got $75,000 to watch my only daughter slowly die."

"I'll pray for you, Sir. Thank you for speaking with me, giving me some closure, and again I am very sorry to bring back all those tragic memories." Pause. Then I change the subject and ask, "How about those *GIANTS?* Do you watch football?" The two of us bantered about football for awhile and then hung up after Mr. Umstadter said again, "Call me whenever you want".

Twenty years later, I would have demanded to see Sarra's chart, called her family like I just did, and offered to testify on their behalf. But back in residency, I was dodging so many bullets already, I didn't think about doing that. Truthfully, I thought that soon after she was discharged from Albany Medical Center on March 22, 1988, she had died and her parents won the lawsuit. There must have been quite the "cover up", like her father told me.

A dead baby is worth a lot less to an insurance company than one who is suffering and still alive.

* * *

BACK IN TIME TO March, 1988, pediatric ophthalmology rotation:

Dick called me into his office, yet again, just before the end of my pediatric ophthalmology rotation. He told me the Vice Chairman gave me a very poor evaluation, wrote that I had "poor medical knowledge", flagrantly unfair. Dick mandated (no shrink appointment), but he dictated "You will be on probation the rest of your residency and I would suggest you tread lightly, because we will be watching you. It is highly unlikely that you will complete your residency here."

I was stunned by his words. I stormed out of his office and burst into tears in the hallway, then I turned with tear-streamed face and marched right back in unannounced. Apparently, I scared Dick a little as he jerked up and stopped lighting his pipe. I vehemently stated, "Before you die, Doctor, you will see me a board-certified ophthalmologist"!

The "good ole boys" never could come close to kicking me out of my residency because I was too damned good. I was one of 5 out of 12 residents to pass the ophthalmology boards that year, *and the **only woman** who passed.* They couldn't possibly get rid of me; they had no solid reason for it except "the little Indian squaw showed up one of the Chiefs." Remember, I was not the one being sued. I didn't even get a subpoena.

Mr. Umstadter also told me that the Vice Chairman is the current Chairman of the Department of Ophthalmology at Albany Medical Center Hospital at the time of this current publication, March 2009.

Those brief stories are not even a snowflake on top of the tip of the iceberg of bullshit that I navigated through during the decade of my working to "be a doctor". Not a fraction of one fucking snowflake.

Medical school, internship, and residency require their own novel, most likely a trilogy.

Chapter 9

What Next?

June 30, 1989, a new Duke Holiday, the day I am finished with hell, the last day of blessed residency, just over a decade since high school and Mr. Kapp's letter. Ten years is quite fast to finish college, medical school and residency. Forget about an extra one or two-year fellowship for me. I'm fried. Cooked. It's time for me to get out in the real world where people try to sleep six to eight hours per night. I am not bitter about all of the time I spent becoming a doctor but then again, maybe I am. If I didn't feel a little bitter, I wouldn't be human. If I had gone to finishing school instead of medical school, where one learns how to give good back rubs and ego rubs, I may be married by now with one or two lovely babies, and a man taking care of *us* instead of me taking care of patients and a man. Nah, I would have flunked out of finishing school; I could never play second fiddle to any man, no matter how much money or power he thinks he has.

There is no graduation ceremony and diploma handout after residency like they have in medical school. It's just like leaving a job you hate, pack up your things into a cardboard box and get the hell out. I don't remember a single blessed thing about that final Friday, except going to the Chairman's office and asking the new girl if I could see my file. She gets it naively without questioning me. I immediately take it to the copy room, lock the door, and copy every single page.

Just as I suspected, none of my letters of recommendation from the doctors in the community of Albany Medical Center were in it; not a single one of the many letters of glowing praise and thankfulness from my grateful patients were in it. Even the Vice Chairman must have had some premonition of my future fervent disclosure of events because he removed his evaluation from pediatric ophthalmology. I wish I had it to repeat verbatim; it was incredibly unfair and "ivory tower doctor bull".

Just like judges who reign and rule, doctors in academia alias "ivory tower" think they always know more than us doctors out in the real world. My response remains "*Au Contraire*". The number one reason to go to a major university setting when one is gravely ill is because there will be more than one doctor available at a moment's notice for a second opinion and possibly also a savvy medical student or resident to get the diagnosis and treatment correct. Unfortunately in the legal profession, only one judge sits on the bench for most family and domestic matters. Do you ever wonder why the violent crimes get a trial by jury but a divorce of many years with several children is ruled on by only one judge? Until the House of Representatives and Senate and Supreme Court consist of one-half women, we women will continue to get put down, period. I am going to continue on this ever-pervasive rant in a humorous way briefly and if one wishes not to read a few paragraphs, just skip to the next "dots".

*   *   *

Truthfully, maybe it is just an inborn error of metabolism that predisposes most men to be control freaks. That would be a nice excuse for them to have. It would make women feel a lot better about men, too.

Can you just imagine two women complaining about their husbands like this?

Women could share their woes with their friends and family and therapists and rationalize their husband's controlling/quasi-asshole behavior with, "You know Amy, my David went to the doctor, that new specialist, Dr. Dick, who deals only with "male problems" and he said my David's enzyme level of *"pricktene"* is ten times normal." Amy's gushing with sympathy response is, "Oh, Emma, you poor dear, how do you *stand* him? I put up with as much shit from my Ryan as me and my therapist can take and his enzyme level of "pricktene" is just *high* normal, not even two times normal, but *ten times*. Heaven forbid!"

"He even has 'prickteneuria'. (Also in the urine.) It burns him Amy! But what's worse is he's turned into some manic psycho-dictator! Some days I just want to stab him a few times while I'm cooking just to stop his bitching!"

"Oh don't do *that*, Emma. I once heard of a C.E.O. of some company or other who got off for stabbing his wife to death because he had untreated 'pricktenemia', but it doesn't work the other way! You *know* what a man's world it is! Hang in there, Honey, maybe Dr. Dick will get things under control. But if he can't, for God's sake, get a good divorce attorney!"

It's the simple one-gene-one-enzyme theory I learned in Biology class in high school. "Pricktenemia" has apparently eluded scientists since Watson and Crick who described the double helix structure of DNA in 1953. Ha, ha…Going back to the story…

* * *

I was especially disappointed the letter wasn't there from a great one-eyed, myopic WWII veteran. He wrote that "For sixty years, I awoke in the morning and reached for my glasses. Thanks to Dr. Duke, I reach for my slippers instead". I operated on three grateful one-eyed patients with dense cataracts that the residents before me at the Veterans Administration Hospital were too scared to operate on. I was given copies of some of the letters, but where were all of the originals? I felt very pissed off, but feeling angry and illegitimately put down had become the norm. So what the hell is one more lousy day?

I can't remember one thing that I did that night either. Not one. And it wasn't because I drank. I just lied in bed numb. It felt too weird to not be banging my head against the wall. That's pretty sick. That's pretty damned sad. All those years of studying and pushing myself and the last day of residency, instead of feeling elated and celebrating, I just wanted to crash.

I do have one claim to fame. I probably was the only ophthalmology resident in the history of the program to graduate without a job or even a fellowship lined up. I was offered a six-month fellowship by a doctor in Albany but hadn't accepted it as yet. Why? I don't know. Maybe it had something to do with Sven. Sven was an Emergency Room physician I dated during my entire residency, while many residents were switching sex partners every three-month rotation change. Sven told me he "loved me to death and wanted to take me to Amsterdam after residency to buy me a beautiful diamond". Yeah, right. I'll never forget what happened the day before my medical school roommate Diz's wedding.

Sven, who was built like a brick you-know-what, lived outside of Saratoga Springs on a huge farm. We were basking in the sun sipping a light beer after a great workout at his gym on one of the rare weekends we both didn't have to work Saturday or Sunday. "Isn't this just the most perfect May day?" I ask him as I leaned back and closed my eyes.

"Awesome," Sven agreed.

Instead of Sven popping the question "Will you marry me?" which would have made me so happy at that moment, a noisy car drives in. I didn't bother to open my eyes to see who it was until I heard a woman's voice say, "Hi Honey, how are you?" I can't come close to her name except one that has five letters and begins with a B. I sat right up and there before me is the permed and bleach-blonde secretary from the E.R. where Sven worked with her two sons in the back seat of her red convertible. She ignores me and walks right up to Sven and plants a wet tongue kiss on him. Her two young boys get out of the car and start running around like they owned the joint. She was also sporting a cigarette. I never did like her.

Sven does not act surprised and instead simply asks her if she wants a drink.

"I'd love a gin and tonic. What a nice day, isn't it?" It was until you showed up, I bitch to myself. I surmised the situation immediately. Sven and Ms. Secretary had something going on, obviously, as I followed everyone into the house. What else is there to do except confront Sven head on? As he's mixing her drink I flatly say, "You have one chance, Sven. You ask one of us to stay and one of us to leave."

I'll give him this. He *hesitated*. That's all I'll give him and more than he deserves. After sitting down and putting both of her boys on his lap, Sven states "I think you should leave." I stared at his downcast eyes, speechless. What utter humiliation he cast on me. Worse than a slap in the face. I had to then walk around his house and pick up my sneakers from one room, dirty laundry from another (since I didn't have my own washer and dryer), jacket, etc. as the Cheshire cat secretary sipped her gin and tonic with a grin.

I speed down the road to the nearest gas station with a pay phone (pre-cell phone era/the dark ages) and call Sven angrily, "You asshole! How dare you humiliate me in front of that bitch! Don't you ever call me again!" That Saturday afternoon was six weeks before the end of my residency *and* the day before we were going to Diz's country club wedding. Groovy. I have to go to a wedding alone. That night in my angry state, I hyper-extended my own right index finger trying to close a sticky window.

I got lost driving to Diz's wedding and missed the dual Catholic/Jewish ceremony. Good thing, I probably would have balled my eyes out. I blew in right as everyone was shaking hands with the bride and groom and acted like I'd been there the whole time. I kissed and hugged my dear medical school roommate and exclaimed, "Diz! You are the most beautiful bride! I am *so happy* for you"!!

I tried to have fun at Diz's wedding anyway. Her father asked me to dance. While he was gracefully swinging me around the dance floor he asks, "Where is your boyfriend, Honey?"

"Sleeping with his secretary; I found out yesterday." Diz's dad danced with me for twenty minutes. God bless him. My demeanor must have told him I needed to exercise off some anger. I danced with everyone who asked me and everyone I asked.

Sven's chair was the only empty one at Diz's wedding. I remember looking at myself in the mirror in the skanky-minus-one-star-cheap hotel room I stayed in that night and thinking to myself, "You're going to be okay, Mary Ann, better to find out now than after marrying him!"

The next day at work I had to make sure that no one found out about my broken right index finger. I knew it was broken; I had broken a few fingers before playing football and had kept the splints. I taped it and said, "Oh, just a little scratch." I *had* to keep on operating and finish all of my cases so I could graduate! No one even *noticed* for six weeks that I held the delicate ophthalmic needle holder with my thumb and middle finger, instead of index, and still operated as well. It was actually a perfect tribute to finish my residency years operating with my middle fucking finger.

I walked into work a little hung over, a few too many gin and tonics at the wedding to numb my broken heart and throbbing finger. There on top of my small desk were two-dozen of the longest long stem red roses I have ever seen. Everyone wanted to know who sent them and crammed into my small chief resident's office. The unsigned note said, "I love you. Will you marry me"? I faked a smile, didn't show anyone the card and simply said, "My secret admirer."

Sven filled sixty-minute message tapes on my answering machine at home, day after day, for weeks. I refused to speak to him when he called me at work, too. He banged on the door of my home one night and I wouldn't let him in. I just sat on my staircase inside the door and cried; then I called my mom and cried some more.

It was high time to high tail it out of the not so all balmy Albany area.

Actually, I did interview in Maryland and D.C. with two doctors, stayed with sis, Elena. She offered to let me live with her in her townhouse in Gaithersburg, Maryland if I wanted to move to the D.C. area, an extremely kind offer and one I will always cherish. My parents wanted me, of course, to move back home. I just could not move back to my small hometown unmarried. I guess I thought I'd never meet my Prince Charming there and wanted to move south anyway. I think they're disappointed to this day, and I often think how different and probably so very much simpler and easier my life's path would have been if I had gone back home and was near those who loved me the most. "Shoulda, woulda, coulda", Dad used to say. I refuse to grow old and bitter. My Baba had a very hard life and I never once heard her talk about regrets. I pray I grow old just like her.

*   *   *

I lie on my back in the backyard of my house, which Elena had helped me buy, just outside of Albany. I sold it a week before finishing my residency and it was closing by the end of July (whether I liked it or not). I didn't have the energy to even *think* about packing it up and moving. I sunbathed for a week and drank beer, just sunbathed with my cat and her six kittens crawling all over me. I got a great tan, and let my charred brain rest.

The phone rang out of the blue at 11:00 a.m. one day.

"Hallo?"

"Hello, Mary Ann... is that you?"

"Yep."

"Hi, it's Ted, it doesn't sound like you."

Ted was my high school prom date, a good buddy, who I set up with his wife. Well, we hadn't spoken in over a year. But Ted is one of those friends like Diz where you don't need to speak to them for five years and then just pick up where you left off.

"Hi, Ted, what's up?"

"I was just thinking about you, so I thought I'd call. Did you finish your residency?"

"Yep."

"When?"

"A week ago or so."

"So what are you doing?"

"Drinking." Pop.

"What?"

"Drinking a beer."

"Already?"

"Yep.

"Why?"

"Feel like it."

"Oh… So when are you going to start a *real* job?" (Slaving in residency, of course, does not qualify as a *real* job. Real jobs are when you get paid sufficiently for the work that you do or at least by the hour.)

"Don't know."

"You don't know?"

"Nope."

"Well, Mary Ann, did you *get* a job yet?"

"Nope."

I must have sounded a little depressed. Ted asks, "How are you paying your bills?"

"I'm not. I can't find my checkbook."

"Duke, have you lost your mind?!"

"Yep."

"How much have you drank today?"

"I just opened my first beer."

"Listen to me, Duke, get a grip! Did you put your house on the market?!"

"It's sold."

"So what the hell are you doing there?"

I can tell Ted is getting just a little frustrated with me, but I'm sipping a cold one and petting three to four kittens. I'm not letting him bother me.

"I gotta move by the end of the month."

"Where are you moving to?"

"I don't know." Now Ted finally raises his voice and yells, "Have you even *had* an interview?!"

"Yep."

Still with a raised voice, he asks, "Did anyone offer you a job?"

"Yep, in D.C."

"Did you accept it?"

"Not yet. I thought this guy I was seeing was going to ask me to marry him but I found out he's sleeping with his secretary, so that's the end of that. That's why I am leaving town. Too many shitty memories."

"Duke! Before you drink anymore, I want you to call the doctors you interviewed with, and get a damned job! I'll call you in a few hours and you better sound better!"

"Yep, thanks for calling."

Before I finished my beer and went back outside, I made the calls. I wasn't too hopeful; for God's sake the interviews were both three months ago.

Well, I got lucky (or so I thought at the time) and the first doctor I called, whose job I preferred, offered it to me. I was to be paid $50,000 and half of what I earned over $100,000. Hip, hip, hooray! That was twice what I was paid as a resident and I certainly planned on generating over $100,000 in billing. The doctor's office was only twenty minutes from my sister's house, too.

I needed to get a Maryland Medical License, which takes about 6-8 weeks, so I agreed on a start date of September 15th. I then called my sister Elena to ask if I could still live with her. She was cool. Good old big sis always comes through for me. I also asked her for a $1,000 loan.

"What do you want $1,000 for?" she asks.

"I need to get away."

"Where are you going?"

"Don't know. I'll figure something out."

"Okay. I'll mail you a check today."

"Thanks so much! You know I'll pay you back."

I then call Nadine at work in San Francisco, my best friend from high school. She's surprised to hear from me.

"Hi! How *are* you?"

"Okay. Can I come out for a few days?" Pause.

"Uh, when?"

"Soon."

"Uh… sure." Poor Nadine. What could she say to her best friend, *no?*

"Okay, thanks. See you soon." Click.

I then called a few airlines, bought the cheapest one-week advance fare ticket I could find, called Ted back within an hour and said all was well, and "I'm back on track!"

By the time I finished my beer, I had accepted a job, decided to move to Maryland, firmed up a new residence, borrowed money for a much needed vacation, decided on California, and informed poor Nadine of my arrival time.

Welcome to my world. Not for the weak of spirit or faint of heart!

*   *   *

I returned from San Francisco forty-eight hours before my house closing. Good thing I was used to going without sleep, because I packed non-stop. The two-family home outside of Albany appreciated over 10% from $66,000 to $74,000. What a joke that seems like now. Some women in Potomac spend more on panty hose over three years than that house appreciated. A million dollars barely buys a new townhouse in Potomac, even with the depressed housing market.

*   *   *

I hated my first job, with a capital H. I only did two Medicaid cataracts in less than six months. Within three months I put an anonymous listing in the American Academy of Ophthalmology's placement exchange seeking employment. The day before I signed a mutual release leaving my first job with a whopping severance pay of $2,782 dollars, my boss called and stated he "wanted to work things out". Sure. I didn't believe one word he said. He never let me operate and never talked about future partnership; I knew I needed to move on before I lost my surgical skills.

Truthfully, it's more cost effective these days for an ophthalmologist to turn into an optometrist, do routine eye exams, and sell eyeglasses and contact lenses. Then, one doesn't have the stress of operating or the risk of malpractice from having something go wrong that is not even the surgeon's fault, such as equipment failure, that leads to a lawsuit.

So now I'm unemployed again. I thought doctors were supposed to make a good living. Baba said I would. So why am I struggling so hard? On top of everything, I became board certified by the American Academy of Ophthalmology (a separate written and oral exam in two different cities that takes almost two years to obtain, besides all of the studying and expense) so I should be able to find a good position anywhere. It was very frustrating. I could have made more money my first year in the D.C. area as some high-class escort with a third-grade education.

One of my friends repeatedly told me "you need a mentor". Perfect, I just need a mentor and a sugar daddy. Maybe Luke Skywalker will loan me Obi Wan Kenobi and I'll give Donald Trump a call; he likes Czechoslovakian women.

How do I find a mentor? I'm not from a family of doctors. I'm the first one, have no connections, am not from the area and didn't even train here. So now what? Call a member of the Orthodox Church! That's it, now I'm thinking like a small town girl again. Maybe I'm not so naïve after all.

It worked. This fellow Orthodox ophthalmologist that I was friendly with referred me to an optician named Lou Williams. Lou was totally cool. He said all I had to do was send him patients for glasses and he loaned me $40,000 dollars, interest free, to be paid back over five years, $666.66 a month. I thought that was do-able. Lou also co-signed a five-year lease in a Potomac office building worth almost $200,000 dollars. Lou *must* have been crazy.

Truly, I loved Potomac immediately. To me it was OZ. Everything was pretty; the wealthy sure know how to landscape. Their beautiful flowers remind me of the ones Baba grew, now transplanted into my own garden. Lou said I was going to do great; all I had to do was "my thing". He said, "just keep smiling, Honey".

Lou was my sugar daddy, but where is a good genie when you need one? Some little elfie-like dude who talks all high-pitched like his balls are being squeezed, a genie who will grant me one wish, to let me finally be successful.

Starting your own practice from scratch is no easy feat, for anyone, anytime. It just isn't. In residency we didn't get one single minute of training on how to do it. How crazy is that? With all of this HMO, PPO, Blue Cross/Blue Shield, Medicare, Medicaid and the rest of them, with all of their different bullshit co-pays and deductibles, it's a wonder any doctor flies solo. If I had any clue that it would be so complicated, I would have done it anyway. Why? Because I was sick and tired of having a boss. (Isn't everyone?) I loved the independence of it, and I truly loved that patients will be coming to see *me,* trusting *me*, and not just showing up at some clinic where I was employed. They were coming to see "Dr. Duke" and I was so proud, and so was my Baba.

It was a rocky start. I saw two patients my whole first week. I used to drive to the office praying the phone would ring that day. The one and only thing that kept the practice afloat in the beginning was treating nursing home patients who couldn't travel. Like the old television western *Have Gun, Will Travel* but instead it was *Have Heavy Ophthalmology Equipment, Will Travel*. And sometimes it was all for only one patient.

Within only six months the $40,000 loan was all used up. I had to call Lou.

"Lou, it's Mary Ann."

"Yes, Honey, how are you?"

"I'm upset Lou. I need to talk to you."

"Okay, Honey, come over to the house after work."

Yeah right, "work", my three patients that afternoon who should have been thirteen to cover my expenses.

Lou lived within walking distance from my office. He was sitting at the head of his kitchen table, as usual, smoking a cigarette. He had given up drinking as it wrecked havoc with his diabetes but he still enjoyed a cigarette. He had his usual quick smile for me. "Would you like a drink?" he asks.

"Sure."

So Lou smoked and I drank. "What's the matter, Honey?"

"I'm all out of money, Lou. I have some Medicare checks due in, but I haven't received them yet and I owe Bausch & Lomb $3,000 dollars and need this month's $2,500 rent. Those checks should be coming in, but not soon enough to pay the rent and B&L."

Lou wasn't fazed. "So what do you need?" he asks, blowing a smoke ring.

"Six thousand dollars. I'll pay you back within sixty days."

"Okay. Come back tomorrow; I'll have it for you."

The next day, Lou gave me sixty $100 dollar bills. Sixty days later, I paid him back, sixty $100 dollar bills.

"You know what, Lou?" I ask him while he's smoking his cigarettes and I'm sipping my wine, "You are my Fairy Godfather!" I got emotional and cried. Lou gave me my start and I love him for that. Less than two months later, Lou died in his sleep. I was so thankful, so very glad that I told him he was my Fairy Godfather that special day.

    I only knew Lou Williams ten months, but I will love him forever.

Chapter 10

Forward to Seven Locks Jail and the Alleged "Killer"

On Thanksgiving Day, two days into jail, I finally reach Edward. One can only call collect and cell phones don't accept those, of course, and neither does his work phone, so I had to wait until after dinner when the phone is turned back on. The phone is only accessible a few hours a day; that's why it is so hard to get a chance to use it. I ate fast and sat by the phone so I could be first. During rehab I realized that I needed to break it off with Edward once and for all. I cannot stay sober and watch him drink every night. But while I am locked up, I need him to watch my home, pick up my mail and the only way to reach Eloise is through him, so it certainly is not the right time to say "Sayonara". I think he's just sticking around and not in love with me anymore either. Quite possible that he's just waiting for me to break down and finally give him "power of attorney" which he most annoyingly requests almost every time we speak.

I used to be so in love with him or so I thought, but now I feel nothing for him except that he is the father of our beautiful daughter. I remember I have to whisper to him or everyone in the room can hear my conversation, unless someone ups the shitty sound on the television. The rumor is Mark Fightson ripped the men's television right out of the wall when he was in Seven Locks. When he got out, Fightson bought them a brand new big screen. The men's television is great. Ours stinks. Edward finally answers and accepts the call.

"Hi.", is all I can get out.

"Hi, how is it? Are you okay?"

"Sure, I'm F.I.N.E." Edward gets it. "I sleep on a metal bed with a thin gym mat as a mattress. It sucks, big time. The food sucks, too. The best meal was the real turkey we had tonight. The rest of the time it is mystery meat; and they only give us dirty dishwater-like coffee every three to four days. Otherwise, it's powdered juice."

"That's a bummer." Edward understands. He loves his Starbuck's.

"All we do all day is read the paper, try to sleep, watch a really shitty, snowy pictured television with horrible sound or just talk and play cards. But today I did sit-ups and push-ups on my upper bunk."

"You did?"

"Yes. I'm going to go nuts if I don't work out a little. My feet were freezing, but a nice girl, who's been in here before, was wearing two pairs of socks so she gave one of her pairs to me. Wasn't that nice?"

"Yes." Such a simple creature comfort as a pair of socks was a huge deal to me. Wow, and many rich Potomac women have a cow when they break a nail between appointments on the door of their Mercedes.

"Can I talk to Eloise?"

"She already went to bed. She was exhausted."

"Oh." I would have loved to hear her precious three-year-old voice. "I need you to do something for me. I can't reach Dieter. I have tried numerous times and am always getting an answering machine, and I need to have him answer and accept charges because I can only call collect. It's only sixty-five cents for a local call, I heard. Please call him and ask him to pick up."

"I'm not calling him."

"Why not?! I need to speak to my kids!"

"I'm not calling him for you." I'm more than exasperated. I need to tell my children that Mommy is okay. I need to tell them that it'll go by fast, and I'll be out before they finish school. Yeah, right, the past 48 hours have felt like 48 days. Forty-eight days in Siberia in a closed space with an AIDS patient with a hacking cough.

"Well, call Jane and have her call him. Tell her to tell him I can only call collect!"

"Okay."

"Okay, thank you. Do it right now, please! It's getting late, and I want to speak to the kids on Thanksgiving. The phone is going to be forbidden soon and another lady wants to use it. I gotta go. I'll try to call you tomorrow. Bye." After the other lady finished her call, I try Dieter for the sixth time in two days. He finally accepts a call. I choke up immediately hearing my children's sad, little voices. "Hi, Mommy," says my eldest eight and one-half year old daughter, Marika.

"Hi sweetheart! I love you! I'm so sorry I had to go to jail. I'm so sorry I missed Thanksgiving with you, Honey! Please forgive me! It's going to be okay. Time will go by fast."

"Can I come to see you?" Oh God, she sounds so hopeful. I want to cry, and hate my answer, "No, Honey, I'm not allowed visitors here. But soon I'm going to be sent to a big new jail in Clarksburg, and you can come to see me there."

"When do you go there, Mommy?"

"I don't know yet. Women leave to go there every day, so I think it will be soon. I will let you know as soon as I know, okay?"

"Okay." She doesn't sound good at all. My poor baby sounds depressed. "Mommy, I cried all night when Daddy told us you went to jail." I choke up again but hold back bursting into tears.

"Please don't cry anymore my angel! It's going to be all right. Daddy will take good care of you and I hope he will bring you to see me soon." A little pause then Marika asks me softly, "How is jail, Mommy?" What do you say to an eight year old little girl who's worried about her Mom? It's the pits? I hate it! I'm claustrophobic and going crazy? No. Not at all. I try to take away all of her worry.

"Well, it's not anything like home; it's a lot smaller; but Mommy's going to be just fine. I'm in a pretty big room with a lot of nice women, and it's really not too bad. Before you know it, I'll be back home, and everything's going to be all right."

Yeah, sure, I think. I've lost my angels from heaven, been putting my over $8,000/month mortgage on credit cards, still owe a boat load for rehab, and now am locked up for six months. I need to go to let another woman use the phone so I say, "Angel, listen, please forgive me for this. I will make it up to you. I promise. I promise I will make everything up to you that I have missed. Please, believe me, Honey, that I love you and your brother and sisters more than anything on this earth, and I promise to make it all up to you. Please, let me speak to James and Nadia, because I have to get off the phone soon. I will call you tomorrow. I love you very much."

"Okay, Mommy, I love you, too." I have very emotional conversations two more times with James and Nadia. James just turned ten and Nadia is only six. After that, I'm *totally* exhausted and just go sit on my slab and stare blankly at Peggy. She looks at me and understands. She spoke to her kids a few hours ago and cried for half an hour when she got off.

I smile at her a little through my tears. "Boy oh boy, they must think Mommy's a real piece of work, huh?"

"Yep."

"I have to make this up to them somehow, Peggy, I *have* to." Peggy pulls her blanket up to her chin and rolls over.

"You will, Mary Ann. You will, somehow."

*   *   *

The local news is very scary the day after Thanksgiving. A young African American male was found shot to death on a sidewalk, multiple times, right in the face, twenty minutes from my home. His name is "John Doe", because he's unrecognizable, and apparently never been in trouble with the law before and finger-printed. "If anyone has any information, please contact your local police department immediately," says the news announcer.

"Gross," I whisper to Peggy.

"Yeah, real gross," she concurs.

"Geez, right on Thanksgiving."

Peggy answers, "Probably over some drugs."

The good news of the day is that the guards finally took the forty-two year old with AIDS to the hospital. I couldn't help myself; the doctor in me addressed one of the guards on Thanksgiving with: "Excuse me, Sir, but I think that woman has pneumonia". At that very moment she was, yet again, spitting copiously into her disgusting reused Styrofoam cup. The guard just looked at me. Maybe he knows I'm an eye surgeon, maybe he doesn't. However, it doesn't take a rocket scientist to know it's not normal to spit up vast quantities of dark green sputum on a fifteen-minute cycle. Twenty-four hours after I commented to the guard, she developed a high fever and was finally taken to the hospital. Thank God.

"Duke?"

"Yes?" The guard is talking to me so I turn and look up from my tattered romance novel. The guard is doing his wall monitor check-in by my corner bed/slab and has never talked to me before. It shocks me a little.

"Do you have two jumpsuits on?!" he asks gruffly.

"Yes."

"Take one off."

I pause for a second, and then plunge on. "But I'm very cold, Sir."

"You can't wear two jumpsuits."

Why the hell not?! I bitch to myself. "Am I supposed to be cold?" No answer. Just a glare. I get up and walk to the bathroom. Oh, fuck it. It's laundry day. I was going to take off the medium underneath and get it washed anyway. I did my socks in the sink with hand soap a couple of days ago. I showered and had to wash my hair with the same limey soap bar. No shampoo or crème rinse in a jail "vanity pack". I was told one can't send one's socks to the laundry, 'cause you'll never get 'em back, and I have to have my warm gift gym socks. Mom always said it's bad to have cold feet. All I need is to get sick in jail. Can't afford that, need all the strength I have just to cope.

At least they're giving me my antidepressant in the a.m. and sleeping pill, which doesn't help, at night.

I return to my gym mat of a mattress and proceed with my workout of sit-ups and push-ups to warm up with my wet head. No blow driers in the wall at Hotel Hell. Some of the women are staring at me. What? Haven't you ever seen a sit-up before? Or does it just look like an impossible feat? Go to hell if you think I'm crazy. Go straight to hell. Oh, how could I forget, we've already arrived.

Three nights in a row, the news remains hauntingly bleak, asking the same question, "Does anyone know who killed John Doe?" Even us jailbirds are spooked. Who can kill an unarmed kid... shoot him in the face in cold blood so even his mother can't recognize him?

The Washington Post publishes the story a few days later. A twenty-two year old African American girl named Venice is charged with the crime of murdering the sixteen-year-old boy on Thanksgiving. Peggy was right; drugs were involved. There was a witness and/or accomplice. He turned her in. Venice supposedly told the two boys in the car with her to "Pull over here. I need to go to the bathroom". The witness said Venice went behind some bushes and came out holding a gun. She commanded the unarmed victim to get out of the car. She then shot the victim more than once in the face. Venice and the witness drove off. The witness said Venice looked back and saw the victim still moving.

I tell Peggy, "The poor kid was probably having a seizure before he died. I've never heard of anyone surviving multiple shots to the head!" Peggy nods quickly in agreement, not moving her eyes from the story. The witness in the car states he was then commanded to drive back and get out and shoot the victim, yet again. Who knows who really fired the last shot, but now John Doe is definitely good and dead, has a real name, and his poor mom knows why he missed her turkey dinner. Peggy and I are still engrossed in the article when the new girl arrives.

"Boy, is she ugly or what?" Peggy hisses to me.

"What's with the shaved head?" I whisper back. The new girl is at least 5'10", close to 200 pounds with shaved head, big buck teeth, and overall too muscular and strong looking. Hope she doesn't take the empty bunk above me. Nope. She picks the one above Glenda. That fits. Looks like there will be a toppling of the monarchy by the young rebel. Glenda, the eldest of us, is no longer queen bee. The new big girl seizes the crown.

I never in my life have met anyone quite like this girl. She talks too loud and is constantly interrupting other people's conversations and basically taking them over to talk about herself. "I's was doin' this, and I's was a doin' that! And kin yous believes this?!" This new girl thinks she's so bloody important. She's pissing me off more and more by the minute with her self-centered speech. I think to myself, "She doesn't even come close to speaking proper English and who cares how many drugs you've sold or consumed"?! I glance over at Peggy and she rolls her eyes in understanding. We both wish she would just be quiet and read a book. Then again, maybe she doesn't know how to read. "Who gives a shit"?! I'm bitching to myself yet again, which I find myself doing more often than not since getting incarcerated.

There is too much adrenaline in my body, so I climb to the bunk above me and start doing my sit-up/push-up routine. I have to hurl my mattress onto the top bunk. I'd bump my head if I tried to do my routine on the lower bunk. The new girl immediately looks up at me and yells, "Wudgee looks at that! It bes Janie Fonda!" She said it so loud that I'm sure everyone in our 20' by 50' jail box heard her.

Oh shit, she's talking about me, bringing attention to me. The other women are used to my exercising and don't stare anymore, don't even look up. I ignore the comment, so she speaks even louder. "Lookee there! We's gots us a Janie Fuckin' Fonda! Looks ats her!" I don't stop my sit-ups, but decide to address the bold new girl, "My name's Mary Ann, not Jane. What's yours?"

"Venice. My Momma named me Venice." And she flashes her big buck-overly-sharp-toothed-grin. GOD HELP ME. It's *her, the alleged killer.*

I'm not the only one who figures it out immediately. Even the dippiest dipshit in the room got it, obviously, because the room went dead quiet. I switch to push-ups, and Venice keeps on talking. Now she's spilling her guts, telling her story. Her side basically is, "He's was on my turf. He's was sellin' on my turf. No one's gonna be dealin' on my turf! But I's didn' kill him! He's was a still movin' when I left him. The guy that be tellin' on me; he's was the one be doin' the killin'! I's didn' do no killin'! He's was a still movin' when we's be drivin' away!"

But there is even more. Peggy informs me after dinner without hesitation, "Venice is a dike." Oh great. Perfect. A killer dike to go "night night" with. *Why* are they putting an alleged murderer amongst us? Shouldn't she be by herself? Guess this is "standard of care", Mary Ann. She may be charged with a crime just like you are, but she's also innocent until proven guilty. I tell Peggy, "I'd rather be locked up with HIV positive Coughing Cathy."

"Me too, plus she's a dike," Peggy whispers. Still it gives me the shivers, being locked up with an alleged cold-blooded killer.

Since I'm banned from two jumpsuits, I now walk around in my metastasizing blanket. But I'm certainly not the only one. It's damned cold. The only time I warm up naturally is with exercise. The only exercise the other women get daily is taking turns sweeping and mopping the floor. We have to clean our "room". And if your arms really want a scrubbing workout, clean the bathroom. We get inspected once a day like in the military. What's to inspect? That my flimsy sheet and Mr. Burlap are tucked just right around my worse than gym mat-like mattress and puny plastic pillow? Inspection of the minus-5-star bathroom is pulling aside the blue plastic curtain and making sure the toilet isn't plugged, the cinderblock shower isn't green with fungus and the metal sink not dull with soap scum.

* * *

I'm starting to go crazy by the end of a week. I need to get the hell out of here, or smother Venice. Her chatter is driving me nuts. On top of that, she's even trying to sing. She can't carry a tune worth a damn. I certainly can't understand the words whatsoever, but Miss Venice thinks she's "Some Kind of Wonderful".

The holding tank, Seven Locks jail alias Hotel Hell, continues on as a place of transition. Some girls leave by finally posting bond after screaming at their boyfriends on the phone to "Hurry up and get some money!" The sweet-faced prostitute is still waiting to be deported. Others are going to the "real" jail, to the new ninety million-dollar facility in Clarksburg. And some of us are just hanging out, wishing we were staying anywhere but at Hotel Hell.

* * *

My nerves are frayed and body sore. I haven't slept or eaten well in a week. My gym mat slab of a bed is hard as a rock and I ask at least five different guards, during those every half an hour state required wall checks (which almost always wake me up), for ibuprofen. Finally, I was given some. (Begging is okay by me in jail. Absolutely.) My lack of REM (rapid eye movement), otherwise known as dream sleep, which one needs to cope with life and feel refreshed, is basically zero.

Also, no fresh air. It snowed a little outside and looked very cold, but I would have loved to run around in that small yard, even coatless and in cheap flip-flops. I had to beg for another pair, because one of mine broke in five days. Peggy laughed at my hobbling around, before I got my nice new size 11s, way too big for me. We can barely walk right with our socks shoved back between our big toe and second toe in our over-sized sandals, much less with me dragging around a broken one. If I gave them up and just resorted to only socks, though, my socks would be filthy in no time and my feet *really* freezing.

I'm laughing as I walk back from the bathroom and sit down next to Peggy, "I need to be issued new shoes. My uniform isn't up to par." Peggy laughs as she looks up over her tattered romance novel at my size L, wrinkled jumpsuit with crotch to my knees. "Ask for a new jumpsuit too. That color doesn't become you and looks a tiny bit big." Peggy and I try to chuckle, but it's really hard to laugh at all. We're in such a sorry state locked up with a bunch of "crazies", us included. Though luckily, we're not as crazy as some.

Venice wakes up one morning and paces around the room like a hungry tiger in a zoo. "I's goin' to wig out! I's jus a goin' to wig out! I's gots to gets outta here!" I'm not exactly sure who alerts the guards, but I think it was Grandma Glenda. Bet she's seen a "wig out" or two in her day. Before I can even figure out what's going on, Venice is changing into a very bright red jumpsuit, being handcuffed and hauled away. Just like that. Venice just bought herself a one-way ticket to solitary confinement. Better late than never. I hope I never see that strange bitch again.

A few minutes later, the guard is back in our room yelling, "Duke!" I don't move, shocked to hear *my* name. "Duke, come here!"

"Coming!" What's up? I'm paranoid. What's going on now? It's not medication time. Oh, thank God, they're not holding a red jumpsuit! For a minute, I thought Venice made something up and got me in trouble, and I was going into solitary, too! That scary girl has been making nasty faces at me like a second grader and picking on me and my "Janie Fuckin' Fonda" workouts mercilessly.

"Yes?"

"Follow me."

I'm led down a gray cinderblock hall with no windows into a very small room. A middle-aged, gray-haired man in glasses looks up at me from behind his desk.

"You're Miss Duke?"

"Yes."

"I'm Mr. Smerck. Please fill out these forms in the room across the hall, and bring them back to me when you are finished." I pick up the pile of forms, and do as I'm told without a word, so relieved I am not in trouble.

But what is all this crap about? They want to know if I finished high school? Of course I finished high school. I was the valedictorian. I *don't* want to write that I finished medical school. Why should I? "Higher education, if any." Yeah, I've got higher education, Mr. Smerck, as high as you can go. But why do I have to tell you? I don't want to be an eye surgeon in jail, no way.

I'm too much in the minority just being white. The only way I would do eye surgery on anyone in Hotel Hell would be under general anesthesia. God knows what their drug tolerance is, so local anesthesia would be out. I wouldn't want any one of them getting anxious in the middle of a cataract surgery and want to bite me either. I'd end up with their retina in my now teeth marked hand, needing an HIV test. (I truly once had a big shot attorney wake up all of a sudden under local anesthesia, in the middle of cataract surgery with an *open eye*, and try to leave the operating room. Luckily his surgery came out okay, but I know my heart skipped a beat, and I'm sure the anesthesiologist's skipped, too.)

Oh, hell, I think. He probably already knows. He probably saw the psychiatrist's report. They made me see the "shrink" the same day I saw the blonde lady who admitted me to Hotel Hell, and I told him who I was. My bad knee was hurting in the cold, and I wanted him to make sure I got some ibuprofen. I also wanted a little respect from a colleague, especially after the blonde lady's matter-of-fact statement, "You're not a criminal."

So I'm as honest as ever on the forms. Mr. Smerck comes to get me and says, "I am from the Pre-Release Center in Rockville. You qualify to go there, but you have to get a job."

"But, I'm unemployed. I don't have a job."

"You can obtain one."

"I've had trouble finding work. I've been repeatedly told, "I'm over-qualified and too old. I can't be an eye surgeon now, and that is all I know."

Now Mr. Smerck is frowning at me, and I have no idea why.

"Do you *want* to go to Clarksburg's jail?"

"Sir, I want to get out of any jail as soon as possible. I heard from the other women that there is a program in Clarksburg, something called J.A.Z. for alcoholics, and if you do that program and work in the kitchen, you get more "good time" and get out sooner." He looks exasperated now and smirks at me.

"A job will get you out in the community from the Pre-Release Center. But if you do not obtain a job within a few weeks, you will be sent back to a cell in Clarksburg."

I'm not understanding at all. I just want out of the whole damned system A.S.A.P., and the other girls told me the fastest way was through this J.A.Z. program. I repeat myself, "I want to do whatever I need to do to get out of jail as soon as possible."

"Okay. I'm signing you up for P.R.C." J. A. Z. or P. R. C., *whatever*, I think, just get me out! Because my luck's been lagging, I repeat my desire for good measure.

"This P.R.C. thing gets me out of jail *the* fastest?"

"Yes."

"But I have to get a job?"

"Yes, you can go now," and there's that little smirk again on his face. Is he actually enjoying this? Or am I paranoid and just imagining it? (Nope. It's just one of the many, many moments I will be forced to endure with this feeling as an incarcerated, white doctor/eye surgeon, that the person dealing with me is enjoying putting me down.)

How the hell am I going to "get a job in a few weeks" when it took almost six months to get two lousy ones that I either got fired from or quit? Oh dear God, I don't know what the hell is going on anymore! I need my medical license back, oh, but I can't add that to my other hundred worries right now like basic survival and not getting sick.

Chapter 11

MORE COURT

I'm barely back sitting on my bed, haven't started to tell Peggy where I had to go, when my name is being yelled out again.

"Duke! Miss Duke!" A new guard is shouting for me.

"Yes?"

"Come with me."

I glance at Peggy who's looking at me with worry in her eyes. I fling off Mr. Burlap and walk to the door. The really nice girl Yvonne had left just like this the day before. She got yelled at by the guard to "Come with me!" and Peggy and I never saw her again.

I follow the guard and immediately feel like sprinting down the hall again. It's a week to the day since I checked in to Hotel Hell, and I'm 1,110% sick and tired of it.

This female guard is much smaller than me, a real rarity, so I don't feel intimidated and ask her a simple question, "Where am I going?"

"To court."

"Excuse me?"

"Court."

"Why?"

"For your theft charge." Oh my God, I think again, didn't the Wizard get my ex-husband, Dieter, to drop it? Obviously not. Twenty-five hundred dollars to the Wizard to represent me for a less than twenty-dollar piece of my own grandmother's, my Dad's Mom's, glass candy dish. It was mine, not Dieter's. I repossessed, not *robbed,* it out of Dieter's house, and the Wizard didn't get it dropped? Terrific.

We walk the long way to the "loading dock" where the paddy wagon waits.

"Turn around." I turn. On slap the tight handcuffs behind my back. I panic and quickly ask, "Don't I get to change into my street clothes?"

"No." Oh, Jesus, I have to go to court naked under a jumpsuit? In flip-flops? With my hands behind my back so my cold nipples show? This is too humiliating. Glenda always gets to change into street clothes on her trial days. What about me? I have to ask the guard, "Glenda always changes her clothes before court, why can't I?"

"She's federal." That's her flat response.

The door opens and a gust of cold November air immediately starts me shivering. I flip flop up the paddy wagon steps, barely a minute of fresh air, and sit my sorry ass on the ice-cold metal bench. As I grab the strap behind me to steady myself, my brain bellows a very bad thought: Is my ex going to have the satisfaction of seeing me in this degrading jumpsuit and handcuffed?! The disgust of that thought makes me want to retch right through the fence-like metal partition at the men. Dear God, what next? What the fuck next?

I try to push the humiliating thought out of my head, but it won't leave, and a second track in my brain starts wailing. What if I'm found guilty? Will I have to be in jail even *longer?* A third brain track is now screaming, what about... *my... poor... children*! I barely hear the "Hi's, Honeys" from the man across from me, but if looks could kill, he'd be dead. Unbelievably, he doesn't utter another word.

*   *   *

The bumpy, cold hard ride to the courthouse feels ten times longer than it is. Might as well be in dreadlocks like the rest of 'em, because I'm in a total state of dread. Perfect. I'm ushered into the same third far cell with the shitty faucet. Just great, I'm already thirsty. I turn to get unhandcuffed. Right, there's my old stalker, mister camera. Why must one be filmed in a cage outside of court without even a bar of soap to choke oneself on?

On the bars five feet in front of the toilet, there is a no more than a ten inch solid square piece of metal, so apparently the camera is blocked from seeing one's private parts when using the metal bowl/toilet. All eight tracks in my vintage brain are smoking in complete stress, way into overdrive, and I sarcastically speculate: Is that metal piece supposed to block the male guards from seeing my private parts if I'm sitting or squatting or both? To pee or not to pee? That's the big question; what indeed do the guards see? That little square probably only blocks a little if I sit on that contaminated metal toilet, and I only squat like Mom taught me to do in public, so they can probably see. But then again, I'm in this stupid jumpsuit that I have to unbutton and pull down below my bottom to go bathroom anyway. So they get to see my boobies, at least, because they took my bra away.

Hmmm, if I had been to jail before like the girl that wore two pair of socks, and graciously gave me one pair, I would have worn two pair of long underwear. Yep, Mary Ann, you are beginning to go out of your mind. Shut your brain down! But why don't they have only female guards in the women's cell area? Why the *hell* are there *men* watching us?!

Oh God, (back to the second brain track) Dieter is going to see me in this stupid jumpsuit and handcuffs. What a nightmare! Do they at least take my handcuffs off before entering the courtroom? Probably not. What a total bloody nightmare. From my starched doctor's lab coat, he always had to respect me in, to this.

How did I let myself lose control of my life? I'm such a strong person; how did I let alcohol take me over? It just did, Mary Ann, with all of the stress you were under for so long. It used to be called a "nervous breakdown", and you had every reason in the world to have one. But I only drank too much for a couple of years. Well, that was *plenty of time* to just about kill yourself, Mary Ann,… several times over. I'm trying to not think, but I can't stop my thoughts. Believe you me, I never dreamed my life would get this bad after how hard I have worked.

*   *   *

I sit with my head in my hands for a very long time. I don't give a damn if the guards are watching me and laughing at me or not. I don't care if they know I'm a surgeon or not. I don't care. I just sit there and pray: Dear God, please help me. Please watch over my children. Please God, please let my babies forgive me. Please God, don't let them give me any more jail time. I'll pay whatever fine, just *don't* make me stay in jail any longer for my grandmother's candy dish.

The candy dish and a couple of old stained table cloths, which aren't even big enough for my dining room table were all I inherited when my father's mother died, while I was in medical school. I was close to my father's mother but my mom's mom, Baba, was everything to me. My dear

Baba who told me over and over to "be a doctor and you'll have a good life". Mary Ann, you lucky little cat, you really have been through eight lives. Better make this last one good, if only for your children. They deserve the best.

I'm so lost in my thoughts that I don't hear the Wizard come in and greet me through my bars.

"Mary Ann!" he says again.

"Oh!" I jump up. "Hi."

"Is your ex-husband really tall and good looking?"

"He's 6'2", nice blue eyes, looks kind of like that one movie star. I can't think of his name."

"I think I rode the elevator with him."

"So, he *is* here?"

"Yes." The Wizard has that "ants in pantsers" mood I don't like.

"Did you get him to drop it?"

"No, the State's Attorney is still prosecuting."

"He's using a State's Attorney? Doesn't he have a *real* one?" Beautiful. I'm unemployed and incarcerated paying $2,500 to be represented for a $20 piece of glass, and Dieter's prosecuting me for free.

"Yes, the State's Attorney is representing him."

I push the Wizard, "Well, are you getting *him* to drop it?"

"He can't. Your ex won't. But I received your father's fax that it was his mother's dish, and I told him we're pleading "not guilty", and I'm putting you on the stand."

"Okay, I'm ready." Right, ready to jump right out of my skin, not only this scratchy jumpsuit.

"There are some cases ahead of ours but we'll be heard soon."

"Do you know the judge?" The one truth I've really come to acknowledge in our corrupt world and coercive court system is it really isn't what you know, but *who* you know.

"I don't know her."

"*Her,* you said? My judge is a woman?"

"Yes." Glimmer. A glimmer of hope.

"Great! Go get 'em. Get me off!" The Wizard grins and vanishes.

I'm a caged, cold animal and start to pace, 'round and 'round, in my claustrophobic gray cell. I don't give a flying fuck who's watching me through the camera. One week in jail will do that to you, you don't sweat the small stuff anymore, and you think too often in four letter words. I'm going to be different when I get out of here. No one will be able to stop me, I hope, or at least I'll be in great physical shape, if not mental.

   *   *   *

Who knows what time it is? How much time has gone by? Who cares. Time to stop running in place. Lunch. I started running in place in socks, because the flip-flops were impossible to keep on, after making myself dizzy trying to walk in tiny circles. I open the paper bag the guard hands in to me. What the hell is this? *This* is what they call *lunch?* I'm looking at four pieces of bread (at least they're wheat) wrapped in plastic, a cardboard container of no-name orangeade, a small bag of pretzels and four white plastic tubes. What are these? Giant mayonnaises and mustards? Where's the mystery meat?

It's too hard to peel the plastic with even strong surgical fingers, so I resort to my teeth. A gob of plain grape jelly plops onto my chin. I bite open one of the harder tubes and have to squeeze it with all my might. Slowly but surely the nastiest looking hard brown peanut butter plopped out. I've never seen peanut butter this color or consistency. I throw back my head and laugh loudly.

"What bes so funny?" the girl, who I can't see at all, in the next cell is asking me.

I'm laughing so hard tears come to my eyes, and I can't respond. My next door neighbor must think I'm crazy, all that flip flop pacing, then running in place, and now I can't stop laughing hyena-like. I finally answer her and wipe my eyes.

"My peanut butter looks exactly like a terd on my bread. How yummy!"

"It be all dat! Jus' likes shit, ain't it? I's agrees wich you."

I'm still laughing. Sheer insanity. It's so hard that even if I had a plastic knife, which of course wasn't included, I couldn't possibly spread it. So I squeeze it out onto a piece of bread like a fat tic tac toe board, glop on some jelly and eat my "terd" sandwich. I always loved a good PB@J growing up, but now PB@J has a new meaning.

*   *   *

Three long, hard, cold hours go by.

I've paced, and run in place, and used up all of my carbohydrate-rich lunch. I still feel like doing air punches like Sylvester Stallone in *Rocky* with my excess aggression. But, now my legs are tired.

Keys, finally, keys in the lock. I'm standing in my flip-flops, and even in those, I'm taller than my Wizard. He is beaming from ear to ear as he shoves in a piece of paper through the bars at me. "001 THEFT: LESS $500 VALUE. Plea- OTHER PLEA Verdict- 'NOLLE PROSEQUI'."

Rock on my soul, I scream to myself! I got it. I *finally* know what that 'Nolle Prosequi' Latin legal mumbo jumbo means. It means nada, nothing, not being prosecuted for, all charges dropped. "How did you pull this off?" I challenge the Wizard.

The Rooster, I mean Wizard, is still puffing out his chest and straining his suspenders with glee. "It's a full house in court today. While your ex was waiting, I called the State's Attorney aside and told him we were pleading 'Not Guilty', and we have a letter from your father, and with all of the cases ahead of us, we were not going to be heard for hours."

"Then what happened? Go on!"

"The State's Attorney pulled aside your ex and told him our plea, probably showed him your Dad's letter, and your ex left with a pretty pissed off look on his face."

"He did?"

"Yes."

I'm overjoyed that Dieter didn't get to see me in a jumpsuit and handcuffs.

Now I feel too exhausted to talk.

The Wizard continues, "I also asked the State's Attorney if he really felt you deserved another eighteen months and to be convicted of a felony over your own grandmother's candy dish, knowing a felony conviction will probably keep you from ever getting your medical license back."

I'm staring at him, not even able to blink, in shock, yet again.

The Wizard sees my amazement, and puffs his chest out yet more. "That's right. I pointedly told the State's Attorney it was going to be on *his* conscience if you could never be an eye surgeon again, because of his prosecuting you for something that was your property!"

I continue to stare at him in disbelief.

Then it begins to register, but not make any sense. I could have gotten *eighteen* more months of incarceration for a twenty-dollar dish that was mine? *And* the Wizard is saying a theft charge, no matter how small, if convicted is a felony, and one stupid felony like that will keep one from reobtaining a medical license?

The world has definitely gone mad. It's not just me, no way. Sometimes I feel a little nutty, but I would *never* have had Dieter arrested, like he had me arrested, for something that was his. I'm still giving him memorabilia of his I find. He should have never taken my grandmother's dish in the first place. Who's really the thief?

I ask the Wizard, "Do many ex-husbands do hurtful things like this?"

The Wizard shrugs his shoulders. Good answer, very lawyer-like, I think, non-committal. "I've got to go, Honey. It's over. Call me if you need me," and the Wizard leaves for good with barely a wave.

Yeah, right, I think, as I plop down on the long cold metal bench. It's over for *you*, my Wizard. Go home and have a cocktail to celebrate. Get a couple cases of Dom

Perignon on me with the $2,500 you charged me for this dubious "theft" charge...but I just started my sentence.

    I close my eyes and clasp my hands together and think: Thank you, God, for letting me win this one time in court, not only to not be convicted of a felony, but eighteen *more* months away from my children would have been totally devastating. I've been away from them for far too long as it is.

    I also thank you, God, for not lengthening my sentence, because I'm afraid Venice would be difficult to escape from for another year and a half without getting a rearranged face, at the very least.

Chapter 12

Dreams, Back to the Spring Before the Separation and Divorce (Four years before jail)

It is May of 2001, my favorite time of year in Washington, but not this year. Dieter and I have been married seven years and our children are five and one-half, four, and almost two years old. Nadia is still in diapers. The Friday before Mother's Day 2001, three weeks before my birthday, Dieter planned a boys' night out. So I planned a girls' night. This was a new one for us, this boys' night/girls' night thing, but I guess we don't go out with each other anymore, so why not?

Dieter was going out with his new carpenter friend, the small guy named Dan, who helped Dieter put some crown molding up in our bedroom. I was going to my backyard neighbor's art exhibition in DuPont Circle, a trendy place in Washington, D.C., with my girlfriend Pat, a urologist.

I run into the house from the office at 4:45 to get some orange juice, because I had missed lunch yet again, and low blood sugar usually makes me feel like biting someone. I need to finish patients and finish *fast,* because it's almost five on a Friday and Rita, my nanny, wants *out.* I ask her between gulps, "Where's Dieter?"

"Downstairs, ironing," Rita responds. I don't believe her. Ironing?!, I think, I *never* saw him iron anything, not one damned thing in seven years of marriage!

"You've got to be kidding me, Rita." Rita just rolls her eyes.

Just then Dieter saunters into the kitchen wearing the peach linen shirt I bought him for too much money last year for Father's Day. It looks perfect, like it came straight from the dry cleaner's.

"You *ironed*?!" I ask him, still incredulous.

"So what?" he blandly responds.

Dieter stunk, too. He stunk up the whole kitchen with too damned much Polo cologne that he continues to wear, even though I prefer different. (Why do most European men wear too much cologne anyway? I've not yet been able to figure that one out. I think they should stick to regular deodorant applications and bathing.)

Something comes over me. I yell, "Bye" to Dieter, give Rita the look that means "I know you want to leave", but instead of finishing a dilated patient, I give my office manager Judy the same look, grab the phone book, and go into my surgery room and shut the door.

I rip open the yellow pages and look under P, then have to flip back to I for "Investigators and Investigation". I call a private investigation firm in Rockville thinking: That's not too far away. They gotta get here fast, because it's ten to five and Dieter is leaving to go out at 6 p.m.

"Hello?"

"Yes, may I help you?"

"I'm in a bit of a hurry, actually very much in a hurry. My husband is going out at 6 p.m., and I think he is cheating on me. Could someone from your firm be at my home at 10220 Democracy Boulevard in Potomac, and be here by 5:45 to be sure not to miss him?"

"Yes, Ma'am, we can be there."

"He'll be driving a tan Lexus SUV, is 6'2", wearing a peach linen shirt, has blue eyes and is handsome enough to be a movie star."

"Do you know the license plate, Ma'am?"

"No. I have no clue. Just hurry, please! Please follow him for four to six hours. How much is this going to cost?!"

"Well Ma'am, it depends on whether we need two investigators or one, probably no more than $1,000, and we need a credit card number."

"Oh God, that's too much! And I can't put it on a credit card because then he'll find out I hired you! I'll pay cash. I'll pay you on Monday. I'm Dr. Duke and I'm good for it. Please cut me a little break for a cash deal."

"Just a minute, Ma'am".

Shit! He put me on hold. I've got to finish patients before any of them gets pissed off at me, along with Rita and Judy!

They must have been having a slow weekend. The young man got back on the phone and said, "We don't usually work without a retainer, but we will this one time."

"Thank you. Thank you very much, but hurry up, so you don't miss him! Call me on my cell phone, please, around ten." I give him my cell phone number, address again, urge him to hurry and hang up.... Done deal. Then put a smile on my face and finish my mildly annoyed patients, to get both my mildly pissed off nanny and office manager out by six.

Our babysitter, my young seventeen-year-old patient, arrives promptly at six along with my friend, Pat. I'm not ready and have no clue if the P.I. arrived in time. I didn't get a chance to look out the upstairs window. Dieter left a little before six. Damn.

"I'll be ready in a second," I tell both of them, when I answer the door in a robe.

My children love the babysitter, and are already showing her some of their toys. I get dressed quickly and decide to do my usual routine, put on a little make-up at red lights.

"I'm so happy you don't mind driving, Pat," as I pull the mirror down in her Mercedes, "I'm a little upset."

"Why? Did you have a crazy day in the office?" she asks.

"Oh, that too, you know how Friday afternoons can be, but that isn't what's bothering me. I just hired a private investigator to follow Dieter tonight."

Pat, the ever unruffled, doesn't need to comb her hair because it's so short and always in place anyway, never wears a stitch of make-up, not even lipstick, squinches up her face and turns to me, "What did you do that for?"

"Because Dieter ironed a shirt for the first time, probably in his life, and he was stinking up the kitchen with so much cologne, that I think he's meeting a woman and not his new friend."

"Wow."

"Yeah, I know. I hope I'm wrong. The evening is going to cost more than I made in the office today. But I just got this weird feeling, and called a P.I. firm an hour ago. I hope they got here in time."

Pat knows Dieter and I have been having a difficult time. She gives me a little smile like, "It'll all work out", and accelerates her Benz. Hmm, I think, Pat doesn't really understand but is still supportive. She's never been married, has no children, and is one of too many women in medicine who sacrificed having a family to be a doctor.

Pat and I enjoy the art show. I buy a painting for seven hundred dollars. I don't know why I bought it, extravagant, for frugal me. I guess just because I liked it. My neighbor sold it to me for half price. It's a beautiful painting. Ethereal. An oil of a woman sitting and cupping her chin with her hand called, "The Thinking Woman". How apropos.

We drive into the district afterwards to go to dinner. I'm starving. On our way down into the parking garage below the infamous "Washington Waterfront", Pat's beeper goes off. She is also in solo practice, so is on call for her patients way too much like I am. In ophthalmology, however, my beeper rarely goes off. Not so fortunate, in urology. There's an emergency patient of hers at Suburban Hospital with a kidney stone. Great. Turn around. Go all the way back almost to home. What bad luck. My first night out in a long time. Pat's disappointed, too, but says, "This shouldn't take too long. Kidney stones are pretty straight forward."

I have to smile at her. We doctors really do put things in another perspective. Pain with a kidney stone is supposedly worse than having a baby or even a heart attack. The patients may think they're dying, but to a physician, a kidney stone simply means a lot of fluids intravenously to help it pass and enough pain medication to get the patient comfortable. No big deal, just an I.V. and some morphine.

I hang out in the doctor's lounge, stomach growling, watching CNN, trying not to think about what the P.I. will come up with. 9:30. Pat is finally finished with her admission. "I'm ready to bite, let's eat!" I exclaim. "Let's go to the Cheesecake Factory in Rockville; they serve big portions."

"Good choice," and Pat pedals the metal on her Mercedes.

Thank God there is no wait, for once, because it's so late. The waiter is prompt, even though the restaurant is jam packed and noisy. "Can I get you ladies something to drink?"

"Two vodka cranberries, please," and I nod at him nicely meaning, "*Now*, please." (A glass of Chardonnay is just not going to cut it.) Pat looks up over her menu a little surprised, "I'm not drinking. I'm driving and still on call." I raise my eyebrows and open my eyes wide, glancing at her over my menu and retort, "I know. I know. They're both for me. I don't want to have to wait for my second drink." Pat accepts that explanation as legitimate and responds, "Go for it," then puts her gaze right back into her menu. The waiter soon returns setting down one drink in front of each of us and takes our orders.

"I can't believe how hungry I am," as I drain my drink in two swallows.

"Me too, bummer we couldn't eat downtown."

"Don't worry about it, Pat. Nothing you could do about it. Isn't my new painting great?!" as I reach over to get the drink in front of her, and replace it with my empty glass. (Don't want to *look* two fisted, even if I *am* two fisted.)

Before she can reply, and before I can take a sip, my cell phone rings. I had almost forgotten about it, but...

not quite. I scramble to get it out of my purse, but really don't want to take the call.

"Hello?"

"Hello, Dr. Duke?"

"Yes?"

"I have some information for you."

"Yes?" I take a long sip of my second drink.

"Your husband drove straight to 'Polyester's' dance club and he has been drinking and dancing with a brunette with very long hair."

"Yes?" I sip some more.

"She's attractive with pretty brown eyes, approximately 5'5", 120 pounds, early thirties." I interrupt him, *"She is?!"* The brunette must be my "best" friend Marilyn. The P.I. told me he wouldn't know her name for sure until he "runs the plates" on Monday. He didn't have to. The woman he described was definitely Marilyn. How could she?! How could he?!

He describes some more, and I stare at Pat in disbelief over my drink. This can't really be happening to *me.* I have been *trying so hard.* And it still isn't enough. Sadly, the well is just about dry, not meaning my drink. *I don't have any more to give.*

I mumble something about bringing cash on Monday; thanks a lot, have the report ready, and close my phone. I bow my head for a minute, as I toss the phone into the bottom of my purse, then flip up my head and look Pat in the eye, pissed off and pissed *on* all at once.

"Pat! Pat, get this! The P.I. told me Dieter was kissing her hands. Kissing her hands! How beautiful. My hands were never kissed. Never. Damn it! My hunch was right. I can't believe it is my *great friend,* Marilyn, though!!"

Pat spits out, "Little slut!" just as our food arrives.

I can't eat, but drain my drink. Dear Pat is the best person I could be with at this moment. She's smart, ha, deals with "dicks" of all kinds on a daily basis (as a urologist, not as a woman) and says her next all-inclusive one liner, "Men suck."

I feel numb. I feel like I think I should be crying, but I don't feel like crying immediately. My first reaction is anger, total venom-producing anger that my best friend is going after my husband, and my husband is out kissing my best friend. "That bitch," I mutter to Pat as she's busy chewing. "She knew Dieter and I were having problems, but who does she think she is going after my husband?!" Pat can only shake her head.

The "thinking woman", *me* (not the damned painting), doesn't know what to do, or how to handle this. "Do I tell him I know, Pat, or keep it to myself? Do I wait until Monday and call an attorney? How the hell can I keep it cool all Mother's Day weekend?"

"I don't know, Mary Ann, I don't know what to tell you. Maybe you should talk to an attorney first."

"I don't know if I can do it. You know how emotional I am." I definitely have a strange buzz from this horrid news, my adrenaline surge, and sucking down two vodkas in ten minutes. "I'm a wild and crazy, you remember *Saturday Night Live*, Czechoslovakian girl! How, in God's name, am I supposed to keep my mouth shut all *Mother's Day* weekend? Oh, I feel so awful."

I almost jump out of my skin when my cell phone rings again, and I fumble to find it. It is my babysitter's mother reminding me that she has to be home by midnight.

I had lost track of time. "We have to go!" I exclaim to Pat. "I like my babysitter, and her whole family is my patients. That was her mom reminding me that she has to be home in ten minutes!" Pat is awesome, throws cash on the table, and we fly to my house in her Mercedes.

Betrayed. Angry. Dejected. So many bad feelings all at once are inside me. No matter how hard I was trying to make my marriage work, it was a losing battle. My dream of being happily married for life is shattering before my very eyes, and I feel totally helpless. What to do?

I slowly climb the long staircase to our bedroom and open the door. The lights are out, and there's Dieter in bed. Surprised, I ask, "Where's our babysitter?"

"I took her home."

"You *what*?!" My blood starts to boil. Too late. The tea kettle is going to scream. I can't believe it. Dieter just left my three babies alone for at least fifteen to twenty minutes, and doesn't think he was in the wrong at all. I am livid.

"I took her home," Dieter repeats.

Desperately trying to retain my composure, I start the inquisition. I just can't be quiet all weekend to wait for an attorney's advice. "Where did you go tonight?"

Dieter rolls away from me, but I step forward and can smell the beer on his breath. "I stopped at Montgomery Mall because Dan wasn't off from work yet." Lie #1.

"Where did you eat?"

"Chick-fil-A." Lie #2.

"Where did you end up going with Dan?"

"Oh, he wanted to go into the District and I didn't, so we never met up."

"So, what did you do?" Dieter is still rolled away from me. I am standing at the edge of our bed with my hands on my hips.

"I went to Circuit City and hung out on the Rockville Pike and then came home." Lie #3.

Three strikes and he's out! I stomp into the bathroom and check the pockets of his pants. Lo and behold, a receipt from "Polyester's" for over fifty dollars. I charge right back into the bedroom, where Dieter is actually trying to fall asleep.

"Oh! You went to the Mall? These receipts say you were at *Polyester's dance club*, and the P.I. I hired to follow you said you went straight there and were kissing and dancing with Marilyn!"

That was certainly enough to make Dieter finally roll over and open his big blues wide in shock, and his face had guilt written all over it.

With yet another adrenaline surge for the night, along with total disappointment, I lost it.

I lunged at Dieter like I was going to slap him across the face, and he leaned back and put his big foot out and kicked me in the chest! He kicked me so hard that I fell back against the bedroom wall and banged my head and my back. I was stunned. Stunned that he actually had kicked me and shocked from the pain!

I had just had the abdominal hernia repair and breast augmentation only six weeks prior, so when he kicked me, it *really* hurt. But I don't know which was worse, the physical pain or the emotional, no, definitely the emotional.

I fell against the wall and slid down. I sat there a while. Not for long. I needed to leave. I hope his damned guns aren't loaded. I'm afraid, and want to get away from him.

"I'm going to call the police!" I yell, as I slam the bedroom door.

"Go ahead!" Dieter yells back, "I'll tell them you hit me first!"

I burst into tears as I ran down two flights of stairs, after quickly opening the children's doors to make sure they weren't awakened.

I didn't call the police. I should have. Most definitely. Tonight, Dieter was one hell of a lot more drunk than I was. I drank only the two vodkas. I could have told the police that he left my babies alone in the house, drove drunk, and my patients could have vouched for it. This particular night the police would have really believed *me*. I could have even shown them my still healing chest and abdominal hernia repair for that matter!

I screwed up. I didn't call them. That night I was too annihilated to call the police, but I knew my dream of living happily ever after, married with children, was over. I can't stay with a man who kicks me. He will deny it to this day and lied about it in court. He testified that "he never hit me" and he doesn't remember doing anything of the sort. Maybe he truly doesn't remember, because he drank enough to blackout. I definitely should have called the police, but was too depressed and too afraid that maybe Dieter would hurt me again if he heard me on the phone. He had never hurt me physically so badly before. But much more than that, he was so angry with me for following him and catching him lying, I thought he might even shoot me. I had never seen such an angry look on Dieter's face before, not even when we had that horrible argument and were throwing things at each other before Nadia was born. Dieter and I had our share of shouting matches, arguing usually over money, but to kick me when I recently had surgery. I cried harder as I locked myself in the basement bedroom.

Chapter 13

Mother's Day and Turning FORTY

A woman knows when a man doesn't love her, especially when there are twelve calls in 2001 to the police, mostly for domestic violence. Most of the time the police officers do not write a report, and truthfully, I think I blocked a lot of that year out of my memory bank. A woman knows that she is not loved, but when the cold hard proof hits one in the face from that P.I.'s phone call and Dieter's kick; it felt like someone was trying to freeze me. It was like liquid nitrogen was being sprayed at me, and I couldn't help but become frozen. All I could do was cry. I slept no more than two hours that night. I didn't know there could be so many tears to shed. Me, dumb ass, the great ophthalmologist, didn't realize the lacrimal gland can keep pumping them out so damned long.

"My poor little babies" I kept thinking over and over. I never ever wanted them to experience divorce. I never wanted to break up their home. I wanted to be married for over fifty years like my parents. They have had their ups and downs, but when all is said and done, they are there for each other. I could continue to be a martyr for my children, and stay in a loveless marriage for them, but not if I am going to get physically hurt. My dear sweet innocent babies' lives are going to be changed forever. I wish I could take on all of their disappointment and loneliness and just add it to my own.

My very highest hopes and dreams of having the perfect, beautiful family and losing it all, and losing my children causes me the greatest pain, every minute of my life. I often wonder how I get up and keep going. So much easier to just stay in bed. That's why I suppose divorce *is* highest on the stress scale, even higher than the death of a loved one. Divorce to me is like living death over and over. The despair, the disappointment, the absolute betrayal and loneliness. How could Dieter do this to me when I was trying so hard to make it work?

It doesn't matter whether Dieter and Marilyn had actually gone all the way. It was the lying that killed my feelings. How many other times has Dieter lied to me? Probably a lot, he's so good at it. Even the lies have lies to cover them up. I had already caught him once, when he went skiing for a few days to Colorado with a buddy, leaving me home six months pregnant with Nadia and sick to death with a bronchitis I even had to take antibiotics for. I had to fly my Mom down on a full fare next day ticket; I was so desperate for help. I was outside pregnant *and* sick, rolling a snowman with James and Marika, as he drove out the driveway. Dieter told me he had to work. When I couldn't reach him for three days because "he was on the slopes", I finally called his boss and found out he never was traveling for work at all; meanwhile, I was still seeing patients trying not to cough on them and assuring them, "Don't worry, I'm on antibiotics". Then I would stumble into the house and lie on the couch wasted, unable to help my Mom with second shift or third.

That ski trip came into my head as I'm lying on top of the quilt, too tired to even pull it over myself, wiping my eyes and blowing my nose with toilet paper. And the kick. One wouldn't even kick a dog like that. He kicked me, oh dear God, I *am* going to have to get a divorce. My greatest dream totally shattered, to be happily married with children. Though I knew on one level, it had been a long time coming; now it was gone, dead. Just like that.

* * *

I have to see a few patients the next morning. They were two of my oldest and very favorite patients, very British, educated, well traveled, cultured, and simply so interesting to me, the little Czechoslovakian girl with a Baba who finished sixth grade. I did Louise's second cataract that Friday, and here she is with her patch on, dressed to the nines, yet again, wearing another unusual piece of her magnificent jewelry from all over the world. Her dandy British husband Blair's work took them traveling throughout the "colonies" for "Her Majesty".

Louise takes one look at me and exclaims, "Darling, you look bloody awful!"

"Thanks. I feel bloody awful." Wearing my heart on my sleeve as usual, I say, "I hired a private investigator last night and caught my husband kissing and dancing with my best friend. And he totally lied to me about it. He kicked me, too. I think I have to get a divorce. I called my best friend a little while ago and told her, 'Only whores sleep with their best friend's husbands!' And I hung up!"

Louise's response is ever quick, just like her mind, "Sounds that way to me."

In the next breath, she is inviting me over to their pool. I respond, "Oh, thank you. It's a lovely invitation, but none of my kids swim, and Nadia is still in diapers."

Louise immediately retorts, "Well, she won't be the first baby who has pooed in our pool! Do come dear. We'll have a barbie."

"I'll have to see what the day brings, Louise, but thank you."

Louise leans into me, "Look at my garnet broach, dear. Didn't you tell me your grandmother gave you her garnets?" The broach is outstanding, and I tell her, "Oh, Louise! It's magnificent. My Baba left me a broach that is very similar! You know I have a wonderful set of garnets from the 1920's and 1930's from her, right out of Czechoslovakia. Oh, how I love to wear them. I think mostly because they remind me of her, and she would be happy I was enjoying them."

"I know you do, Dear. You have shown them to me and some other unique pieces I have seen you wearing in the office."

"Yes, I just loved going to estate sales and buying antique jewelry inexpensively. My Baba would be delighted at my collection of real jewelry. She only wore costume, except for her precious garnets. Baba and I loved jewelry more than anything, except each other!" I was grateful Louise changed the subject and reminded me of Baba.

She seemed to read my mind and said, "I hope you come for a swim."

A most gracious offer and a lifesaver for me. I need to get out of the house. Dieter hasn't said a word to me, nor I to him. After lunch, I pack up five-year-old James, four-year-old Marika, and two-year-old Nadia for a big outing of swimming. Great, three total non-swimmers to keep from drowning, on two hours sleep.

The children and I have a great time, despite everything. Blair is awesome, helping me watch the kids even at eighty-three, but the best part of the day was when their handsome son drove in, Edward, showing off his new BMW. Hmm, I didn't expect this. He's cute. Beautiful green eyes, gorgeous wavy full head of blonde hair, six feet tall and broad shouldered, just the way I like 'em. And, with the added bonus of a sexy British accent.

Mary Ann, you idiot, what are you thinking? Suddenly, I feel very self-conscious. I'm a married woman in an overly conservative bathing suit with three small children, hanging out with two eighty-plus-year-old patients. On top of everything looking ultra-unattractive with no make-up, wet hair, and a tired, cried out face.

The weather cannot be more glorious; it is a perfect May day. My beaten down spirit gets a little lift by the pure, unadulterated sunshine. (What a strange choice of adjectives, "*un*adulterated".) Edward changes into a suit and "Wow!" I think, "He even has sexy chest hair and great legs". Shut your mind off, Mary Ann. Better yet, shut off your hormones. Guess it just felt great to have a nice looking, intelligent, fun man giving me positive attention, instead of moping and bitching about not ever having enough "stuff" like Dieter, and most especially nice after last night's total trauma. On top of everything, the kids are really enjoying playing in the pool with Edward. Uh, oh.

We all stayed for the "barbie" and had a lovely time. I never called Dieter nor he me. Louise invites us to come back the following day, "The weather is supposed to be as nice as today, do come back." (Guess she was happy with her cataract surgery too, ha.)

"Oh, thank you very much, but Mother's Day is a family day."

"No, no I insist, do come back, Dear, and bring your lovely children."

I did not plan on coming back. No way.

*   *   *

Marika's adorable, tan face and bad breath wake me up at seven a.m. on Mother's Day, in my new basement bedroom. "Mommy, I need some cereal."

"Honey, ask Daddy to get you some."

"Daddy's gone."

"Gone?"

"He went for a bike ride on his BMW." Gee, thanks for making breakfast for me and the kids on Mother's Day.

I am still exhausted from the night before, but obviously Mommy duties have already begun, without the slightest reprieve, even on Mother's Day. Around noon I call Louise.

Her invitation is genuine, "Yes, of course you must come over." Dieter finally came home from his all morning ride. We speak for the first time since Friday night. "I'm taking the kids swimming over to my patients', the Everett-Monroe's home."

Dieter says simply, "Be back by six-thirty. I'm making spare ribs for James." That's it. No eye contact. He didn't bother to ask what the girls and I wanted for dinner. No apology. Nothing but a little Mother's Day card with a thinking woman on it (how crazy after the painting I just bought), a very short cold saying on the inside and *no* "Love" signing. Looks like a card for an ex-wife I think, if ex-husbands even bother to get one. Bet they don't. (I never have; that's for sure.)

The children and I have another wonderful, fun day. Edward puts arm floaties on all of the kids and is patiently teaching them how to doggy paddle. I'm sipping ice cold Chardonnay and lounging, seems like the first time I've had my feet up in years. Behind my sunglasses, my eyes well up with tears for a moment as I think, "Dieter should be doing this, not my patients' son".

I thank the Everett-Monroes for another lovely day and we get back home right on time. No sign of Dieter. Oh my God, he's standing us up on Mother's Day? I'm in shock. James asks, "Where's Daddy?" I can't believe this. He's not here? I look in the refrigerator. Where are the ribs? The children are hungry!

"He must still be at the grocery store, Honey."

"Mommy, I'm hungry," says Marika. Cute little Nadia looks up at me expectantly with her beautiful eyes, which are just like her father's.

"I'm sure Daddy is on his way. Let me put Barnie on for you," and I put a few towels on the couch and let them sit, wet bathing suits and all, and grab them each a juice box.

Fifteen minutes go by and I panic for a second, then pick up the phone and call Louise, "Is your invitation for a barbie still all right?"

"Of course, Dear." It was easier to be invited back than to call Dieter and be rejected, yet again. The food should have been ready when we got back. The kids usually eat by six, and there's no sign of Dieter at a quarter to seven. I make up an excuse to the children, "Daddy must have had to go to work."

I grab some hot dogs and diapers and load the kids back into the car, before I would have burst into tears. "The thinking woman", the overly emotional Czech woman is going to need every ounce of chutzpah and overall stamina to get through this train wreck of a marriage. I was still living off that stamina, but the supply of perseverance was getting pretty low.

The evening is festive, illegal fireworks, sparklers and all. I'm so happy the kids had a blast. Those poolside evenings pretty much became the norm for the summer. At least my babies were learning how to swim, and having a little fun, despite the escalating tension between their Mom and Dad.

*   *   *

Dieter's grandfather died the end of May, so he took family leave and flew to Germany for several days. He could have come back for my 40th birthday, June 6th, if he had any inkling of a reunion. But no, he stayed until the very last moment and arrived back on the 7th, for Nadia's birthday on the 8th. That was a slap in the face, ignoring my 40th, a no show, with no gift, not even a card.

The dye must be irreversibly cast. Never, ever again without an iron clad prenuptial. Better yet, never remarry, why be legally tied to anyone? Who cares to be a wife or called Mrs. so and so? I certainly don't. I seemed to have been the husband and the wife, and was called Dr. Duke anyway! Being married has been scratched off the "to do" list… forever.

A few days before my birthday, I still didn't know when Dieter was coming home and if we had a chance to work things out. In my soul I didn't want a divorce, but I knew with my heart and my head that it was inevitable. Seven years only. The classic "seven year itch" by Dieter, but we have these three little angels from heaven. Don't we still have to work it out for *them*?

"Hello?"

"It's Dieter."

"Hi!" I haven't heard from him since the funeral at least four days ago, when he really only wanted to talk to the kids anyway. "When are you coming home?" I ask. He knows full well my 40th is Wednesday.

"Thursday."

"Thursday?"

"Yes, for Nadia's birthday."

"Why don't you come back a day sooner?" I'm thinking for *my* birthday. I know he flew on one of those tickets that was open ended for family emergencies and could easily have changed it. The funeral is long over.

"I don't want to."... Stab... Just stab me in the heart yet again, Dieter. I want to run upstairs and burst into tears, so I just ask him, "Do you want to talk to the kids?" And then I sprint upstairs and do just that, leaving Rita to hang up the phone so my kids don't see me crying, before I have to compose myself and finish patients.

An hour later five o'clock arrives, all of my help turns into pumpkins as usual, and the phone rings again.

"Hi, it's Edward."

"Oh, hi!" Felt like he had e.s.p. (extra sensory perception) or something.

"It's a beautiful evening. Do you want to bring the kids over for swimming and a barbie?"

"Absolutely. Thank you." Just what the doctor ordered. Escapism and maybe a little wine. But, unfortunately, the Everett-Monroe home was not the best place to escape to. Not unlike a hotel, it had its own bar.

I guess I looked upset, and Edward asks, "What's wrong?"

"Well, I thought my husband was coming home today or tomorrow. I'm forty in two days, and he's purposefully not coming back for my birthday. He said, "I don't want to". Pause.

"Well..., do you want me to take you out for your birthday?" Longer pause, *much* longer.

Now *I* was the one crossing the line. I was the one "cheating" and going out with another man on my husband. But, I think, we can go out as friends, right Mary Ann? And forty is such a monstrous milestone for a woman. After forty, most men just don't consider a woman young anymore, unless they're fucking *eighty*.

I stare into those gorgeous green eyes for a long minute. Edward's eyes are looking back at me kindly, not like he wants to take advantage of me, just like a new friend that wants to take me out for my birthday. So I smile a broad smile for the first time all day and respond, "Yes, thank you. That would be very nice."

Edward calls again the following day and asks if I've ever been to Morton's restaurant in downtown Washington.

"No, I haven't, but I heard it's very nice." Wow, he's asking me to go there? I've heard it's pretty posh and quite expensive.

"Would you like to go there and then maybe go out somewhere in D.C. afterwards?"

"That would be lovely. I'll ask my nanny to stay late. Actually, I took Thursday off because Dieter is coming home, so I *can* stay out late."

Oh dear God, what an idiot, I think, not for the first time, there I am mentioning my husband again. Well, you *are* a married woman and a *good girl* Mary Ann, remember you were branded as a young girl that sex was "bad", and only "bad" girls had sex before they got married? But when you don't get married until you are almost thirty-three, it gets a little rough. Young girls should wait at least until they're eighteen. And be demanding, not submissive, like I always thought I should be.

Unfortunately, I don't believe in the institution of marriage anymore. I wholeheartedly believe in the sacrament of marriage, and if one is lucky enough to meet their soul mate before they are twenty-one and stay a virgin until then, great! But, the legal system has ruined the sacrament of marriage in the United States. It takes twenty minutes to have a beautiful church wedding ceremony, but it takes almost two years and God knows how much pain, aggravation and outrageous money to attorneys to extricate oneself from a bad choice.

Here's the big question for God: Are we supposed to stay in an angry, hateful, cheating marriage just because it is a sacrament? Or are we supposed to persevere and move on and be happy in our life, because we do only have *one* life and really aren't cats?

In our age of over 55% divorce rate, and by 2010 there will be more broken families in the U.S. of A. than "real" families, is one supposed to get married to have sex and children and then stay married and be miserable in that marriage in order to not commit a mortal sin or break a sacred sacrament and get divorced? Is getting a divorce so damned expensive and difficult because you want us to suffer, so we stay in horrible, cheating marriages to save our souls? Even if we are married to atheists who don't even believe in you?

Married women don't go out with other men even if it is their 40th birthday and their husband is caught by a P.I. dancing, and kissing the hands of their best friend and drinking to the point of kicking them.... You know what? Yes, indeed, I'm a good girl and this is exactly what good girls do at this very moment.

* * *

How to write about my 40th birthday and not make it X-rated. Impossible. Here goes: Morton's was excellent. I'd never felt so special at a restaurant before. Maybe Edward told the waiters in advance that it was my birthday, or maybe that's just what money buys (I think that's the right answer, the money thing for sure.); money buys great service. You do get what you pay for. A bottle of Dom Perignon to start, steaks, oh so delicious, and chocolate flambé to finish. We both needed all of those calories for what we certainly didn't expect was yet to come.

I was in a blissful state for the first time in a very, very long time, despite turning that "F" word, F-O-R-T-Y! (Oh screw it. I love being forty now. I'm so much older, wiser, and happier with myself now that I *finally* know myself.) Maybe it was the Dom or maybe it was the compliments Edward gave me. Maybe it was the beautiful Australian opal necklace he gave me as a complete surprise. Maybe it was just being out in a first class place for the first time in years. Who knows, but I am having a total blast for the first time in a very long time after seven years of martyrdom-exhaustion-mania.

* * *

I didn't even begin to *pray* for any relief, because I thought this martyrdom-thing was the way "it" (marriage and motherhood) was supposed to be. Not so. Life lesson 101 *finally* learned; I am going to give total unconditional love and understanding to my children like my Baba gave to me. I am going to make sure that every single one of them, boy or girl, never doubt their self worth for one second, ever. I *have* to teach them that looking out for number one is absolutely vital, because once you start neglecting yourself and play the martyr, you risk losing everything. I never want my beautiful babies to ever feel a fraction, not even 1%, of the misery I live with not being able to see their happy faces daily, nor even often. I pray not one of them suffers like I have. Nope. Not on Mommy's watch.... Just a moment of truth. Back to turning the big 4 0.

*　　　　　*　　　　　*

We decided not to go out after dinner and just go back to Edward's for a nightcap. We sat with our brandies and stared at one another and started to talk about how devastating divorces are. Edward stated that he had been divorced for one year.

"I was married for almost ten years", he said. "I have two children, a girl and a boy, and I rarely get to see them. They live in England with their Mom. I wish I could see them more."

"Oh, I'm sorry. How old are they?"

"My daughter is a few years older than your son, but my son is almost the exact same age" and his voice trails off. He sips his drink and I can tell he is thinking about them right now. No wonder he enjoys teaching James to swim so much, since he can't do that with his own boy.

At that point, my curiosity got the better of me. I hesitate for a minute and then ask, "Was there any infidelity?"

"Not that I was aware of. Certainly I didn't stray."

I asked softly, "Have you been with anyone since your wife?"

"No, and we hadn't been together for some time."

I am shocked at his response, but then again I wasn't. My marriage did not die overnight. With no hesitation, I reach over and take his hand. I look into his stunning green eyes and quietly ask, "When was the last time someone made love to you?" I can see in his eyes that the answer was a long time ago.

    I squeezed his hand, stood up, and made him follow me into his bedroom. As I walked into his bedroom I could not see very well as we didn't put the lights on. I turned my body into his and put my arms around his neck and kissed him passionately. At that moment, we both knew exactly where this was leading.

    Being that it was my first time of unfaithfulness, I had real misgivings. But when one is starving for affection, the emotions do take over, not the brain, and I reached up and started to unbutton his shirt. While we undressed each other hastily, we continued to kiss and caress passionately, like two lovers who had longed for each other a long time.

    We walked hand in hand together to his bed; there was no turning back now. As we lay there exploring, kissing and caressing, I thought "Wow, could I fall in love with this man"? Oh, Mary Ann, you always wear your heart on your sleeve, and then I'm falling into the abyss of ecstasy well over the top,… totally losing count of orgasms. Is this really happening?

    After we were both spent and feeling glorious, we lie quietly, my head resting on Edward's chest enjoying the beating of his heart. But it was getting late, and I felt I should go home, so I ask softly, "Could you take me home now?"

    "Of course."

    On the way home as I lean back watching the stars through the sunroof and think, "What an exhilarating time; I hope this never ends". I glance at my watch. It's not midnight yet, my birthday isn't over! So I turn to Edward and ask, "Would you like to join me in the hot tub?"

Edward turns to look at me with a smile; I think I must have been grinning from ear to ear with a twinkle in my eyes. "Sounds just perfect," he responds.

After I showed Edward the way to the lower deck and around the side of the house to the hot tub, I tip-toed upstairs where the nanny was sleeping with the children to grab some towels.

It was such a beautiful full moon and warm night that we undressed each other quickly. (It's not like we could have undressed inside and risked being caught by a few little tikes, or worse, *the nanny*, now is it!)

We slid into the hot tub and I purposefully left the jets off. Edward pulled me to him and lifted me close. I could feel his manhood and the passion started to fly again. He slid into me easily like it was so natural; I gasped as glorious sensations overtook my senses again and again. After drying each other off and getting dressed in my office, we started to kiss again. (Needless to say, not a lot of dressing was accomplished.) Slick-backed, wet-haired, half dressed and overall giddy, I give Edward "le grand" tour of my office. We end up in my surgery room, door closed, playing with the controls of my surgical chair.

Edward tried my chair, and before I knew it I had the controls reclining him slightly; I lifted my skirt and we resumed our journey toward that lust of passion.

…My oh my, guess that chair positions itself well for other things beside patients' operating comfort. It'll *never* just be my "O.R." chair again.

I'm positive that Edward slept like a baby that night, with a smile on his face. I certainly did. (Wow, what a wild and wonderful, climax to my 40th birthday!)

Chapter 14

Just the Facts, Ma'am

It's a few days after my 40th birthday and I'm enjoying the hot tub for the second time all year, by myself, naked as a jay bird. I don't think I'm ever going to go in it with a bathing suit on ever again unless I'm with my kids. Skinny hot-tubbing is awesome, I finally figured out on my 40th.

"What *are* you doing down there?!" Dieter is questioning me none too nicely from the upper deck off of the back of the house.

"What does it look like I'm doing?" I am nonchalant. Dieter just stares down at me.

Probably the first time he's seen me naked in six months. The last time we had sex was Super Bowl Sunday, most likely because we bought a 750iL BMW that afternoon.

It's after dark and the kids are in bed. Dieter put the four back spotlights on before he came out so he can see me just fine. In March I had surgery under general anesthesia, for I developed an abdominal hernia after my third almost nine pound baby. Jeepers, my belly button was sticking out further than my breasts. Since I was going under general anesthesia anyway, I decided to do a breast augmentation and a chemical peel of my face all at once. All of my freckles did *not* pop off during my deliveries along with my crow's feet so I thought, why not?

I used to think having plastic surgery was nuts until *I* wanted it. My surgery was not out of sheer vanity though. Flat chested my whole life, then after breast-feeding babies and two biopsies and a lumpectomy, my poor breasts were like irregular pancakes with a strawberry in the middle. Knowing my marriage was all but over, I certainly didn't want to go "back on the market" with those.

Dieter got a nice view of them for the first time, I think, instead of through a steamy shower door, and I don't recall him ever touching them.

I flip over and do a short breaststroke to the other end of the hot tub, buns up.

"Do you mind please turning off the spot lights?" I ask politely.

Dieter turned to go back into the house after a brief comment, "You're pathetic." Well, on that beautiful starry June night, naked and feeling pretty and very relaxed from the hot jets and moreso from my fantastic 40th birthday celebration, I was feeling *anything* but pathetic.

*   *   *

I'm grateful for that one relaxing birthday evening, because the summer screamed in with heat--heated discussions, that is. Beautiful way to get up and get ready for patients. Just two weeks after my birthday, Dieter and I are in the ring again first thing in the morning, arguing viciously, yet again, about money.

"Where is our checkbook?" I ask Dieter.

No response from Dieter. He's not even looking up from the *Washington Post,* sitting with paper up and legs crossed casually, at the kitchen table. "Aren't you going to answer me? Or are you just going to ignore me?" I ask a little louder.

"What?" is his only response. I again repeat, "Where is *our* personal checkbook?!" My face is a little red because I just came in from running, but getting redder by the second as I feel my blood pressure rising.

"I'm sure if you look for it, you will find it."

Now I'm angry. Dieter does all of the billing in the office and pays our personal bills, so basically I do not know what is coming in or going out. I only know I have to work very hard to pay the bills.

Dieter recrosses his legs, still holding the newspaper so I cannot see his face. "Where is the checkbook? You are the only one who ever uses it! Tell me!"

I need to shower and get ready for patients, but I had a feeling we were short again this month and I wanted to know how short. I was worrying about it a lot while out running, even with *The Rolling Stones* blaring on my "Walkman".

Dieter says, "I don't know where it is. I'm sure you can find it."

"I have patients in ten minutes. I don't have time. What the hell is going on with you this morning? Can't you even put the paper down to look at me when I am asking you a question?!" I stomp across the kitchen and yank down the *Post* so he can see I mean business. Dieter surprises me by jumping up and lunging towards me with a full cup of coffee, obviously pissed I grabbed his newspaper, and half of his hot coffee lands right on my chest. (Maybe it was an accident, but also maybe not.) Luckily I had a thick running bra on under my tee shirt or I would have been burned. I am stunned yet again, although I did start it, and Dieter out of the blue yells, finally looking at me with hatred in his usually beautiful blue eyes, "You will have to give me half a million dollars to get rid of me!"

I back away quickly and run into my office ignoring the look on my office manager's face, which means: Why aren't you ready for patients, we start in less than ten minutes?! I think, as I'm scurrying into my surgery room to use the phone, "Damn it, Judy, didn't you hear our argument"?! I'm sure she had to. I have a simple two-step commute from my home into my office. If I can hear a little baby crying inside, I'm sure Judy heard two adults' raised voices. I don't worry about Judy's look. I'm busy thinking, "Where in God's name does Dieter get off expecting half a million out of me? He hasn't earned nearly that our entire marriage"!

I have my new highly recommended $7,500.00 retained attorney's phone number already memorized. We met a few days ago, and I didn't like him from the get go, but since he came so highly recommended by one of my most successful patients, I painfully wrote him his fat check.

From here on he will be referred to as "Fat Bastard". You know, one of those middle-aged men, who hasn't walked into a gym since mandatory phys-ed in junior high. He's inherited his mother's wide hips, so he's got that pear-shaped thing going on that goes with, "I'm worth it. I over-indulge-myself-too-much-béarnaise-sauce-body". However,... "Fat Bastard" did get laid in the movie by Austin Power's sweetheart played by Elizabeth Hurley. But...not Moi! I would never have slept with my "Fat Bastard" in my horniest blackest blackout. After a couple of minutes on the phone with him, I hang up and simply exit the office informing Judy, "Cancel all of my patients today!"

No explanation. That's it! I'm going to the courthouse to file an emergency "Ex Parte" order like Fat Bastard instructed me to do.

The one and only time I have ever won in court with Dieter (except the stupid theft charge) was with that wonderful thirty day "Ex Parte" order. I filed, "This morning at 8:15 my husband was arguing with me about how much money I will have to pay him to get a divorce. He has told me how much he hates me, and how he wants to hurt me and ruin my life. I argued with him and have called him a compulsive liar and he lunged at me with his right hand. He had a hot cup of coffee in his left hand, and it landed all over my chest". (I brought my tee shirt and bra to court.) I also filed that Dieter "kicked me in the chest and I fell across the room the day before Mother's Day", and noted that he owned a "357 Magnum, an automatic Glock and a shotgun".

I was granted a "Petition for Protection" for thirty days, and Dieter was served to move out. Two police officers came to the door after nine p.m. that very night. I did make sure the children were in bed. The police stated: "Violation of this Ex Parte Order may be a state and/or federal crime or contempt of court, or both, and result in imprisonment or fine or both. This Ex Parte Order may be enforced by another state or jurisdiction, which may impose additional or different penalties for the violation". Guess I had to go this route to get him the hell out for a while, and truthfully, I was simply doing what my attorney advised.

Too bad Fat Bastard turned out to be just that. He took my money and did nothing those thirty days Dieter was out of the house. The four of us had a few meetings with me, Fat Bastard, Dieter, and Dieter's attorney who I'll name Saddam because he's now retired/dead or at least dead in the practice of law. We got nowhere in those meetings. Fat Bastard and Saddam should have sat on the same side of the table so they could have stroked each other easier. They yanked (get it?) money out of Dieter and I at the dual rate of, at least, $650 per hour.

Welcome to Washington, attorneys like those are everywhere, slapping each other's backs. I recently heard a quote that I hope is not accurate, but very well may be.

"There is one attorney in the District of Columbia for every nine people". Terrific, and they are all so sub-sub specialized (way worse than medicine) that one attorney won't answer a question about a simple traffic violation, because he just does divorce and custody cases. Or another one has no idea about estate work, because he's a public defender. Jeepers, if I didn't have a decent knowledge about the rest of the body, and just knew eyeballs, I'd be a pretty darn bad doctor! And lawyers are certainly the cover-my-ass-queens; they rarely sue each other, just doctors.

I love it, too, when they talk to each other for half an hour, but, of course, the bill is for an entire hour, since there's two chatting. Doctors never charge a patient when they are running something by another physician. We should. Insurance companies should grant it a CPT and ICD-9 code. (Insurance billing mumbo jumbo.) I had no clue what any code meant when I started in practice in 1990, or that billing codes even existed, I just gave patients a receipt for an "eye exam" on one of my prescription pads. Dear God, what a rude awakening "coding" was, and a total pain in the documentation ass!

Why shouldn't a doctor bill for phone calls? Why not? Isn't a doctor's time trying to save lives most definitely as important as any attorney's conversation? Sure it is. Back to Fat Bastard and Saddam:

I can just imagine a phone call: "Saddam, do you mind holding for a minute? I need to pop outside and have a cigarette while we're chatting".

"Oh sure, Fat Bastard, no problem. Did you see how the weather is supposed to improve for the weekend? I can't wait to take out the boat!"

Puff, puff. "Oh, ya, I did see that. Gee, it's getting nicer out already. I think I'll leave the office early tomorrow and start the weekend off at noon. Want to get a few holes in before we're supposed to be home?" Puff, puff.

"Great idea. I'll pack the clubs tonight. Everything I'm working on can wait until Monday. Now what were we discussing"?

Puff, puff. "I forgot, oh ya, 'The Duke divorce', God, aren't those two *nuts"?!* But, of course, the bill*s* for the consult started for both attorneys with the first "Hi"!

Just too many attorneys in the D.C. area. Supply and demand. Every single one wants to be successful, have a nice home, afford their kids' college, and be able to buy off their spouses if necessary. (I truly don't have an accurate account of how many different attorneys I went through in the past seven years and still am paying them. Thank God I don't have to switch doctors so often to find a "better" one.) Fat Bastard tried to impress me with the framed cover of his firm on *Washingtonian* magazine. I was not particularly impressed. "I'm in Potomac", I remember thinking, "where everyone's important, or at least think they are, because they have property value".

Our first four-way meeting was so bad, I walked out early or maybe stormed out is a better description. The four of us met in my attorney's conference room boasting a beautiful wooden table with comfortable chairs and wall shelves stocked with law books. I sat on one side of the table with my attorney and Dieter sat across from me with his. Dieter turned his chair towards his attorney and crossed his legs away from me so that he was facing the two men in the room and ignoring me. I don't think he made eye contact with me once, sitting there complacently with his hands folded in his lap. I was definitely out numbered. It felt like the two attorneys enjoyed dragging out our supposed "settlement out of court" as long as possible. Why not? Time means money even though both of them informed us early on that it was "cheaper to settle out of court".

Saddam states, "Dr. Duke's husband is entitled to alimony and a percentage of Dr. Duke's future earnings." I was more than furious at the audacity of his request. I started my practice four years before Dieter and I had even *met*. It's not like he put me through medical school and supported me through residency. Au contraire! I'm the one who paid off *his* school loans, and Dieter clicked into six figures only our last year of marriage. How dare he ask for more, especially after he was out with Marilyn?!

"Forget about alimony or any part of my practice or future earnings. Kiss my ass," I politely stated and left. Dieter finally made eye contact with me with great disdain.

Another great meeting was when Dieter did not want to pay a dime for college. Do you know that Maryland law does not require a man to pay a dime in child support or for college whatsoever after the age of eighteen? Saddam informed me of this fact. I looked Saddam right in the eyes from across the table and asked, "Do you have a daughter"?

"Yes, I do", he replied proudly, "She is a lawyer".

"Oh, that's wonderful"! I piped back. "Did you pay for her education"?

Dead silence. Another time that I stood up abruptly and walked out.

Thirty days went by for well over thirty pieces of silver. I am still trying to figure out what Fat Bastard did with my entire retainer except take his family to Europe. Late one afternoon, I was in my car, driving up Old Georgetown Road from Suburban Hospital, tired after operating. Fat Bastard calls my cell phone and states categorically, "We don't have a meeting of the minds: I can no longer represent you."

"Excuse me?" I *really* didn't think I heard him correctly.

"I can no longer represent you."

"What?! What's going on? Why are you doing this?"

"I just told you. We do not have a meeting of the minds."

"You are firing me?!" Pause. This is unbelievable; Fat Bastard is firing *me?!* He didn't get anything done for me except the master bedroom back after the judge let Dieter back in after the thirty day "Ex Parte" was up. $7,500.00 to get my bedroom back and now *I'm* being fired.

Attorneys don't fire their well-paying clients. Bullshit. He is clearing off his desk before he is going on vacation. He had already told me he was taking his family to Europe next week, sure, with my retainer.

I need my file, I immediately think, as I'll need to hire new counsel. My God, I scream to myself, I have to have my file! I gave Fat Bastard so much personal and financial information and hadn't kept a copy for myself! I trusted him, and as always was too busy to plan an attack, and didn't even have legal paper for copying in my office anyway.

Fat Bastard retorts, "You can't have your file because you owe me money." Now, instead of being fatigued, my adrenal glands are squeezing out adrenaline again. I could probably run a marathon, and I angrily retort, "I am coming over to your office right now and picking up my file!", and I hung up on him.

"Good afternoon ladies", I say and smile at the girls at the front desk of Fat Bastard's office. "I'm Dr. Duke and I'm expected," as I walk straight back to Fat Bastard's lair. Fat Bastard does not look pleased to see me but not surprised either. He insists "You cannot have your file until you pay your bill in full. The balance is this." He shoves a paper at me. The paper's balance is over $6,500.00. I am flabbergasted. $14,000 in a little over four weeks? What did he do? Bill me for dreaming about me?

"You did not even file divorce papers for me, and you expect all that money?!"

Fat Bastard does not like me raising my voice in front of his staff. His blood pressure must be up a bit; his face is really red.

"Call the police," Fat Bastard yells to his receptionist, "and have them throw Dr. Duke out of my office for disturbing the peace if she does not leave in the next two minutes," and he opens his office door and leaves. I'm livid and let him have it in front of his entire front desk as I follow him to his office entrance.

"You call yourself a good attorney?! You call yourself a man?! You should be ashamed of yourself! You have *no honor*!"

Fat Bastard looked like he was about to burst as he waddled out the door.

* * *

The police were called, because I guess I was in too much shock to move for his fucking "two minute warning" and plainly did not want to leave without my file. I wait for the police cruiser in the parking lot. I tell the officer everything, all about the domestic violence, thirty day ex parte order, over $14,000.00 bill for nothing, and say, "You know what officer? I am a doctor, and a patient can owe me a million bucks, but I am still required by law to give them their records for probably less than twenty-five dollars. Officer, please go in and ask those secretaries to give me my file, because I gave him my originals, trusted him, and I need to have my file!"

"I'm sorry, Ma'am, but there is nothing I can do. I do believe it is the law that he doesn't have to give you your file unless you have paid him in full." I'm too pissed to respond.

"I'm sorry, Ma'am."

And attorneys wonder why they get a "bad rap"?

*   *   *

I think Saddam retired on all the green backs Dieter paid him. Or indirectly *I* paid him, because Dieter "cleaned up" in our final divorce settlement. My one savvy and crazy patient told me, "It will only cost you $36,000 to get rid of Dieter. I know someone". Yeah, right, and eternity in hell.

Dieter put all of the bills in my name. Phone, electric and gas bills bounced (Ba Da Bing!), and I didn't know he wasn't paying the bills any more out of our joint account. Instead, he maxed the account out and even took the $3,000 line of credit before I could stop him. He gave me $1,500 in June towards an $8,400 mortgage. Thanks a lot. I'm sure that made a big dent in his $10,000/month salary.

So in July Dieter's back home. The judge admitted "This case is a sad case".

No kidding, your Honor. Dieter's back in the house, and I'm told to put dead bolts on my office and bedroom doors that very day. I immediately call a devoted patient who drops everything and puts the locks on for me. There I am, back in the ring, back in the first round, without gloves or even a trainer with a retainer. At least I got the master bedroom back, small consolation prize for a $14,000.00 bill.

*   *   *

There isn't a sharp enough machete to cut the tension in our home.

*   *   *

I call Fat Bastard's office every single day until he *finally* sends me my file. Now what do I do?

I rack my brain in between working my ass off in the office to make money, then on to second shift M.o.m.m.y. duties with our three children, five and one-half years old on down to two, but "no worries"; Dieter has made my mind up for me. He serves me with divorce papers on August 15th, just three weeks after he's back in the house, and poor me is still in a way hoping to save our marriage.

I call my dear Mom for advice and she pleads with me on the phone, "Work it out, Honey. Ask him what he wants. Ask him what he needs. You *have* to work it out, Medka. (Remember, "little Mary" in Slovak) Marriage is one of the seven sacraments. You can't get a divorce. You *can't* break up your family." The ultimate guilt trip.

So I do exactly what she asked a few nights after Dieter had me served with divorce papers. He is watching television in the living room, as usual, while I get the kids ready for bed. After they are asleep, I walk into the living room and state, "I really need to speak with you." Dieter ignores me. I walk over to the television and push the power button off. Dieter just powers it back up with the remote. I click it off again. He hit the remote on, even though he can't see the screen because I'm purposefully standing in front of it. I repeat myself again, amazingly keeping my cool, exhausted at the end of the day, and repeat, "I really need to speak with you", hitting the power button again, "*It's important.*" Dieter still will not look at me, but leaves the television off.

I used Mom's exact words, and I plead with Dieter. "What more can I do to save our marriage? Marriage is one of the seven sacraments. We have three beautiful children. We need to stay married for them. I am working so hard. I really can't work any harder or make any more money. What do you want? What do you need? What more can I do?"

Dieter, without looking at me and clicking the television back on, yet again, flatly says, "More blow jobs."

Dieter's reply feels worse than the sharpest slap in the face.

I am speechless, too hurt to reply. It is over.... God give me strength.

The television is blaring; Dieter doesn't look up still, as always the stoic German. I shuffle to the refrigerator before a tear falls to get my painkiller, a cold bottle of Chardonnay, my "Screw Pull" bottle opener, wine glass, and trudge slowly up to bed.

*   *   *

"Where is his chart?!" I'm rummaging furiously through the M's.

"Whose?" Judy gives me a wee bit of a dirty look. She doesn't like it when I mess up her well-filed charts. (Like they're really hers.)

"That nice lawyer I did Lasik on, Ben Masters." Forget another "excellent" referral, I'm going to ask my patient if he will represent me. I like him, gees; I hope he's a good divorce lawyer!

Judy jumps up and finds his chart immediately. "Thank you" and I retreat to my new phone boudoir, my surgery room.

Ben gets on the phone right away, "Hello, Dr. Duke."

"Oh, please, call me Mary Ann. Ben, do you do divorces?"

"Yes, of course."

"Great. I need help,… like yesterday. I'm having a really hard time. Could you meet with me late tomorrow?"

"Sure. That would be fine. Is three o'clock all right with you?"

"Yes. Great. I'll be done with surgery by then. Where is your office located Ben?"

I scribble down directions even though I plan on plugging it into my GPS anyway, as driving in the D.C. area is the worst.

I'll never, ever forget Ben's first words to me, "You should have filed for divorce while Dieter was already out of the house with the "Ex Parte" order. You could have kept him out. *Why didn't your attorney do that?"*

Chatty Kathy me is beyond speechless. All I can do is stare at him, then I just want to sob with frustration. Oh…my…God. That makes complete sense. Why the hell wasn't that done for me? Fat Bastard was just too busy planning his vacation on my $7,500.00 plus the $6,500.00 he'll get in his next life.

But, no time to sob! I'm not paying for someone to watch me cry no matter how much I need to. The truth is it takes two people to get married, but only one to file for divorce. One cannot keep a marriage by oneself. Two must want to stay married, just like it takes two to tango.

*   *   *

It took over five months from that fateful Mother's Day weekend to get Dieter to move out. Five tense months that felt like five years. "The sum of $155,000 shall be payable by the Wife to the Husband within thirty days of the execution of this agreement... The sum of $35,000 shall be payable by the Wife to the Husband within 365 days of the execution of this agreement...The Wife has accumulated $57,000 in credit card debt for family-related expenses throughout the marriage, and the Husband has accumulated $14,000 in credit card for payment toward the parties' 2000 taxes. (Yeah, right, simply because *my* cc's had a higher limit.) The Wife will assume the credit card debt that she has incurred on her credit cards. In consideration for the excess credit card debt assumed by the Wife, she shall be entitled to a credit in the amount of $21,500 against the purchase price which the Wife is to pay the Husband for his interest in the marital home of the parties".

His interest?! His fucking interest?! *I* paid the mortgage for the last seven years. Do the math. Dieter grossed just over $400,000 total during our seven years of marriage, which nets out to approximately $250,000. I had to give him $190,000 cash (which would have been $211,000 except for my gracious cc credit), in addition to a

$60,000 plus Lexus SUV with only $11,000 left on the note, furniture, art, BMW bike, Polo everything, etc...

I gave Dieter more money/possessions in the divorce post tax dollars than he earned post tax dollars the entire marriage, and, oh, by the way, he was out with *my* best friend, remember?

Does this make any sense to anyone whatsoever? If it does make sense to you, *you* should be locked up, and the key thrown away.

Dieter pulled into the driveway the day he was to move out with an eighteen-wheeler. I thought the heavy truck was going to leave dents in my driveway. Nope. Not unless it was full, Mary Ann.

"Dieter, what did you hire such a big truck for?"

"I need to get my things," he says without looking at me, of course.

"I really think you could have hired a smaller truck," and I'm a bit shocked as these three huge men follow him in who could have all played on the defensive line in the NFL.

"I need my things."

Sure, I think, bet you can empty the entire house with that truck and 50% plus of what is in this house is mine (premarital) and the remaining 50% we're supposed to split in half. I'm forever grateful a friend told me to hire his MD state trooper buddy for Dieter's move. My $125/hour state trooper was all of 5'9", however packing a piece on his shoulder strap. We walked room to room together and when Dieter asked for something like a dresser drawer in one of the children's bedrooms, I shook my head, and my hired trooper would say "You can't take that." I couldn't believe he wanted to break up the children's bedroom sets on top of wanting the complete master bedroom! Dieter even asked for the McCormick spices in the kitchen; my trooper didn't have to look at me.

"No" he simply said. That was the best $375 for three hours I have ever spent. (Remember this every reader.)

But within a year Dieter sued me for more. Proclaimed, "I didn't get enough of the household possessions". Well, maybe he didn't because he didn't deserve them!

Doesn't matter. I don't know why I even bother walking into a courthouse. For me it's like trying to wade through quicksand. The more I try to fight, the quicker I'm sucked down. Dieter won again even with a female judge. Ah, not too much more, just the best Persian rug in the house, a little 10' by 14', my favorite. Another sum of money, too, $10, $12, or $14,000 in cash, I can't remember exactly, and a whole bunch more stuff I don't *care* to remember losing. (Do lawyers really like to screw doctors over, or is it just a figment of my imagination? Or is it because I'm a woman who calls a pink pig, a pink pig, on top of being a doctor that they don't like? The answer is c. Both.)

Dear Ben Masters copied just what papers he had of my divorce proceedings, and the stack is well over two inches high with an "Index of Pleadings" of upteen items. PLEADINGS. What an awesome word the legal system uses. Maybe if I had just pleaded a million times more, along with overt begging and a lottery win, we could have stayed married and not broken up our family. I totally understand the saying "cheaper to keep her" now, and don't forget the tens of thousands in attorneys' fees.

I asked what a "Pleading" was for the benefit of y'all. I know every non-lawyer reader is just dying to know. I obtained a simple, ambiguous answer: "A

'Pleading' is basically anything that is filed with the court". Thank you for clearing that up for me so succinctly, counselor. I feel like it's the same as a lawyer asking me, "What do you have to dictate in an operative report?" and I answer, "Details about the operation." That covers it, doesn't it?

I'm convinced of two truths in life so far. We all die, and we all pay taxes because too many attorneys have too much discretionary power running our great country.

*   *   *

I did win two things: 1. Primary custody of the kids (which was snatched away just over a year later causing me the greatest pain every day of my life), with a whopping $749/month child support for all three, even though Dieter's salary clicked over 100K the year we got separated and even higher the year we divorced. And, 2. "The parties agree to share equally the cost of a four-year college education for each of the minor children of the parties: provided, however, in no event shall the cost thereof exceed 1.5 times the cost for tuition, fees, room and board for an in-state student at the University of Maryland".

Every woman in America should get their ex-spouse to commit to some college expense. I wanted two times the cost of the University of MD. What if one of the kids is super bright and makes it to Harvard? Dieter wanted one time, thus a settlement at 1.5. So I guess when I talk Marika and Nadia into law school so they can both become judges and help make this country a little more fair for women some day, I'll be covering that by myself. No problem, where there's a will, there *is* a way. I do love my children and don't use them as pawns in a settlement.

*   *   *

Welcome to America. The land of opportunity, for men, *white* men, because that is what most of the judges are.

I was the man of the house (the "usual" primary bread winner), the woman, and the M.o.m.m.y. in my marriage. Yet I had to give even more money/possessions to Dieter than he had earned the entire time we were married just because the house appreciated. I, me, *alone* was paying the mortgage for all those years, and going through three full term pregnancies and taking care of the babies, and trying to save the maximum of 30K for retirement as best I could with a spendaholic spouse, whom *I* had to pay off after he filed first for divorce and was found out with *my* best friend.

Is that fair? Is that *justice*? Is this the new American Way? Does this make any sense at all? No, it doesn't. It's called "white male justice robbery". And it's all premeditated bullshit.

Are women supposed to be men, too? Are women supposed to take care of their husbands like they are their little babies? Get real. Last time I looked I still haven't grown a penis, so I really shouldn't have had to provide for a wife I never had.

I think there are some balls in my abdominal cavity somewhere though…or just that overdose of chutzpah in every cell.

Who doesn't want a cold one after reading that?

*   *   *

The legal system in my humble, but still learned, opinion has swung way too far in the wrong direction and discriminates against working mothers. In the good old days when women were stay-at-home-Moms, if they didn't get "half", there wouldn't be a roof over their heads for their children, food, clothing and health insurance.

But things are different now! There are two family incomes; most moms are earning money, often more than their spouses, working full-time and still trying to do everything else. When there is no pre-nuptual whatsoever, and the woman makes more money, she's absolutely screwed.

Does the white male dominated legal system really think in the new millennium the man should get half the house and half of everything else when the man initiates the divorce, is unfaithful, and the wife paid the bills the entire marriage? (Well, I didn't have a snake camera under a doorway, but I was brought up that husbands weren't supposed to kiss and dance with their wife's friends.)

Isn't that some kind of criminal/spousal abuse? When the husband is in good health, has a good six figure job with future salary increases, isn't fighting for full custody, but just wants the children the exact minimal number of days to pay the absolute minimal amount of child support?

Yep, it's the *law*. Frustrating. Plain old unfair. Why should the wife pay so exorbitantly to the husband when he's the one who wanted the divorce? It's insane and abusive. It certainly is a man's world.

Pre-nuptials are now in vogue but don't always hold up. Pre-nups are a must in life. My daughters hopefully will learn from my mistakes. James, too. Why buy the cow when the milk's for free? The excellent corollary is: Why buy the whole pig when all you want is a little sausage?

Also, whatever happened to infidelity? Guess you do need one of those snake cameras under the door to catch them naked in the act, but in my divorce I don't think an X-rated film would have helped one little bit. I'll never know the truth about whether Dieter and Marilyn went all the way but my hunches are usually right. It isn't called "women's intuition" for nothing. What do those male judges think? Gee, your husband must have cheated on you because you didn't give him enough? It *must* be the woman's fault the man strayed. Fuck that.

    The laws need to be changed.

    I thought being married was this enchanted state of being like Cinderella. Instead of living happily ever after, the disillusioned, very disappointed and depressed forty-year-old falls in love with wine and just about loses her mind.

Chapter 15

911 and Baby Bliss

My internist started me on Prozac right after that fateful Mother's Day weekend. I took it for post-partum depression with every one of my children and then stopped it after three to four months. But this time, the antidepressant wasn't helping. I couldn't even sleep. I prayed to God: Please make Dieter move out. I can't take the stress. It was so bad that Dieter walked around the house holding a tape recorder, right in front of our children, and taped our conversations. I needed that harassment like a hole in my head. We certainly weren't preparing for Oprah. He stopped the tape recordings, of course, only after my attorney called his attorney.

Anyone who has ever been through a bitter divorce, especially involving children, knows the tension heightens until finally one spouse or the other moves out. The tension in our home needed two six-foot chain saws (way past the machete stage), if it could be cut at all.

To this day I do not know whether Dieter taught barely six-year-old James to call 911 if Mommy was sleeping on the couch out of true concern for the children, or if he was already starting a plot to take them from me. If it was the second reason, instead of paying only $749/month child support, Dieter could receive a fat check from me. Most of all, if he wanted to hurt me the hardest, taking our precious children from me would be the #1 way to annihilate me.

James dialed 911 or "the fire trucks", as he called them twice in September. Exactly what I needed for my boring, mundane existence, multiple police officers climbing over my fence, denting it many times and then breaking in my front door. I was revived right away both times and certainly am not proud that I can't remember every moment until I fell asleep. It's called retrograde amnesia. One can easily not remember falling asleep and can even sleep walk from certain sleeping pills by themselves. But when these pills are stupidly mixed with a little alcohol, one definitely can have a longer period of retrograde amnesia. Thinking back, I was in my very own "catch 22". If I didn't take a sleeping pill or have a glass of wine, or worse both, I would lie awake worrying about all of my financial problems, office overhead, mortgage, etc. (and now high attorneys' bills) all by myself. Remember, I rarely wrote a check after getting married. Dieter took charge of the money.

Damn it! Not one, but I have two huge regrets. I have finally forgiven myself for them while writing this book and pray my children forgive me, too. But the judicial system has not stopped punishing me one little bit for my mistakes and now is downright abusing me. (If you heard it once, hear it again: A penis prevents problems.)

#1. I should have gone to a rehab center *before* Dieter and I even divorced to get off of the sleeping pills and alcohol before everything escalated and just got some "R&R". I *never once* even thought of it and truthfully no one else suggested rehab until the worst had happened.

#2. I totally regret never having live-in help from the get-go. I'm so angry with myself for thinking I could "do it all" and not taking in help so I might not have turned to drinking too much, in a vain attempt to drown my sorrows over my divorce. I want, at least, my children to learn from my bad choices.

Both times 911 was called, I called my nanny and she came over immediately. The first 911 police report called me an "ill person" since I had slipped on the stairs. (wasn't hurt) The second 911 call was at 9:43 p.m. and the police wrote "child neglect" on their report and sent a copy to Child Welfare Services. I didn't know this fact whatsoever at the time.

*   *   *

Dieter moved out just after those two 911 calls. I thought he would really never leave after the terrorist attack on September 11, 2001. I couldn't blame him, truthfully. I have hardly flown since that horrible day, but Dieter has to fly a lot for work. I understood his fear. But fear of flying and claustrophobia galore didn't stop me from getting on a plane a few weeks after we were legally separated.

I desperately needed a vacation, so Edward took me to San Diego for a long weekend as he was attending a psychiatry conference. He's gone most of the day to his "shrink sessions", I call them. What do they talk about besides the new medications or how much crazier my patients are than yours? God bless them. I couldn't do psychotherapy all day and listen to other people's problems if my life depended on it. I have enough to do trying to keep my side of the street swept.

While Edward was at his conference I holed up in the hotel room opening two months' worth of mail and writing two months' worth of bills I was behind on, instead of sunbathing. I hauled the stupid mail all the way across the country in a huge suitcase. How many people do that on a long weekend? Hopefully, not a lot. I missed a couple of birth control pills that weekend. Just a couple days without a little hormone and each ovary must have seen its chance.

I became pregnant with *twins at 40.*

Finally legally separated, but still eleven months from being divorced, since it takes one full year after legal separation in Maryland, and then, yikes! I'm pregnant! What were my patients going to think? Twins to boot! Oh, there's that small-town-girl from Johnson City, New York mentality molding my brain again. Who cares what they think? I know I'm a good person, and I don't give a rat's ass if anyone thinks I'm being "bad". Would it be better if I tell everyone I just aborted twins? Kill two? I can't. No way. But how can I afford twins? I'm barely making ends meet now. Most of all, I have three gorgeous children and I adore them. I know how truly wonderful it is to be a mom, and I do have a limit to what I can take, some of the time.

A divorce and an abortion in the same year *are* too much for me.

*   *   *

Eight weeks pregnant with twins at Christmas, 2001 and everyone is trying to pour me a drink. No one knows. I can't tell anyone because I still don't know what the hell I'm going to do! For the very first time in forty years, I keep my own counsel. So not a soul knows, amazing I could hold it in.

"Here, have some seriously spiked egg nog", and I'm trying to nurse the same glass of chardonnay for four hours, but it's not working. Oh, I'll just have one and a half.

Edward will be fifty by the time the baby is born. He assuredly wants absolutely nothing to do with even the thought of having a child. He's told me point blank, so I went back on the pill for us. Great. *Twins.* I'm in double trouble. Two weeks later at the ten-week ultrasound there is only one heartbeat. One of the fetuses is dying, no heartbeat, starting to dissolve. That happens with twins a lot. I don't remember that either from medical school;

however, the one remaining heartbeat was very strong. I stared at the little heartbeat and thought, "Only the strong survive. This is going to be a strong little baby".

I told Edward I was pregnant on an evening my children were with Dieter. I couldn't hold it in anymore; I was starting to show! I waited until he finished his second drink so far for the night and was sitting down.

"Edward?"

"Yes?"

"I have something very important to tell you." Edward looks up from his laptop at me. Without pausing, I look straight back at him and state "I'm pregnant."

Edward's big green eyes bulged out as he bolted upright from the kitchen chair.

"Pregnant? How can you be pregnant? You're on the pill!" Edward's whole body stiffened. With his red face and neck with pulsing veins and his bulging eyes glaring at me without a blink, it was obvious that Edward was furious.

He downs his scotch. "You can't have a baby! You have to have an abortion!" as he slams down his glass on the kitchen island. I look away from his angry eyes and speak quietly.

"No, I don't."

"Yes, you do!"

"No, I don't." I speak louder this time as I turn my gaze back to his. Edward looks away from me like he can't stand the sight of me, grabs his bottle of scotch, and pours another drink without getting more ice.

"Yes, you do! You're too old!"

"No, I'm not. I had twins inside of me until two weeks ago."

Now I *really* blew his mind. I'm glad we're arguing with the big kitchen island between us.

"Twins?!"

"Yes…One dissolved."

"What are you going to do with the *other* one?!"

"I'm going to have a chorionic villous sampling next week, you know Edward, where they take a piece of placenta and find out the chromosomes early, and if it comes back normal, I'm going to have the baby."

"No. You're not." Edward's running his fingers nervously through his curly blonde hair. "Why bother having the C.V.S?! Just *have an abortion*!" and he pounds his fist down hard on the island. "You're supposed to be on the pill! How in God's name did you get pregnant?"

"I missed a couple of pills."

"You what?! When?"

"When we were in San Diego."

"How did you do *that?!*"

"Well, we were going out to eat and drinking every night; then we'd get in late, and I just missed starting my next pack on time." I look down at my clasping and reclasping hands. I knew Edward was going to put all of the blame on me and be pissed off and his beautiful eyes were too full of anger to look at.

"You've got to be kidding me! You can't keep it!" Edward takes another swill of his scotch and I think, "'Prince' Edward really does drink too bloody much".

"It's my body." I finally meet his gaze and if looks could kill, I'd be dead.

I felt very sad and also pissed off. I knew Edward didn't want another child, but I guess I was hoping he wouldn't be *so* angry. I turned and stomped upstairs to change my clothes. I thought, if you were that adamant about not having another child, Edward, *you* could have taken responsibility for the birth control and had a vasectomy after your divorce… or worn a condom! Women can still get pregnant on the low dose birth control pills that are out now, and why should I have to take the pill over the age of forty when women can have terrible side effects, even a stroke!

Edward will not control me and my decision.

Pregnancy is the one and only moment in the history of mankind that a woman has complete control; the men know it, and they HATE it! I believe if the roles were reversed and the men had the burden of pregnancy, the human race would be declining, probably on its way to extinction, instead of escalating.

That was the very evening our relationship started to die. What a shame. A new life to be born to two lovers, killed the lovers' relationship.

*   *   *

I hoped for a boy; maybe Edward would change his mind about an abortion if it was a boy. A week later, I found out that the fetus was a chromosomally normal little girl. Idiot me cried a little because it wasn't a boy. But I cried mostly because she was normal, and I definitely was going to keep my baby.

Thank God, Eloise Duke *is* normal. I was stressed out her entire pregnancy, drinking both too much coffee and too much chardonnay. I had already tested my "alcohol-will-kill-off-weak-genes" theory with Nadia and won, for my dubious efforts, but I was now over forty and worried about everything.

Small consolation Dieter's health insurance paid for every single one of my ultrasounds, labs, C.V.S., etc., and he was getting the explanation of benefits in the mail. Maryland law dictates he had to provide health insurance for me until we were divorced. (A damned small coup, huh?)

Within a week of telling my children that "Mommy is going to have a baby", Dieter sent me a letter via his attorney requesting I supply "a certified letter that this is indeed not his child". I laughed out loud when I opened it so hard I almost peed my pants. I called Dieter's cell phone immediately.

"Dieter?"

"Yes."

"I am in receipt of your attorney's letter. Listen, unless this is the gestation of an elephant, this is not your baby, get it?" Pause. No comment. Click.

God knows I was certainly not a "teetotaler", not by any stretch of the imagination, during this pregnancy. I definitely needed one cold glass of wine after work to deal with Edward's abortion aggravation and my patients' daily questions.

"Oh! Dr. Duke, I'm so happy for you. So you got back together with your husband"? I was so sick of that question; I finally just ignored it and countered "And how *are* your eyes today"?

I should have broken up with Edward then, but I didn't have the gumption. I was too needy and way too vulnerable and too damned insecure. If I had done it then, my life wouldn't be such a mess now. And if I had live-in help, I wouldn't have burned my candle at both ends, had a little time to myself, and not abused alcohol. C'mon now, Mary Ann, there must be a reason for all that has happened. No regrets.

I never once heard my Baba regret the past in the thirty-one years I knew her and she had one heck of a hard life. That's pretty remarkable. What a way to be… Happy. Content. Content with one's life just the way it is. Content with oneself; not very many people are.

*   *   *

Every damned night Edward told me that I shouldn't be having this baby, even after we knew she was normal by the testing. Over and over like a broken damned record, "You shouldn't be having this baby". Even his eighty-two-year-old mother told me "You shouldn't be having this baby".

My parents, on the other hand, were mute. They didn't know what to say. They don't believe in abortion, and they don't believe in having a baby out of wedlock either, a pure catch 22 for them. So they were basically numb, then happy. Probably the last grandchild they would see, unless my baby brother banishes big, bad, beautiful bachelorhood and starts procreating. "Make sure you are eating right" my mother said at every phone call.

My parents came around, but not Edward. He kept it up, kept it coming, nagging me to have an abortion. Night after night. And the ranting was fueled by more and more alcohol. He could down three scotch-on-the-rocks before dinner, a bottle of red during, and sip cognac or *whatever* until he went to bed. The more he drank, the more I heard, "You should have an abortion"!

I thought Edward was drinking too much, but I certainly couldn't stop him. He berated me with dagger sentences like: "You can't afford another child". "You are too old." "You're just a medic"! I made him explain that last one.

"What the hell is a 'medic'?" I yelled at him as I turned from looking for something to eat in the refrigerator.

"You're just a body mechanic".

"That's right Edward", as I flushed crimson. "I'm a body mechanic and an *eye surgeon"!*

Jane, my friend that took me to court and the die-hard believer in marriage, unbelievably was the one who kept telling me to break up with Edward, pregnant or not. But I was afraid to go it alone, financially and emotionally, so I endured the arguments, almost every one over the baby. I didn't have quite enough chutzpah to break up with him, because I thought no one will ever want me with all of my baggage, four young children and two very difficult-to-deal-with-"ex's".

In my ninth month, I screamed at Edward one night after work, "Will you shut up already? I am not flying to California to have a fucking third trimester abortion"! Edward stormed out and left me wrung out after work to feed and bathe and put my three children to bed. So then I could toss and turn and never get comfortable with my big belly all alone in my king sized bed.

I lived every day extremely distraught and over tired, from pushing myself to see as many patients as I could, and taking care of my three children all night and distressed over Edward's verbal abuse.

But all I really knew from relationships was abuse of some kind or another, right?

*   *   *

Edward leans over the hospital bed and kisses my cheek, "You did good."

I can't respond. I was too busy crying and breathing and straining to see my new baby girl.

Dr. Belizan was barely done with me and Whoosh!!! There was James, not yet seven, Marika, five, and Nadia, just turned three, running into the delivery room all screaming, "Hi Mommy! Hi Mommy! Hi Mommy!"

I shrieked to myself, "How did they get in here so fast? What if I was still pushing"? I pull away my oxygen mask, not to scare them, and all I can do is point and yell, "Look at her!" I'm smiling and crying at the same time. I am so proud of all my little angels. Eloise checked out A.O.K. and is handed to me. James, Marika and Nadia all yell at once, even louder, "Can I see her? Can I touch her? Can I hold her?"

Rita, who has never been blessed with a child, looking like she was about to faint, is apologetic. "Mary Ann, they all ran down the hall so fast the nurses couldn't stop them from entering your room!"

My retort is simply, "No problem Rita, but a few minutes sooner and they would have seen her being born." That sight probably would have shocked my small children but in a way, would have been beautiful.

*   *   *

By noon the next day I'm discharged with Eloise on a hot, humid August day. I had no guilt asking Edward to get a bottle or two of champagne for us on the way home.

Since Edward preferred scotch, he bought his single malt, and the two champagnes ended up both mine.

I got good and drunk within twenty-four hours of Eloise's birth. I rationalized drinking too much that night (which I now know there never is a "good enough" reason to get drunk), because the worry was over and Eloise was born to my tired forty-one-year-old body normally. Thank God. Little did I know at the time, however, that the worrying had just begun.

*   *   *

Post-partum depression reared its ugly head like a giant medusa with deadlier venom than fifty water moccasins. I felt down and out and decided to see a psychiatrist. I picked one of my favorite patients.

"How are you feeling today?" asks my new shrink/old patient.

"Tired and depressed," as I lie back on his comfortable couch.

"Are you breast feeding?"

"I'm trying but I'm so tired; I'm not making much milk."

My psychiatrist pulls out his prescription pad. "Let's try some Celexa. It's safe even if you breast feed."

Within a week after giving birth to Eloise, I was seeing emergency patients. Just thirteen days after her birth, I worked a half-day. The next two days I worked full days in the office, including Botox injections and Lasik consults, who then allowed me to operate on them only two days later. On a Friday afternoon, just sixteen days after Eloise was born, I'm back in the O.R. at Johns Hopkins with the same nurses who last saw me forty pounds ago.

Crazy, huh? Doesn't every woman do it? Without a wet nurse? Just not sleep at night, feeding and changing a newborn, work within two weeks post-partum, operate on eyeballs, and watch three additional small children all evening without a nanny, husband or even live-in boyfriend?

Doesn't every man? Work all day, see as many patients as possible and operate as much as possible to save the home/office? (Now that I'm paying all the bills by myself. Dieter's $750/mth child support barely covers my nanny for one week.) No savings, month to month, credit card debt, and work on getting another loan on the house, as Dieter is getting another major cash infusion before I can be divorced. Spend more than you earn, the good old American way? Doing everything totally physically and mentally wiped out?

Isn't that what every good man does? Sure, maybe five thousand years from now when they're all bionic. And men think they are the "stronger sex"? I've got one perfect double-four-lettered-word for that: BULLSHIT.

I'm not saying women are stronger than men but we are at least equal and should be treated that way. I can't stand that "glass ceiling" crap, the term for where women can "see" higher positions but never obtain them a.k.a. "glass ceiling". It's bullshit, too

*   *   *

I'm getting "shrunk" again a few days later, back on my psychiatrist's couch.

"How are you feeling? Is the antidepressant helping?" he asks me.

"I don't know if it is doing a damned thing. I'm tired, worried and depressed."

"Why?"

"Because I am."

"What do you mean?"

"Because I just am! I'm already back to work within two weeks, totally exhausted, feeling fat and depressed!" I yell at him loudly, and I like my sixtyish shrink. He really seems to care with his compassionate, big brown eyes.

"What are you worrying about?" he calmly asks, ignoring my outburst.

"Everything! I still can't believe Edward called 911 on me Saturday night because I was a little out of it, you know, just sleep deprived to the point of babbling." (August, 2002, two-and-one-half weeks after Eloise's birth.)

"I told you my letter will take care of that situation, but let's discuss it again if it will make you feel better."

"I don't want to deal with Child Welfare Services again. My attorney said they are vultures! Last Fall, (2001) when James dialed 911, it took five months to get them off my back. Why didn't Edward cut me a break for just having his baby and going back to work too soon? Jesus, he's a shrink like you! What the hell?! I'm so stressed about money, too. Oh, fucking everything sucks! I just can't believe Edward dialed 911 Saturday night, just because I was a little out of it. He could have taken care of Eloise for once! I was simply exhausted and needed some rest. For God's sake, I drove to Hopkins and did Lasik surgery the day before! What more can I do?!"

"I want you to stop worrying about Edward's 911 call."

"Well, he did write an apology letter to me." I take it out of my purse and my psychiatrist's nodding head means "go ahead".

"He wrote: 'I am so sorry for my obscene behavior and all those things I shouted at you, which I did not mean.

I know that you are an excellent, wonderful and caring mother'".

"I'll give you a copy but let me read the last paragraph to you." Another nod. "Your professionalism and caring did not deserve the disrespect that I gave you the other night. It will never happen again. I love you dearly and pray that we can move forward—please forgive me. All my love, Edward." Then I thrust it at my good shrink and blurt out, "Why the hell then did he call the police?"

"I don't know, Mary Ann. He should have known better. Here's a copy of the letter I wrote to Child Welfare Services: "Dr. Duke had an unusual drug reaction to Ambien, Flexeril, Klonopin, and Celexa. I carefully reviewed Dr. Duke's medications, obtained all the relevant details from her, and came to the conclusion that the particular combination of her medications caused her to experience a period of amnesia, agitation, and irritability on August 31, 2002." And he reads the rest.

"That sounds good. Go ahead and send it."

"How are you sleeping?"

"What's that?"

"Mary Ann, I'm serious, how are you sleeping?" my dear shrink reasks.

"I'm not. I have totally broken sleep, up changing the baby, and my best hour is probably the first hour after I've had some wine."

"How much are you drinking? You should not be drinking at all with your post-partum depression and on Celexa. You are defeating the purpose of the antidepressant."

"No kidding. But sorry, Doc, I need one cold Chardonnay to relax a little after a day of patients, before I start my second shift job taking care of my four small kids. C'mon, don't you have a drink after listening to all your patients' bitching and moaning all day? Edward certainly does."

"We're not talking about me." Silence. "Okay, I'll give you a few more Ambien (sleeping pills) to sleep better, but you are going to have to ask Edward to do some diaper changing at night, because you must get some good sleep. Here are a few samples and a prescription for more Celexa. Is your back feeling better? Are you still taking the muscle relaxant (Flexeril) and the Klonopin (anti-anxiety) that your Internist wrote for you? I need to speak with him in advance so that our combined meds don't cause you this problem again."

"Yes. I'm off both of my Internist's medications within a week. I'll ask him to call you."

"Good. See you next week. Get some good rest; you'll feel less depressed."

"Sure." He smiles at me and I attempt a weak grin back at him and leave.

I feel a need for a vat of valium after that $200 hundred/hour "shrinking" and a one way ticket to St. John. I don't think Edward's going to do much diaper changing.

Two months later, after many meetings and phone calls, Child Welfare Services sends a letter stating "child neglect could neither be proved or disproved. The investigation disposition is 'unsubstantiated' and the record will be destroyed after five years *if there are no additional reports"*.

Chapter 16

More Reports

Three weeks post partum (just a few days after Edward's 911 call) I did cataract surgery at Suburban Hospital. I kissed one dear nervous patient on the cheek before operating on him. Then I happily operated to the Eurythmics and my surgeries came out beautifully. I never expected to get called into the Executive Director of the Medical Staff's office a few weeks later. I took Blair, Edward's father, with me as a witness.

I introduced the Director to Blair and they shook hands. He asked us to sit down behind his massive desk and handed me a piece of paper.

"What's this?" I ask.

"A complaint was filed that you had alcohol on your breath in the operating room, September 9th, 2002."

"Who filed this complaint?" and I hand the paper to Blair. The name on the complaint was blacked out with magic marker. Blair's countenance looks confused. He wrinkles his brow as he read the very brief complaint.

"I'm not free to discuss that with you."

"Why not?" asks Blair in his distinguished British accent.

"I'm just not."

"I'm just not."

I thought this situation was weird and plain old wrong and I state, "Sir, there is no way I smelled of alcohol in the operating room. I even kissed one nervous patient on the cheek, without a mask on, and I am certain if anyone could have smelled alcohol on me, it would have been my patient. As nervous as he was, *he* would have cancelled his surgery and reported me."

"Well, it is my job to address this complaint. I want you to go to Physician's Rehabilitation Center in Baltimore." I am shocked by his words and indignant.

"If someone thought I smelled of alcohol and wrote a complaint, why did they let me continue to do *eye surgery*? Why wasn't I stopped immediately before cutting an eye open and allowed to prove my innocence? Why wasn't I just sent to the E.R. for an evaluation?"

No reasonable answer, just "This complaint is a part of your record at the hospital now and the hospital wants you to make an appointment with Physicians' Rehab in Baltimore."

I'm pissed off and glance at Blair and Blair re-asks, "Why does Dr. Duke need to bother with that?"

"I insist."

Blair sighs, "Well, if they insist on it, Dear, I'll take you."

I stand up and say, "Fine. May I, please, have their phone number?"

The Director scratches it down and hands it to me. What can I say? Thank you for making anonymous, unproven trouble for me and making me lose a day's income in the office going to Baltimore to meet with someone else? Nope. I simply state, "My surgeries both came out perfectly."

"Good day, Dr." and the Director looks down at his paperwork on his desk.

I never liked the Director. I thought he had a "Napoleon complex" which unfortunately too many people in positions of power suffer from. (Possibly a high pricktene level, too.)

A few weeks later Blair and I go to Baltimore and meet with the Head of Physicians' Rehabilitation. The "Head Man" of Rehab was much nicer. He agreed the "allegations should have been proven at the time and I should have been stopped from operating". I said to him, "I was told by the Director that they didn't like my rock and roll music. Too bad. I don't play it too loud. I'm the surgeon and I play what I like after I first ask my patient their choice of CD. Jeepers, I remember doing a blepharoplasty (droopy lid surgery) while an elderly vascular surgeon took the varicose veins out of one of my patient's legs. He was singing loudly 'I Can't Get No' and waited for me to sing back 'Satisfaction'. The Rolling Stones were blaring the whole time"! The Head of Rehab smiled.

Blair and I both left there thinking "that was a waste of time". Little did I know it at the time but that erroneous, anonymous complaint became the first black mark on my career.

*   *   *

The Head of Physicians' Rehab wrote a letter to the Director which I received a copy of five years later. (In 2007) His last few sentences summed it up: "Dr. Duke's question as to why she was suspected of drinking prior to surgery and no one intervened is a good one. However, there are certain aspects of her personality that would easily be seen as arrogance. This could make her a *target...* "
Yep, the Head of Rehab hit a bull's eye. In a man's world,

a woman isn't supposed to be a better doctor than a man, certainly not make more money, and *definitely* not speak her mind all of the time *even if she is right.* That's not arrogance. That is being a successful woman with chutzpah whose parents and grandparents taught her to not be afraid to "March to your own beat, Medka". "Illegitimi Non Carborundum", Latin for "Don't let the bastards get you down". The corollary is: "Just because you're paranoid doesn't mean they aren't trying"!

*   *   *

Eight months later, Saturday, May 3, 2003 started out as a beautiful Spring day, not a cloud in the sky. James, Marika and Nadia were spending the weekend with Dieter and Edward stayed over Friday night. I actually got to sleep in that morning and Eloise did, too. I walked into the kitchen to find Edward sipping coffee and reading the *Washington Post.*

"Edward?"

"Yes?" he responds without looking over the newspaper.

"I brought down the baby monitor. Do you mind listening for Eloise so I can do some weeding?"

"Fine." He still doesn't look over his newspaper. I saw my chance. I grabbed a cup of coffee, and happily went outside to weed around all of Baba's transplanted flowers. My yard is two acres so there are a ton of weeds to pull. I love gardening even if it is only pulling weeds. I always feel close to Baba when I garden because she loved it, and she taught me to love it, too.

Several hours later I come in for a quick lunch. Edward's drinking a beer. Usual and customary for him to start drinking around noon on weekends. His cold beer looks good.

"Wow," I address him as he's watching television, "It's already two o'clock! Where's Eloise?" I grab two yogurts out of the refrigerator and see a cold bottle of chardonnay.

"Down for her nap. Are you finished weeding?" he asks and looks up at me as I'm shoveling in my second yogurt.

"Hardly. Do you care if I go back out and work some more?"

"Go ahead. Knock yourself out." Edward didn't offer to help me. Four hands pull twice as many weeds as two and we could have taken the baby monitor outside, but then again, I never really expected him to help me.

A few hours later, I come in because I'm thirsty. Eloise is still sleeping and Edward is lounging on the couch still reading, with a fresh beer by his side. I don't remember buying the wine; Edward must have brought it. (He always preferred drinking with me "his drinking buddy" than alone.) The power of suggestion got the better of me. I opened the bottle of chardonnay, put a bunch of ice cubes in a glass, and went to the backyard with my glass in one hand and the wine bottle in the other. (Hindsight 20/20, a very bad move for a dehydrated human with a virtually empty stomach.) Sipping chardonnay in the full afternoon sun, I pulled one hell of a lot of weeds to make room for Baba's flowers.

I finally came back into the house, sweaty, tired, hungry and happily drunk.

Edward was not happily drunk. He was trying to feed nine-month-old Eloise and did not appear to be having much success. There was more cereal on Eloise's face and high chair than she could have possibly eaten, and she was wailing.

"It's about time you came in!" Edward angrily yells at me.

"Oh hush, child, and eat your cereal!" he yells now at Eloise. Eloise wails louder after his harsh tone.

"Eloise doesn't need to be shouted at to eat. Maybe she doesn't like the cereal. Did you mix in some fruit?" I ask Edward. Edward gives me a look of disdain and picks on me instead of our baby, "Well, you've had a fine day, outside all day. You haven't helped me with Eloise one bit!" I smell scotch on his breath and glance at the clock. Yep, it's after six; time to change from beer to scotch, I think. I also do not care that Edward is feeding Eloise. Nor do I care that he watched her all day. I do 90% plus of her childcare on weeknights and weekends. Edward can do one Saturday's baby watching. I don't feel guilty at all, seems like Eloise slept most of the day anyway; and Edward drank beer and read his book on the couch.

Everyone knows a bottle of wine is equal to about four drinks. In medical school I never experienced a blackout on four drinks. Either the argument that ensued between Edward and I was so horrendous that I blocked it out or had a brief blackout or both. All I recall is dialing 911 and telling the operator, "He's beating me up"!

The Maryland Medical Board or "The Board" (as they will be referred to herein) made public my personal life. I am sure I am the very first doctor in the entire state of Maryland to ever have had a nasty fight with their significant other on a weekend after alcohol was consumed who dialed 911. An irrational and most dubious honor bestowed upon the one and only Dr. Duke.

This is what the Board wrote verbatim as a matter of public knowledge:

"On May 3, 2003 at 8:26 p.m., Montgomery County police responded to a 911 call from the Respondent's home from a woman breathing heavily saying, 'He's beating me up.' According to the police report, when police entered the Respondent's home, they found her naked and sitting on the floor, 'screaming wildly' into the telephone. The Respondent's nine-month-old baby was found crying on the floor several feet from the Respondent. There was no one else in the house. After the officers provided the Respondent with a coat, she 'stormed into the kitchen' and made a telephone call to an unidentified person. The Respondent 'screamed in a rage' into the telephone for several minutes. The reporting officer heard the Respondent repeat several times during the call that she will 'kill them all'. After the Respondent completed the call, the officers handcuffed her. The Respondent 'continued to scream in a rage' stating, 'If you keep me from my kids, I'll kill myself'.

The officer completed a Petition for Emergency Evaluation and accompanied the Respondent to Suburban Hospital.

On May 3, 2003 at 9:45 p.m., the Respondent arrived at Suburban Hospital in restraints and was reported to be 'combative, yelling profanities at EMS/police/nurse'. During her psycho-social assessment, the Respondent admitted that she drank (two drinks/night), every night, and had had three drinks that evening. The Respondent refused to submit to a breathalyzer test or blood sample upon admission: however, a urine sample indicated that her alcohol level was 0.22 (percent alcohol). The Respondent's assessment was stopped until her blood alcohol was below 0.1 (percent alcohol)". (I learned in medical school that one cannot *accurately infer* a blood alcohol level from a possibly concentrated urine, but I was obviously not without a bottle of wine in me that day.)

"On the morning of May 4, 2003, the Respondent was discharged from Suburban Hospital. The discharge note states that the Respondent was 'very apologetic...promises no more alcohol, wants to go back to children'".

I've read those paragraphs at least 50 times.

On first read, I agree with every shocked reader. Wow. She really *is* a wild one. She's a raging drunk, homicidal, suicidal, a neglectful mother and everything in between. She's not coming near my eyes, not a chance. She's out of control of herself, crazy, so how can she be my doctor, especially my *eye surgeon?* ... Lock her up and throw away the key.

On 50th read, however, my conclusions are different. Remember, this is a part of the "public record". First of all, it's 8:26 p.m. on a Saturday night (not a work night) and I'm naked with Eloise because we were just coming out of the shower. I thought Edward was yelling for me, not the police. (Did our nakedness really need to be a matter of "public record"?) The police report said I was "breathing heavily saying, 'He's beating me up'". Why would I make that up? And it's on their 911 tape! Edward must have got his ass out of my house as fast as he could. He must have been drunk, too, or why leave?

The police report said they "didn't know *who* I was talking to?" C'mon. I'm vocal, *loud*. I must have said Edward's name at least twice, and the officer had been to my home before? He knew *exactly* who I was yelling at.

Why didn't the police just ask me who I had called? Why didn't I get asked if I was hurt, since I dialed 911 "breathing heavily, he's beating me up"? For God's sake, who the hell would*n't* have been pissed off if they had just gotten shoved or hit by their boyfriend, and then *they* were handcuffed and restrained (found naked), and taken away from their nine-month-old baby girl and home? Sober or not, I'm sure anyone would have been wildly frantic at that moment.

Crazy! I was obviously talking to the hospital staff: I was refusing testing, talking about how much I had drank that night, etc. All I could think and repeat out loud since the police hauled me away in handcuffs was, "Who has my baby? Where is Eloise"?! No one answered me as they tied me down, all four limbs to the bed. I was put in a room by myself with no windows and the door shut a.k.a. the "Psych room". My left wrist was killing me. I couldn't sleep a wink because of my wrist pain and the damned tight restraints. Who the hell can sleep tied up and spread-eagled like an X? I kept yelling "Nurse! Nurse! Doctor! Someone *please* help me"!! (Looking back, possibly that bloody sterile box of a room is sound-proofed and certainly all fours tied down to the rails of the bed, I couldn't possibly hit a button to call a nurse *if* there even was a button to push!) I could have choked on my own vomit, and it seemed like no one was listening to me or even seemed to care when I continued to yell, "Where is my baby"?!

"I need an x-ray of my left wrist. Please x-ray my left wrist"! I begged and pleaded for hours for an x-ray every time someone came in. Finally, at 4:30 a.m., the E.R. doctor allowed me one pain pill and an x-ray. The radiologist missed the fractures. Suburban Hospital sent me home with a broken wrist in two places and no pain medication. I found out three weeks later, since I was still in a great deal of pain while continuing to carry around my baby, after I went for an MRI on my own.

Last, but NOT LEAST, *what happened* to Eloise? The police *must* have called Edward to pick her up. "An *un*identified individual", yeah right. The police knew damned well who I was talking to, now didn't they? (The same police officer who investigated my burglary and wrote $41,000 worth of valuables lost. Wrong. No way does the FBI come to investigate a $41,000 robbery. It was *$241,000* robbery, officer. Who conveniently left out 20 zeros on the police report so the burglary looks $200,000 less than it really was?!) I have tried to get my FBI report for over two years through the FOIA, "Freedom of Information Act". I've sent everything certified, notarized, you name it, and received nothing. My Dad calls it "passing the buck". (I call it lazy beurocracy bullshit and quite possibly plain old corruption.)

Truly, doesn't Edward look guilty leaving me alone with our baby if I was so "out of it"? Did the police do a breathalyzer on him when he arrived to pick her up? Doubt it, or they would not have let him get behind the wheel of a car.

Once again the truth is the truth: a penis prevents problems. I'm a man in a woman's body. I don't want to be a man; I like being mommy. But I am supremely confident that if I was a man, none of my personal life would be plastered up on the internet like some old-fashioned, now outlawed, huge McDonald's sign. Why didn't they write whether I had a bikini wax or not? If you want to go…all…the…way, *just do it*.

On 50th read, I understand the date, also. I'm in the throes of "Magnificent Martyrdom", still fighting post-partum depression and the trauma from my divorce, absolutely at the end of my rope. I was putting up with Edward's abuse, because I was downtrodden. I was working furiously and sleep deprived. Then the next morning, "I'm apologetic and go home"? I was discharged with a prescription for six low dose anti-anxiety pills and simply told to "take one tablet twice/day and follow up in three days with my *Internist*"?!

What happened to the homicidal/suicidal wild woman? Was everything all better in her mind just because she was sober at eight a.m.? Hell, no. I was a tired train wreck! Why wasn't I "admitted for observation" for a few days or plain old *help and rest*? Why wasn't I, at least, referred to a psychiatrist and why was my broken wrist (in two bones, bring back memories of Baba?) missed and not even Tylenol recommended for pain?

Terrific. Two monkeys/vultures on my back now, Child Welfare Services and The Maryland Medical Board.

Chapter 17

My Children, My Life

Child Welfare Services swooped in first. An "Assessment Social Worker" called me on a busy afternoon at work. I had already received a pile of paperwork from her, which I hadn't filled out yet with Edward. Of course, I wanted his expert psychiatric opinion before answering the multiple questions and his name was on every page, too.

"Ms. Duke? This is Liz Mandoval-Gewell. I am the social worker from Child Welfare Services investigating the suspected neglect of Iloise Duke."

"Good afternoon. I think I heard you say 'I'loise? My daughter's name is Eloise with an E, and please, call me Dr. Thank you. What can I do for you?"

"We have not received any of our forms back from you," she states in a challenging tone, not pleasant at all. I try to keep my tone light.

"Well, yes, Dr. Everett-Monroe and I have both been extremely busy and, truthfully, he has also been out of town for work. As soon as possible, we will answer your requests," I reply nicely.

"Your case is *high profile.* Child Welfare Services will not tolerate tardiness," she boldly states.

I cup my hand over the receiver so my patients cannot hear my conversation that are sitting patiently in the waiting room.

The office is so busy; no lunch again; I don't even want to take the time to walk into Exam Room 2 a.k.a. the "phone boudoir". I just want to get off the phone, period, and back to my waiting patients. A quick glance at Judy, my office manager, and I can tell she "was all ears", too.

"Excuse me, Ms. Mandoval?" I do not like her tone of voice and was confused by what she said. I'm not "high profile". I'm a "hunkie" from Binghamton/"Bingotown" alias "Bumfuck", New York. What the *hell* is she talking about?

"My name is Mandoval-*Gewell*."

"I'm sorry. My office is a little noisy. Could you repeat what you said before, Ms. Mandoval-Gewell?"

"Your case is very high profile. If you do not cooperate fully with me, I will take you to court and you will lose everything, your children, your home and your practice!"

I can't believe what she just said! She is a social worker calling me for paperwork. I lose my cool a little and speak softly but very firmly back, "Is that what you do as a public servant? Get off on *ruining people's lives?!*"

"Get the paperwork done and my boss wants to set up a meeting with you and 'I'loise's father as soon as possible. I'll be calling you." Click.

Wow, she actually threatened me! As soon as I finished patients, I banged out a letter on my typewriter. Embarrassed to admit, but me, the "vintage" ex-wife had still not learned how to turn on a computer in 2003 and was afraid of them, still am. (Such a dinosaur, Mary Ann.) But I banged out on the typewriter, "I was baffled by the tone and the nature of your phone call earlier today. I was particularly puzzled by your verbal threats of 'I will take you to court and you will lose everything; your children, your home and your practice'. As a loving mother and dedicated physician, I am deeply concerned whether your statements actually represent the views of the Child Welfare Services". I wrote a little more and cc'd my shrink and my attorney, made copies, and put them in the mail. I do not like that woman and do not trust her one little bit. Does she get a feather in her cap to take me down, this "high profile" case now it's called? Who knows?

I called my state trooper buddy (same one that was at the house when Dieter moved out) and he emphatically stated, "Dukie, you would have to be running up and down Democracy Boulevard, naked, holding your baby and endangering her life, high on crack cocaine or heroin, before you will *ever* lose custody of your children".

His words made me feel a little better, but not really.

Child Welfare Services made Edward and I get evaluated by I don't recall how many people.

The Maryland Medical Board then swooped down with their own talons and expensive hoops for me to jump through.

I had to see a forensic psychiatrist of *their* choice. She added absolutely nothing to my treatment except a laundry list of "must rule out diagnoses". Her letter to the Maryland Medical Board stated I "had been under an extraordinary amount of stress for the last several years". (No shit, Miss Sherlock Shrink, doesn't take a forensic psychiatry degree to deduce that; a four-year-old pre-schooler can diagnose it.) She also wrote verbatim: "She is clearly a very talented individual who has accomplished a lot on her own. She is dedicated to her children and to her work but could lose both if her mental illness is not brought under control. (Terrific, now I'm labeled *mentally ill* to the Board and they obviously are trading paperwork with Child Welfare Services. Why didn't they both just get together and burn me at the stake and save money on ink, paper, stamps and typists?!) She continues…"I recommend life-long contact with a psychiatrist for medication management…I have *no evidence* that her *illness* has impacted her work but it has the potential to do so".

Thanks for the all-encompassing-cover-your-ass report. I bet every one of her patients, including herself, have the "potential" to do just about *anything.* Miss Sherlock Shrink's laundry list of "must rule out diagnoses" are Bipolar II, Rule out Bipolar I, Rule out anti-depressant-induced mania, Alcohol Abuse and she suggested yet another $200/hr. shrink.

*   *   *

I know I am not Bipolar I or I would have done myself in with the medication roller coaster ride the Board's shrink has been insisting I ride on nauseously. The Board forced me into a corner and now I'm dictated to see the female shrink they recommended who never talks. She just stares at me. There I sit in her tiny, but well furnished Chevy Chase office. I speak first, "I went to the supposed 'Doctors' AA' meeting at the Del Ray Club in Bethesda."

Her one word response, "Really?"

"Yep. The room was full of anything but Docs. There were medical technicians, nurses, just not a lot of M.D.'s. I got a list of the members."

"Really, may I see it?" I dug in my bag and handed it over. For the next forty-five minutes she poured over the two-page list, even lifted up her distance glasses and held it right up to her nose to see it better.

I wanted to ventilate and I did; however, I don't think my new highly-recommended-Board-dictated shrink heard a single word I said. So much for Alcoholics

"Anonymous". Many of the people on the list signed their full name and gave both home and cell phone numbers. At the end of my $4/minute, fifty-minute session, she had the audacity to ask, "May I make a copy"?

"No", I immediately responded and gently tugged the two sheets from her grasp.

A most excellent way to waste $200 cash. On my way out she chimes, "I'll see you on Thursday". The Board wants me shrunk (that's my word for seeing a shrink (obviously)…to get shrunk) twice a week. $1,600/month to go crazy. I'm so pissed off at her for being a busy body and wasting my time and money, I want to *scream.*

After my second appointment, she matter-of-fact states, "Mary Ann, I want to change your medication. I think you may be Bipolar II."

"No one in my family is bipolar whatsoever. Isn't it hereditary?" I ask, but I already knew the answer.

"Bipolar I is hereditary, yes. But I think you are Bipolar II and it is not necessarily hereditary at all," she responds. "But you will need to change all of your medications."

I lean back in her lounge chair and stare at the ceiling. I don't want to keep changing medications, but I desperately want to feel better and sleep better. "Doc, personally, I think I'm tripolar." She half smiles at me. This shrink has summed me up at least enough in two visits to know that when I feel like it, I often resort to a little twisted wit. (Tripolar is not a legitimate diagnosis, ha, yet! I think it stands for tired, stressed, and abused.) I rant on: "I'm manic in the office to make ends meet (thus "tired"), depressed from divorce and post-partum (thus "*stressed out*"), and just totally fucked up in the synapses in my brain from all of the medication changes in the past year (thus "ABUSED").

It is always the same story with her, "Here are a few samples. Try this."

"I am sorry, but I would like you to try something for Bipolar II," and she hands me a new sample of something or other.

I think, "You aren't 'sorry'; you're just a pill-passer-outer type of shrink".

God help me. The only drug that seemed to work at all…was alcohol.

In a fifteen month time period, I was prescribed the anti-depressants: Prozac, Celexa, Lexapro and Zoloft, the anti-anxiety drugs: Xanax, Valium, Klonopin and Librium, the muscle relaxant Flexeril, and the sleep medications: Ambien and Trazadone. Add to that the various drugs for "Bipolar II". Listing them: 1. Zyprexa- On Zyprexa I gained fourteen pounds in fourteen days and basically developed diabetes so my Internist gave me some Phentermine for appetite suppression.

2. Topamax- Didn't do anything for me, but at least I lost the weight I gained.

3. Gabitrol- Gave me a terrible red rash from my feet to my knees.

4. Geodon- Simply made me feel like a zombie.

5. Lithium- The Worst Tremor! I looked like I had a fifth of vodka the night before during office hours when I had no alcohol whatsoever. And in surgery, under the operating microscope, the tremor was worse than the worst case of Parkinson's! I *had* to be non-compliant so that I could operate. One can't have shaky hands and do microscopic eye surgery,

no way! Propranolol 20 mgs. was supposed to help with the tremor and anxiety, and it didn't work worth a damn.

Of course, I was given Antabuse, the drug that interacts with alcohol so if you drink any alcohol with Antabuse in your system, look out! It is time to vomit and be violently ill. I didn't have the pleasure of that experience, because Antabuse all by itself without any alcohol at all, gave me a horrible headache and the worst stomach cramps. They are both well-known side effects of Antabuse, but the "Board" wasn't happy about me not taking it.

God help me. Again, the only drug that seemed to work at all…was alcohol.

*   *   *

Adding insult to injury, my back was causing me a great deal of pain. I never was one to have back pain, and so I thought it was just too much lifting children and/or running. I go to the doctor and he sends me for an MRI which revealed a herniated disc in my lumbar spine (lower back). Not much to do for a herniated disc, unless surgery is required, except rest and pain medication. Ibuprofen alone was not easing the pain so my neurosurgeon gave me a prescription for Vicodin (Acetaminophen with Codeine). "Bed rest" and "No heavy lifting" weren't viable options.

On top of everything, Dieter sues me for more money and possessions from the house and, of course, *he wins both*, the beginning of my flagrantly foul month. Then Edward's mother, Louise, had a heart attack on a cruise boat and came home in an urn at the end of the same month, October 2003. Edward was of no help to me the entire month because he was either at his mother's ICU bedside in South America or taking care of his grieving father after her funeral. I offered to fly Louise home in an

"ICU in the sky". I spent one entire afternoon making calls and was willing to put the $22,500, that it was going to cost, on *my* credit card.

I always loved Louise. But no one listened to me (I have "poor medical judgment", right?), so Louise came home in an urn two weeks later. Edward and his sister thought it was "too much money". What is "too much money" to probably save your mother's life? And dear God, I offered to pay the *entire* amount!

*   *   *

Child Welfare Services swoops back down with a letter: "The information obtained during the neglect investigation supports the conclusion that *neglect did occur.*" (The May 3rd incident when I dialed 911.) Both Edward and I were charged with "indicated" neglect. "A social worker will be contacting you in the near future to work with you to assure the protection of your children." Super, I thought, why don't you send a couple of nice women over this weekend? One can help me with the children and the other can cook and clean. Maybe if I call Liz directly, she'll buzz right on over and start changing "l"loise's diapers. Dream on, Mary Ann. Your fatigue is showing right through your thin skin. You must have forgotten to grease your back this morning after showering so that everything can roll right off of it like a God damned duck.

I'm all alone after work taking care of my four beautiful children, eight years of age on down to fifteen months with multiple medication changes from the Board's "super shrink", and now taking Vicodin for back pain which made me even more tired and constipated.

*   *   *

"Yes, James, Honey. Go ahead and put the Barney tape on for your sisters."

I'm feeding Eloise in her high chair on the "Splat Mat" in the middle of the living room. It's Sunday evening and the weekend was beautiful, weather-wise, that is. The children were in and out of the back door. I was up and down the stairs from the deck to the back yard to check on them every ten minutes. Heaven forbid one of them accidentally gets hit in the head with a swing, punches the one who let the swing go at the wrong time, and the punched child falls into the third knocking her down so all four of them are crying when Child Welfare Services decides to make a "wellness check".

I swear I worked harder from Friday after work until Sunday when they all went to sleep than I worked in a five-day work week in the office. By this particular Sunday night, with my back pain worsened by the lifting of children and infants in and out of tubs, beds, car seats, etc…I was sincerely about to collapse.

I didn't want to bother him with his Mom's recent funeral and all, but I called Edward and got his cell phone. "Hello, this is Edward Everett-Monroe; please leave your message after the tone".

"Edward! It's Mary Ann. I really need your help. I am in a lot of pain, *extremely* tired and I really need your help getting the kids to bed. I wouldn't be calling you if I really wasn't in dire need! Bring your father if you want. I'd love to see Blair and it might be a good break for him." Edward never returned my call. (Sunday night football) Next, I call my daytime nanny, Rita. No answer. I leave a message, "Rita, I really need your help tonight as I am having back problems. Could you, please, help me bathe and put the children to bed? Please, call me as soon as you can. Thanks, it's Mary Ann." Rita doesn't have a cell phone.

I called my girlfriend, Jane. No answer. That's right, I think, she always has church group on Sunday nights, probably has her cell phone turned off.

I call a neighbor and friend who lives less than a mile away. "I'm sorry I can't help you. My daughter has strep throat and mine is a little sore, too."

"No problem", I said, "I don't need a house full of strep throats".

I call my girlfriend who lives four to five miles away. No answer. Then I remember she was going to her parents for the weekend and may not have driven back yet. Now I am getting desperate. I wish my sister, Elena, still lived in Gaithersburg, but she moved back to Johnson City. It really is tough raising four children with no husband and no family in the area and no live-in help.

I call Edward again. He must check his cell phone between the four o'clock football game and Sunday Night Football, right? "Edward, please come over and help me. My back is killing me and I need help, *please*!"

I'm running out of options. God, I wish I had a valium for my back spasm. I break down and open a bottle of wine. "I'll just have a little," I tell myself. I just have to feed and bathe and get the children to bed before I can fall into bed and cry frustrated tears. Frustrated from everything, just everything! The wine hits my brain and I hurry into the office, after making sure all of the children were watching the Barney video in the living room and one of them hadn't wandered downstairs to play in the cat's litter box, like it was a sand box (that was not pleasant), and I grab two more patients' charts that are very nice, may be willing to help me and do not live too far away. No answer at the first patient's number. I don't bother with a message.

The second patient is in. It's my construction-working buddy Dave. He has no children but is strong. I'm so relieved to hear his "Hello?"

"Hi Dave! It's Mary Ann. I know this is an inconvenience, but I have called six or seven friends and I haven't been able to reach anyone!" I must have sounded ultra- harried because Dave said, "What is wrong? Do you need my help? When?"

"I really am sorry to bother you like this, Dave, but I have severe back pain, and I am totally exhausted right now. I have to get my children fed and to bed. Can you, please, come over *right now* and help me? I would be so grateful!"

"I'll be right over, Mary Ann."

"Oh, thank you so much! Thank you! See you soon!"

Dave came to the office door. There is no doorbell there. I didn't hear his knocking on the office door over the blaring Barney video and children's chatter inside the house. He left. He just didn't think to come to the front door and ring the doorbell, which I would have heard. Dave could have saved my life. I collapsed from exhaustion and combining a little alcohol with my medications.

James dialed 911 and the "fire trucks" came. Dieter arrived. Edward finally appeared out of nowhere. But, it was too late for me, too late for M.O.M.M.Y. The police told Dieter to take into his custody James, Marika and Nadia. It all happened so fast. "Mr. Everett-Monroe?"

"Yes?" Edward responds to the policeman.

"The baby is your daughter?"

"Yes."

"Are you willing to stay here and take responsibility for her tonight?"

"Yes, officer."

"All right then. We're leaving. Dr. Duke, I suggest you find a good attorney."

*   *   *

I was in shock. I really was in shock. I couldn't talk. I couldn't think.

I let Edward put Eloise to bed. I call Dieter and say, "I'm coming down to get the children."

"No, you're not!" Click.

Rita finally called, but it was too late. The police gave my children to Dieter to take care of. I said blankly, "Rita, they took my babies and gave them to Dieter."

Rita has been working for me for over four years. *She knows how hard I work.*

Rita says, "It is going to be okay. Don't worry. They can't take your children away from you just like that. You are their mother! You will get them back soon. My sister does not like her job. She will quit it and come to work for you. When I leave at five or six p.m., she will take over and sleep in your home. We will work something out."

Thank God for Rita and her sister. The plan gave me some hope, but I have no idea how I slept that night or got up the next day and saw patients. I made an appointment on Tuesday to see two attorneys with good reputations.

Dieter called my cell phone Monday after work. "Mary Ann?"

"Yes, Dieter? How are the children? May I talk to them?" I'm trembling from nervousness, pain, exhaustion and simply fear of the unknown.

"No" Dieter said, "I'm fucked. I have to go for full custody or they are going to split the kids up and put them in foster care."

"OH MY ***GOD!!***" is all I can respond.

"I've got to go. Bye." Dieter dropped a bomb.

I let the phone fall out of my hand to the floor. This is unbelievable. This can't really be happening. Dieter is getting remarried in six weeks to a woman who is childless. I have to speak to my *two* new attorneys tomorrow and get my children back with Rita and her sister! My babies need to be home with Mommy! I'm here all of the time with the home/office. Dieter's always gone for work! Oh, my God, please, help me!

I went out for a few groceries after work. As I'm trudging up the long staircase to my bedroom, hadn't needed to turn the lights on yet, still reeling about Dieter's phone call, I see several police cruisers drive into my driveway through the large foyer window. I'm afraid. The police bang on my front door. I sprint up the remaining steps, hunched over like Quasimodo so they can't see me and run into my son's room in the front of the house to peek out the curtain. I hear one of them yell: "She's got to be in there! Her car is still warm. We'll have to break in, if she doesn't come to the door!"

Dear God, I think, what have I done now? I race into the nearest closet and hide under a quilt.

Bang! They broke into my front door. My mind is racing; I didn't do anything today but work a hard Monday in pain. I can't be in trouble for anything with the law! I didn't do anything wrong. Should I come out?

Heavy feet running in and out of rooms, flashlights, so many people running all over my home. Oh my God, they are opening my son's door. They open the door to the closet where I am hiding; I hold my breathe.

"She's not in here!"

"Maybe she went out the back door. I'll check the back yard, but it's getting dark. She could be hiding anywhere. But she can't keep her baby quiet without smothering her!" More heavy footsteps, but they seem to have left my son's room, where I was in the closet mildly freaking out. I flip open my cell phone and call Edward.

"Edward!" I whisper urgently.

"What? Why are you whispering?"

"The police just broke into my home! A whole bunch of them! Can you come over? They seem to be looking for me and Eloise! Why? And they are not leaving, because one of them said my car was still warm and I must be around!"

"Why don't you ask them what they want?"

"I'm scared! I haven't broken any laws; I'm hiding in James' closet! They couldn't find me."

The police were definitely not leaving. "I can hear them talking outside, but I can't hear what they are saying. Why don't they *go*?!"

"Oh, for God's sake, I'll be right over." Blair's house, where Edward is now staying with his father grieving, is just over a mile from mine. Edward arrives quickly, but it feels like an hour. Edward talks to the police for awhile. I can't make out their conversation. Finally they all leave, including Edward.

I think for a little while and then grab a few clothes and drive to Blair's home. Edward and dear Eloise are there and I can't wait to hug my baby! I need to hug and kiss her dearly even more so because Dieter wouldn't let me talk to James, Marika or Nadia. My poor children, what must they be thinking?

My nerves are beyond frayed; they are shrayed/shredded. I walk into the Everett-Monroe home, with its abundance of alcohol, craving a glass of wine.

Blair looks exhausted and stressed, but he has good reason to with Louise's recent death. He looks up at me and says, "Sit down, Dear. Edward, get Mary Ann a glass of wine." I sit. Edward promptly brings me a glass of red from his open bottle, knowing full well I prefer white.

Something is wrong, very wrong, and I gulp down half my glass.

"Where's Eloise?" Neither of them speak. I am confused. I stare at Blair and repeat louder to be sure he heard me, "Where *is* Eloise?"

Edward speaks because Blair can't, "Child Welfare Services came and took her to a foster home."

I'm in complete shock *yet again* at his words and cannot reply. My heart starts beating too fast and too hard. Tears well up in my eyes. I look at Blair and can tell from his face that what Edward just said is true.

I jump up out of my chair. Luckily, the red wine Edward gave me was half drunk or it would surely have spilled on their oriental rug. "What in God's name is going on?! What is going on with my children? Yesterday they make Dieter pick them up, and he doesn't want them now, damn it! He's getting remarried in a few weeks! *Now where the hell did they take my baby?!*" I am screaming and crying huge tears that fall straight to the carpet.

Both men blankly stare at me.

"What foster home? Why couldn't she stay here? *When can I see her?!*"

"We can see her on Wednesday from ten a.m. until noon at the county facility. I don't know where they took her. They took her right out of bed," monotones Edward. Oh my God, Edward is always composed. He looks like he just got shot in the chest.

I'm so appalled and so grief-stricken all I can think of is I need something to calm down.

"We have to wait *two days* to even see her?!"

"Yes," Edward repeats, "We can only see her on Monday and Wednesday mornings from ten until noon." I can't listen to any more horrific news. I have to calm down! I have to stop crying and shaking with my heart beating so fast. I need some dinner, but I set down my glass and head straight for their liquor cabinet.

"What are you doing, Dear?" questions Blair.

"Pouring a scotch! Do you want one?!"

Scotch on the rocks. Not my drink of choice, but most definitely my dinner of choice that Monday night. I don't know how I slept that night. I lost what mattered most to me in this life, all of my children, in the past twenty-four hours. You didn't sleep, Mary Ann, you passed out.

They took my children, they took my children; they just took them away from me! That thought kept spinning in my brain over and over like a broken record.

They took them, they took them was all I could think. Child Welfare Services, those vicious vultures, just swept down and took my children! My great state trooper buddy was gravely wrong. I didn't have to be running up and down Democracy Boulevard naked and high on crack or heroin, not even close.

All I could think was that I need to get them all back. They need their strong, sweet Mommy and I need them. That's all there is to it. Please, God, help me get them back; please, help me. I need you. I need a real deity to convince those "good ole boys", those mostly white male judges, no God damned different than like it is in medicine.

November! I will always hate the month of November. All of the terrible things in my life happen in November: my car crash and broken neck after Baba died, my first drunk driving arrest, going to jail and the worst of all, losing primary custody of my children. The only good day in November is Thanksgiving. I don't know how I got through that November losing my children and Eloise in foster care without, at least, three suicide attempts.

Every day was filled with the monotony and chaos of the office; then the total dichotomy of going to an attorney's office and getting spanked with a new set of problems or a new bill. Seeing fifteen-month-old Eloise on only Monday and Wednesday mornings for only two hours at the county facility in Rockville, and then having to say "Good bye, Angel", and kissing and hugging her one last time and watching her yearning look and outstretched arm over the shoulder of her foster care mother broke my heart into smaller pieces than it already was.

*   *   *

I always cried on the way back to the office with Blair driving. I was too much of an emotional wreck to drive, and Edward took his own car to go the other direction to work. Every time I told Blair, "I can't take much more of this", and then I would replace my eye make-up and start seeing patients to try to pay my enormous bills.

On top of that, only sparingly seeing my older three children was killing me, too, along with the new quiet in my home. I only saw them every other weekend with Rita supervising, and every Wednesday night from four until eight p.m. On the Wednesday before the weekend that they would be with their father and I was not going to see them for an entire week, I tried to hold it in until they were out of earshot, then I would sob and shake all of the long ride home. Rita would try to calm me down, "You'll appeal and get them back soon". (Well, you know how the appeal went…nowhere.)

Then when I walked into my now quiet, big home I would start crying hard all over again.

Mothers with addiction problems should be demanded to go to rehab before losing custody of their children. Period. Do all the poor African American women in D.C., our great capitol, lose their children as easily as I did? Or are they sent to some addiction clinic and allowed to keep their children, because there aren't enough foster homes in our country's great capitol for all of the neglected or abused African American children, and who wants them anyway? I know that sounds very terrible but doesn't it ring true? Wouldn't a white Montgomery County family prefer a white child to any other race? Probably 90 out of 100 families would vote: Yes.

A few days before Thanksgiving, I signed over custody of Eloise to Edward. I had to in order to get her out of foster care before Thanksgiving. Rita asked me, "Why are they giving her to Edward? He drinks much more than you do and he was charged with the same neglect. Why does *he* get custody?"

"I don't know, Rita. I have no clue." If I had the rested mind that I have now, I would *never* have signed those papers. But then again, he may have won her anyway, because a penis prevents problems.

But how could I give thanks on my favorite holiday if my baby was in some foster home and not with her Mommy? I wasn't *very* afraid of signing over custody of Eloise to Edward because we were still a pseudo-couple and I saw her all of the time. And that is what my *attorneys' advised* me to do. I thought I could get her back soon, too!

The Child Welfare "vultures" had backed me into a corner and were pecking at me so hard, before I was even dead, that I was bleeding from everywhere and had no choice. Why didn't I get a choice? Just one chance? Why didn't I get sentenced then, if not before, to a nice long rehab, instead of having to sign over Eloise?!

I'll never forget Edward's female attorney's comment, "You may never want to give custody back." She didn't think I heard her words when we were standing just outside the courtroom, but I heard every single one. His attorney was right. He didn't want me to have her, fought with me nightly to get rid of her, and now he enjoys keeping me from her.

*   *   *

Losing custody of my first three babies to Dieter is just as bad, multiplied times three.

*   *   *

Do all women lose custody of their babies for an alcohol problem at home after a nasty divorce and no bad thing happened like a broken bone, bruises, or physical signs of neglect? Or was the judge harder on me, not sentencing me to a thirty or ninety day rehab (which is what I needed), because I was a doctor and should have known better?

Women *and* men should *never* lose custody of their children for an alcohol problem before a judge sentences them to a good rehabilitation program!

I was drowning. Drowning in loneliness, depression, debt, guilt and anger. The medication roller coaster ride the Maryland Medical Board's "expert" psychiatrist had me on went faster and faster and still, the only drug that worked at all was damned alcohol. I just couldn't stop drinking by myself, alone in my despair.

Doctors aren't born with a little extra chromosome blessed with fortitude and perfection. We're regular garden-variety Homo sapiens like everyone else, so why the higher standard? Damn it, don't people know we've sacrificed our twenties when we should have been having more fun, more sex and more sleep? It would be nice if someone could cut us a break for working and sacrificing so much of our youth *to help people* instead of this "higher standard" shit! Just because someone has less college, is it okay for them to make mistakes but not forgivable of a physician?

*　　　　　　　*　　　　　　　*

Chaplain (Captain) Emile Joseph Kaupan of the 8th Cavalry Regiment, First Cavalry Division said, "It doesn't matter what happens to you. *Anything can happen to anyone.* It is how you handle it that counts". Retired Lieutenant Colonel Samuel R. Shumaker III told me that quote in 2008. That quote came from Prison Camp 5, North Korea, 1951. Lieutenant Colonel Shumaker's quote from 2008 is, "It is only out of confrontation, that the sparks of illumination come"!

Well, Mary Ann Duke, M.D., it is high time to live up to those great men's quotes.

Chapter 18

My Major Medical Mistake

I needed more pain. For some reason, no one had felt that I had had enough pain on my own, losing my marriage, my best friend, and my retirement money, that I had to also lose my most precious possessions of all, my glorious children.

Sure, bring it on. I like pain. Doesn't everyone? No. I'm being facetious. No one likes pain. That whole insane period of my life, God knows how long it lasted (actually, it still isn't over), almost ten years but feels like a hundred, I wanted to kill myself and have no one know. I just wanted to die so as not to feel the pain of not seeing my children and not tucking them in at night. That thought of killing myself still creeps into my conscious mind unwillingly, but suicide is the easy way out. Carrying on through hellish frustration and brutal stress, and striving to be happy is how I want to be remembered.

Always persevering, *no matter what.*

Also, I couldn't let anyone *really* know I was in such despair, because I am "The Magnificent Martyr". I was also afraid if my patients found out how devastated I was, they would probably think I couldn't concentrate well enough to maintain my excellence as their trusted ophthalmologist. That excruciatingly difficult period of my life isn't over. Not at all. But there is a big difference now.

The difference, is that I don't want to punish myself for the past anymore nor be a martyr.

I just want to live in the now with my children and have them grow and attain all of the goals that they want to attain with as little pain as possible. Never do I ever want them to suffer like I have suffered.

*   *   *

The day after I received the court papers that officially stated I was no longer the primary custodial parent, I walked into my quiet home and burst into tears. My heart isn't heavy; it's been torn to shreds. I miss my children! What are they doing right now? I'll call them. No, not yet, they're probably eating dinner.

I undress and put on my favorite red robe. I feel the softness of it and it brings back memories. It's the robe a friend bought me after my car accident in 1992, a few months after Baba died suddenly of a heart attack. My neck was broken in that head on collision. I had a C1C2 fracture (the first two vertebrae in one's neck); the vertebrae that break and cut through the spinal cord when a person hangs himself. It is called exactly that, a "hangman's fracture". It's the same fracture that the late Christopher Reeve suffered. After a hangman's fracture, one is either dead, a quadriplegic or absolutely fine. I wore a "halo" contraption for three months, even saw patients that way and now my neck feels fine. Guess it wasn't your time, Mary Ann, and God must be watching over you, but you ticked away another one of your nine lives.

I examine my cried out face in the bathroom mirror. I look terrible. Look at all of those crows' feet and wrinkles under my eyes from crying so much in the past six weeks ever since Child Welfare Services took my children. I decided I needed a pick-me-up. After looking in my medicine cabinet and finding two left over Valium and two Vicodin from my lower back problem, I decided to do a chemical peel on my own face. Never had I done my own face, but I had done plenty of patients. I went to my office, grabbed the supplies needed, opened the refrigerator and saw a half bottle of wine, poured a glass and went upstairs.

I took one Valium and one Vicodin before starting the chemical peel just like I would have given a patient in the office. I mix up the acid in the correct proportion but I leave out the blue tint. I didn't want the additional stress of looking like a "Smurf" for a few days. Big mistake. Huge. I thought I had done enough of these facial peels to know when to stop; however, it's easier with the blue tint to know when to quit applying the "magic wrinkle remover". I finished my glass of wine, ate a TV dinner, took the last Valium and Vicodin for sleep and prophylactic pain and went to bed.

First thing in the morning, I need to see my result. Walking swiftly to the bathroom, I realize that my face hurts quite a bit. I cringe when I see my super puffy and very red face in the mirror. Oh, well, maybe it's a good thing that I don't see my children for a week. But little Eloise won't care and I definitely need something stronger than Tylenol or Motrin. My face really hurts so I call Edward, "Hi, it's me. Do you still have any pain pills left from your neck surgery?"

"Why do you want to know? What did you do now?" I ignore his impatient sigh.

"Well, I did a chemical peel on my face last night and I think I may have over-did it a little. My face is pretty red and it hurts."

Edward grunts a "humpf" and says, "I'll give you a couple Tylenol #4 if you really need them."

"Thanks. I do. Is Eloise up?"

"Yes."

"Can I come over and see her?" I basically beg. Edward has been staying at his father's home more than mine because of Blair's grieving, and must be grieving the loss of his mother, too, because he has been so damned negative and bad-tempered. I feel like he's taking *everything* out on me including his new responsibility of caring for Eloise.

"We are about to go to the mall." Bummer, I think, I can't go with them. I can't go out in public with this face.

"Well, can you, please, wait for me to come over for the pain medication before you leave?"

"All right!" Edward sighs again, "But hurry up."

I throw on some clothes and arrive within five minutes. "Where is Eloise?"

"In her car seat," Edward deadpans.

He is always so impatient, too, I think crossly. If it wasn't for Eloise, who knows what I'd do?

Edward begrudgingly gives me two of his Tylenol #4's.

"Thank you. Will I see you and Eloise later?"

"I'll call you after the mall" is his reply. I would have preferred a simple "Yes". Driving back home, I chide myself for not thinking this chemical peel thing all the way through. Now I have to depend on Edward for pain pills. If I were one of my patients, I would have a prescription for Percocet and not need him. Oh, well, too damned late now.

I write bills, waiting for Edward's call, and try to not cry over my children. It doesn't work. I let a few tears fall and the salt in my tears burns my acid-burned face further. You know, Mary Ann, you were only thinking of the smooth end result and not how painful the first few days are.

Edward finally calls and asks me over to dinner. I gladly go to see Eloise and to check on Blair. I slept over. Oh, shit, I think when I first look at myself the following morning; I'm even redder and puffier today *and* in more pain! I definitely over did my peel without the blue tint. I basically gave myself almost second-degree burns without wanting to go that deep.

"Edward, can I have one of your stronger pain pills? My face is painful."

"Yeah, it looks it. Here is an Oxycontin, but go easy, they are very strong."

"I know. I took them when I had my abdominal surgery. I won't over do it."

I needed a sleeping pill to fall asleep that night. I had to do cataract surgery at Suburban Hospital and needed some real rest. I have never cost a patient any sight loss under my hands. I am eternally grateful for that blessing, especially because I did so many one-eyed patients in my residency and my very first year in private practice, that other doctors didn't want to touch with a ten-foot pole.

"One-eyed" means they have already lost sight in their other eye possibly from an old trauma, or glaucoma, or age-related macular degeneration or maybe were just born with one good eye. Truthfully, it takes balls to operate on a one-eyed patient. Obviously, if something goes wrong, even *out of my control*, for example a spontaneous intra-ocular hemorrhage at the time of surgery, the patient may never see again; it's all over; and who do you think the family wants to blame?

Plus, I had cancelled these two cataract patients the week before, because I indeed had the flu, thus didn't want to cancel them again. As I recall, for both of them it was their second eye, and they both had a very nice result with their first eye, so they were confident in me. I wasn't in pain Monday morning anymore, so I too felt confident and with my red face went to Suburban Hospital to operate.

I walked into the operating room waiting area with my still red and kind of scary face. I have no idea who did it and why (except my face was red, big deal, I'm going to wear a mask in the O.R. anyway), but someone called the Medical Director right away. The tiny new Medical Director, whom I had never had the displeasure of meeting, appeared instantly. Jeepers, I don't think he came up to my armpit, and he had the charm of a cobra. He said, "I'm Dr. Gruffini, the Medical Director. We want to draw your blood."

"Why?" I ask.

"You don't look normal" he states.

"I know, Dr. Gruffini. My face is red because I did a chemical peel on Friday. In two to three days, the skin will not be red and will be back to normal."

"I still would like you to come with me to draw your blood."

"All right." I still didn't know why he was doing this, but I was getting afraid. The pain medication I took is going to be in my blood and the Valium from Friday night. I still thought that I wasn't the first surgeon to operate with a little pain medication in them from back strain, neck pain, etc. And I didn't take any today, just yesterday.

I should have sprinted out of the closest exit.

"We are drawing your blood because there was a complaint that you smelled of alcohol," Dr. Gruffini bluntly states.

"I didn't have any alcohol, Dr. Gruffini." I allow them to draw my blood and then go back upstairs and talk to my first patient, Mrs. Hartzstein. I explain the situation to her. "Mrs. Hartzstein, I did a chemical peel on myself on Friday. I over-did it a little, but I am okay. Do I smell of alcohol to you? I'm a little late for your case because I was sent for blood work, because someone said they thought I smelled of alcohol." I leaned into her face so she could smell my breath.

"You don't smell like alcohol to me, Honey."

"I didn't think so, Mrs. Hartzstein. I didn't have any. I would hate to cancel your surgery again, but they may make me do it."

"Oh, dear."

"I promise you, Mrs. Hartzstein, if they make me cancel your surgery today, I will reschedule you on any day at any time you want."

Little did I know at that moment that I would never operate at Suburban Hospital again.

I had no idea that something like this could happen to me. My blood draw had every possible damning chemical in it to make me look like the biggest "druggie" of all time. There were three forms of pain medication, mine from my back pain, then the two different kinds from Edward's surgery including the Oxycontin. Oxycontin is basically pill form heroin, and probably the most expensive black market prescription pill ever. That was only the second time (and also the last time), that I ever had Oxycontin, the first being when I needed it after abdominal surgery and I told Dr. Gruffini exactly that.

Dr. Gruffini struts towards me like he's won some victory. "Dr. Duke, you have three forms of codeine in your blood, benzodiazepines (Valium) and some alcohol. You have to cancel both of your cases." I'm shocked. How did alcohol get in there? I think hard. Then I remember a half drunk glass of scotch next to the lazy boy I usually sit in at Edward's. Dear God, I must have had trouble sleeping, woke up in the night and drank half a drink and don't remember it from the Ambien.

What an absolute nightmare situation for a surgeon to be in. That weekend with the chemical peel "pick-me-up" turned out to be the worst possible thing that has ever happened to me as a doctor. Instead of a "pick-me-up" after losing in court, the peel completely ruined my reputation. If I didn't have bad luck, I certainly had no luck at all. Instead of a public malpractice case to tarnish my excellent reputation, I just needed to self-destruct myself.

One over done chemical peel and now everyone thinks I'm a pill popping druggie. Just what the doctor didn't order. I may be a binge drinker, and that gets me in a heap of trouble, but I am not a druggie.

The very next day I drove to Physicians' Rehab in Baltimore and volunteered my story. I told the head man, same man whom I had previously met, everything that happened, and I wanted him to see my face. I wasn't hiding anything and even told him about my children. My mental state was beyond depressed.

"Despairing in abject agony" is a more suitable description.

My cell phone rang on the way home from Baltimore.

"Hello, Dr. Duke? This is Dr. Gruffini."

"Yes?"

"Your case was discussed by the Executive Committee, and we have decided to offer you medical leave."

Wow, I paranoidly think, already? It was only twenty-four hours ago, and the big shots are already getting rid of me? I didn't know what "medical leave" meant, and I just thought they were terminating my privileges. Dr. Gruffini did not offer any explanation whatsoever. He was silent, not helpful *at all.* I made a too quick decision without thinking it through: I'm going to resign from Suburban. I always hated it there anyway, too many jealous nurses and too many good ole' boys. I'll just get privileges at some surgery center like most of the other ophthalmologists in the area use, and get rid of hospital "Peyton Place" politics once and for all.

I believe I was the first female ophthalmic surgeon on staff at Suburban Hospital in 1992. Over $4,000 in attorney's fees, way back then to fight to get in, because the men didn't want me to join *their* hospital. Both Shady Grove and Suburban made obtaining staff privileges as tough as possible. I was humiliated by having to be "proctored" (watched by another eye surgeon) for several surgeries. I don't know a male doctor who had to be watched; that is what residency is for!

In 1997, when I joined Johns Hopkins, it was a breeze. It is very basic to understand. The male ophthalmologists wanted to keep me out of the area hospitals I needed to use because I was local competition. Johns Hopkins didn't see me as competition but as a referral source and they gave me credit for being board-certified, published, and granted several awards. It's always about money. Always, and throw in a little chauvinism.

"I don't think I need to operate at Suburban again, Dr."

Dr. Gruffini's tone almost (but not quite) changed to cordial, "Okay, that's fine. We will need a letter of resignation from you. You can send it to the Medical Staff office." Click.

Without consulting an attorney, without consulting *anyone,* stupidly, I sent a letter.

In the interim, I obtained privileges at a nice surgery center and operated on my two waiting cataract patients. A short time after I sent in my resignation letter I talked to one of my Hopkins' ophthalmology buddies. He told me the cold, hard fact that I had forgotten, but should have remembered. If a doctor resigns from a hospital staff while the hospital is investigating that doctor for *anything,* the hospital has the right to turn that doctor in to the National Practitioners' Data Bank as an adverse action, and that doctor's reputation will be tarnished forever. Just like that. Instead of a perfect record with no malpractice suits filed whatsoever or anything negative at all, a hospital turning me in like this will be damaging and stuck to me forever like a scarlet "A" branded on my chest. The Data Bank's record can hinder me getting hospital privileges elsewhere in the future and possibly keep me off insurance plans. With my luck, it'll even make my malpractice insurance go up.

I immediately call Dr. Gruffini as soon as I hung up with my colleague and politely state, "I will be very grateful to accept the Executive Committee's offer for medical leave from Suburban. I am coming over with a letter rescinding my resignation right now, please. Thank you; see you soon."

I still don't know what medical leave will entail. I'm sure I will probably have to have my blood drawn regularly at my own expense, who knows, maybe attend some outpatient rehab deal on my own dollar, too. I'll probably have to jump through a thousand hoops, but anything is better than tarnishing my perfect reputation with some negative report to the National Practitioner Data Bank, as was adamantly insisted would happen by my Hopkins' colleague.

Suburban Hospital is just a few miles from my office. I scratched a few sentences on a piece of my stationery and was in Dr. Gruffini's office in no more than fifteen minutes.

"Dr. Gruffini is not in" his secretary said crisply. I'm surprised and tell her, "I just spoke to him, Ma'am, and said I was on my way with an important letter. I need to get back to patients. Do you know where he went?"

"You can leave the envelope with me, and I'll give it to him."

Something about her tone didn't make me feel comfortable doing that, so I repeated myself, "It is important that I see Dr. Gruffini briefly. Do you happen to know where he went, *please?*"

The secretary sighs and says, "I think he went to the Medical Staff office."

"Thank you," and I rush down the hall.

I burst into the Medical Staff office, and there is Dr. Gruffini directing one of the secretaries on the computer. "Good afternoon, Dr. Gruffini. Here is my letter rescinding my resignation."

Dr. Gruffini ignores me and keeps on directing the secretary to "Enter this, and enter that….Okay. That looks good." After several minutes he finally turns away from the computer and matter-of-factly states, "It's too late. We have already sent you to the National Practitioner Data Bank."

I feel like I'd been slapped. "But I told you I was coming over with a letter," and my voice trails off. I'm stunned, because all of a sudden it hits me. Dr. Gruffini ignored me, because he was having that secretary enter *me* into the computer. He just scurried over to the Medical Staff office when he knew I was coming over, to make sure I got my black mark before I could give him my letter.

Sure enough. When the National Practitioner Data Bank sent me my copy of my damaging report from Suburban Hospital, it was dated the exact day I was there. You know the old saying, "Just because you're paranoid doesn't mean the bastards *aren't* trying to get you down." Just a few days before Christmas, 2003.... Merry Christmas, Mary Ann.

The surgery center got the report, too, and politely dumped me even after I had scheduled more cataract patients at their facility. I had to give those surgery patients away. Oh well, at least the two devoted patients of mine that were cancelled twice at Suburban were completed before I got dropped and both came out 20/20. My grand finale to cataract surgery.

Thanks a lot, Dr. Gruffini, for being so gracious and *not* taking just a couple of minutes to explain "medical leave" to me during your first phone call and then slithering away so fast to type me in to the National Practitioner Data Bank when you knew I was on my way over. Would all two-and-one-half inches (oops!), I mean, five-feet of you have had the balls to do that to me if I was a man?

Chapter 19

WHY?

    I know I was drinking too much. I know my drinking chardonnay went up, up and away during my "War of the Roses" divorce. Dieter is telling everyone that my drinking is the reason he filed for divorce. I think my drinking increased the year we separated when I met Edward who drinks a lot daily. My reason for divorcing Dieter is because he lied to me many times, and I don't want to grow old with someone who doesn't tell the truth. Dieter never ever sat down and explained to me why he wanted a divorce. Maybe his reason for filing is something very basic like he just fell out of love with me or never really did love me. Whatever, that ship has sailed. My dad once summed up Dieter when he spoke to Dieter's mom on the phone. Dad said, "Dieter should have married a Saudi Arabian princess, then maybe he could get everything he thinks he deserves".

    Anyone who has been through a divorce knows full well that marriages do not die over night and are rarely blamed on just one party.

    My attorney told me about Father Martin Ashley's 28-day rehabilitation center. I was going to miss my children and a full month's earning in the office, but I needed to go. I truthfully wanted to get away from my $400/week shrink and get off my medication roller coaster as much as I wanted to be alcohol free. It was not court ordered at all. It was my own decision. I also had enough of the Board's constant harassment about my children, then about Suburban, paperwork, shrink appointments, Lithium levels, med changes, etc. All that crap would be gone for awhile if I went to rehab.

Father Martin's is a beautiful facility in Havre de Grace, MD with a magnificent view of the Chesapeake Bay with sailboats and sunshine and even a nice place to run, and I *hated every single minute of it.* My mom and dad paid for it out of their precious retirement account. I will always be grateful to them for that. I certainly didn't have a dime, much less $18,000 for 28 days of rehab after my divorce. I've refinanced my home twice in two years, to take money out to pay Dieter off, and am still drowning in debt.

I vow after those 28 days, "I will *never* drink again." I also vow if I ever have to say "The Serenity Prayer" more than once a day, exception being an AA meeting, I am going to scream!

That's all rehab is about, finding serenity so one does not feel the need to "use" alcohol or drugs. People are making millions writing books about rehab. Rehab is first a potentially life-saving detoxification process especially for abusing alcohol. The withdrawal from cocaine, marijuana and any kind of pain pills, including Oxycontin, and even from heroin is not life threatening. The drugs that are prescribed in rehab do make any form of withdrawal more palatable. The Basics of Rehab are:

1. *Forced abstinence from one's drug of choice.*

2. Forced lectures about any and all drugs that can be addictive.

3. Forced AA/NA meetings. (Alcoholics Anonymous/Narcotics Anonymous, overall the NA meetings were much livelier.)

4. Forced living quarters with other sick/weirdo supposed addicts who hate rehab more than you.

5. Forced dining of okay tasting, however, very nutritious food with people who don't feel like eating. (And last but not least.)

6. Forced repeating "God Grant Me The Serenity To Accept The Things I Cannot Change, Courage To Change The Things I Can, And The Wisdom To Know The Difference" at least fifty fucking times a day.

That's all there is to it, almost $1,000/day for that. Everyone should try it. Maybe I can get a license to put one in my back yard. Potomac could benefit from such a facility, and it sure would rake in a lot more cash treating addicts than seeing regular patients. Rehab is a piece of cake when all is said and done because one's *forced* into abstinence.

The hard part is not going back to one's old ways, once back in the stress of the real world.

Some great doctor needs to come up with a pill that stops addicts from craving and abusing alcohol and drugs. That doctor should then win the Nobel prize and be given enough millions to retire well, because the sale of that pill will put Prozac, Viagra, Valium, pain killers, and birth control pills all put together to crying shame. Many people think addiction is the new number 1 problem in America, probably in the world.... IT IS! Whether one is addicted to drugs, sex, money, power, alcohol, gambling, pleasure, food or any combination thereof.

*   *   *

Dieter never brought our three children to visit me even once while I was at Father Martin's.

Edward picked me up on my last day of rehab in September 2004 with cute little two-year-old Eloise in her car seat. I am higher than a kite to be out. I give my ninety-two pound roommate named Kristin (who can still tip back at least a fifth of vodka a day) a big hug. Then I hug Tony, our funny, short Italian buddy, who lives with some Baltimore Ravens' football players twice his size, and their drink of choice is vodka/Gatorade. Either one of them could drink me under the table and into the pavement. Tony has five DUI's and came to rehab to avoid jail. Kristin is independently wealthy, and simply has too much loneliness and time to drink. I'm sure Kristin and Tony are going to date when they get out. "Bye guys, hang in there, I'll be in touch!" I yell to them as I start running towards Edward and Eloise.

It's a beautiful fall day, crisp and clear. We have the windows down and the sunroof open. This is absolutely the happiest and the best I've felt in years. No alcohol for four weeks certainly helps. We start down the long driveway out of Father Martin's, and I'm not looking back.

I'm allowed happiness for five glorious minutes.

We're not even off the property when Edward blankly says, "Brace yourself."

"What?" I quickly turn and look at his handsome profile but he doesn't look over at me, just keeps staring down the road. He looks very serious, and I immediately think something dreadful has happened.

"What? What's wrong?" I feel my heart pounding fast.

"Just brace yourself."

"Okay, okay, tell me already!" My first thought is that someone died or is ill. I quickly flip around and look at Eloise; she looks fine, just contentedly sucking her thumb.

"Did someone die?"

"No... you were robbed." All I do is stare at him with my mouth open, too shocked to speak. I actually could not believe his words.

"Robbed?... I was robbed?!"

"Yes."

"Oh my God!" I feel instantly like I want to vomit, anxious, afraid to find out what was stolen and what really happened. Afraid to know how much I lost, then I *really* worried.

"Did they ransack the office? Is my office okay?" I have a beautiful home/office, a perfect set up that I'm sure most of the doctors in the area would like or are envious of.

"Were they looking for drugs? I only have eye drops!"

"I don't think they even went into the office. The door was still locked between the house and the office," Edward replies.

Now, I become even more of a nervous wreck when I think of what some careless thieves could do to my beautiful home. My heart is pounding right out of my chest.

"What *did* they steal?!"

"All of your jewelry."

"Did they find my Baba's garnets? Did they steal them, too?!" I scream at Edward.

"Yes." I am too mortified to talk. I close my eyes and try not to think, but it doesn't work. The memory of all of Baba's precious garnets pops right up in my brain like a photograph. Edward drives and thankfully left the radio off so I can think in peace.

I *LOVE* jewelry. I love jewelry more than food, more than alcohol, even more than men,… sometimes. I owned enough jewelry for ten little girls to inherit and was looking forward to giving mine all away to my three girls when they grew old enough to appreciate it. It wasn't because I "wanted to keep up with the Joneses'" at all. I collected jewelry simply because it was shiny and pretty and my dear Baba instilled a love for it in me.

All I did every weekend for my first ten years in the D.C. area was go to estate sales and buy some ignorant somebody's grandmother's jewelry at ten, twenty or even five cents on the dollar. It was my favorite thing to do, treasure and bargain hunting on the weekend. I went every weekend right up until I had my third child in four years. Then the logistics of maneuvering three babies up and down staircases, with crowds of people, diapers, and bottles, just got to be too much.

I had scads of gorgeous, antique, you-name-it, pearls of every color, diamonds, rubies, sapphires, emeralds, platinum, rose gold, white and yellow gold anything and everything from hair clips and earrings, necklaces and rings, right on down to ankle bracelets. I'd rather buy jewelry than clothe myself any day of the week. And none of it was insured, only a very few pieces, because I had bought them so cheap. Why pay $45 dollars to have something insured that I only paid $90 for? (Because it would have been appraised for over $1,200, Mary Ann, and now this.) So many, many pieces of jewelry I owned like that, antique, one of a kind. On top of that, Blair had been giving me an outstanding piece of his late wife's gorgeous collection almost every week, trying to make me feel better after losing custody of my children. I should have run to Bailey, Banks and Biddle in the mall for a weekly appraisal, but I was too busy working all day and then drinking in the evening, a vain attempt to ease the pain of missing my children.

"*All* of it?!"

"Yes, everything from your jewelry boxes." I feel violated, almost like being stabbed, and am bleeding too fast. I burst out crying and lean back in my seat, just letting the tears stream down my face.

"What about the alarm?"

"They were pros; it never went off."

"It has a battery back up. Why didn't *it* go off?"

Edward finally turns and looks at me now, hands me a pile of tissues and repeats, "They were professionals. They cut all of the power to the house and phone lines, and the bastards got to the alarm box before the battery backup could go off."

"But that's only twenty seconds."

"I told you, they were pros. Many homes were hit in seven days. (Turns out to be only three in all of Montgomery County.) It was on the news. The F.B.I. is working on it."

"Oh my God" is all I can respond through my tears. "So they got into my jewelry box in the locked closet in the bedroom?" Smarty me keeps my jewelry locked in a closet with a deadbolt to keep it from the cleaning ladies. The thieves probably went straight for it!

"Yes."

"When did this happen?"

"About two weeks ago."

"*Two weeks* ago! Why didn't you tell me?!"

"Everyone didn't want you to leave rehab."

"Did they take anything else?"

"I don't know."

"I keep *everything* in my closet! All of my credit cards, home equity line checks, everything! I needed to cancel everything immediately! The thieves can have run up several hundred thousand more! You should have told me right away!"

"We all wanted you to finish rehab."

Bang! Why did this have to happen?

Just like that, my natural high from leaving rehab is dashed away, gone, gone forever. I lost about $250,000 worth of jewelry, who knows how much it would have all really appraised for, but at least that and I only had four pieces insured totaling under $20,000. One solace was the thieves didn't take Baba's costume jewelry.

After getting home to coffee stains all over my off white bedroom carpet, the bastard thieves even drank coffee while they stole, having to cancel all of the credit cards they took, $100,000 of home equity line checks, stolen savings bonds, stolen passport and social security card, opening a month's worth of mail and *bills*, who knows how they will get paid? Then filling out police reports with over six hundred valuables, those that I remembered, for both the local police and the F.B.I., meet with the F.B.I. and look at 1,200 pictures of unique jewelry, not one picture matching any of mine, and trying to catch up on a month's worth of business in the office and patient demands, I lost my resolve.

I drank the drink Edward poured for me.

*   *   *

Only two months after rehab, on November 10, 2004 I remember having another fierce fight with Edward, but I don't recall how it started. Probably the way our arguments always started, after a few drinks. Very, very stupidly, I got in my car in a total blackout and drove off. That was my first drunk driving charge in my life and it sure was a "doozy".

I was arrested for everything but the kitchen sink. Seven tickets. "DUI, DWI, attempting to elude the police, failure to drive right of center, reckless and negligent driving", "Failure to stop after unattended property damage" (took out a few mail boxes), to be arrested and handcuffed in a complete blackout. The police report said I even tapped the police cruiser as I fled. What a nightmare.

How humiliating, Dr. Duke handcuffed and hauled away in a police car, and I don't remember a single second of it. I don't remember getting into my car. For God's sake, if I was even half in my right mind, I never would have driven. Upon coming to, in the Emergency Room, the first person I focus on is a man in uniform, a police officer, and I remember wondering, "Why is *he* here? Where the hell am I and why am I in restraints"?

Beautiful, Mary Ann, you just needed a corpse. But thanks to God Almighty, I didn't hurt anyone. But I disappointed myself, my children, my whole family, my patients, everyone.

Chapter 20

Persevering Can Be Painful

The August 30th robbery is not an excuse for a relapse. Even if my parents had both died in a fatal accident is not an excuse to get drunk. I realize that...*now*. But relapses occur with most people who drink or use drugs. It doesn't justify them, but it's the "nature of the beast". Addiction is a deadly disease. It's like a malignant cancer; one can go into remission, but it can always come back.

I could easily have had a fatal car accident with that first DUI on November 10th, 2004; however, I needed to be wide-awake for another nightmare in that hateful November, on the very last day of the month, the 30th. Exactly three months from the day I was robbed while away at rehab trying to get better. Not as awful a daily nightmare as living with losing custody of my children, but a tragedy indeed.

My first arrest for drunk driving can still be turned into a "Peanut Butter and Jelly", the Wizard calls it, which stands for "Probation Before Judgment". A "PB&J" for a first offense means no jail time, just probation. I hadn't gone to court yet; it was only two weeks since my arrest and the office phone rings.

Judy covers the receiver and wide-eyed whispers, "It's the "Board. It sounds very official." Judy quickly passes me her phone.

"Hello, this is Dr. Duke. May I help you?"

This is Ms. Kranekey, the Compliance Analyst for the Maryland Medical Board, and we want to come to your office and talk to you on November 30th at 10:30. We want to talk to you about rehabilitation." I roll my eyes at Judy. Ms. Kranekey is not one of my favorite people. I've met her before and disliked her condescending attitude, basically a "Napoleoness/female Napoleon".

"Could you, please, hold for a minute while I check my schedule?"

"Fine," she responds. "Thank you," I quickly say. (You know what I think of every time I hear that word: Fucking, Insecure, Neurotic and Emotional.) Good choice of words, Kranekey, that's exactly how I've been feeling.

Judy is nodding her head vigorously up and down meaning "Give her what she wants".

"That would be a good day for me, too," like the Board gave me a choice, *not!*

"Good day, Dr.", and Ms. Kranekey abruptly hung up without even asking for directions. Well, I certainly wasn't going to call her back. I think "Kranekey probably has a broom with GPS".

I take a deep breath, give Judy a nod and point at the time and date in the appointment book. She writes it down. Heaven forbid I forget *that* appointment.

"Okay, F.I.N.E.", I think, as I walk into the house for a glass of juice. I'll go back to rehab if the Board wants me to. It'll be true torture, especially with the holidays coming up, but I'll go back if I have to. No problem. I'll do whatever they want; I resolve in my head. I have worked way too many years and way too hard to lose my medical license over a DUI. How did the Board even find out about it so fast? Who called them?

I wonder if the Board will help me pay for a forced second rehab in six months? Maybe if I ask the Board for some financial aid, you know, just donate $10,000, maybe half, they will help me. It's for a worthy cause; I'm an excellent ophthalmologist that the State of Maryland should be proud of.

Yeah right, Mary Ann, the Board won't help you with a nickel. All you need, Dukie, is to have a reversible sex change; get a quick law degree so you can represent yourself, to save money on attorneys' fees, then change back to Mommy. Too bad that's not yet possible, but then again, I think it is!

*   *   *

The phone rings again within hours. Judy answers and pipes "It's the Medical Director's secretary of Johns Hopkins Hospital!" I grab the phone.

"Hello?" All of a sudden I'm afraid and a chill goes down my spine.

"Dr. Duke?"

"Yes, this is she."

"This is the Medical Director's office of Johns Hopkins Hospital calling. He requested that I call you to set up a meeting on November 30th with him and the President of the Medical Staff."

I feel numb, not just a chill went down my spine, but more like a stun gun zapped me. First, the Board calls, and now my favorite hospital to operate at, Johns Hopkins. This does not sound like good news at all. Why would the two biggest big shots want to speak with me except to bear more bad news? Think positive, Mary Ann, maybe they just want you to go to rehab, too.

"What time would the doctors like me to be there?

"Is 8:00 a.m. all right?"

"Fine, I'll be there."

"I can fax you directions to the Medical Director's office."

I give her my fax number and barely remember to say "Thank you" and "Good bye."

I immediately call Blair and don't even say hello because I'm feeling agitated and worried. "Blair, do you have a doctor's appointment on November 30th? If you do, can you cancel it and go with me to Johns Hopkins? I need you to come with me. It's important!" I rush the words out.

"What's the matter, Dear? You sound quite harried."

"I am. Can you come to a meeting with me?"

"Yes, I believe I can."

"Thank you very much Blair! I appreciate this! We have to leave no later than 6:30 in the morning."

"Okay, do call down. Where is this bloody early meeting?"

"At Hopkins. It's some meeting with the Medical Director and the Chairman of the Medical Staff!"

"What do they want to meet with you for?" Blair asks calmly.

"I don't know. Thank you again. I'll call you later. Bye!" I definitely need Blair to go with me. I need his eighty-six years of wisdom, his 6'4" height, royal British accent and prime minister like presence. Not much fazes Blair. I need his support, *and* I want a witness for this meeting.

*   *   *

November 30th my alarm blares at 5:45 a.m., an ungodly hour to rise. I quickly shower and put on my best suit. Blair, as always is on time, while I'm a few minutes late.

"It's a little weird; don't you think Blair? That I have two meetings on the same day?"

"Possibly a coincidence."

"I'm not so sure" I firmly state as I press the accelerator.

Traffic on the 495 Beltway and Interstate 95, beautiful, gotta love it, the absolute worst traffic in the country. I'm going to be late yet again, so am speeding just a "wee bit" to get there on time.

"Blair, why do you think the big shots at Johns Hopkins want to meet with me?"

"I don't know, Darling, but you had bloody well slow down!"

Somehow, Blair and I arrive on time, luckily aided by his handicapped-parking pass.

The usual handshakes and pleasant greetings. Both men appear in their sixties and very nice, but I still want a witness, "Can Mr. Everett-Monroe, please, come in with me?" I politely ask.

"No" almost in unison. ... Damn. "Why not"? I ask myself. I should have brought a hidden tape recorder like I've done so many times before, got some great C.Y.A. (cover your ass) tapes in my collection, but I really thought they would let Blair come in with me.

I'm in for it, a barrage of questions regarding my "consumption of alcohol". I answer them all truthfully, told these two strangers about my extremely difficult divorce, robbery, rehab, relapse, DUI, everything. I also say, "I am so very proud of my privilege to work at Johns Hopkins, extremely proud. I am an excellent, caring physician. I have never harmed a patient, never been sued, not even close. And that's a pretty big thing for any doctor in the D.C. area to say with its super high concentration of attorneys. I have been in practice over fourteen years, and the average physician gets sued every seven, so I'm *way* overdue. Also, because I practice in Potomac, I call it the "Beverly Hills" of Washington. It's where all of the lawyers live! Every one of my patients either *is* an attorney or is *married* to an attorney or at the very least, *knows* a good one! It's pretty amazing I have never been sued over something stupid, really pretty amazing!" Both men smile for the first time.

"Thank you for your candor, Dr. Duke, we truly appreciate your honesty. Could you please leave the room and sit outside with Mr. Monroe for a minute while we discuss this?"

"Oh,… sure, of course." I walk out to where Blair is sitting.

Blair looks concerned. He wrinkles his brow, "What's the matter Dear?"

"I think they are going to kick me off of the staff!"

"You what? Why?!"

"I don't know why."

Several minutes pass until I am called back in. "I'm sorry, Dr. Duke, but we have to suspend your privileges."

"Why?"

"I'm sorry, but we just have no choice." Then they give me the name of somebody somewhere that monitors physicians who have had their privileges suspended and told me to contact him. I scribble it down. They didn't even have his business card for me.

Who cares, I just start crying, but I shake both of their hands and tell them as tears are pouring down my face, "I very much hope that my privileges will be reinstated in the very near future. It has very much been an honor and a privilege to work at the Johns Hopkins Hospital".

I manage a small smile and leave the room. "C'mon Blair, let's get out of here!"

I whimper to him. "They did it Blair. They took away my privileges." Blair stares at me in surprise and hands me his handkerchief. Then I plop down next to him and just cry, who *cares* who sees me, I'm not coming back here for a while.

"You can drive home, Blair, I'm too upset. But step on it. I can't be late for the Maryland Board people either, at 10:30." So I let the eighty-six-year-old-one-eyed bandit Brit drive back.

*   *   *

It's an hour from Johns Hopkins in Baltimore to Potomac without traffic. By the time we get to my office I am composed with brand new eye make-up and lipstick. Good thing, because there is Mrs. Biche, one of my more demanding patients, who just happened to pop in with a hundred questions, that my poor new office manager can't possibly answer. On top of everything, Judy had quit.

Back to my patient, Mrs. Biche, the one and only negative to practicing in an affluent area is that the patients are more demanding than average. Patients with money on the whole (but most certainly not all of them) tend to be more educated than the average "Joe Schmoe", thus have a lot more questions.

While I'm under interrogation, now by Mrs. Biche, Ms. Kranekey and another terse-faced woman from the Maryland Medical Board enter the waiting room. I politely interrupt Mrs. Biche for a second and address Ms. Kranekey, "Are you on a time schedule? Do you want me to resume my meeting with my patient at another time?" Why not, it's not like Mrs. Biche had an appointment, she just showed up. It's Potomac. Patients drop in on their schedule, not necessarily on mine.

Ms. Kranekey is in a perfect little suit, with her perfect make-up job, must admit she does do a great lip liner, and with her perfect pucker quips, "Oh no, you're *fine*, finish with your patient."

"Thank you. Now what were you saying, Mrs. Biche?"

Blah, blah, blah. "Oh my, really? Well, why don't you try this?" Blah, blah. "Yes, just like that. You are absolutely right. I agree. Here are some free samples, yes, your welcome, *no*, thank *you*." And she left with enough samples of dry eye teardrops for her entire family and friends.

Thank God. I'm on my very best behavior because "Patience" is not my middle name, and Mrs. Biche was really trying mine, but the "Board" was in attendance, so I am traveling above and beyond gracious, somewhere to "I'm starting to kiss your ass and I never ever do that" planet.

I really can't stand Ms. Kranekey's perfect pompous pout, but I'm not going to let her get to me, even though I'm tired from the Johns Hopkins' ordeal, and my ungodly hour of awakening. No way, so I give her a big, bright smile and a nice hard handshake. "Hello, may I help you?"

"Yes, Dr. Duke this is my associate, Mrs. Smugg." (Perfect name, matches her face.) Mrs. Smugg gets the same big smile and strong handshake. "Nice to meet you, Mrs. Smugg." She returns my smile with her vain attempt at a "Mona Lisa".

"What can I do for you today?" I politely inquire.

This mission is for Ms. Kranekey, she's the Board's scud missile, seems to me like Mrs. Smugg is just a foot soldier, standing there mute, waiting for a command.

"We are here today as representatives from the Board and we need to have you sign some papers, and we need you to surrender some items to us."

"Excuse me, but you told me that you were coming here today to talk to me about rehabilitation."

"Who told you that?"

"*You* told me that on the phone." Ms. Kranekey frowns at me like I'm a little child who has displeased her. I ignore her frown and look back at her expectantly.

"We need you to surrender your original Maryland medical license."

"Hang on a minute here, Ms. Krankey, you specifically told me that you were coming to discuss rehabilitation, so why don't we *do that*?"

"We did not come all of the way out here to discuss rehabilitation with you, Dr. Duke. I have an order from the Board to suspend your Maryland medical license," she announces loudly. She doesn't even look up at me, because she's furiously digging with her pile of papers until she finds the one she wants and thrusts it at me.

If I was a violent person, thankfully I'm not, I would have strangled her scrawny neck with my bare hands until she was dark blue, and I knew she was good and dead. Instead, I read the paper in front of me:

It reads: ORDERED that on presentation of this Order, the Respondent SHALL SURRENDER to the Board's investigator the following items:

1   Her original Maryland License D38796;

2   Her current renewal certificate;

3   DEA Certificate of Registration BD7503729;

4   Maryland Controlled Dangerous Substance Registration M78301;

5   All controlled dangerous substances in her possession and/or practice;

6   All Medical Assistance prescription forms;

7   All prescription forms and pads in her possession and/or practice; and

8   Any and all prescription pads on which her name and DEA number are imprinted; and be it further ORDERED that a copy of this Order of Summary Suspension...............

I have read enough............... And be it further ordered by Dr. Duke that the Maryland Medical Board is a lying sack of shit, and they can kiss my royal "DUKE" ass.

The Board lied to me, plain and simple. Ms. Kranekey's eyebrows are reaching for her hairline.

"Excuse me?" I inquire.

"Your medical license."

"I thought you were coming here to talk to me about *rehabilitation*!" I JUST CANNOT BELIEVE THIS IS HAPPENING!!!

"No, the Board wants your medical license for the *unforeseeable future.*"

The Maryland Medical Board stabs me in the back and kills a part of me, kills a wonderful part of me forever. They totally annihilate my cherished belief that Medicine is fair and ethical, finally, finally, once and for all. No more naïveté. This is real. I give Ms. Kranekey my license to practice medicine in the State of Maryland off of the wall. I gather everything together for her as fast as I can. I simply can't stand the smug smiles on these two women. Even with a hangover from hell, my brain is faster than the two of theirs put together. I want these two Board patrolers to get the hell out of my office and off of my damned property as soon as possible!

I really can't believe this! Hopkins at 8:00 a.m. and now this at 11:00! This is the worst God damned fucking morning of my life! They are taking my whole life's work away from me! Stealing my life from me, stealing what I LOVE. I LOVE being Dr. Duke, and my patients LOVE ME! This is an OUTRAGE! I've never ever done anything to harm a patient in any way. If anything, I'm going the extra mile and diagnosing problems other doctors would have missed, because I actually STUDIED in Medical School and I know and remember A LOT about the whole damned body! I'm a great Doctor, I never miss anything, I even CARE!! I LOVE HELPING PEOPLE!!!

"How long until I can appeal this?" Mrs. Smugg is already loading my "stuff", only everything I need to practice medicine, into their car. What a stupid little foot soldier she is, couldn't she at least have had the brains and the decency to take my medical license out of its beautiful lacquer frame and given me my frame back?! I just want them to go. Ms. Kranekey is loving this, her little power trip. Good for you, I bitch to myself, I rather prefer to enjoy sex, than watching someone get put down. She hands me a stack of papers. "This is your copy," she chimes, like it's some sort of Christmas present.

"Excuse me for a second, please," I say as I turn abruptly. "I'll be right back." Then I run up the two steps into my home with the papers and scream softly at Blair, "Could you please look at these?"

I calmly walk back through the door to my office and ask "Are you finished?"

"Yes, just please sign here and here and here, thank you very much."

Yeah, I think in my head, thank you and fuck you for ruining my life, but instead I smile at both women and say, "I'll have my attorney call the Board this afternoon, this is obviously a mistake." They both give me a smug smile and leave.

"Remember to cancel your patients!" Ms. Kranekey yells out the window as they whisk away like two damned witches from the west on their dirty brooms.

I certainly could have used a second chance at rehab instead of a back stabbing loss of licensure.

I give my new office manager the rest of the day off after she calls and cancels the day's patients. Like always, I was planning on working the afternoon, even after Hopkins and the Board. "Please remember to put the answering machine on; I'll see you tomorrow" is all I can say.

I slowly walk into the house. Blair turns and stares at me. He is standing by the window to get good light for his one good eye and looks like he just finished reading. His face is redder than ever, and he looks shocked, wide eyed and staring again at me. Blair has only one comment, only one, and in his beautiful accent exclaims, "This is *absolutely Draconian!"* (Like Draco, the Greek Athenian ruler remembered for his overly severe punishments.)

"Great description Blair. Just great. Been one ***hell** of a morning, huh?!"* I'm starting to have a total body quiver, probably from the immense amount of adrenaline that must be pumping out from a full morning of total mental devastation.

"Blair? How am I supposed to pay my $8,063/month mortgage and support my family? How am I supposed to *eat?!* You know I don't have any money in the bank and barely 30G's in retirement after my damned divorce, just debt! I have to call my attorney; this is outrageous. It *must* be a mistake! They weren't coming to talk to me about rehab *at all*! The Board blatantly lied to me! Can you believe that? Oh look, it's noon already, well, I guess I've got the rest of the day off."

I must call my attorney, but first I'm rummaging in the refrigerator. I thought I had one in the bottom drawer. "Oh, here it is. Would you like a nice cold glass of French chardonnay? I'm having one with or without you!"…

"Yes, Dear, please, I need one too."

Chapter 21

Out of Control

December 2004 is a complete blur. I escape into alcohol after taking the Board bullet. I hire a doctor to help me in the office. I have to have someone to work in the office, my lawyer and faithful patient for over ten years, David Goldstein, advises me. "Dukie", he always calls me, "Dukie, hire someone to work in the office because *you need to eat* and pay your mortgage, and we haven't had a hearing before the board yet, so we really don't know how long this suspension is going to be. So get someone in the office as soon as possible so you don't lose all of your patients!"

"Okay, Davie, okay, I'm on it!" I love Davie, he reminds me of my Baba, just in the male form with coke-bottle glasses. Like Baba, he's as round as he is tall, and every ounce of him gives off positive energy and compassion, just like she did. He makes me laugh too, a real rarity in an attorney, especially because he doesn't charge me for our bullshitting time.

I have a female doctor in the office within a week. She works all of two days then sends me this letter, after a brief phone message, "I can't work for you anymore".

"Dear Dr. Duke,

I was contacted today by the Maryland Board of Physicians in connection with the services that I provided to your patients at your office on December 6 and 8, 2004.

The Board informed me that your medical license had been suspended and that, therefore, your office should not bill nor accept payment for any services rendered during the suspension period, including the two dates mentioned above.

The Board requested that I write you this letter and suggested I indicate to you that you are not authorized to use my provider numbers in the billing from your office and to please inform me if you have already done so.

Yours truly,

Gotsum Pasta, M.D."

What? Que pasa? Of course, my office manager used her provider numbers; we certainly knew we couldn't use mine! The big bad billing is gone to the insurance companies within 48 hours, because I never get paid for at least another 30 days, so of course it already went out! What are they doing to me now? Am I just supposed to leave my good patients high and dry?! The phone is still ringing; patients are asking to see *me!* Am I just supposed to tell them I'll call them back in the *"unforeseeable future"?*

What am I going to do? The phone is ringing off the hook, for regular eye exams, contact lens refills, potential Lasik candidates, everything. I can't be unavailable for the holidays forever! I think, as I hang up the phone, "That's the second or third time I've put off Mrs. Reenkal for Botox". (I am answering my own phone now. Who can afford an office manager with no income?) Hmmm, what's the big deal? One doesn't even have to be an M.D. to administer Botox injections. Before the manufacturer caught on to it, nurses were ordering it themselves and having "Botox Parties" in their living rooms.

It's not like it's rocket science or even close to being surgery for that matter. It's harder to start a good I.V. than it is to give Botox. It's not like I'm doing an eye exam and handing out a prescription. I don't want to waste the bottle; the damn thing costs almost $500.00. I really need the money. I'll call Mrs. Reenkal back and tell her I'll do her Botox whenever she wants. It's not like I'm "practicing medicine"; it's just a little Botox.

On January 24^{th,} I finally gave Mrs. Reenkal a little Botox. No big deal… Well, it turned out to be a very big deal. Wrong move, I put myself right into checkmate. Should have called Davie first, but I truthfully didn't think I was practicing medicine, since non-nurses do it in doctor's offices, and the doctor never even sees the patient. Well, *someone called* the Board, told them I gave her Botox, and within a week I was delivered a "Cease and Desist Order". Cease and desist, great, now I'm charged with "Violation of the Order for Summary Suspension".

"This conduct also constitutes the unauthorized practice of medicine, in violation of the Board's Order for Summary Suspension and of H.O. & 14-601 and H.O. & 14-602, for which she is subject to penalties pursuant to H.O.& 14-607." What the fuck is this?! Doesn't sound too good, "Cease and Desist". Maybe I should just "Cease and Decease". The Board would probably approve of that, since what they've done to me is slowly killing me anyway.

"Davie?" Thank God, Davie answers right away.

"Yes, Dukie?"

"What the hell is wrong *now*?" I ask him.

"Dukie, what did you do?"

"I just did a little Botox, used up my last bottle. Botox isn't "practicing medicine".

"To the Board it is, Dukie, and that's all that counts now. Do not do *anything,* nothing at all. Listen, I'll take care of it. I got our hearing date. It's April 6th."

"*APRIL?*"

"Yes."

"Davie, what am I supposed to do until April with all of my bills?" Pause. "This is outrageous! I'd better get a fucking good paying job, and fast! Oh my God, I'm so stressed out!"

"Well, don't drink Dukie."

"Yeah, right, I've got to find someone else to work in the office, and just pray the Board doesn't scare them off, too. The phone is still ringing; I've transferred it to my cell since I let my office manager go."

"It's going to be okay, Dukie, hang in there, just don't do anything else in the office without calling me first."

"Okay, Davie, sure, bye."

Gee, the sun's out and it's raining. There must be a rainbow somewhere. Maybe if I run fast over to the bottom of it, I'll find the pot of gold. Better hurry and get to it first, since there aren't any leaves on the trees in the backyard yet. Oh, Jesus, Mary Ann, you *really are* losing your mind this time. This is for real! No screwing around anymore. Get a job *now*! You're going to be out of credit card space by summer. Oh God, don't make me sell my home and my practice. It's all I have left. Help me God, please.

I call Tony from rehab. That little lucky guy was making over $200,000/year as a surgical sales representative, and had bragged in rehab that he only shows up in the O.R. to sell equipment three days a week. I can handle that, in a heartbeat. First time I talk to him since rehab, "Hi Tony baby, it's Mary Ann. How are you doing? Have you heard from Kristin, my old roommate?"

"She's right here, would you like to talk to her?"

"Ha, ha, ha," I can't help but laugh with him. I knew they were going to date when they got out, even though they live four hours apart.

They put me on speaker phone and Kristin is screaming, "Mary Ann, how *are* you?!"

Short pause, "Pretty shitty, Kristin," and I recap as briefly as I can, *everything*... "Life sucks right now, but can you believe I still have my driver's license? The day my Beemer (BMW) came out of the shop, I'm back on the road! But, I can't be a doctor anymore to pay for gas! This isn't just a social call. I need to talk to Tony about getting a job, or I'll *have* to sell my home/office and probably start working at Starbuck's; I heard they give health insurance. But tell me, how are you Kristin? Are you staying sober?"

"Are you *kidding me*?! I was so sick of that fucking rehab; I drank on the way home! Tony and I are splitting one of those big bottles of merlot right now!"

Wow. That was the very first time I ever heard Kristin swear, and I lived with her for almost four weeks. Guess she hated rehab, too, but she drank her first day out? So much for sobriety. What'd she waste $18,000.00 on rehab for if she wasn't even *planning* to stay off the bottle? Tony yells, "Duke! Listen, get on the web and go to med reps.com. You can send your resume on the internet to hundreds of jobs, and here's the name of my head hunter in Baltimore." I write the name and number down, while still complaining.

"I don't even know how to put a computer on. I'm not on the web and my resume is fifteen years old. Beautiful. I should just become one of those high-priced call girls in D.C., probably will make a boat load of money, and have a lot more fun."

They both laugh. Sure they're laughing; they're drunk! And Tony still has his job, and Kristin's father left her so much money, she has never had to work a day in her life.

"Thanks a lot for the tips, I'll be in touch."

"No, we'll call you, Duke, hang tough, you're strong." Sure, I think, we're all strong; that's why we're all relapsing.

"Talk to you later, bye." Resume. Shit. All I have to add to my old one is that I've been in solo private practice for almost fifteen years and am desirous of a career change. Perfect. No sweat. I'm sure I'll be hired on the spot. With my body, the escort service really can be an option,… I think I need a drink.

I meet with Tony's headhunter within a week with a new resume, and have already sent almost one hundred resumes out on medreps.com with Edward's begrudging help. Thankfully he rewrote my resume on the computer, since I still don't even know how to use Word. Edward is vainly attempting to teach me how to use the internet. (I hate computers, never took one class in college, yuck!)

The sixty-year-old headhunter takes one look at me and my resume and honestly states, "I don't think I am going to be able to place you anywhere, Dr. Duke. I'm sorry, but you are over qualified and too old."

"Too old? And too over qualified? How can one ever be *over* qualified, and I'm only forty-three, and can probably pass for thirty-three on a good day. What's up?"

"I'm sorry, Dr., that's just the way it is. Sales companies are looking for young, hungry, college grads; they do not want to hire a doctor."

The ride home is the pedal to the metal, can't wait for a cold one, and maybe I'll have a bite on the internet if I can figure out how to log on by myself. For God's sake, Mary Ann, you don't know how to do *anything,* but be a doctor. You can't even go to work for some insurance company, because you are such a computer illiterate! That escort service idea is looking better by the minute. Maybe I should give Captain Kirk a call; didn't William Shatner do that movie on beauty pageants? Just kidding, but I'm beyond desperate at this point, lost on Pluto, drinking to make myself feel better yet again, and getting sicker by the hour.

Finally, I get one bite and am offered a job to be a sales representative for a medical supply company over the phone. The Vice President even flies in from Oklahoma to welcome me on board and give me some on-the-job training.

I hate it, hate every single minute of it! Cold calling, me, cold calling cardiology offices, introducing myself as *Dr.* Duke" and many times still getting a "No"! or a "I'll have to call you back"! from the office manager, and not even being able to speak Dr. to Dr. There is no deferential treatment in medicine anymore; that went swirling down the drain right along with reimbursements.

Why don't they automatically suspend your driver's license for sixty days in Maryland with your first DUI like they do in Pennsylvania? That makes a hell of a lot more sense than taking away a doctor's license for the "unforeseeable future", don't you think? I'm driving myself silly all over Washington area for this job, buying the doctors lunch on my credit card, then waiting to see him or her (gave me new perspective on making my patients wait), however, introducing myself as "Dr. Duke", then try (because I never learned how or more aptly refused to learn how) to "suck up" to make a sale. I certainly did not go to medical school to be a "sales rep"; I only went to *be a doctor and help people.*

All that education and now I'm selling cardiac event monitors, day after day. I need a second demo to wear 24 hours/day on myself in case *I* have V-tach! (Ventricular tachycardia, when the two large chambers of the heart start beating out of control. One can easily die from V-tach, especially driving in the D.C. area.) I definitely should be wearing my own monitor. Maybe if I open my blouse, and show the male doctors how to place the electrodes and test them, along with my breasts, I'll bring those accounts right home.

One month later the party is over, well before dessert. My boss, the V.P. Mr. Hartatak, calls from Oklahoma, "Mary Ann? This is Mr. Hartatak."

"Hello, Mr. Hartatak, how are you? Did you see the new accounts I got on board last week? Isn't that great?!"

"Sure, that's fine, but what you did to the office manager at that large practice in Rockville is not acceptable, not acceptable at all." I don't recall doing anything wrong so simply ask, "What did I do?"

"You don't remember?!"

Uh, oh, by the tone of his voice I know I'm in big trouble. "No" is all I respond.

"You were rude, extremely rude on the phone, because he didn't want to work with you. He told me you sounded intoxicated. *That* is unacceptable."

"I'm very sorry, Mr. Hartatak." Oh God, I think, it must have been that depressing morning last week I started the day with a drink instead of coffee. Did I blackout? I must have.

"I'm sorry, too, Mary Ann, but we can not have our employees treating potential customers like that. We are going to have to let you go."

"What? Are you firing me?! Please don't fire me, Mr. Hartatak. Please, forgive me! Please, give me another chance. I have to have this job!"

"I am sorry, Mary Ann, but I do not want you to call on another office. We will send your earnings as soon as we receive the demo model back."

I have never been fired in my entire life from anything, never ever. (Except for Fat Bastard, of course, and he doesn't count.) It took four months to land this job. I can't lose it even though it really stinks, and on top of which it pays by straight commission only, with no expense account. I beg Mr. Hartatak,"Please give me another chance."

"I'm sorry, Dr. Duke, but I can't. Excuse me, but I have to take another call, good bye."

My W-2 for 2005 for a month's work plus all of the extra studying I did, I can probably now pass the American Academy of Cardiology Board Exam, is a stupendous $131.65, not even enough for my cell phone bill, much less gas and lunches. I *lost money* on that shitty job. *I paid* to go to work! "FINE", I bitch, "JUST FINE"! (No reader will forget the acronym.) I hated the damned job anyway! Sure, great, the accounts I *did* generate, the money comes in thirty days later, and I am already fired. That $131.65 is most likely from my first day of work, and doesn't even cover my dry cleaning and panty hose. I know I can get paid a lot more to escort. Hell, I've got some great pumps for the job!

Dear God, why did I drink that morning? I rue the day I became an alcoholic.

I feel desperate. I *am* desperate.

Chapter 22

The Maryland Medical Board

April 6th, D-day, off by a couple months, same concept, the day of my hearing has arrived, and it's time to scale the cliffs of the Maryland Medical Board and dodge some serious bullets. Davie drives an hour out of his way from his house to pick me up, "to talk to me on the way there", he said, but I think he was worried I would be late if he didn't. He has been my devoted patient and experienced waiting for the good doctor before. Davie's not stupid.

We arrive early, then have to wait almost two hours. The Board is behind, but we're not patients in an office where we can get ticked off with the wait and walk up to the front desk and reschedule, we *are* being examined today.

The Board's attorney, Penelope Peperre, great name for an attorney, everyone needs a "hot tamale" for a lawyer. I like her look immediately. "She has balls", I think, to wear her hair very, very short, blonde and spiked like that great Eurythmics lead singer. Mine is unspiked today, but I am wearing make-up and a designer pastel peach suit one of my wonderful patients gave me after she gained weight from *her* divorce.

Davie already had told me in the car that I looked nice, not over dressed, and "I'm supposed to look like the successful, good doctor that I am, right? I don't have anything to be ashamed of. I've never harmed a patient.

It's not like I'm the first doctor in history who has ever gotten a DUI".

"I know, Dukie, I know that for sure", Davie responded.

"Dr. Duke", oh, Davie is addressing me by something other than "Dukie" and I don't respond as quickly, "Yes, Dav...Mr. Goldstein?"

"This is the Board's attorney, Ms. Peperre."

"Nice to meet you", as I smile and shake her hand.

"We have been discussing your case, and attorney Peperre and I have agreed to recommending a one to two year suspension."

"One to two *years*?"

"Yes, Dr. Duke", Davie is looking me right in the eyes as he speaks. "Six months have already gone by, and attorney Peperre believes that one year is the best deal we are going to get. You can get by another six months, right, then start up again?" Of course, Davie, if you loan me some money, but I already owe you! I reply, "That's as good as it gets?"

"Yes," answers Davie bluntly. Now it's my turn to stare him down, and I read it in his eyes. He's doing the best he can, because the Board did charge me with that "Cease and Desist" dogma over a bottle of Botox.

"Okay, I'm fine with that," I respond, but I certainly would have been more fine just going back to rehab last fall like they promised.

We enter the hearing room. The Board is sitting behind a string of folding tables. Attorney Pepperre sits behind her folding table, and Davie and I share the other one facing them. All of a sudden I have a very sick feeling in my stomach like I need to throw up.

Fuck. They're almost all men. I see only two women. Look at those smug faces, just *not* what the doctor ordered. They're a bunch of "good ole' boys"! I've had so many of them in my life I can spot one a mile away. Why aren't there more women?! I'll be damned, over 50% of medical school admissions are now women, but…only a very few are in positions of power yet. The good old boy network is still in power, alive and well, in medicine, still in 2005 and it's going to take at least twenty-thirty years for them all to die. And even if men become the minority in medicine, you bet your ass, they are still going to try to remain in power.

For the record, there are currently fifteen men and only six women on the Board, but there aren't twenty-one people in this room, and only the two women. Great. Time for the bullets. I am sweating now in my beautiful suit of peach armor.

"Yes, yes of course………No……….I truly would *never* have administered Botox if I thought I was breaking the law……….No, I have not been convicted of DUI, no Sir, I mean Dr., I have not gone to court for the charge yet………Yes, I have a sponsor and attend regular AA meetings. (A little white lie there, my meeting attendance is *ir*regular and spastic, just like my colon right now.)………….I deeply regret anything wrong that I have done, but I am a very caring, exemplary doctor and have never been sued, not even close, and I *need to be a doctor* again. It's all I really know, and I have a family to support, and have had tremendous difficulty securing a decent job of any kind."

"Thank you for your candor, Dr. Duke. (Sound familiar?) Could you, please, step out while we make our decision?" Davie, Peperre and I go back to our tiny room to wait some more, but not for very long, and we're called back in. Hmm, quick decision, maybe everything's all right.

The next three sentences from the Board change my life forever. "The Board recommends a five year suspension of licensure. Dr. Duke must enter into a contract to be monitored at the Board's discretion for the next five years. However, since Dr. Duke has stated she is destitute, we will not impose the $50,000.00 fine for practicing medicine without a license."

I glance over at attorney Peperre. Her jaw is on the floor. So is Davie's. The Board didn't even consider their own attorney's recommendation, blew it right off! Five, not one-two, but *five whole years*. I'm so stunned, slapped down so hard, I can't move, much less think.

"C'mon Dukie, it's time to go," Davie whispers in my ear and takes my arm to help me up. The three of us again go back to our room. Attorney Peperre looks like she wants to say "I'm sorry". She looks apologetic and stunned herself. They both look at me worried, like I'm going to faint or flip out or both.

The only words that come out of my mouth tell it all, and I'm sure neither attorney will ever forget them: "Well, you know, I have been taking it up the ass for so long in medicine, what's another damned lousy day?"… No response.

Ms. Kranekey pokes her head in. With her perfect pout cheeps, "We'll be sending the paperwork to you very soon for you to sign. Nice to see you." Sure, fine, smile at me, I'm not obligated to return it, but that old grit of mine makes me grin back anyway, like she's doing me some big favor.

I should have been sent to the funny farm right then and there. Or, better, taken straight in an ambulance to the psychiatric floor at Johns Hopkins and sedated with intravenous valium for at least the next four to six weeks. Valium, not alcohol, would have been a much superior drug of choice, and hospitalization, even if restraints were necessary, would have been preferable to driving in blackouts.

The Board takes away my medical license for five full years and puts me out of business. Just like that. Takes away the only way I know how to make a living and what I love to do. Bang! Just one bullet to the back of the head, but my head's so damned hard they still didn't kill me. Maybe I should have gotten on my knees and opened my mouth for them, so their bullet could have penetrated better. I most definitely should have been heliported to Hopkins for a good while, and then on to a nice long rehab in a nice sunny place.

Instead, I go back to my beautiful home/office and put the lights on. I look at the dust collecting on all my patients' charts and my equipment. The waiting room walls filled with framed certificates of achievement and Exam Room 1, where I toiled and gave my soul for almost ten years (almost fifteen years total, after five years of leasing space), with its largest wall completely covered with diplomas, honors and awards, all in beautiful lacquer frames. And the little wall holding my past medical licenses from New York, Virginia and the District of Columbia, but just a hook and nail where my Maryland medical license used to be.

Hmm, I do still have my driver's license. Maybe I will start a true escort service and even pick up my red light "District" clients in my big BMW, since Scottie from Star Trek still hasn't fixed the transporter to get me to Sunset Strip. I don't think he even knows where my molecules are; I think I'm lost, out of this galaxy, maybe gone along with Pluto. It's okay he can't find me. I could never be a call girl.

*   *   *

I sit on my examining chair and put my head in my hands. Five years. I'm going to lose all of my patients in five years. If it was only one to two years, I wouldn't lose them all. I'm going to have to sell my home. I love my house, my yard. It's all I have left.

Finally, after a good, long cry, I slowly walk into my kitchen and plop myself down at the kitchen table and sit staring into my beautiful back yard. As always in trying times, my mind wanders back in time to sitting with Baba in her cheery kitchen. My dear, kind Baba, do you think being a doctor is so good for me now? And dear Baba, what do you think of your words now? "Be a doctor, Honey, you'll get respect and have a good life". That would have been true if I were a man.

A man would have received a hand slap from the Board and maybe a sentence to a thirty-day rehab in my situation. (I can prove that.)

Oh dear Baba, and all I ever *really* wanted to be was a Mommy. It is going to be harder than ever to get my children back now. God give me strength.

Chapter 23

Papers, Cars and Candy (Six weeks after the Board hearing, May 2005)

"Dukie, it's Davie. What are you doing?" Davie calls me out of the blue.

"Trying to find a job on the Internet."

"I thought you were working."

"I was Davie. It's kind of a long story. What's up?"

"Come on over to my office if you are not busy."

"Busy? That's for bees. I'm a cat, remember? I sleep a lot."

"Right, those nine lives of yours. Well, the papers from the Board arrived and I'd like to mail them right back."

"What's the big hurry? They've got five years. Another two and they can hatch an elephant, but maybe not. I think they're all sterile."

"Very funny, just get your sweet you-know-what over here."

"Fine."

If I didn't sign a "voluntary suspension" (which I was adamantly opposed to doing, "voluntary", my eye!), on *public record,* the Board was going to revoke my license for five years. A revocation is much harsher than a suspension. A suspension is lighter, after five years it's lifted, and your license renewed, done, you're back in practice.

A revocation is total annihilation. It's like you never were a doctor in Maryland ever, and the whole application process has to start all over again, and there is no guarantee that you will be granted a license again. Period. The Board can keep me out of Maryland forever, and that means I am history in the other forty-nine states, too, because of the incredible Internet. Before the Internet, if physicians lost their licenses in one state, they just moved far away. I doubt I could get a medical license even in St. Thomas.

The Board has one more dagger. The five-year suspension starts from the end of May 2005 when the papers are signed, not from November 2004 when they actually took my license, flagrantly unfair.

"Davie! What the hell is this? It is five-and-a-half years instead of five! This is bullshit!" Davie nods as he passes the papers to me. I sign where I'm supposed to sign in my first sober fucking blackout. I'm glad I don't remember, ha, maybe Ill be happier without being a doctor in this state, or at least not lorded over by some totally corrupt Board… Intense thought.

*   *   *

Oh, this "discretionary" democracy we live in. America, "the land of the free", a true fallacy. One's life's work, one's total future can be dictated by one judge or one Board and the Board is hand-picked, I was informed by the Head of Rehab, by the Governor, so we're down to one man again. Americans are not free. We're pawns of the more powerful. I always believed good conquers evil. Well, we'll see in this new millennium, now won't we?

* * *

The very night I "voluntarily" (sarcasm) signed the five-year suspension of my medical license; I walk to my car dealership owner patient's house. I've known him and his wife for years and always got along with Mr. Kirkpatrick. I give the dear man an ear full and tell him everything. Mr. Kirkpatrick graciously offers me a job and I start the very next day. Super duper orgasgissimo! Now I'm selling cars but maybe I'll learn, and it will be some form of preventive medicine for my now beat up BMW.

But, what the hell do I care are the differences between an Accord and a Camry? Who has even thought about fuel efficiency with a V4 or a V6? My V12 is always thirsty. I understand thirst, but I cannot keep the nuances between a Honda, Hyundai, Ford, oh Lord, stab me with a sword. Please, put me out of my misery...This job is soon going to be history.

I do like Farouk, though, my turban-headed, big bearded mentor. When I'm not having an engine lesson, I'm helping Farouk sell cars. Farouk is on the phone, so I run out in the rain to greet a potential customer. I cannot sell a car and get a commission by myself until my training is complete, and who knows when *that* will be.

I approach the elderly couple wearing a big smile and a big umbrella. "May I help you?"

"We are looking for a Toyota Camry."

"Well, we certainly have plenty of those!" I'll never forget the first time Farouk took me up to the huge storage lot. The Camry collection went on forever, it seemed. It reminded me of the American cemetery in Normandy that I saw as a little girl, when the white crosses went on as far as the eye could see. To think Mr.

Kirkpatrick had amassed that amount of wealth in his lifetime, starting out as a simple car salesman himself.

"What color do you want?" I ask the couple, like the color is the absolute most important reason to buy a car.

"We don't really know."

"I think you should buy this silver one. It doesn't show dirt." Great sales pitch.

"Honey, what do you think?"

"The silver's okay; do you like it?" the husband responds.

"Well, the nice lady has a point that it doesn't show dirt." See, my idiot comment worked. Elderly people aren't out in their driveways washing their cars, and they don't want the additional expense and effort of driving to a car wash like a black car will demand.

"Do you like this one?" I inquire, as I peek in the window. "No, you don't want this car, because it doesn't have leather seats and you must have leather seats."

"Well, we've never had leather seats."

"Oh, then it's high time you treated yourself to them!" I exclaim with a smile. By the time Farouk got off the phone and came outside, I have them buying the V6 with leather seats and every other option I can remember after my first morning on the job.

Car salesmen live in a dog-eat-dog world. They don't take turns with customers, not that I ever saw. If one isn't inside writing up a sale, then their eagle eyes are constantly doing 360's outside the showroom peering for the most probable buyer. I ran out into the rain and accosted the poor elderly couple before anyone else could seize them for their own prey.

Undeniably, Farouk likes me back. I am good at sales (lucky first try), not afraid to be forward, and at least was helping *him* make money. I introduce Farouk and he takes the couple inside to do the paperwork. I must admit there is more paperwork to selling a car than scheduling a surgery and most of it is done on a way-too-complex computer. I'm completely overwhelmed looking over Farouk's shoulder. I'm never going to make a damnable sale until I learn all this computer crap. I'm screwed.

I *certainly* did not go on to higher education for the equivalent of twelve years after high school, and spend another two years becoming a board-certified ophthalmologist to sell cars with high school dropouts who do it *better* than me. I am the best dressed salesman, but that's as far as it goes.

After my first day of work and the *day after* I signed my career away; however, my first car sale with Farouk, I drive to my ex-husband's home to pick up my beautiful children. My visitation is only every other weekend and every Wednesday from four to eight p.m. I left work early my first day.

Waiting patiently just inside the screen door, I glance around the living room, and then spot something. There it is, right smack in the middle of his coffee table, my father's mother's (not Baba's, but my other grandmother who I also loved dearly) antique peach glass covered candy dish, all three sections filled with different kinds of candy. The only inheritance I received when she died was a few stained tablecloths and two peach candy dishes.

I had been missing that pretty dish, had wondered if the thieves had taken it. Mildly wild, I reclaim what is mine. Why not? After Dieter moved out, I gave him everything I found that he forgot to take that was from his family. I dump out the candy under the table, ran, and put it in my car. (I should have kept the candy, but then that would have been stealing, right? The candy wasn't mine, but the dish *was*.) I've never stolen anything in my entire life.

My children are always so happy to see me. I always give a big hug and kiss to each one. James is tall and handsome at nine-and-a-half. Marika is eight and has gorgeous brunette hair with red highlights, that looks more lush every time I see her, and Nadia at only six is so pretty and already carries herself like a model.

We walk to the park near Dieter's house. It was a nice May afternoon, and the plan was to play in the park and then go to dinner. With only four hours to visit, I didn't want to spend time in traffic and the children asked me to take them to the park.

"Will you push me on the swing?" Nadia chirps.

"Mommy, I want you to push *me* on the swing" Marika asks also. James has scampered towards a friend he saw and I say to him, "Don't go where I can't see you, Honey." James nods without turning around. I turn back to the girls and say, "Angels, I can push you both; don't you worry!" I think back, as I'm pushing them, to the swing set in my back yard that has two swings and a bucket-type swing for a baby. I used to push all three of my little girls, Eloise in the baby bucket, all at one time. But Eloise rarely sees her siblings now. Edward and I are drifting apart more and more, and I think he punishes me for my losing interest in him by not letting me see Eloise. I shake my head a little, trying to put that sad thought out of my brain and luckily it leaves. The sun is shining down on us and Marika and Nadia are yelling in unison, "Push me higher Mommy! Push me higher Mommy!"

Barely fifteen minutes have passed, and I hear Dieter's angry voice, "C'mon kids, you're going home with me!"

"Why?" I ask him and poor Marika and Nadia both have scared and wondering looks on their faces as they turn and see their father striding fast towards us with a red face.

"I called the police," he angrily barks at me. He's dead serious.

"*What*?"

"You stole from me!"

"No, I didn't, it's mine."

Dieter looks like he is going to explode, stops both swings, takes our two little girls' hands, and yells, "C'mon James, now!" James also looks bewildered and his wide eyes tell me he's frightened, too. Dieter starts dragging all three away with him. "James is bold and says, "Why Daddy? We're playing."

"Just c'mon home!" Dieter dictates.

"Why are you doing this?" I ask Dieter.

"You know why! The police are going to be here right away!" My poor babies all look disappointed and now even more terrified, all three wide-eyed, and having to run to keep up with their father's long legs and brisk pace.

I think, "Oh my God, he *really did* call the police"! I am frightened, probably most of all, and I start running. Every time I have fought Dieter in court, I have lost except with the one African American judge in Montgomery County who believed me about the coffee spill and granted me the thirty day "Ex Parte". Every court date since, I have totally lost against him. *(Why is that? Simple. I'm a female doctor. Let's fuck her over extra hard and put her down. I think lawyers hate doctors even more than we hate them*.) My adrenals are starting to do their thing. Now I'm definitely running out of luck; it's all gone. Less than twenty-four hours after signing my career away; my ex is calling the police to get me arrested for the theft of my own grandmother's candy dish!

As I jog past my children, I turn a loving look at them and say, "I'm sorry, Angels, but Mommy has to go." Now tears are streaming down my face, and I can't help myself from saying, "Sometimes your Daddy isn't very good to me. I'll call you in a little while." I sprint to my car, and start home. I turn down the usual street. I'm crying so hard; I can barely see to drive.

Shit! There's a police car. I turn onto a side street. Fuck! There's another one! It's over. My ex called the police to have me arrested for theft and my children were traumatized, and *my time* with them is taken away yet again. I stop my car and roll down the window. Two policemen approach me.

"The candy dish was my grandmother's, Officers," I offer first.

"Well, Ma'am, your ex-husband says it's his, and you stole it from his house."

"How could I steal something that was mine?"

"Will you, please, show us your license and registration and give us the stolen property?"

I give them the dish and think to myself, "This is insane". The two police officers have obviously radioed somewhere and have probably seen my seven charges pending from six months ago. Who do you think they believe?

I arrive back home in a daze, alone, and in trouble with the law again. And most of all, worried about my children. Miss "goodie two shoes", who has never cheated anyone or stolen a single thing in her life, arrested for stealing. I lie on my couch and stare at the ceiling. Dear God, I pray, are you listening or have you forgotten me? I think I *am* losing my mind. Nothing makes sense anymore. I wish I could have one of my heart-to-heart talks with my Baba right now. God, I really miss her. The tears start flowing down my cheeks. I'm so lonely. I get off the couch, walk into the kitchen and open my special cupboard, the hiding place for my vodka bottle. (Chardonnay has been surpassed by vodka in the past few weeks.) Oh, I sigh, thank God there is half a bottle.

      The very next day I get my second drunk driving arrest in another total blackout, (a screwdriver for breakfast that morning instead of a cup of coffee), and then a third arrest three weeks later; I think the day my car came out of the shop from the second, and both of them within a mile of my home. Why didn't I just sell my Beemer and by a moped after the second arrest in May? Why did you even get a *second* DWI? You know why, Mary Ann, because you were not thinking clearly at all. Normal people don't get two drunk driving arrests in a three week period unless their lives and their minds have completely spun out of control, and my world was certainly out of control.

      Yes, for sure, an ambulance ride straight to Johns Hopkins Hospital would have been much more preferable the day of the Board's decision, with several weeks in the hospital on intravenous valium was *exactly* what I needed, instead of more arrests.

      It's blatantly obvious to me now that my sanity was depleted and only a desire to drink and a feeling of despair was left, probably along with a death wish. I was not thinking at all, had lost my mind, was giving it long baths in alcohol, sterilizing and killing brain cells, in a lame attempt to forget…*everything and all my pain.*

Chapter 24

The Few Months Before Jail

The office phone continues to ring, so I place an ad to hire an ophthalmologist. Dr. Jones answers my ad. He agrees to pay me $2,000/month basically to rent my fully equipped office space with the added bonus of having patients wanting to be seen. That's not a quarter of the mortgage, but still 2G's in the black. I'll take it.

The Wizard commands me to go back to rehab. I do just that.

The Board called Dr. Jones a few months later while I'm in rehab in Atlanta, hemorrhaging over $30,000 in fourteen weeks, just for rehab, on top of the mortgage, utilities, child support, etc… Dr. Jones was told by the Board that "Dr. Duke's practice is no longer an entity and *she cannot earn a living through it*". I wasn't earning a living through my practice, not by a long shot. The $2,000/month Dr. Jones paid me didn't even cover the cost of rehab per week. (That's crazy, too.) But the Board can do whatever they want to do. He was commanded to take down my sign and close up shop *or else*. Just like that. The Board threatened him over the phone; they didn't have the balls to put it in writing.

Dr. Jones then sent me a fat contract to purchase my practice while I was in Atlanta at rehab. He offered me so little I was ashamed of him for him. He offered me $20,000 plus $2,000/month until I sold my house. He knew I was thinking of putting it on the market. Even if it took a year to sell, 12 months times $2,000=$24,000 plus the initial $20,000 wasn't a fair price; my equipment alone was worth more than $44,000. Isn't one usually close to death before the vultures start circling? I politely told him to go fly a kite.

*   *   *

Rehab in Atlanta is more than stressful. I am having a hard time convincing my psychiatrist that I don't need lithium. How many times do I have to say, "I can't tolerate lithium. My hands shake, for that matter, *I* shake and *I can't stand it"!!*

"Well, I think you may be bipolar I, and you need the lithium" is my stoic shrink's reply. Sure. *F.i.n.e.* I'll take the lithium you are prescribing for me, stuff it under my tongue, and spit it down the toilet as soon as I leave the nursing station. So it went for fourteen weeks. I only swallowed the lithium (the bedtime dose I was given to take on my own) the morning I had to have a blood test for it. Rehab. Yeah, Rehab. You know what I think of it. Forced this and forced that. But lithium is where I draw the line. I hate that drug. Enough about that. I still think I may be tripolar (You remember, up, down and in between, aren't we all? Stress alone can make anyone seem crazy, I think, all by itself.), but the diagnosis "tripolar" hasn't made it to the big fat DSM-IV psychiatric textbook yet.

On top of everything to deal with in rehab, being away from my children and my home, strange roommates, strange shrinks, strange food, no fun…I still have to deal with large envelopes of mail and bills Edward is sending to me, and the worst, an occasional certified letter.

I'm really blown away when New York State revokes my medical license (out of nowhere!) while in rehab almost two months *before* Maryland revokes me. Maryland revokes me *also* while I was in rehab in Atlanta because I wasn't compliant with *their* "Voluntary Consent Order" which meant peeing in a cup twice a week. I'm already peeing in a cup randomly in Atlanta for rehab; does the New York and Maryland Boards want to send a leer jet for me so I can pee in a cup in Maryland and then fly on to New York within a few hours to make sure I don't have a drink on a commuter flight that will be metabolized by the time I get to either state anyway?! (Maybe I should have just named this book "INSANE".)

    I didn't even know I *still had a valid* New York medical license to revoke! I surrendered it in the early 90's and never paid them another cent. But they revoke me before my home state of Maryland where the suspension first occurred? Now isn't that interesting when the current Chairman of the Ophthalmology Department of Albany Medical Center Hospital was the Vice Chairman who took care of the little girl that woke up brain dead, and I thought her asthma should have been checked? Yep, Chiefs don't like it when their little Indians look better than they do *and* are female. Again, I wasn't the one with the fat subpoena. Being a man, though, bought him a big cover-up. He has been the Chairman for seventeen years in Albany. I wonder if there have been several other giant cover-ups?

    *   *   *

    Finally, *finally* I'm home from that excruciatingly long rehab in Atlanta. All I do every day, after opening the mail and juggling bills, is lie on the couch and watch Oprah or HBO and most of all, worry about going to jail.

    I need to talk to someone, *anyone* who cares and *might understand.* I decide to call Bruce, the first man who ever asked me to marry him (before Sven). I know that Bruce will always love me, and if anyone can understand, he would. Bruce is an ophthalmologist, too, and he has a history of cocaine abuse.

"Hi Bruce, it's Mary Ann."

"Hi, Mary Ann, how *are* you? God, it has been *years* since we talked to each other. I'm so glad to hear your voice!" Bruce sounds very pleased to hear from me.

"I'm not doing so good, Bruce, not good at all. It's a terribly long story; I want to tell you everything, but first let me ask you, did you retire already? You're so lucky. I called information for your office number, and then your office said you were no longer working."

"Well,...not exactly. I have my license suspended for cocaine abuse for one to two years."

"You do not!"...I'm floored…"What happened?" Misery does like company, and I'd rather listen to his story *(I thought at that moment)* than pour out mine.

"Well, my wife turned me in."

"Your *wife?!*"

"Yep. We're separated now, but she was really worried about me because I had a couple psychotic episodes with too much "coke" on board. So then I was monitored by the Physicians Monitoring Group, but after that I used again and had a positive urine, so then I got suspended and I'm still being monitored. I'm going to request to be reinstated soon."

"You mean you only got a *one to two* year suspension for *cocaine*?" I'm astounded, because I heard the New York Medical Board was *the* toughest in the country. (They were on me, anyway.)

Bruce answers, "Yes, I need to stay clean for a good eighteen months, and then I'm going to try to get my license back." I can't hold what happened to me in any longer and I take over the conversation, "Listen to me now, listen to this!" And I go on and on and on…

"Jesus Christ!!" is Bruce's response. I obviously shocked dear Bruce. He tries to console me. "You won't go to jail, I promise you. You won't. You just won't!" Then he changes the subject, maybe to get my mind off of my tragic mess. "Listen, Mary Ann, remember the married retinal surgeons, the Dr. Schwartz's? I turned them in because I found out he was writing narcotic prescriptions for her. She became a total addict to pain pills, Oxycontin, everything."

"So they both lost their licenses? For how long?"

"No, not at all. She just got a one year suspension, and I think he paid a fine."

"Jesus, Joseph and Mary, they let *him* off? He's the perpetrator! You're not supposed to write prescriptions for your wife, *especially narcotics.* That's malpractice. I can't believe it!"

"Well, it's true. That's all he got."

"That's totally fucked up. *He's* the one that should have gotten at least a two to three year suspension, and she should have been sentenced to rehab." I hate the discrimination, just hate it so much! I start crying again out of frustration.

"You're telling me! I don't know what the hell happened to you, but I know a lot of doctors that have gotten DUIs or DWIs or a bunch of them, and they haven't lost their medical licenses for one minute. And they are certainly *not going to jail!* They are just being monitored."

"Bruce, are any of them women?"…Pause.

"Umm, no. The only ones that come to mind are men." My turn to pause. What more is there to say?

"Mary Ann, I have to go pick up my daughter. I have your number in my cell phone. I'll call you very soon. You're going to be okay. But, you have to appeal the Board's decision; it's too severe."

"I know Bruce, I know. Call me soon."

"I will. I promise, bye for now."

I sit at the kitchen table and stare into the backyard for a long time after that conversation. What Bruce said made me more angry and more despondent, all at once. The male doctors with drunk driving charges in the toughest state in the Union get a hand slap. It's not a fair world, but this is ridiculous. I have to tell Davie. We have to start working on an appeal right away, terrific, more legal bills. My trees aren't growing any more money leaves.

I think some more about what I've just heard. I'm convinced, more than ever, having a penis prevents problems.

But my sex change has to be reversible. I like being a woman, being Mommy, and I like my multiple orgasms. Maybe that's the crux of the whole matter; men in power are just jealous of women because we can have multiple orgasms, when they have trouble achieving one. Too bad boys, that's our bone-us for giving birth. (ha) Oh, who cares, sex is the furthest thing from my mind these days. (Well, not really, but I like to think it is, instead of missing it.) I'm struggling with the most basic needs for survival, like eating and sleeping.

*   *   *

One stupendous example of perfect penile prevention presented to the Maryland Medical Board several times over almost twenty years:

Dr. Rose's repeated hand slaps are totally laughable on one level, but truly perverse and tragic in complete context. Verbatim records except for the doctor's name.

(Sorry about the grammatical errors, Board's secretaries' fault.)

"Case Number: 2003-0027:

II. PROCEDURAL AND FACTUAL HISTORY

A. Prior Criminal and Disciplinary History 1988-1996

Dr. Robert Rose was first implicated in a prescription drug fraud case with his wife in 1988, while he was still a resident in the University of Maryland Medical System's ("UMMS") general surgery residency program. At that time, Dr. Rose was charged with, and admitted to obtaining controlled dangerous substances ("CDS") for himself and his wife writing prescriptions from 1985 to 1988 for narcotic substances for himself and his wife using fictitious names and taking the prescriptions to pharmacies to obtain the drugs".

This doctor/surgeon was making up Joe Schmoe lived at High Grove Rd., for example, and had a gall bladder surgery on such and such a day, then he was filling the prescriptions at different pharmacies acting like he was the patient. I *love* this example. Everything I'm quoting is indeed public knowledge. This gets "fantasmigorical", (You know, a term from Dick Van Dyke's classic, *Chitty, Chitty Bang, Bang!)* It's almost unbelievable, but it's all true.

"Dr. Rose admitted to "recreational use" of drugs which included Hycodan syrup, Oxycodone, and Vicodin. Dr. Rose was fined $1000, and received probation before judgment in the criminal case. (Boy, bet his hand was really red after that slap! Three years of fraudulent illegal prescription writing, *while a lowly resident,* repeated federal offenses, and all he gets is a "Peanut Butter and Jelly" and a 1G fine?) In 1990, Dr. Rose also tested positive for marijuana, and received treatment as an inpatient for chemical dependence, followed by outpatient treatment and monitoring." Meanwhile he defaulted on his "Health Education Loan or Scholarship Obligations". (H.E.A.L. loans, I remember those; I had some. What nerve he had to ignore them. Guess he inhaled? And with the cost of pot et. al…who has money left to pay one's school loans?)

"Dr. Rose entered into a Consent Order with the Board in 1990 in which the Board concluded that he had violated the Medical Practice Act, (ya think?), by practicing medicine other than in connection with the university's unlicensed medical practitioner's postgraduate training program (All that mumbo jumbo means he was still a resident-in-training, but again, this is verbatim Board's documents.), and by willfully making and filing false reports or records in the practice of medicine". (Remember he was a *surgical* resident too.) "Under the terms of the Consent order, Dr. Rose was *granted a medical license and placed on probation for five years…*.Following successful completion of the probationary conditions, the Board terminated his probation in 1996".

That hand slap didn't even turn pink! Well, don't want to hurt his surgeon's hands, now do we? He needs to cut people open and be a great general surgeon some day. *If Dr. Rose was a <u>woman</u> and not a man, in my opinion, she would have been kicked out of her residency program and never operated on anyone in the real world <u>ever.</u>* Guess he has the right name; how could a doctor named Rose come out smelling like a skunk? Keep reading. The truth is more appalling than any fiction.

B.   Criminal Proceedings 2001-2003

"In June, 2002, however, Dr. Rose was again charged with prescription drug fraud following a criminal investigation in 2001 by the Anne Arundel County Police Department. The investigation revealed that Dr. Rose had written numerous prescriptions over a *long period of time using fictitious names* for Oxycontin, Percocet and Phentermine, all of which are CDS. (Controlled Dangerous Substances) These illegal prescriptions were intended for his drug-addicted wife and another individual, whom Dr. Rose knew to be his wife's drug supplier. (footnote 1) Dr. Rose entered an "Alford plea" to *one count*, (I'm kidding, right? Nope, would I lie to you? I couldn't make this shit up in a million years.) of prescription drug fraud, received a six-month suspended sentence, (*No jail time yet again?!* Just another peanut butter and jelly sandwich? *The doc sounds like a drug dealer to me, writing scripts for his wife's **supplier**?) and a fine of $1,000, and was placed on supervised probation for one year".*

My God, talk about coming out smelling like a rose! The good Dr. Rose apparently has been writing fraudulent prescriptions and breaking the law for almost two decades, and all he's had to do is attend a little rehab, grab a few PB &Js, and pay 2Gs in fines! I'd say he smells like the whole damned National Botanical Garden! I *have* to find out the name of his attorney, pronto! That lawyer's not a wizard, he/she/it's a God.

The footnote 1 above stands for this: "In his ethics paper, Dr. Rose noted that his wife's drug addiction cost $150,000 a year". (Poor baby, in a later paragraph Dr. Rose indicates that he has)… "financial debt and federal and state income tax liabilities resulting from unpaid taxes from previous years".

Perfect, guess $150,000/year to buy drugs doesn't leave much left for Uncle Sam.

*   *   *

Has the Board had enough already, or are they just waiting for him to drive drunk?

*　　　　　　*　　　　　　*

This last quote just can't be left out: "In one expert's view, Dr. Rose lacks psychological insight about his relationship with his wife, mishandled her drug addiction, (no...*really?*), was *unable to act independently of her, and allowed himself to be victimized by her throughout their marriage.*" (That was an *expert's* view? Expert in what?! How to cover a man's ass? That's easy, just wear the pants in the family, but a lot less of that going on in our new millennium. The women are wearing both, the pants and the skirts.)

I don't care if that expert was Dr. Phil or Dr. Ruth; I don't want his or her name for sure. You gotta admit, that "view" is a crock of crap and it smells just like it. That's right, *blame it all on his wife.* The big strong surgeon has simply been a poor victim of his wife. She must be some Amazon woman to be able to tie him down, make him chew a few Percocet, *inhale* a joint, then free up one hand to write her and her "supplier" a few hundred narcotics' prescriptions. I should have played the victim..., but I didn't have a wife to blame everything on.

I am just a victim of the system. Having no penis gets one more punishment, plain and simple.

Oh right, the good Dr. copped an "Alford plea", another legal loophole, and pleaded guilty to only <u>one illegal Rx.</u> It must have been some big ole' Rx with several hundred refills, since it rang up $150,000/year for a "long time". And he "pleaded guilty to a crime involving moral turpitude"..."Dr. Rose also agreed not to petition for reinstatement of his medical license before December 31, 2003."

I really want to meet him and touch his robe, or kiss his ring. The good doctor gets <u>no jail time for repeated criminal felonies</u>, and only an eight-month suspension/vacation from his practice, not even a year. Is he a saint or *what*? (Is the Board getting paid off? Doesn't it make you wonder about total, unadulterated, *full-blown* despicable corruption? Is it just simple discrimination, or both? Who knows? Maybe he treats members of the Board's habits, oh, I mean pain.)

I dial 411 and ask for Dr. Robert Rose in Baltimore. I want to take Dr. Rose out for a $200 lunch on my prime-plus-three-and-a half-percent home equity line just to meet this lucky leprechaun, and of course get his Godlawyer's name. I get a first year surgical resident finally on the phone. She says, "I've heard of him, but he was before my time. I think he's at GBMC now." (Greater Baltimore Medical Center) I dial 411 again.

All I know is what his new secretary told me: "Dr. Rose is such a sweet man. He started with us March 2nd, 2005. Right now he's on paternity leave, yes, he is remarried, and I'll be sure to have him call you, Dr., when he returns."

"Thank you so much, I can't wait to meet him." Dr. Rose never called me.

Almost two decades of illegal prescription drug fraud and substance abuse and Dr. Rose is cutting open abdomens again with less than three years of total suspension. I guess it's better to "willfully flout criminal drug laws…prescribe drugs for illegal purposes…and violate the code of medical ethics by inappropriately prescribing for a family member" (well, it is her fault for *victimizing him),* and her drug "*supplier*", than to be a depressed, divorced female alcoholic.

I wonder how many addicts died from overdosing on Dr. Rose's <u>twenty years</u> of prescription writing drug fraud? 5, 10, 20, 200? Did the Board ever ask themselves that? Nah. Apparently, the judicial system of our great country didn't give a damn, either.

* * *

On the contrary, I definitely deserve to then have my license totally revoked a few months later for not peeing in a cup for the Board immediately and doing a little Botox, because I was too busy stealing my own grandmother's candy dish back and blacking out and trying to kill myself in my car. Thank God for my strong BMW or I most surely would have cracked at least another neck bone, or put a rib through a lung or two, or just be cold and deader than a door nail. So now my medical license is completely wiped away, and I can't even begin to reapply for almost six years, and then the new Board can say a resounding, "NO!", but who's counting. (I don't think my count counts.)

*The fact of the matter is, there is not one licensing Board, (not one including Medicine, Chiropractic, Optometry, Nursing, Dental or even Law, etc.), in the United States of America that has a statute that can put a time limit on a <u>revocation,</u> except for one…the D.C. Law Board. And that's why past President Bill Clinton had to wait five full years before being reinstated in D.C. after he lost his license for the little Monica Lewinsky problem. It doesn't take five to six years to get rehabilitated from alcohol, cocaine, heroin, oxycontin, or any drug for that matter… and an addict or alcoholic is always at risk for relapse with their disease. What have I done to deserve such special treatment? Is a drunk driver worse than a drug dealer? Who **really** has the potential to kill more people? Is the Board allowed to make the rules up as they go along?*

Scottie, damn it, where's my phaser, at least? I have to, at least, shock and stun; I can't let the good ole boys have all the fun!

Are not women supposed to be able to feed themselves and their children? Or am I just supposed to bend over, "be victimized", say "thank you" and then shrivel up and die like some fragile flower? Are *only men allowed to be forgiven*?

Chapter 25

"Real" Jail, Seven Locks and on to Clarksburg

Peggy looks up questioningly from her romance novel when I walk back to my "own little corner" after my excursion to court. (Ain't no Cinderella, not even close.) I'm still more than a little taken aback by the "candy dish" and the "get a job" thing. I had no idea that you can go to work while you are incarcerated, even though the Wizard had mentioned something about it. I thought that I was just going to sit behind bars for six months, claustrophobic.

"What's up?" Peggy asks.

"I don't know. I'm exhausted. I got off today on my grandmother's candy dish deal I told you about. But before that, they talked to me about some place in Rockville. It's still jail, but they let you go to work in the community eight hours/day."

"That sounds good." I just look blankly at her. I can't hold it in any longer and get up and sit on the edge of her bed and whisper in her ear so I can't be overheard.

"Peggy, listen. I'm a doctor, an eye doctor. The Maryland Medical Board took my license after my first DUI last year, *last* November. I had a bitch of a time trying to find a job. I even sold cars for awhile. Hated it! I don't know how to do anything, but be a doctor."

"I knew you were smart!"

"Don't tell anyone. When the Board gave me a five-year suspension, the very next day I was arrested for the candy dish and within three weeks I got two more arrests for drunk driving. I should have been locked up on a mental ward with I.V. valium. I just lost my mind. I don't remember any of my driving arrests. *Please,* don't tell anyone."

"I won't. Guess what, I have breast cancer!"

"What?"

"I have a lump in my left breast."

"Didn't you get it out?"

"No."

"Why not?! How long have you had it?"

"A year."

"What?!" I speak too loudly and a few girls in the room look over. I lower my voice and hold my finger over my lips so Peggy knows to be quieter, too.

"My boyfriend felt it a year ago and I had a mammogram. The doctors told me they thought it was cancer, and I need to have it out, but I don't have any health insurance."

"Peggy, you have to have it out! You can't just ignore it!" I whisper loudly in her ear. My first instinct is to ask her to let me feel it; I want to see how big and how hard it is. *That* would go over real big in here. We just get rid of one gay girl, but who's feeling up who? Think again, Dr. Duke.

"I know I need to have it out."

"Listen, Peggy, listen carefully. I don't care whether you have health insurance or not. You have three children. They don't want their Mom to die in her early forties of breast cancer. This is America. Poor people without insurance should still get treated for cancer. Just go to the emergency room. Lie. Say you just found a lump that hurts. That's right; just say it hurts. The E.R. Doc will have to work you up. They'll find out if it is cancer and someone will operate on you. They *won't* send you home (I sincerely hope not, back to her van) with a tumor!"

Peggy starts to cry a little. "I'm afraid."

"Of course, you are! But you don't want to die of cancer!"

Peggy cries harder. "I don't care if I die."

Oh, God help me, I pray. This woman is really suffering from depression, too. "Peggy, you have to get back on an anti-depressant. You have to ask to see the shrink, *today.*"

"I know. I feel terrible."

"Please, tell the guard in half an hour that you used to take an anti-depressant, and you are feeling very depressed and need to see the doctor. Then when you see the shrink, tell him you have breast cancer! Maybe they'll take care of you right away. Then you can go to the hospital, have your surgery, and get the hell out of here for awhile! Sure would be a lot better to be in the hospital taking care of your cancer than lying around thinking about it in this hell hole!"

Peggy wipes her eyes with her sleeve.

"Do that today!"

"Okay."

Peggy gets an appointment to see the psychiatrist in a few days. I don't know what happened; however, because two days later my name was called. I guess I'm going to Rockville now. Well, I need to find a job, but

Rockville's better than Clarksburg, closer for my kids to come and see me. I haven't seen them in almost two weeks, and our phone calls have been getting increasingly difficult. Their sad little voices keep asking, "Mommy, when do we get to see you?" Even little Eloise is asking. My ignorant response is always, "I don't know, Honey, but I'm sure it is going to be soon." Soon. What the fuck is the definition of "soon" in jail? Basically, there isn't one. "Soon" is a figment of one's imagination while incarcerated. Nothing is ever "soon". "Soon" is bullshit.

"Miss Duke, get your things together. You're leaving." I dash a quick look at Peggy. I'm leaving? I can't leave Peggy! I'm actually going to miss her. She's been a friend. She never told anyone my business, and she really is a nice person. A nice girl with an addiction to crack cocaine, three kids, depression and cancer, who lives in a van. God bless her, her life is outrageously much, much shittier than mine. Please, God, help her.

I grab the tiny pencil we share to keep track of our card games and scribble my cell phone number on a scrap of newspaper. "Call me if you want. But I guess not for six months. I hope your stupid cousin drops the charges!"

"Thanks. Good luck to you, Mary Ann. You'll be all right."

"Thanks. I hope so." The rest of the women in the room are paying attention now, if they know English.

I don't give a damn. If I have to go out in the cold and sit again in some paddy wagon, I'm not going to freeze my ass off. I'm yanking on my large jumpsuit right in front of everyone, on top of my medium, shoving the collar of the medium down so the guard hopefully won't notice.

"Bye, Peggy." We lock eyes and Peggy's well up with tears.

"Bye," is all she can say and puts her face back into her tattered romance novel.

I walk to the door, waiting for the guard to come back. "I said, Duke, bring your things!" the guard barks once the big door is finally unlocked.

"I have everything," as I pat my breast pocket where my court papers are.

"Get your bedding, Duke!"

"Oh!"

I scurry back to the corner and pick up Mr. Burlap and my sheets. I had already thrown out my cup, toothbrush and basically empty tube of toothpaste.

"Pillow, too." I have to flip flop back yet again. Peggy looks up with a little grin, I am glad to see, and we roll our eyes at one another. I wink at her, and I'm off to the races… Right.

*   *   *

Two other girls are going with me from the big "holding tank" room at Seven Locks Jail. We are handcuffed before the door to the outside is opened. The fresh air feels great. Wow, I'm blinking, just like they do in the movies, when they're let out of jail. The sun really does seem bright after being inside so long, but I'm confused. The other girls said, "We're going to Clarksburg". I thought I was going to Rockville, so I ask the guard. "Am I not going to Rockville?"

"Well, maybe you are, and maybe you aren't. But you only go to Rockville two days a week, and this ain't one of those days."

I push it, "Well, can't I just stay here until I go to Rockville?" I'm thinking, at least I know what it's like at the Hotel Hell, and Peggy's here, how much *worse* is Clarksburg going to be?!

"Orders are to take you to Clarksburg." That's it. No talking back. I stumble up the paddy wagon stairs.

The ride to Clarksburg is longer than I thought it was going to be. Damn. Dieter isn't going to want to drive this far with the kids. Probably Edward won't want to either. Oh, God. This sucks, and I'm freezing again even in *two* jumpsuits. Please, don't let me get really sick.

The entrance to Clarksburg is imposing, a very high solid concrete wall with a huge automatic steel double door that opens slowly, and seems to close even slower. Hurry up and wait again. Bureaucracy. Government employees. Are they always in slow motion? I think about how I used to run around my office like a chicken with my head cut off doing three things at once. Patients waiting, patients dilating, phone calls on top of doing eye exams and an occasional stye or lid tumor surgery or laser surgery or Botox injection. I'm slamming all of the correction officers at once in my head thinking: Most of these people would never make it out in the real world! They'd be fired! They *have* to work for the government. Too damned slow, freaking caterpillars. I should have landed some government job; at least, I'd have some retirement money and not have to work at 100 miles an hour.

Hurry up and wait again. The three of us sit shivering in a "lobby" near the doors and wait for our duffle bags/ jail-carry-ons (*whatever* you call 'em). I unzip mine. What goodies do we have in here? Two flat sheets, a microscopic pillow, same Mr. Burlap blanket (Oh my God, he metastasized here!), basically an over-cloroxed dish towel for a bath towel, along with a new one-inch toothbrush, tiny tube of toothpaste and soap, with the great addition of a small black comb like my Dad used in the sixties when he still had hair.

Also, a walkman-type radio with headphones. For a brief second, I wonder if this headset comes with a television in my room/cell. Dream on, Mary Ann. Now march. Don't talk to anyone, which is extremely difficult for a Chatty Kathy like me. I'm reprimanded once for speaking and am surprised by the guard's harsh tone. I say nothing more. We walk in single file up a tan hallway in our tan jumpsuits and I briefly ponder, "So real jail is tan instead of gray"? It's still beyond boring, and this long hallway can only be described as the "highway to hell". It even seems to narrow as we walk.

Lucky me, a corner room again with a view, double the draftiness and a scene out of a tiny four-inch by eighteen-inch vertical window of a ten-to-twelve-foot fence with two-feet-plus of dense, curly-Q barbed wire at the top. There are approximately ten feet of small stones with barbed wire flowing in curly-Qs across them going up a hill, followed by another ten-foot fence with two-plus more feet of barbed wire perched on top. No one can escape Clarksburg with any skin left, better to be shot trying I suppose, if it gets that bad.

However, the window view is totally secondary to my roommate/cellmate. She's scarier than the barbed wire fences. Her hair is stringy and below her shoulders with four inches of solid grey and then blond. (Guess she's been in for awhile, 'cause she's in desperate need of a dye job.) Her face is pale and very wrinkled, but the most notable feature is her lack of teeth, not even one.

She gives me a big, gummy smile from the top bunk and says, "My name is Sue but everyone calls me Grandma."

I reach up and shake her hand. "My name's Mary Ann."

"Nice to meet you. Which bunk do you want, Honey?"

"Umm, I'll take the lower one if you don't mind."

"Sure. That's fine. I'm already up here anyways."

Great, I think. You can have the upper one. I'm afraid I'll roll over and fall five feet onto concrete. Grandma seems happy to see me. (What the hell is up with women being happy in jail?)

"Would you rather me call you Sue or Grandma?" and I give her a weak smile.

"Oh, call me Grandma. Everyone else does, and I'm proud to be one already."

"How many grandchildren do you have?"

"Just one. One granddaughter. I had my daughter when I was seventeen, and my daughter was nineteen when she had hers. I have a nine-year-old granddaughter", she says proudly.

"That's nice" is all I respond and give her another weak smile. Oh Jesus, I think, (I was always good in Math and think fast), 17 + 19 + 9 = 45; Grandma's only *one* year older than I am. Dear God, she looks at *least sixty*-five. Thank God I didn't tell her my age or guess hers out loud. I remain speechless, and Grandma continues to chat.

"What are you in for?"

"DUI,... you?"

"Oh..." Grandma responds, "I just stole from Home Depot when I was drunk and I served my time, but then I didn't go to see my probation officer, so I got sixty more days." She's scared the pants off of me already with her aged appearance, but now I'm also wary that I'm on probation for three years and I'm *never* going to miss one of *those* probation officer appointments. It's one thing to skip a post-partum appointment with Dr. Belizan for work; he wouldn't lock me up. Sixty days for missing one time with your probation officer sounds harsh. I hope Grandma's lying and she missed several, to get a full sixty more days.

Grandma keeps right on chatting. "I started drinking and smoking cigarettes when I was twelve, hard habits to break, but we can't even smoke in here."

"Yep" is all I respond, still in shock how old she looks at just forty-five, but now, at least, it makes a *little* more sense. Over thirty years of alcoholism and cigarette smoking can do that to you, but I still feel bad for her. I never saw anyone in all my years of medical school, internship and residency look so damned old at just forty-five, no teeth and so wrinkled. This Grandma also must have had a very hard life.

I give her a relaxed, kind smile and say, "We are going to get along fine. You let me know if I do *anything* that bothers you, okay?"

Grandma gummily grins back, "Sure, Honey, better make your bed before they yell at you."

Bed, I think, yeah, right, as I reach down and start tucking the rough flat sheet under the gym mat.

Grandma's watching me "unpack". "Hey!" she yells, "You got a pillow! I didn't get a pillow. You better give that back! You can get in trouble for having that!"

I blankly look at Grandma and respond, "How can I get into trouble for something they gave me?"

"Well, I didn't get one." (She's jealous of my hard, plastic, disgustingly small headpiece.)………..This is going to be a long six months.

*   *   *

My claustrophobia kicks right in. Our cell is one hell of a lot smaller than my master bath. And, I don't have to *share* my bathroom. I almost wish for bars instead of our solid steel automatic door with tiny window, which seems smaller than the window in the wall, even if everyone could see in, just for more open air flow.

Oh, dear God, it really *is* another metal bed and gym mat mattress. And is that supposed to be our toilet? There is this two-and-a-half-foot metal sink like an R-2, D-2 with a giant gun coming out of the side. The "gun" a.k.a. "toilet" has no lid, and that is it, our metal all-inclusive sink/commode, jutting right out of the middle of the wall. Not even a blue curtain, just a big belly button like indentation where a roll of toilet paper sits.

Everything is attached to cement, no loose chair or anything. The one-inch toothbrush comes to mind. Nothing at all that would represent a weapon, not even close. I don't know how people hang themselves in a cell. Where does one attach the sheet? Thankfully Grandma interrupts my stream of thought.

"Time for dinner!" she pipes as she jumps to the floor. How can she be so lithe in flip flops?... Practice.

Just then the steel sliding door opens loudly, and I feel a little better in the hallway until I look up. Dear God, there she is! My nemesis, Venice. She sees me at the exact same moment and a wicked little smile lights up her face below her shaved head, "Well ain't it bes Janie Fuckin' Fonda!" Oh fuck me, I think, I was hoping to never see her again in my life! And now it looks like I have to eat, shower and sleep on the same floor with the killer bitch. Terrific. Just beautiful.

    I've had such an overwhelming day already with leaving Peggy and going to a bloody awful cell in Clarksburg with Grandma instead of to the Pre-Release Center in Rockville, and getting "out in the community" with God only knows what kind of job, I don't give a damn and just glare right back at Venice as she shoves ahead of me to get down the stairs to dinner. My glare says simply: Fuck you! And her glare back is one of a little shock, and I catch it right away. (Always the ophthalmologist, right? I look into eyes for a living, or at least used to for twenty years.)

    I shocked miss two-hundred-pounds, all muscle Venice, probable killer in cold blood. A quick shot of adrenaline squeezed out, and I smile a little and think to myself, "That's how I survive in here. Act like you *are* tougher than they are, Mary Ann, and take not one ounce of their shit, then they will respect me and leave me alone, even if every single one of them is bigger and meaner". I bet Jane Fonda would be proud of me.

                  *   *   *

    My adrenaline high is short-lived, however. Dinner, if one can call it that, lasts fifteen-twenty minutes, no television, and it is back to the cell. On my way to dump my milk carton out and turn in my tray and plastic spoon (That's all we get to eat with, a spoon that *must* be turned back in, no fork and certainly no knife, even if shitty plastic, not allowed, 'cause I bet Miss Venice could get a plastic knife into a carotid artery no problem), Venice dumps her orange peels on my tray.

    I stop and truly without thinking about consequences state to her, "Get your garbage off my tray."

Now it's her turn to glare at me. "Whats yous be sayin' to me?!"

"Take your trash off of my tray," and I glare right back at her.

"I's not takin' nothin' off yous tray. Want to make sumthin' outta it?!"

Go to hell is on the tip of my tongue, but instead I repeat monotonally, "Take your trash off of my tray. I don't take out your trash."

Holy shit! You'd think I just slapped Cleopatra. Immediately there are five or six girls rallying around Venice, and big, bad Venice is leaning her huge frame into my face and screwing up her features and big lips into the most menacing look anyone in my lifetime has ever given me.

Just then two guards enter our dinner area from their guard station and yell at *me,* "Duke! Duke! What are you doing?!"

I whirl around at them with an innocent look on my face, because damn it, I *am* innocent and reply, "She's throwing her garbage on my tray. Am I supposed to throw her garbage out, too?" and I try to stay monotonal.

"I's didn' do nuthin' likes dat!" exclaims Venice.

I'm no longer Chatty Kathy in this joint. I've turned into Monotonal Mary, "Yes, she did."

"You two get yourselves back in your cells! Venice, throw your own garbage out. Where are your spoons?"

I immediately turn away from Venice, throw out my trash and hers, hand in my spoon and walk back to my cell.

Good show, Mary Ann, jolly good show. You've been incarcerated in a cell less than an hour, and you've already pissed off two guards and even better, confirmed enemy status with the meanest, most dangerous girl on the unit. And she, obviously, has reinforcements, and they look pretty nasty themselves. Just beautiful. Perfect entrance, just grand. Grandma walks in and the steel door slams behind her. She gives me a look that simply says, "You shouldn't have done that." And then she shoots me a small toothless smile and twinkling eyes for a second, as she climbs up to her bunk and immediately puts her radio on so we don't speak.

But her smile spoke volumes: Grandma is proud of me. I think she is happy she has a roommate with some balls, even if I left my brains back in the paddy wagon.

Chapter 26

HELP!

Somehow that first night in real jail I slept, naked still under two rough jumpsuits with my gift gym socks on, under Mr. Burlap. Slept that is until before dawn, when the sliding steel door banged open at 5:00 a.m. for breakfast. Venice surprisingly doesn't say a word to me. The modus operandi of breakfast appears to be to eat in fifteen minutes and go back to sleep. With no coffee and nothing to do back in the cell; this was definitely everyone's M.O.

I have to ask Grandma one question at breakfast as I watch the guard take a tray and put it through a small slot in a steel door on the first floor. "Why is she doing that?"

Grandma looks at me half asleep like I've grown a second head overnight.

"That's solitary confinement," she whispers to me. "You don't want to go in there. You'll be stuck in there alone for a week. You aren't even let out to shower or eat."

I think of the trickle of water to wash in from R-2 D-2 and the small basin not even fit for a bird bath, much less for a "P.T.A." bath my great aunt used to call them. (pussy, tits and armpits) I gulp my juice and silently agree with her and nod. I better be on my best behavior today. Curiosity gets the best of me, and I walk quickly over to the narrow slot in that door and bend down to peek in on my way upstairs

Oh my God, it's Yvonne, my engineer buddy from Chicago, the educated crack head. What did she do to get in there? She looks up at me with sad eyes. Definitely. I'm not going to say a word today, not one.

Between breakfast and lunch, I start to go really crazy for the first time, and that edgy, claustrophobic feeling is getting worse by the minute. Time for my Jane Fonda workout. I work up a sweat, even in just one jumpsuit, so now feel gross on top of caged. One hour after lunch. One hour after lunch, we get to make collect calls and shower. It's called 23-1 lockdown--one's first week in real jail. I eat lunch fast, talk to no one and hiss to Grandma, "I'm running into the shower because Venice is on the phone. Please, if you see her come up the stairs, please, try to warn me."

I give a small smile and a wink to Yvonne in solitary, throw off my sweaty jumpsuit and run in the shower. I look around and quickly start the shower. Great. No lock on the door. Perfect. Venice could simply slip in, grab my head and hurl it against the cement wall, or better yet, position it just right and put my temple through the hook for one's towel. *Or,...* just fucking snap my already once-snapped neck!

I never stood with my back to the door to face forward into the shower's stream. Not a chance. Definitely the fastest, backwardest shower of my life. I'm half wet, throwing on my large jumpsuit to run back to my room to use the bathroom before Grandma comes up. And I have to hurry because I want to call Edward. I can't call my children because they are not home from school yet. I won't be able to call them until the weekend, so I want to also call my parents or my sister and ask them to, please, call my children and tell them, "Mommy is okay". (Sure I am, one giant claustrophobic gerbil in a small cage with no treadmill.)

I rush pass Venice coming up the stairs without looking at her, but I can feel her glaring at me. Who's afraid of the big bad bitch, tra la la tra la la? Not not me, not not me. (*Sure*, I'm not.) Damn! The phone is already being used by another screaming hyena, this time not in English. My heart is pumping fast, so I sit down and blankly stare at the soap opera I've never watched before on the television in our eating area. It's soundless, and I don't have my headphones on to tune into the station.

Someone sits down next to me and gently touches my arm. I just about jump out of my skin and quickly turn my wet head. It's my buddy from solitary. "Oh, thank God" I think and smile, "It's just you, Yvonne". My eyes ask, "How are you and what the hell did you do to get in there for a week"? She whispers to me, "I refused to live with *her*."

My eyes widen, but that's all she needed to say. I would have done the same damned thing. I would have taken two to three weeks in solitary confinement without a soul to talk to and no showers, to having to share a tiny cell with a big, strong girl who is charged with murder, supposedly gay, with a tendency to "wig out". Absolutely.

The guard walks in. Shit. Time's up already. I never got to make even one call. "See you at dinner. I'm glad you're out," I whisper to Yvonne and trudge "home" to Grandma after I grab a three-year-old Forbes magazine on my way up the stairs. All of the romance novels are gone: pickings at the reading rack are slim.

I kill the afternoon with my Forbes. On the cover are the ten richest Americans. I jump out of my bunk and show the front-page article frantically to Grandma. "Look!" I yell at her, as I'm jamming my finger at one of the names. I try to keep my voice down, because I have felt since minute one in jail like my cell is wired for both audio and visual. (I try to go to the bathroom only when Grandma is sleeping, but I still feel like I'm being watched. It's creepy.)

"See that name?" Grandma pulls off her headphones and just replies, "Yep."

"I went to rehab in Atlanta with that person and what an asshole. Can you believe it? One of the top ten richest people in America with everything in the world, *billions,* not millions, and just another flaming alcoholic. And not a nice person either."

Grandma's reply, "Yep. Money don't count. An alcoholic is an alcoholic." That's all she says. "Grandma is a wise woman", I think, "even if she does like to rob Home Depot in front of cameras and blow off her probation officer".

*   *   *

Dinner is way too quick, as is every meal. I barely get to talk to Yvonne. Probably because Venice is vainly attempting to be a Donna Summer again, and her wailing drowns out everyone else's conversation.

She really is one sick unit, I bitch to myself. She's insane. She probably *did* murder that sixteen-year-old, and now denies it and shows no remorse. But she shouldn't get off on any kind of insanity plea. No way…and get let back out on the streets to do it again? She must have been on something to shoot a sixteen-year-old, not once, but three times in the face. Here we are pouring all this money into Iraq when we should be taking care of addiction and escalating crime and homicides at home. Gees, if I was President I wouldn't be corrupt and keep wars going to make money. I would just clean house and clean up this country. Corruption is corroding the United States of America. This country has gone to hell since the Kennedy assassination. Venice is still singing away. God, is she ever going to shut up? I give Yvonne a disgusted look and hiss at her as we empty our trays, "You did the right thing. She would have driven you nuts." Yvonne stares back at me and says sarcastically, "*That's* an understatement."

Venice couldn't have heard our exchange, but like an animal she must have sensed something, and whines at me, "What's the matter with you, Fonda? Yous gots a problem?!" I ignore her. That pisses her off more, and she starts walking toward me. I don't look up. Before she can get within arm's length, the guard comes around the corner and yells, "Back to your cells!"

Thank you, Guard, very much.

I return the Forbes, like anyone else in the joint might read it besides Yvonne. Grandma certainly didn't want to. I see a romance novel. Praise Jesus. I snag the beat up book and head upstairs thinking, "I'm not going to shower tomorrow. I don't have a clean jumpsuit to put on anyway".

*   *   *

Day 3 starts out with a real jolt. 5:00 a.m. breakfast with coffee! I drink mine in one gulp, as necessary, because it resembles dirty dishwater, has no taste and is lukewarm. I usually take mine very hot, sweet and light, but no Splenda or Coffeemate in this hell hole, just greenish/black, weak, disgusting coffee once or twice a week. Grandma doesn't want hers; neither does Yvonne nor the next girl nor the next three girls. I imbibe seven cups. I don't know why. I guess after almost two weeks of incarceration and lack of stimulation, I feel like some serious caffeination,…so I get it.

Grandma climbs up to her bed/metal slab and immediately starts snoring. All seven cups of coffee in jail probably equals one "Vente" Starbuck's, so sleep is not an option for me.

I sit on the hard metal stool in front of the metal jut-out/desk and stare out of the slit shaped window over the barbed wire and watch the color of the sky change. The sun is just coming up. Ernest Hemingway's famous book title comes to mind, *The Sun Also Rises*. Some day, I ponder, the sun will rise when I am happy. Some day, the sun will rise when you are on top of the world again, Mary Ann. Just keep holding on. You used to have the world by the ass. You will again, just keep holding on, I tell myself, as I get my pen.

My prison pen, if one could even call it a pen. It is four inches long and of flexible plastic, absolutely an impossible weapon to put through someone's carotid and/or eyeball. One has to hold it very tightly right at the tip or the whole thing will flex, and writing is like trying to force a wet noodle to hold still upright. Damn. I don't have anything to write on. Yes, you do, Mary Ann, as I dig under my gym mat. There they are. My court papers, getting straightened while I sleep on them after being folded many times and stuffed in the breast pocket of my jumpsuit. All nine pages of them, including the Nolle Prosequi theft charge. I smile a little as I leaf past that one, my only victory, however insane the original charge was.

I flip that one over first and start writing.

By the time Grandma rises I have covered all nine pages with the tiniest handwriting I can muster with my incredibly poor prison pen. (My first book draft)

*   *   *

I finally get to use the phone that afternoon. I think for a second as I sit, holding the receiver, and decide to call my retired parents. At least, *they* might be home to take a collect call. Dad answers.

"Hi Dad! It's Mary Ann."

"Oh, hi."

I don't really know what to say next. There's so much to say, so many apologies to make. What does a daughter, the only doctor in the family, the valedictorian and track star of her high school, say to her obviously mortified father from jail;…how's the weather?

"Is Mom home?"

"No, she went to the store."

"Oh." Mom was always less of a disciplinarian than Dad. Since Baba died we have become even closer. It would have been easier to talk to her, but I have to ask for some help and talk fast, because the next girl is already breathing down my neck to use the phone.

I talk quietly and rapidly. "Dad, I need your help. Please, call Edward and Dieter and tell them that I cannot call them to speak to the children, because I am only allowed to use the phone between one and two p.m., when the kids are in school. Please, tell them I will call them on Saturday and that it has to be collect, and to please, be home then and pick up. Dieter has been refusing most of my collect calls. They are only sixty-five cents for a local call, and I have told him so more than once. But I have been very frustrated, because he doesn't always accept them. I haven't talked to the kids in days."

"Okay." No other comment.

"I have to go now, Dad. Another girl wants to use the phone. I'll try to call Mom over the weekend."

"Okay, I'll tell her."

"Don't tell Mom, Dad, she'll worry, but jail is really terrible. It's awful."

Dad pauses just a second, then states, "That's how it's supposed to be."

Now it's my turn to pause for a lot longer than Dad did. That's not what I wanted to hear. There were no words of comfort or encouragement or wisdom, or maybe that was the wisdom. I'm shocked by how harsh his words felt.

"Bye, Dad."

"Bye."

I feel put down by my father. Does he really feel I deserve all this? Especially after almost four months of rehab? I really didn't expect Dad's response, wow.

*   *   *

The rest of the day is miserable. I can't sleep. I don't feel like reading. I'm out of paper, so I can't write. Grandma told me I can't ask the guard for paper, that I have to wait until I've been in jail a week. Then I can buy some from the list of things one can buy from the "store". It's not really a store; it's just a list of things one can purchase, small creature comforts, like a chocolate bar; but first I need some money.

So what the hell am I going to do for four more days until a week is up? Oh God, I shouldn't have drank all of that coffee this morning. I'm wired. "Like a cat shot in the ass" my father used to say. Fabulous. I'm a cat shot in the ass in a tiny room without even enough air.

About nine p.m. I lose it. I have my first full-blown panic attack from claustrophobia, and I push the button for the guards, that is supposed to be used only in emergencies.

"What do you want?"

"I think I'm having an asthma attack! I can't breathe! I need some air! May I come out into the hallway so I can breathe?"

No response. I turn my wild eyes up to Grandma, and she looks at me worried but doesn't speak. I stutter to her, "I can't breathe!"

I stand up quickly, and now I'm light-headed. Just then the steel door opens. I rush right through it and almost shove the guard.

"Oh, thank you!" I gasp through my hyperventilating breaths. "I can't breathe!"

"Do you have asthma?!" the guard, a large woman, yells at me.

"Well...no...I mean, I've never had it before, but I think I have it *now*!"

Just being in the open space of the hallway looking over the common area makes me feel a little better, and I relax a bit. The guard repeats herself, "Do you *have* asthma?"

"No."

"Well, then get your sorry ass back into your cell!"

She said it so nastily, and was towering over me menacingly, that I abruptly turn and walk back into my cell. Grandma watches everything from her high perch. I stand just inside the steel door as it slams shut and look up at her with fear in my eyes. "Grandma,...I can't take a whole lot more of this. I'm claustrophobic!"

Grandma is so wonderful. She jumps down and immediately comes to me and hugs me tight. "It's going to be okay, Honey. You are going to be okay." I hold her tight and try to slow my breathing. She holds me until I do.

I'll always be grateful to her for helping me in my time of need. It was just nice, too, to have a hug.

But needless to say, I slept ever so fitfully that night. I need to get out of this box.

*   *   *

The following day is Saturday. Somehow, someway, I'm first to the phone. I call Edward. He answers right away.

"There are visiting hours today. Will you, please, bring Eloise to see me?" I decided during my fitful night that I am *not* going to ask Dieter to bring my older three children. Reason number one is I don't want them to see Mommy in this place and ever have the memory of Mommy in "real" jail. Reason number two is I don't want to have to cope with the rejection of him saying, "No", either.

But Eloise is just turned three-years-old, so she won't remember Mommy in jail, and I need to hug my sweet little baby.

I tell Edward what exit to take off of the 270 highway and say, "It's easy to find. Just follow the signs. May I, please, speak to Eloise?"

"She already went down for her nap."

"Oh." I'm disappointed not to hear her cute voice but am excited they are coming to see me later. Two girls are panting to use the phone now, so I get off quickly with Edward, but ring up Dieter to their loud protestations. Shouldn't have bothered, no one picked up. Oh, well, maybe Dad didn't get through yet. I'll have to try tomorrow on Sunday, or I won't speak to the kids for God knows how long. That'll be hard.

I walk up to Yvonne and whisper, "I think my three-year-old daughter is coming today."

She smiles and responds, "You are lucky to be getting a visitor. It gets you out of that fucking cell for more than one hour a day."

I remember Yvonne is from Chicago, but ask, "Do you have any friends or relatives here?"

"Not any who would bother to visit me."

"I'm sorry" I say and pat her arm. All of a sudden we both turn our heads. Venice is on the phone, screaming into it so loud I think they can hear her in the unit across the hall. "What yous be lettin' da police into mys apartment fo?!" She's yelling, "Whys you be lettin' them take my wallet?! Whys didn' you go gits my wallet?!" Yvonne and I roll our eyes at each other. Of course, the police can search your apartment and confiscate any damned thing they want. You're charged with first-degree murder!

I swear Venice has some seventh animal type sense and reads my mind, even though I'm not near her or looking at her, and now she's yelling at me, "Yous be listenin' to my conversation, ain't you, Fonda?" I ignore her, yet again, so she reattacks *me* verbally while still taking up phone time. "Don't yous be listenin' to my conversations!"

Dear God, because I despise and fear this woman, I think, "You are a screaming hyena, you wild thing, *everyone* can't miss hearing every word of your lousy jive talking you think is English". A part of me feels sorry in a way for Venice, but my instinct is to survive, and this alleged killer has a hatred for me. I need to really be on my guard every minute when around her. I whisper to Yvonne, "I'm going to get a very quick shower since she's on the phone. Watch my back, will you?" and I look her dead in the eyes. Yvonne understands; she knows one is most vulnerable in the upstairs shower, so far from the guards. Lucky Yvonne is on the first floor, and doesn't have to share her shower with Venice.

Ignoring Venice as I run upstairs, I take *the* fastest shower of my life.

*   *   *

The afternoon drones on. I'm totally un-caffeinated today, had a horrible night's sleep, but can't nap to save my life. Finally the steel door opens and there is a guard. For a second, I panic and think, "I'm in trouble for something and they are taking me to solitary".

"Duke! C'mon Duke, you have a visitor."

I'm out of bed in a flash, flip flopping my way in step behind the guard. Oh *great*, Eloise must be here! I haven't seen my baby in two weeks since Edward left in a huff with her the night before court.

Down, down, down the long tan highway to hell we walk. It seems like the damned hallway widens as I hurriedly move down it now. More hallways, more turns, I'm lost. "I never would be able to find my way out of here", I think, "and I certainly can't fit out the window". But negative thoughts stop entirely as I get more and more excited to see Eloise.

I am told to stop at a large desk where another guard sits. Before he can speak I blurt out, "I'm Mary Ann Duke; do I have visitors?"

The guard barely looks up and just points to the left with his arm. I turn swiftly and face a row of cubicles. The sight hits me in the face like a ton of bricks. It's just like it is in the movies. Oh, my God, we are going to be separated by a big window, and I am going to have to pick up a phone to talk to them, and I won't be able to hug Eloise! My disappointment jolts away when I see her. Oh, there she is! I scramble into the chair and hurriedly pick up the receiver. Eloise is standing on the table on the other side of the partition holding both hands against it, getting it good and smudged. I reach my hand up and tap both of hers as she is banging hers back. A huge smile lights up her face, and I jump out of my chair, stand and lean my face right up to the partition like I am going to kiss her. Eloise reaches forward and kisses the partition, and I, like a knee jerk reaction, kiss her through it and start blabbing, "I love you Eloise. Mommy loves you so much!"

My dear little blonde three-year-old is still tapping the partition and kissing it. I try to kiss her through the partition again and continue talking to her. "I'm so happy you came to see me, Angel! I'm so sorry that I cannot really kiss and hug you, but Mommy loves you so much! You look so pretty." I reach up and tap back her tapping little hands, when there is Edward's all too serious voice in my ear, "She can't hear a word you said."

I stare at him blankly for a second, then his words register and monotonal Mary Ann takes over. (Edward can be a professional "kill joy" when he wants to be, probably could win an academy award for it.) "Hello, Edward. Thanks for coming and bringing Eloise. Could you please put the phone up to her ear?" Edward acquiesces and Eloise immediately starts babbling after my first, "Hi, Angel!"

"Hi, Mommy! When are you coming home? I want to play with you!" (Eloise is fantastically verbal and articulate for her barely three-and-one-half years.) Her words speak volumes. I *have* to give her hope.

"Mommy will be able to play with you very soon, but I cannot come home with you and Daddy today.

Mommy still has some work to do here, okay?" Eloise nods, smiles, and keeps right on tapping. I think briefly that she understood me. All of my children know from experience that M.o.m.m.y. works, works hard, and has to, to pay bills. They seemed to have figured that out from the first moment they could think, period.

Edward takes the receiver from Eloise and says, "You look good." Strange compliment from Edward, tan jumpsuits aren't becoming, and I don't have on any make-up, obviously, but I respond with a "Thanks." I can hear the girl's conversation in the next cubicle so decide not to say much. For all I know, every phone in Clarksburg is bugged just like the Wizard told me the phone in the big room at Seven Locks was being recorded.

Edward reaches up and takes Eloise away from the smudged partition and sits her on his lap; so I sit down, too, but am still staring at Eloise and her adorableness. I haven't seen her in it feels like forever, and who knows when I'll be able to see her again.

"How's it going?" asks Edward.

"F.i.n.e."

"That bad?"

"Pretty much. I have *no idea* how people do this for years. I hope I get to go to Rockville soon, but I'll only be able to stay there if I get a full time job."

"When will you know if you can go there?"

"I don't know. Somebody told me they take people there on Sundays. Dear God, I hope I get to go tomorrow. I am so claustrophobic in that damned cell!"

Edward is silent for a minute. Guess I stumped the great Brit briefly. Even *he* cannot fathom it. No one can.

No one can truly understand how it feels to be a caged animal unless they have been one.

"Can I, please, speak to Eloise again?" I'd rather listen to her innocent chatter than field questions from Edward. Eloise and I chat a little about school (daycare), her new shirt and shoes, as she lifts her chubby little leg, and I must tell her at least six times how much I love her.

Time flew by. That was the quickest hour I have ever lived. Blowing kisses and waving to Eloise, as she stared longingly at me over Edward's shoulder, and not knowing when *I* was going to be able to hold her again or even see her, is a horrible feeling. But just think, Mary Ann, I encourage myself, some women do it for years and years. You've got six months. You can do anything for six months. Anything. Anything except let my older children see me in this jail. I don't want them to see me here in this disgusting jumpsuit behind a partition. I pray silently on the way back to my cell, "Please, God, get me out of this jail and my awful cell soon. You know I'm an alcoholic, not a criminal. Please, help me to see all of my children, and rescue me from this insane asylum before I go any crazier".

*   *   *

Grandma looks up expectantly as I walk through the metal door to "home". I smile at her and say, "That was great." Grandma smiles back, and I gush on, "Eloise looked so cute. She kept tapping on the partition with her little hands and trying to kiss me through it. It was so wonderful to see her and to hear her little voice,"...then I trail off unexpectedly as the sharp reality hits me that I'm back in a cell with Grandma, and I don't know when I am *really* going to be able to hug her and kiss her.

My smile is gone, and I ramble on like I'm on some psychiatrist's couch. Instead of lying down, though, I'm standing with my arms folded on Grandma's upper bunk with my chin on my hands, because my head is too heavy to hold up. "Grandma, I have to get out of here. I have things to do. I have a home. I put it up for sale while I was in rehab. I didn't get any offers. I'm all out of money. I can't foreclose on it. I can't give power of attorney to Edward, because I don't trust him. My family all lives too far away to deal with it. I'm all alone. I'm almost out of credit card room. Everything's a mess. When are they going to let me go to Rockville and try to get a job? I don't want my children to see me here."

Grandma pats my arm. "I think they take girls to Rockville on Sundays. Maybe you will be going tomorrow. Just wait 'til tomorrow, Honey."

What would I do without Grandma? She's really been very kind. Her next sentence says it all, "At least you had a visitor today." I smile sympathetically up at her.

No one came to see Grandma.

Chapter 27

Gray to Tan to Yellow...and I like RED

Please God, I pray over and over, please, get me to Rockville and out of this cage. I've had no caffeine since my overdose two mornings ago, but I still can't fall asleep to save my life. Three workouts today, instead of my usual two, and I should be tired. But after two weeks of sleeping on a gym mat over a metal slab, my body just feels tense and cramped, like some new diagnosis of fibromyalgia or rheumatoid arthritis.

I glance at the emergency button and smirk. That would go over *real* big tonight. I think the same guard is working who "came to my rescue" forty-eight hours ago. Just give the button a little ringee-dingee and politely say, "I'm having trouble falling asleep and am a little sore. Could you please bring me 800 mg. of ibuprofen, and an Ambien or Halcion, (sleeping pills) whichever you have"? Heaven help you, Mary Ann, you are going nuts; you really are. It's not like you're a V.I.P. calling room service at a 5-star hotel. Pushing that button will probably inflate the emergency slide right into solitary confinement; then what chance will you have of going to Rockville tomorrow?

Grandma's snoring loud enough for both of us. I put the radio headphones on low and pray in between catnaps all night.

*   *   *

I can't help myself after breakfast and ask the new shift guard as I'm handing in my spoon, "Am I going to Rockville today?"

"I don't know. We don't get the list until later."

I push it, "But it *is* Sunday that they go there, right?"

"Usually." Usually. Thanks for giving me such high hopes, as I turn away so the guard doesn't see my pissed off face.

I'm frustrated, tired, cold and totally cranky. Grandma senses it. She heard me talking to the guard. Before she rolls over and goes back to sleep, she gives me her winningest gummy smile and matter-of-factly states, "They always go on Sundays. You will be going today, Honey, don't worry."

I love Grandma…I think we both snored our way into lunch.

*   *   *

A short time before dinner, I had just about given up hope of a rescue (from my next off the Richter scale claustrophobia attack), when the door banged open. "Duke! Get your things together. You're coming with me."

I leap out of bed and swiftly cram everything into the duffle bag and stuff my written-all-over court papers and "flexi-jail-pen" into my jumpsuit pocket, barely a ten second pack. I look at Grandma, and feel really bad all of a sudden that I am leaving her alone. I whisper to her, "Can I do anything for you?" Grandma's ripping a page out of her book and scribbling a number down. "This is my boss's number, well, he's kind of my boyfriend, too. Please, call him and tell him to come visit me next Saturday. It's his cell phone." I nod and understand. She hasn't been able to call him at all, because we all know cell phones won't take collect calls.

"Sure. I will, as soon as I can." I reach up and squeeze her hand and whisper, "Thank you for your support."

"Duke. Duke! C'mon!" I grab my duffle bag and run out of the cell. Immediately the heavy door slams shut behind me. I turn to give Grandma a good-bye smile, but her head is already bowed back into her book.

I can't help but feel very sorry for her. I was crawling out of my skin in less than six days in that bloody awful cell; poor Grandma has to get through sixty. I have absolutely no clue how people do it for life.

I would rather be dead than in a cell for life.

*   *   *

Single file back down the optically-illusioned widening hallway, two African American girls and me. My thoughts are scattering, but first off I'm relieved to be leaving Venice's lair. She'll be pissed not to have me to pick on anymore, but she'll find someone else. Did she pick on me because I was white or because I stood up to her? Probably both. White women are certainly in the minority in jail.

The only place better to be African American is in jail, because that is what, at least, 75% of the populace, and the guards are. What a horrible thing. Only 13% of our country is African American. Is only 13% of the population really committing over 75% of the crimes? Or are the white girls getting off with only probation by the mostly white judges and the African American women being harshly sent to a cell?

I think the only thing harder in this world than being a white woman punished by white men is a minority punished by the white man. African American women have it the toughest. Their leading cause of death in their child bearing years is Acquired Immuno-Deficiency Syndrome (AIDS), and they get it from "their significant others", not from I.V. drug abuse or prostitution. Their significant others are either on the "low down" or practicing bisexuals, or sharing needles. Not much in the news about AIDS anymore, but it's out there, *for sure*, and the number one killer of young African American women. If AIDS was the number one killer of young white men, would things be different?

Of course. What a nightmare. What are you thinking about all this for Mary Ann? Oh, probably because the two African American girls walking ahead of you look like they have been locked up one hell of a lot longer than you have. It's something about the way they carry themselves, how they are holding their heads. They seem so passive, so damned beaten down.

Dear God, please, don't ever let me walk like that.

*   *   *

Our duffle bags are searched (For what? Like we've confiscated a hand gun and some cocaine while incarcerated?), and confiscated, then we are led toward the door. Before going outside we are handcuffed, and better yet, shackled together at the ankles. Now we really have to walk "N Sync", or one of us will trip and fall and most likely bring us all down. These shackles are bullshit. They didn't shackle us on the way *in* to jail. Are we more fucking dangerous on our way *out*? These ankle shackles are humiliating and decidedly overkill.

I can't make any sense of it, but who cares, right, not me, as I trip and am hurled forward up the paddy wagon steps.

The sun is going down and the air is cold along with the hard metal bench, my good knee bruised; but the weight on my shoulders is much lighter. I hope we arrive in time so I can call my children and tell them, "Mommy's out of jail".

Wishful thinking. We first have to stop at Seven Locks and get our clothing from court. Hurry up and wait. It took hours to get our things, but lo and behold, there was my rose gold watch. It wasn't stolen after all; I just had to dig in the bottom of the bag to find the crystal face which had somehow popped off. I changed by myself in the bathroom with a guard within reach. My suit jacket was on a hanger, but my skirt had fifty wrinkles from being crushed in the bottom of the bag. Out of a jumpsuit and flip flops and into my own clothes and shoes, I started to feel a little more like myself, even a little happy, however hungry.

We finally arrive at the Pre-Release Center in Rockville, and I'm disappointed that it's too late at 9:00 p.m. to call the kids, as I eye a pay phone on the way in. I don't have any change and will have to call collect. Outrageously, Dieter has been refusing to accept my collect calls, even though I told him they are unlimited local for only sixty-five cents. I am sending him lucky number $13.00 dollars extra to his December child support check for twenty calls to prove my point. I don't think I've talked to the kids even five times since I've been incarcerated; I'm certainly not pinching pennies to try to speak to them. Are you kidding? I've lost somewhere between $300,000 and $500,000 in just one year since they took my medical license; it sickens me to think about it. Being unable to earn a living as a doctor for twelve months and still paying a humungous mortgage, for rehab, car accidents, attorneys' fees, child support, food, etc…that $13 dollars to talk to my children isn't even *a* peanut.

I suppress the disappointment of not being able to call them and replace it with disgust as I glance around. What the hell is this supposed to be, someone's grotesque attempt at the yellow brick road to OZ? Who on earth picked the paint for this place? *Cinderblocks* are definitely *not* supposed to be neon yellow.

"Miss Duke. *Miss* Duke, get over here and get your things!" The guard was yelling at me twice, because I was lost in my own thoughts again. I quickly step forward and get handed a plastic box of what I assume is filled with "prison particulars" like the duffle bag at Clarksburg. The three of us then follow the guard down another neon hallway to a large common area, around 20' by 30' and two stories high where a few girls are watching "BTV" on a small television and don't bother to look up. (There must have been a sale on it. God, I still can't believe the color of this place. Yellow "rules". Maybe the walls are supposed to symbolize one big caution sign.)

Face the facts "*Miss*" Duke, I admonish myself, you are *still in jail,* but, at least, minus big, bad Venice. I shiver remembering her snarling face. Never is it too soon to encounter that mean girl again.

The guard unlocks the door to my room, then surprisingly hands me the key. There isn't anyone else in the room. "There will be dinner for you in the cafeteria for the next fifteen minutes. Hurry, if you want to eat."

"Thank you." What more is there to say? Can I get room service if I'd rather eat in my room, please? I drop my bedding on the first empty twin bed, but immediately decide to claim the second because it has a small lamp on a tiny night stand. Neon yellow walls, with a bright orange closet, but three cheers for a twin mattress, albeit plastic, a small formica desk with orange plastic chair, and a large window without a view of barbed wire *and*…drum roll please…my own bathroom complete with a *door.*

I'm so excited with it I have to use it right away. The toilet flushes okay; the shower has a curtain, and the water out of the tap is warm and flowing hard. You've definitely arrived, Mary Ann, to the "good life". A sarcastic yet wholly relieved smile crosses my face.

I grab my room key and run, a lot faster now in my tight tan pumps than flip flops, in the direction of the cafeteria. My new jail "cell" is an overly retina stimulating box, but it kind of reminds me of my first college dorm room, and, at least, doesn't make me feel claustrophobic. I'm in happy shock. At least this *yellow* "hotel hell" has a little privacy, and a slightly better blanket. Wow, maybe tonight I won't hear snoring.

*   *   *

More amenities. Breakfast is at seven instead of five, with real silverware and believe it or not, *real* coffee. One doesn't have to eat in breakneck speed either to go back to one's cell/cage. I enjoy breakfast, the food that is, not my fellow way-too-chirpy jailbirds. The female "birds" are quieter, but we share a high-school-like cafeteria area with the men who are loud enough for both sexes.

I don't make eye contact with a single one of them except the kitchen boy who asked me if I wanted "hot or cold cereal". As I sit by myself, and sip my first sweetened and lightened cup of coffee in it seems like forever, I am barraged.

"How's yous today? Whats be's your name? How's yous be feelin' today? You sure do look fine! Yous new, ain't you? Wants some company?" Why so much attention, I think, in my wrinkled, boring brown suit, stockings with runs, un-made-up face and un-blown-dry hair? Duh, Mary Ann.

To that last comment, I glance up, look at the questioner and respond with a brief, "No, thank you." I said it sharply enough that the chatting tables around me, and the big guard, who just happened to walk by, heard me loud and clear. I just said good riddance to Venice, well, it looks like now I'm dining daily with men of every race, creed and color who all have one thing in common: they haven't been around women for a very long time.

Truthfully, however, for some reason, I'm not afraid of them. If any one of them gets fresh with me, I'm sure they will be in big time trouble and probably would be sent back to a cell for a good while. With Venice it was different. She was already arrested for first-degree murder; what more does she have to lose if she rearranges some white bitch's face?

I dump my tray. It feels weird to turn back in real silverware, and I hurry back to the women's unit to call Edward at home, collect, and catch him before he goes to work, "Hi! It's me." Ever the pragmatic bloke, Edward responds, "Yes, I know. I just accepted your collect call."

I'm impatient with him, but need him, so try not to sound annoyed that *he* doesn't sound happy or surprised to hear from me. Same old Edward, mildly hung over every morning, despite his protestations to the contrary, and not highly functional until forty-five minutes after his Grande Starbuck's.

"How's Eloise?"

"She's already in her car seat."

"Okay, f.i.n.e," I whine a little. By his response I know he's in a hurry and won't let me talk to her. "I'm in Rockville. I got out of Clarksburg last night! I need some clothes, and definitely some shoes. The pumps I wore to court are killing me. Can you, please, bring me some sneakers and jeans and stuff? And a roll of quarters for phone calls?"

"I can't tonight. I have a late meeting at work."

"Damn. Can you come tomorrow, *please?*"

"Yes, okay."

"Thanks, Edward. If I can't get to a phone tonight, I'll call about this time tomorrow with a list, okay? I'm not sure what we are allowed, have no clue; but I really want my blow dryer."

"I have to get to work."

"Yes, yes, I know, just pick up the phone tomorrow, please, and…my mail! Remember to bring all of my bills and my checkbook. I can't be late again on my mortgage! Thanks. Bye. Kiss Eloise for me!" Edward hangs up before I finished my request, and I sat there a few seconds staring at the receiver before I hung it up.

Three women are sitting on the orange plastic couches. They turn their heads away when I look up. What's the big deal? I'm just asking for clothes and my mail. We've got some kind of "orientation" all week. I'm sure I'll figure this place out by the end of one week. Yeah, right. Such a naïve little girl you still are at forty-four, Mary Ann, so damned utopianly naïve.

Chapter 28

Nice Inmates and Those Not So Nice and...Napoleon

My fellow citizens of incarceration and the guards remain just about 75% African American. No worries. If I went to jail with one ounce of prejudice toward any race, creed or color, which I don't think I had anyway, I left jail with only compassion for the minorities, especially the women.

From my experience, minority women get much more jail time for the same crime than white women. The most striking example was the white thirty-something cute little rich girl from Connecticut, cocaine dealer with double-D fake boobs and wiggle in her walk. (She admitted her drug-dealing boyfriend had beaten her up and popped each implant on two different occasions, so she actually had three boob jobs total, yikes!) She was sentenced to eighteen months. I think she may have sold more cocaine with her boyfriend than the next three women combined. The three African American cocaine dealers I recall, were also thirtyish, however, not wealthy, but were *mothers* of two to five children. Those women each served five to seven years, not a measly eighteen months.

Five to seven years *lost* of their precious babies' childhoods, how unfathomably painful that has to be. I'm confident the white girl got a much lighter sentence, because her rich parents hired a hot shot expensive attorney, and didn't use a public defender. Plus, of course, she is Caucasian.

One African American girl's comment at an AA meeting at P.R.C. will *never* leave my brain. She said, "When the mens goes to prison for a long time, theys learn somethin'. When we's womens gets locked up aways from our childrens, *we's just gets bitter"!!!*

There's something to be said for that comment; it really stuck with me; I agree.

*   *   *

Orientation week was such a pain in the ass that I think my brain didn't waste synapses remembering it. So I can't, but here are some of the highlights:

Our "Job Readiness" coordinator, who is supposed to teach us how to "apply, interview, and secure a job in the community", is an African American woman I like. She's six feet and still wears high heels. Good for her, not afraid to tower over men and undeniably intimidate them; she's got chutzpah/balls. But her lecture is killing me with boredom. I could be giving it: "It's important to have a professional looking resume. Do you all know what a resume is?" Remember I sent mine to over a hundred surgical sales companies and I was repeatedly told I'm "over qualified and too old"?

Dear God, if I couldn't get a decent job in six months of effort in the outside world, how the hell am I going to get one from jail in a few weeks? Moreover, how is anyone else? Almost everyone at orientation does not speak grammatically correct English, if any at all.

The magic amount of time one gets to stay at the Pre-Release Center is less than a month. We are supposed to submit three job interviews a week to our case manager, and if one "cannot secure full time employment within three weeks, no excuses, it's getting handcuffed and sent back to a cell in Clarksburg". Is that really what she just said? Three weeks? I raise my hand straight up.

"Yes, Miss, your name is?"

"Duke, I mean Mary Ann, excuse me, but did you just say we only have three weeks to find a job or we have to go back to Clarksburg?"

"That's correct."

I swallow hard. This is indeed bad news. I need to get a classified section of the *Washington Post* right away. I shall get a job. I cannot go back to being a claustrophobic animal going slowly insane.

A fifty-year-old big guy sitting next to me, sporting a long black ponytail and perfectly plucked black eyebrows, leans a little towards me and whispers, "Don't worry. I heard they always give you an extra week." Great, I think, still mortified. One month searching from jail for a job is going to be easier than six months from home? I'm in agony and then hear, "There is one phone on each unit that is only for local job calls from 8:30 a.m. to 4:30 p.m., and the pay phones cannot be used during this time." I gasp to myself, "That makes no sense! Why the hell not"?

"There are a few computers in this room to type your resumes on, but they are not on the internet yet." More bad news. This is incredible. Over twelve women have to share *one* phone job hunting, can't use our own money on the pay phones and no internet access? I've heard enough and raise my hand again.

"Yes, Miss Duke?" (I'm still annoyed whenever I hear *Miss,* but shrug it off, yet again, for the "unforeseeable future".)

"Do we have access to a newspaper?"

"Yes. One *Post* comes daily for each unit along with the weekly *Montgomery County Gazette*."

This *is* outrageous, one phone, one daily paper and no internet to find a job. I need some air and squirm in my stool when the absolute most fucking brilliant question of the day is asked, "What be dat raaysuummayy thing yous be axxin' about"?

Unable to control myself, I turn and roll my eyes at Mr. Ponytail. He gives me a big grin. I lean towards him and whisper, "We've got a whole week of this? I'd rather be banging my head against a wall." He nods, and gives me a look that says, "Grin and bear it, Honey; it can be worse".

I couldn't wait for lunch, even if I get fifty comments about "How's nice yous be lookin'" in my wrinkled make-uplessness.

"Yous be lookin' fine." "Whats yer name?" "How is yous, Honey?" On and on…I ask one girl if she wants some company and she says,"No." "Wants to sits down wit us?" "Heys, yous can sits here!" I finally respond, "No, thank you" crisply, and something leads me to set my tray down with Mr. Ponytail, who was sitting alone. He looks up from his food, smiles and motions graciously with his long arm to the empty chair next to him.

"My name is Pat," as he extends his hand, and we shake.

But, I hadn't wanted to shake hands with anyone before lunch. Why? I don't know. I just washed my hands and planned on picking up my pizza with them, but did Pat wash his? Oh, get over it, Mary Ann, this whole jail experience is making you overly paranoid. One can't get AIDS from a handshake, but I pick up my knife and fork and start to cut my pizza anyway. Before I can take my first bite I am shaking two more men's hands, who apparently know Pat. Pat is throwing his arms around like an excited psychiatric patient who hasn't had a visitor in over six months and wants to show her off to his "old cronies" on the psych ward.

"This is Mary Ann! She came from Clarksburg last night!" Pat states gleefully.

The first man I meet seems very interesting because he has this aura of calm, like a preacher. I soon find out many years of incarceration can do that to some, but definitely not all. He is fiftyish, African American and has an extremely kind face with no wrinkles, chiseled features and a perfect white smile. He is handsome and speaks perfect soft-spoken English without a hint of what I refer to as "jive" accent. "Nice to meet you, Mary Ann. My name is Lenny."

This man doesn't belong here, I think; he speaks like a gentleman. I wonder why he is in jail. The next man hands over his wet noodle of a slimy gross handshake and simply says, "Hi, I'm Doc." Doc is white and overweight, especially in the face, with a thin strawberry blonde wamp low around his fat white head. An over-sized yamaka *might* be able to cover his bald top, but instead Doc has fifteen or maybe as many as twenty-five of the thickest, most horrendously fake-looking hair plugs I have ever seen. What a trio. I instantly like Pat and Lenny, but Doc gives me the creeps.

I can't help myself. Maybe it's the botched hair plug job that is annoying me. So I bluntly ask, "Are you really a doctor?"

Doc doesn't hesitate, "Yes, I'm a plastic surgeon." I try to suppress a smile. I don't believe him. If you are a plastic surgeon, how the *hell* did you let someone do such a poor plug job? And for the record, you need about twenty-five hundred more. But instead of making an enemy and attack, I eat.

"What are you in for?" asks Lenny.

"DUI," I answer. "What about you?" Lenny gives me that one word answer I have become used to, "Drugs."

Pat seems to feel like he organized this lovely luncheon as he takes over the conversation. I learn quickly that most people in jail *love* to tell you their story; love to talk about how and why they "got caught", and Pat is on a roll. "Oh, you know Mary Ann!" as he flops his right hand at me, "We're all in here for *drugs* for one reason or another. It's true! Doc wrote prescriptions for narcotics for *years* before he got caught." Doc says nothing and just keeps looking at his food, so I have to suffer with a view of his nauseating head across the table. Pat is chatting away again, so I turn my gaze to his plucked eyebrows.

"I got addicted to Oxycontin after my car accident with all my back problems. My boyfriend became addicted, too, and we went through the $300,000 I got from the accident *so* fast. He was jealous that I was still friends with my ex-wife, so the asshole got me framed for dealing. But, I really wasn't selling very many. I'm just an addict. I loved Oxycontin, but when I ran out of money and prescriptions, I *had* to deal a little. I served eighteen months for just a few Oxy's. Can you believe that? Doc didn't serve hardly any longer for *all his antics!*"

"Wow." I don't know how to respond to Pat's last five or six sentences. I'm still trying to assimilate the boyfriend/ex-wife blurb, so all I come out with is "Wow". Okay, no problem, Pat is bisexual. (I always loved that *Saturday Night Live* character named Pat. To this day no one knows what gender "it" really was supposed to be playing.) Or maybe this black-haired, plucked-eye-browed Pat is just gay, now divorced, or whatever! I don't care.

Pat's very outgoing and funny, and I think he's nice, at the very least, *a true individual*.

Lenny is somehow reading my mind and says, "We all love Pat. He's a hairdresser, and he's been on a high since the counselors let him buy hair dye two days ago, and he got to dye his hair back to black."

Pat chirps, "Look, Mary Ann, I even did my brows!" as he raises them up and down like Jack Nicholson. I laugh out loud. "They look perfect, Pat. I wish I could pluck mine so good." Pat is laughing now, too. Lenny joins in, and Doc picks up his tray and blandly states, "See you guys later." I think Doc's self-conscious and just couldn't handle all this "hair" talk. Both Lenny and Pat have a full head.

The three of us can't stop laughing long enough to even say, "Bye". Maybe we just needed to hear ourselves laugh. "What's *his* problem?" Lenny asks Pat.

"I have *no* idea!" exclaims Pat with another patented hand toss. "He's been so grumpy lately. And he refused to give another urine sample the other day. Maybe his wife is slipping him something when she comes to see him, because he is always refusing urines after her visits. I *can't stand* living with him," Pat tells us in a hushed tone.

"If he keeps it up, he's going to get sent back to federal," Lenny states point blank.

This whole conversation has been beyond bizarre for a simple pizza lunch, but animated to say the least. I'm more than a little taken aback. "What kind of surgeon did he say he was again?" I'm amazed Doc even has a wife.

Lenny answers, "He *says* he's a plastic surgeon." Pat gives a series of furious nods in agreement.

I smile and can't help saying, "Well, what the hell? Did he do his hair plugs himself?"

Pat starts laughing and it's infectious. The three of us are roaring again. "I know, Honey," Pat chokes through his laughter, "They're hideous." Hey, the hairstylist said it, not me.

I ate lunch with Pat and Lenny, dinner too, as often as I could. We laughed so loud and so hard we were constantly being asked by the tables around us what we were laughing about. Even the counselors/guards on duty for dinner were curious and grinned at us like they were in on our private jokes. Maybe they did that, so the rest of the inmates thought that *they* knew what was so funny so as to be in control. But they didn't know "diddly-squat". It was like a gasoline spill to fire, when Lenny, Pat and I saw each other, we knew we had to make each other hysterically laugh in order to get through another God-damned miserable day in jail.

I swear to God, if I didn't have them to be silly with a little bit every day, the numerous multi-colored, multi-sexed "Napoleons"/counselors/guards that I had to put up with at the Pre-Release Center were going to drive me stark raving mad.

*   *   *

I came *way* too close every day to speaking my mind and legitimately telling someone off. If I *did* lose my cool, I would wind back up in a cell in Clarksburg and even risk serving the last six months of my sentence which are now "suspended", but can still be ordered to be served even after I'm home on probation for three years until November, 2008. My first week at P.R.C. (what we all called the Pre-Release Center) I saw a young man hand-cuffed in front of everyone and sent back to Clarksburg. We never found out for what reason except that he cursed out a counselor.

My initials aren't M.A.D. for nothing, and if there is one thing in this world that I absolutely positively cannot stand is when some assholes pull a power trip on you and hurt you for no reason, except just because they can.

Think about it for a second. *People in power hurt people for no good reason.* It's not because it will be this big beneficial learning curve to hurt this person, but people hurt other people just because they are jealous, insecure with themselves, or *just because they can.* They do it *for fame, for wealth, for power,* or all of the above; people hurt people and reign over them just because they can, and they perversely enjoy the power trip. Is that too often why one runs for public office? To get ahead selfishly at the expense of others, and *not* to be public servants and help the less fortunate? Too bad most of the super wealthy haven't figured out that all the gold bullion in the world does not buy one a seat next to God, and certainly can't be melted down and fit in their urn along with their ashes.

*   *   *

But I can't go back to a cage/cell, so I'm on a mission the next morning, up early and the first one to grab the *Washington Post.* Should I look under "M" for medicine or medical doctor? No. Don't look under "M". They took away your medical license; look under something else, Mary Ann. But something makes me look under "M" anyway along with everything else. I take down so many phone numbers, I am unanimously the most frequent phone user and disliked for it. Many of the girls "wants mees to gits off rights nows"!

And many of them amazed me by not furiously searching for a job, and just plopped themselves in front of the television. Didn't they care about going back to a cell? Or were their lives so bad on the outside that "three hots and a cot", as jail is referred to, *preferable to being free?*

I asked Lenny and Pat what they thought at dinner a few days later. Lenny summed it up for me with one word. He said, "Probably". I stared at him. Lenny continued, "I grew up in such a nasty area that most of the men either became pimps or drug dealers to make money. I didn't want to pimp, so I started selling drugs to pay the rent and eat".

What an education, I think to myself. I grew up in such a sheltered, comfortable environment. I cannot imagine there are women on my unit that are so miserable or find the real world so hard, that they don't care if they go back to a cell for their "three hots and a cot".

I ask Lenny, "Didn't you ever think about going to college?"

"Nope. I didn't finish high school. I got my G.E.D. in jail," replies Lenny while looking at his plate.

"Oh."

The conversation is getting too intense, so perky Pat changes it and asks me, "How's your job hunting, Mary Ann? Got any interviews yet?"

"Sort of. It's kind of a long story."

Lenny looks up and smiles at me. "Well, fire away, Mary Ann. It's not like we're going anywhere. I'm sure your job hunting is less boring than ours."

I put down my fork, lean back in my chair, and smile at both of them. "Guys, I'm going insane. Okay, I'll talk fast, because I have to hurry back to my unit and wait for the pay phones to try and call my kids again, but here goes. I looked under 'M', right, for medical doctor or medicine or something? I get 'medical receptionist'. I call several doctors' offices and speak to the office managers. It was so demeaning. Here I am an M.D., and I have to explain to some office manager that I need some 'receptionist' job? When I found out what they pay, I gave up. I can't put myself through that all day long. It'll be a bore, plus I don't have enough patience for the job. I know how demanding patients can be on the phone. I'd probably tick someone off my first day and get fired, so I gave up on that idea, but not until I *really* humiliated myself." I stopped talking and played with my chocolate pudding, too depressed to even make eye contact.

Lenny's soft spoken voice simply asks, "What did you do, Mary Ann?"

I look up sadly into his understanding eyes and continue, "I stuck my tail between my legs and called three of my doctor friends asking them for a job. I told them everything. None of them had a position for me. C'mon. Do they want to hire a friend who used to make as much money as them to work for them in some menial low paying job? They would feel embarrassed to hire me and ask me to work for a small wage. And even though they would be keeping me out of a cell, I understand their hesitancy, absolutely. I felt so embarrassed and humiliated after I called them. I still do. Oh, screw it. Then I answered an ad at the Veterans Administration Hospital for an ophthalmic technician. I can certainly handle that half asleep. It took three phone calls over three days for someone to get back to me. Get this. The V.A. will be interviewing for three to four months and then will be hiring. I couldn't believe it. But you know government bureaucracy moves, like a caterpillar. I need a job in three to four days, not three to four *months*!"

Both Lenny and Pat laugh in understanding, and their nods urge me to continue. "I still think I should work in the medical field, so I answer an ad for 'Mobile Insurance Physicals' out of Vienna, Virginia. They don't pay worth a damn either. God, I'll be commuting over an hour back and forth to work, to probably get car sick in the back of some van every day, driving around for these 'mobile' bullshit insurance physicals. You know guys, I get extremely car sick very easily, so I nixed that one, too."

Pat exclaims, "Oh, you would have had to anyway, Mary Ann. I'm trying desperately to work as a hairdresser, and I got an offer in Virginia! But my case manager won't let me take it, because I'll be gone too long each day."

"That's right," says Lenny, "You can't have too long of a commute. I think I'm going to have to stock shelves at Giant. But keep on going with your job story, Mary Ann. It's much more interesting than mine."

"Hardly, Lenny. Do you think Giant has room for me? Check out girl, that's perfect. I'll just be a checkout girl and wear a little red apron and a badge. We can all try to work the same shift and ride the bus in together."

"Oh, please, do stop it!" Pat yells at me with a double hand flop. "You'll get a much better job than running a cashier. C'mon, what else are you up to?"

"Not much. I'm constantly being yelled at to get off the phone. I still can't believe we have only one phone amongst at least twelve of us." I lower my voice, "Do you think it's bugged? I'd rather put coins in the pay phones and let everyone hear my conversations looking for work than stand and wait in the hall. My attorney thinks the phone was bugged at my first jail, Seven Locks. Do you think it's bugged here?" Lenny and Pat both nod ignorance, but the look in their eyes says, "I wouldn't doubt it".

"It's frustrating, to say the least, especially when the girls yell into that echoing phone room to 'Hurry its up'! I just pray I covered the receiver in time before their bitching started." More nods of understanding.

"Well, then I got the great idea that I can teach. Sure, why not, I think? I can teach high school or grade school or anything, Biology or Math or Chemistry or even Physics. Hell, I can probably wing Latin or German if I had to. I can just see it, 'Guten morgan class, I'm Fraulein Duke.'" We all take one of our laughter breaks. (God knows I needed one.)

I stop laughing first, though. "Even with an M.D. degree, I can't teach a damned thing in the public school system, because I need some kind of certificate out of Baltimore that will take *way* too long to get. One secretary told me to try the private schools. I called five of them: Landon, Holten Arms, Norwood, Bullis and Holy Child. I'm hitting brick walls at every one. They don't need this Maryland State mandated certificate, but no one is hiring in December half way through the school year. I feel so helpless and frustrated. It's like I need some science teacher to be struck by lightning so there will be an opening."

No comment. They both understand.

"I'm going nuts, you guys. I even called three different *pre*-schools, and they want some kind of teaching certificate, too, for a less than ten dollar/hour job. It doesn't matter one bit that I have all these degrees and four children of my own. Even the pre-school my children used to attend told me I have to get a certificate before any interview. I have to get, at least, a couple interviews quick or my case manager is going to lock me up and throw away the key. All I'm doing these days is bathroom duty, and it's totally gross."

I lean forward, put my elbows on the table and put my head in my hands. Lenny and Pat are silent. What is there to say? Life sucks? At least, in jail there is no question that it absolutely does, especially when you are white and educated and your case manager decides to dislike you.

*   *   *

After my first glance at my case manager, I changed his name from Tyroleon to Napoleon. Tyroleon is 5'5", with a seventies Michael Jackson afro, and thinks he has it "all going on". He is Lenny's case manager, too. We all have a good laugh over my nickname for him. Lenny, both the same sex and race as Tyroleon, is given a hard time anyway. Lenny announces one night at dinner, "I'm going to stock shelves at Giant. Tyroleon won't give me any more time to look for a better job, that mother fucker." I stop chewing and stare at Lenny. That nasty term has been the *most common two words in a row* since hour one in jail, but I have never heard them come out of Lenny's mouth.

"Oh, that's terrible," is all I can say. Great. Just perfect. I feel an instant surge of stress. I *have* to get a job soon.

Pat says, "I'm sorry, Lenny. I've got an interview tomorrow at a hair salon in Maryland."

Lenny categorically restates, "I hate that mother fucker."

I have no clue why, but "Napoleon" walked around P.R.C. like he owned the joint. It seems to me, in my old middle age, that people, who walk around like their shit doesn't stink, are really the most insecure of us all. Napoleon doesn't have anything good to say about anybody, and once he knew that I was a doctor, even better, an eye surgeon, well, he wanted to slice me up. Yep, just slowly slice me up with a tiny cataract blade and watch me bleed. Then ask me how my bleeding felt, and bring me to my knees to lick myself up, to try to stay alive.

I think he needs a shrink more than I *ever* did. His office is the corner office of the women's unit with windows on two full sides. He watches us hang out at night until he finally leaves at eight or nine p.m. Napoleon gives me a much worse case of the creeps than Doc, big time.

*   *   *

Napoleon calls me into his office for the first time. I dreaded our first meeting, especially after Lenny's comments. "How do you like P.R.C.?", he asks, while looking down at his papers and not at me, like he doesn't care to look up. I want to say, "It's horrible", but instead use my all-knowing:

"F.I.N.E."

"Have you found a job?"

"Almost."

"Almost?"

"Yes."

Pause. "Well, what work have you been looking for?"

"Something in the medical field. I haven't had an interview yet, but I should have three by next week."

Napoleon finally looks up and sneers, "You'd better."

Pause. "I'm sure I'll have a job by next week."

"Just *see that you do.* You're dismissed."

"Um, but I want to ask you why you denied my two-hour leisure pass with my children."

"You cannot do leisure activities with family."

"I don't recall seeing that rule anywhere."

"It's not written down, but that's the rule."

He stumped me for a second. That makes no sense. I push on, "I always enjoy leisure activities with my kids."

"No leisure time allowed with family."

Okay, I'm getting nowhere with this senseless dictator/case manager on that score. However, I *do* need credit for last night's in house AA meeting I forgot to get my slip signed at. "I forgot to get my AA slip signed last night, but everyone knows I was there and can vouch for me."

"It does not matter. You can't have anyone vouch for you. You can't get a retroactive."

"But the meeting was here at P.R.C... Everyone saw me."

"You're dismissed." Napoleon looks down at his desk and I leave without saying a word, but wish I could call him an asshole.

I'm afraid. Even though my three weeks are not up yet, I know Napoleon must be responsible for making my life hell. It has to be *his* dogma that I am cleaning the toilet where all of the addicts give their urine samples every day. We have to give three urine samples/week and three breathalyzers/day. One time I forgot to do a third breathalyzer. Total bummer when it happens by accident. It causes one to get "written up" and get a black mark.

Napoleon punished me hard. I was always on the "bathroom list" for clean up. Even if I was the second or third alternate on the list, I am the one mopping and wiping down that disgusting urine-sampling room or the visitor's bathroom. The girls ahead of me on the list weren't stupid. They know if "Duke" was after their name, they didn't need to do a damned thing.

It was a game to them. The other girls knew it was their turn, but they knew about Napoleon being hard on me. If they saw my name after theirs, they did nothing. Whether it was hallway mopping or garbage duty, anything at all, the other women knew the "Duke" would clean it, even if my name was last. I was in the major minority. That's all there was to it.

I double gloved. That urine-sampling room probably hasn't sparkled the same since I stopped cleaning it. Baba and Mom taught me how to clean right; that's for damned sure.

I still felt really bad for the other women, even though they dumped on me. Somehow I knew I had a much better upbringing than these women could ever dream of giving their *own* children, and I felt sorry for them.

But after a few weeks of over punishment, I really did have the entitlement to call Napoleon one angry motherfucker. Oh, shit. He's just going to justify being such a reverse racist and say it's "Okay, I treated that white bitch doctor unfairly, because look at my life. Being an African American male has not been easy".

Well, Napoleon, if you were a *real* man, no matter what color your skin is, you'd still have been fair.

*   *   *

To save my own ass and sanity, there was only one way out. I followed the advice of an African American counselor (who could have been a defensive lineman in the NFL) that was fair and apparently had a little compassion for me. He told me how to "file a grievance". I filed a nine-page grievance against Napoleon and backed it up with several other inmates' complaints. I included everybody.

A couple of African Americans (including Lenny), Caucasian, Hispanic, male or female. The grievance could not have been more politically correct. One other white girl turned in Napoleon, too. She said that, "He told me I'd better keep wearing my push up bra, that I look better in it". The key to her defense was a couple of African American inmates witnessed the exchange and backed her up.

My grievance, hers, plus a few others much, much shorter than mine, yet strongly indignant, got Napoleon relocated. He was sent to Unit 4, the most dangerous unit. Unit 4 is an all male unit, the baddest of the bad, rapists, murderers, you name it. They even have their own cafeteria. So no longer was Tyroleon basking in his fish bowl view office of us women, and especially for me, no longer my case manger. "Good riddance and Hallelujah"!!!

Chapter 29

Breaking Every Rule For My Children, Risking "Hell/Cell"

I can't wait to see my children. I am yearning to see them. I have not seen them all together for a month. Jane agreed to pick up my older three and bring them over on Sunday afternoon for visiting hours and Edward was bringing Eloise.

Truly, I feel mortified for them to see Mommy in jail. *Totally mortified.* But the joy of seeing them *at all* and being able to hug and kiss them, without some wall between us, is overwhelming anticipation and delight. I completely understand that one woman's comment about years in jail away from one's children making one bitter. It must be incredible pain to see one's children through some kind of partition, yet not be able to hug them, for *years.*

Oh, my God, there they are! Each one looks like they've grown three inches. My thoughts completely stop when I see them. There they are, my little angels from heaven running towards me! My mind is blank but my emotions are everywhere as I run towards them up the ramp from the cafeteria with my arms outstretched. I have never felt such relief and joy and pride and unconditional love all at once.

They all look so happy to see me that their happiness appears to overpower any fears they may have of seeing Mommy in jail. "Hi Mommy!" "Hi Mommy!" "Hi

Mommy!" "Hi Mommy!" All I can do is hug all four of them and kiss all four of them at once without crying too hard and losing what little is left of my self-control.

I feel so blessed. My angels from heaven still love me and want to kiss and hug me even if Mommy is in a disgusting jail.

I will be forever grateful to God for my outstanding children. Every day, to this day, I live in pain that the courts took them from me. Not one hour goes by that I wonder for a period of time how I go on, even get out of bed, after I lost what was most important to me. I must fight for my children to see them more, to nurture them and teach them, so they never make my mistakes and suffer so dearly for them.

Every minute I spent with them at P.R.C., most especially because of the time I've lost irrevocably through custody loss and rehab, I tried to make extremely happy.

What does one do for a two to three hour visit in a loud jail cafeteria to keep one's young children amused and not afraid of the unusual characters/inmates surrounding them? Anything possible. We played cards, "Go Fish" and "War". We scribbled notes on papers and tried to draw cartoons. I had asked Edward to bring me some chocolates for our first visit; so now we were all on a much needed Hershey High. The chocolate kisses high became the norm. If my kids were coming, I always had a huge supply of kisses, real and chocolate. All four always had mini-chocolate moustaches.

We played tic tac toe, told stories, talked about school, and all I wanted to do was to tell them over and over "I love you" and hug and kiss them for every single last second of the visit. Sadly, the time I've lost being with them is exactly that, forever lost. Like every parent, I want my children to love me for me, regardless of all the shit that overloaded my plate, and turned me to alcohol, which then brought me down so terribly low. Just so they learn from Mommy's mistakes. *How can they not?*

Our visits are such a fanfare that many commented on our shenanigans, especially my new buddies, *who truly were glad to see me happy*. It's a rare feeling to receive from one incarcerated individual to another. You know, misery loves company, but Pat and Lenny are great. "Can I have one of your chocolates?" says Pat to my son. James gives him a good once over and then looks at me. I look James in the eyes and say, "Honey, give Pat a chocolate. Lenny, too. Be nice and share your candy with Pat and Lenny; I know them; they're nice." So James shares his kisses with them, and Lenny and Pat carry on a very nice conversation with my son, while Edward snubs his nose at them and won't make conversation.

Dear God, my drug dealing buddies, and my mental saviors.

*   *   *

I call my children every night before bed with the quarters Edward brings. God bless them for always being happy to hear from me, too. I feel so guilty about being in jail, the rule breaking is inevitable. If $1/100^{th}$ of my daily "sins" were found out, I think some judge would have *extended,* not "suspended" my sentence. I never thought I could be so devious, not even close. If a goody-miss-two-shoes-brought-up-right educated person like myself can be so devious while incarcerated, imagine how devious the *real* criminals are?

Where to even start the confession of my sins/rule breaking. Certainly not like a true confessional with "Bless me Father for I have sinned". I don't consider my rule stretching/overt ignoring/ a "sin" whatsoever. Breaking the rules and risking going back to solitary confinement is a damned necessity for survival.

The tiniest sin is how much money I spend on chocolate. We arre only allowed $25.00 on our person at one time unless "approved" for the maximum, which is a whopping $45.00. We can't spend a dime unless it is preapproved except on food. Well, is chocolate not a food? Yes, it is. It is in its own food group under "Happy Food". I spend at least ten dollars a week on chocolates; well worth it for the smiles it puts on my children's faces.

There is a thirty-six page Guidebook filled with impossible rules. I can't remember receiving one, but apparently I signed a paper that said, "I have read the Guidebook and I agree to comply with all terms, conditions and guidelines. I realize that if I violate any part of this agreement, I can be immediately removed from the program and placed in security confinement, and I will be subject to loss of Pre-Release status and privileges and to the penalties provided by law".

I should have, at least, *read* that bottom paragraph on the page I signed.

My new roommate shows me hers our first night together. Jeanetta is great. She helps me stay sane along with Lenny and Pat. Jeanetta is the young African American girl that came shackled at the ankles with me down from Clarksburg. We barely have said "Hello" to each other since. After a week of gratefully living alone, without having to even share a bathroom, she approaches me. Jeanetta asks simply, "Can I share your room with you?"

I am taken aback. Jeanetta was living with two other African American girls, and my first thought is, "What do you want to live with *me* for? Aren't you going to take some heat for that"?

I swear she reads my mind. She says, "The girls I live with stay up late and play hip-hop every night. They keep me up and then I have to get up and shut their radios off after they fall asleep."

I don't hesitate.

I am certainly one who can appreciate not getting enough sleep, and how it makes one feel from residency years and having babies, and Jeanetta is different from the other girls. Number one is she actually is trying to find work. And most notable, I haven't heard her swear *once*, brag about her drug deals, sexual escapades or scream on the phone to anyone.

If I say "Okay" to living with her, than the other bed in my room won't be filled soon by a girl like the two she is trying to get away from. It's a "no brainer".

"Sure, Jeanetta. I'm okay with that." She smiles her thanks. That first night we have a bonding talk. She knows I am in for DUI, but I know nothing about her, and ask, "What did you have to go to jail for?" Jeanetta hesitates for more than a minute, but then admits, "I robbed a bank."

Shocking. I didn't think people still got away with robbing banks with cameras and everything. It's not like we're back in the Wild West. But hey, obviously, Jeanetta *didn't* get away with it, because there she sits across from me. I want to know more; what the heck, go ahead and ask, right? She's going to be living with me for quite a while and I'm intrigued. Everyone on Unit 1 already knows *my* life is a giant soap opera. Like some combination of *Grey's Anatomy*, *The Young and the Restless*, *Sex in the City*, *L.A. Law*, and God knows what else, so why not ask about hers?

"How'd you do it?"

"With an empty gun and a piece of paper."

"What?" That doesn't make sense to me. She must have been on drugs. I ask, "Did you wear a mask or something? What did your paper say?"

"No. I didn't wear a mask. My paper just said to give me all of your money." Jeanetta looks down at the floor.

I'm getting a memory from approximately a year ago, while out running and listening to the radio, about a girl that held up a bank like this and got caught right away. Despite my period of drinking, I still have an excellent memory, thank God. Now my questions are more pointed. "Did this happen in a Mall?"

"Yes, White Flint."

"How much money did you get?"

Jeanetta's voice becomes hushed, "I got an eighteen month sentence for only

$1,200."

"Was it for drugs?" Jeanetta lifts her head up quickly and looks me in the eye.

"No!" is her adamant response. "I've never done drugs."

"Then why did you do it?" I'm staring right back at her.

"Because my friends had done it before and gotten away with it, so I just did it. It was my first time." She pauses a few seconds and then finishes with, "I got caught at the Metro."

Now the whole story comes flooding back to me that I heard on my Walkman. I remember the radio announcers making fun of her, because she didn't wear any disguise and was caught so quickly at the White Flint Metro closest to the bank.

I look sympathetically at Jeanetta for having to serve eighteen months, then the corners of my eyes turn up, and I can't stop from breaking into a big smile and "bust her chops" with, "Jeepers, Jeanetta, don't you know bank robbers are at least supposed to have a *get away car?* What the hell were you thinking getting on the *Metro?!"*

I can't stop from giggling. Jeanetta isn't offended and she grins back slightly. I'm laughing at the *incredible insanity of both of our lives*. I'm just as bad as her getting into a car after drinking, albeit in a blackout. My eyes speak volumes to her along with my understanding words, "We're never going to mess up our lives again like this are we?"

Jeanetta nods in agreement. "I'm actually glad I got caught my first time."

Her comment silences me. My mind wanders back to my first DUI, and then I lost my medical license just twenty days later. Who called the Maryland Medical Board? How did they find out I was arrested for a drunk driving charge and decide to take my medical license away from me in less than three weeks? We all know how slow the systems are i.e. legal, governing, etc...*They crawl.* Hmm, I hadn't even been convicted of the charge, maybe could have even "gotten off" completely. Like so many first DUI charges are dropped totally with the "right" judge.

Also, the Board told me that they were coming to talk to me about rehab. Call me a little paranoid, but I bet my life that I am the first doctor in the State of Maryland, possibly the whole U.S. of A., who had their medical license taken away for the "unforeseeable future" for one single, and yet unprosecuted, drunk driving charge.

Maybe the good ole' boys just got tired of my individualism and my "inappropriate for an ophthalmologist" eye makeup. Ha! Just plain old asinine to stop someone dead, with so much hard-earned education, who has devoted her life to helping people and preserving their sight for the "unforeseeable future", who has never once been sued nor even come close.

Then I get a five-year suspension instead of one to two years like their own attorney recommended. I then lose my mind and get two more arrests in three weeks and the ex's theft charge for a candy dish. Most definitely I should have been a V.I.P. for temporary insanity on Johns Hopkins' Psych ward, for, at least, a few weeks, if not a few months after the Boards' decision.

I don't feel "glad" like Jeanetta. *Not at all.* I feel "screwed" with a capitol S.

Jeanetta asks, "What are you thinking?" I shake my head fast to throw my thoughts away and don't feel like telling her. Then, I would have to relive it yet again. The tragedy forges a path through my frontal lobe way too often as it is.

I change the subject and get right to the point, boring a hole right into Jeanetta's pretty eyes, "Listen, Jeanetta, this place sucks. I'll help you any way I can; just watch my ass too, you know what I mean?"

Jeanetta nods without hesitation. She reaches over and hands me her Guidebook. "You better read this, *tonight.*"

*   *   *

Fuck that Guidebook. I might as well read a twelve-year-old issue of *Bride* magazine looking for a dress for divorce court.

I never finished it, impossible for me to follow those rules. I'd have an easier time tanning on Mars. A brief excerpt:

I just read the "***DON'T'S***": for the first time this past instant for this chapter. I truly don't remember reading them before, but they are so damned obvious, maybe I did read them, *guffaw,* and as the late Rodney Dangerfield would say, "Forget about it!"

"DON'TS":

1. No unauthorized absences. (Unauthorized absences are considered an "escape" after two hours, which means many more moons of jail time.)

2. No drugs, alcohol, or weapons. (No kidding.)

3. No violence or threat of violence. (I think swearing at Napoleon would have been considered "threatening", especially because he was so much smaller than I. Good thing I refrained, but came very close.)

4. No crime! (....................No shit!)

That's exactly how it is typed in the Guidebook. (Except all of the parentheses are my tidbits, of course.) But it is *their* exclamation point at the end of "No crime!" Did *that* really need to be printed? Of course, one cannot commit *another* crime, duh!

What's infinitesimally scary to me is that there are people so uneducated or just so damned not gifted in the common sense department...or worse...so...desperate, that they need the rules spelled out in complete black and white. i.e. No Crime!

Well, spelling them out for me didn't help much apparently, literate and all, because I never read them until now.

*   *   *

Edward brings me my mail as I begged him to. I have no clue whatsoever that my mail is supposed to be screened. Perfect example of ignorance is bliss. Instead I open scads of mail in front of inmates and counselors alike in the cafeteria setting aside bills for Edward to write. He's paranoid of my surroundings and takes all of my mail trash home to be shredded. Good paranoia, Edward. I do remember one rule that said something like, "You are not allowed to write a check for more than is approved by your case manager and is more than your salary".

Right. Okay, F.I.N.E. How the hell am I supposed to keep my $8,000 plus/month home from foreclosing if I can't spend any more money than I earn, which means zero since I haven't a job, and every check I write would have had to be preapproved by my good buddy Napoleon. (Thank God he was moved!) Give me a break. Only way around that is Edward signs my name, after he writes the bills I tell him to write. Period. "But, sorry Edward (for the fiftieth time), I just do not want to *burden you* with becoming my power of attorney". Thus, I can say *I* "didn't write any checks."

These games are new to me and not to my liking. Still I am forced to play. Again, are only men allowed to be forgiven?

I am forced to use the phone for "job interviews only" for personal business. How can I let the other women, most of whom are in jail for drugs and/or theft, or like my wonderful roommate, robbing a bank at gun point, know my finances?

Of course, I need privacy, which it barely is anyway. If I don't talk very low, the woman waiting outside can hear my conversation through the door and get me in trouble. My loud Slovak family is awesome, but not a soft spoken lot.

I talk the quietest in my life in jail, so terrified I am of being caught. Totally stressed I am every day, praying that phone isn't being recorded during one of my calls. Sometimes I hung up mid-sentence if I saw a guard walk by. What a frantic state I lived in.

I have to call my mortgage company first. "Hello? Oh dear, I'm so sorry. I've been out of town. Would you, please, not charge me that horrible three-hundred-dollar-plus late fee? I've been out of town with a family emergency". I'm really not lying, right? It's not every day one goes to jail unexpectedly, now is it? "Oh, thank you so much. Yes, indeed. The check is in the mail'. I am amazed one of my fellow inmates never turned me in. No wonder they *did* complain about how much I used it, though. I had to call my credit card companies, utilities, and every innumerable bill I was late on.

My stress level is so screaming high, I don't know how I slept while incarcerated. How am I supposed to keep my home from foreclosing, and my dubious "business as Dr. Duke the ophthalmologist" from filing bankruptcy without being allowed to even *write a check* for six months? I've been living off credit cards for over a year already. Time's up. No more credit card room. What next? Put my house back on the market from jail? Call my old realtor who is already mad at me for not lowering my price and selling while in rehab?

Davie is appealing the Board's decision in Montgomery County Circuit Court. I call him every forty-eight hours to find out how the appeal is going and he tells me "It's going to be heard in March, Dukie."

"But, I'll still be in jail!"

"That's okay, that's okay, you don't have to testify."

"Why not? Shouldn't I be there?!"

"No, probably better if you weren't. It's just a judicial review."

"Davie, I need to open my office again in six months and be an eye surgeon again. I need my life back that I worked so hard for."

"I know, Dukie, I know. I've got to go now. Call me anytime."

"Fine." Click. Bang, bang, bang on the phone room door. I ignore the pissed off looks on the girls' faces and meander back to my neon yellow bedroom and close my eyes. On top of everything, New York State *wants me to appear* for a hearing in Albany. Impossible, not this December, guys, can't make it. Kiss my New York State medical license good-bye.

I simply *have* to break the rules. Also, the rules seem to vary according to who one asks for clarification. Frustrating, to say the least, so who cares about the rules? Napoleon makes up his own as he goes along like, "No family leisure". It was very clear, however, that one was "*not* to incur any increased debt".

Well, you know, sometimes it rains at the most unpredictable time. One of my longstanding patients sends me a postcard from Chase Manhattan for home equity lines. Perfect. I'm on the "no increased debt allowed" and "no personal calls allowed" phone, asking for money.

"Hello, is this Miss McKenna?"

"Yes, this is Evelyn."

"Hi, this is Dr. Duke, Mary Ann. I just got your postcard about home equity lines."

"Oh, yes, sure. Do you need one?"

"Absolutely I do, like yesterday."

"How much do you need?"

"At least $200,000."

"Do you have enough equity in your home?"

"I hope so." Then I lower my voice to a whisper and tell her I need the money to pay for rehab, credit card debt, and that "I am in jail right now for DUI."

Pause..., and then she says, "Okay. I think I can help you. How can I reach you?"

"You can't. I have to go now. I'll call you tomorrow. I have to go! Thanks! Bye." There's been knocking on the small phone room door for, at least, five minutes by two other women. "I'm sorry" is all I say as I scurry out of the room. I hope to God they didn't hear my conversation, or I'm straight back to solitary confinement.

I do love my patients. Ms. McKenna came through for me. I have no clue how.

I can't carry over twenty-five dollars on me or write a check, but am supposed to pay child support plus an eight thousand plus/month mortgage, while my harsh decision by the Maryland Board of Physicians of five years, as the mother of four children and soul provider for most of their lives, is being appealed.

Sheer insanity.

I sign for a loan while at the mall on a brief pass. I'll never forget that day. The settlement attorney was, believe it or not, the second Lasik patient I ever operated on. He came out excellent, or I'm sure may have sued. I remember him asking me three or four times for a video of his surgery. My answer? "I'm sorry. Johns Hopkins will not allow that". Thankfully, that *is* their policy and I was right, because he asked a nurse on the day of his surgery at Hopkins, and she concurred. If she had said, "Sure, you can have one", I wouldn't have taped his surgery, even if he cancelled.

I want a lawyer or any patient for that matter to have on tape if anything went wrong? Blatant evidence for court? He had specifically asked me, too, "How many have you done"? I answered honestly, "One". Wow, talk about "blind faith". If someone wanted to operate on me *anywhere,* and it was only their second case of that kind, I'd most likely high tail it home. But it's the old motto from medical school, "See one, do one, teach one".

This attorney had closed multiple loans for me before, during, and since my divorce. He wasn't surprised at my tenacity to keep my home. He was now closing me again on a quarter million dollars even while I'm in jail, and $125,000 was immediately paying out to credit card debt. Yep, living on borrowed time and borrowed money. Both are almost gone.

If only Napoleon knew what deal went down.

Chapter 30

"Real" Work

I still need a job, and need a job *fast*; the three week grace period is coming to a halt. I call every store in the mall I know of: Nordstrom's, Wilson's, The Leather Store, Kenneth Cole, J. Crew, Coach, even Crate and Barrel and I don't like to cook.

It's just before Christmas when everyone's shopping for gifts. What would I be good at selling? Jewelry. That's the ticket. I know jewelry. I don't have any anymore, but I know a lot about it. So I call Kay Jewelers, Shaw's, Zale's, Bailey, Banks and Biddle, Hellsburg's Diamonds, Lillenquist & Beckstead, and even Swarovski. (Shit!) I can't remember *all* of the jewelry stores I called for a job. I'll be damned, even the one that is supposedly a glorified pawnshop, didn't need me.

Nah, let's put it this way, those jobs were not offering me enough, and I didn't need *them*. While in Montgomery Mall, *finally,* some interviews, I saw a job offer poster for a department store called Hecht's and decided to fill out an application.

I ran in there as was on an extremely tight schedule. I *cannot* be late back to P.R.C. and considered an "escape", especially because I hadn't put Hecht's as an interview on my day pass. (Another broken rule.) The human relations manager took my hasty application and listened to my story. I was humble.

"I have to get a job to stay out of a claustrophobic cell. I am a doctor, an eye surgeon. I suffered a brutal divorce, drank too much, got a DUI, lost my medical license and now am incarcerated. I have four small children. To get out of jail eight hours/day and avoid being locked back up in a cell, I need a job. I'm dreadfully claustrophobic. I hated that cell. I will work very hard for you and not let you down".

She sized me up quickly and I think was especially compassionate, because she was pregnant. Within ten minutes, I am hired at Hecht's Department store, and am scheduled for training within forty-eight hours, if approved by the work release manager. (Hey, if they don't hire me, an honest doc for extra Christmas help, who the hell do they?) Luckily, the work release manager didn't notice "Hechts" wasn't on my day pass, or I would have been written up, yet again.

*   *   *

It is so stifling in jail that my pass to go to Target for a "black belt and toiletries" was denied because I didn't spell out exactly each toiletry. For God's sake, that denial came from a female, too. I have no idea how I kept from talking back with my quick tongue to the omnipresent put-downs. Sheer fear, I guess, fear of that hellish cell.

God did me a big favor. If I had landed a job in a jewelry store, I would have missed all of my jewelry that was stolen, day after day. I could just see myself trying to sell a three-carat tanzanite to a customer and describing the four carat and diamond tanzanite ring that was stolen from me. Every day, every sale, would have been one bummer after another reliving my burglarized home and how violated I felt after it.

That night at dinner, I told Pat and Lenny what transpired. "Listen guys"! I exclaimed. "I went to

Montgomery Mall for three interviews at three different jewelry stores. It was a waste, because the 'regulars' didn't want competition for their Christmas sales and only wanted me to be their 'wrapping girl'. I would have made no commission and basically nothing overall for wrapping jewelry boxes. Then I ran into Hecht's Department Store, because they had a sign 'Hiring for Christmas'."

"Guess what? I'm going to be a check out girl *after all* for only nine dollars/hour, no commission. See, you should have taken me to Giant with you after all! We could have had fun on the bus ride. But really, I would rather work amongst clothes and shoes and whatever in a big department store than be salivating all day in a supermarket. I hope they let me take the job." Then I whisper, "I have a Hecht's credit card and they give a 25% employee discount."

Lenny is happy for me. So is Pat. They know how much I was stressing to get a job within three weeks. "Good for you, Honey!" Pat exclaims wholeheartedly. "Maybe you'll find a few great sales!"

Lenny concurs, "You know, Mary Ann, you'd rather be shopping in a big department store with everything you need than a grocery store."

They both made me feel successful about landing a "real" job. Yeah, right, with an M.D., I am pleased as punch to earn nine measly dollars an hour. How much college does one need to earn ten? Yeesh!

Here's the punch line: I had to turn in 10% of my income to P.R.C. for savings, and 20% of my gross salary P.R.C. keeps.

One has to pay to go to jail.

Every last penny remaining I spent blissfully on my two fifteen-minute breaks and lunchtime to kill the boredom of being a check-out girl. One of my "big shot" supervisors was suspicious that I may be shopping and on two different occasions I saw two counselors from P.R.C. trying to catch me. (Luckily, I was on the correct side of the cash register, checking people out instead of purchasing!) If the work supervisor found out how outrageously, even borrowing money from Edward sometimes, I would have been awarded to serve my "suspended" six months back in a cell in Clarksburg. I did get written up once for an $8.99 cent shirt and got two days added to my sentence.

    I couldn't help myself from shopping. I really *don't* like shopping, unlike most women, but the sales were too fabulous to pass up! Hecht's was being bought out by Macy's and many things were 90% off. A $280 Michael Kors bag was $28 minus a 15% coupon, then 25% more employee discount, so now under $20. I still carry it every day. Baba and Mom taught me to love finding a great bargain.

    I was called a "floater". I worked in every department sometimes two and three in a day. They used to call "Mary Duke" on the overhead speaker and say something like "Go to bedding in the Home Store". I was good at sales in any department, from children's clothes to men's ties. "Floating" around the store, I found all the best buys. I enjoyed Hecht's especially working in "Teens". The music was different, modern, not elevator-like in the rest of the store. Standing on one's feet all day was tiring, but in teens I always danced a little behind the register. I wanted to apply at Nordstrom's for the live piano music, but Nordstrom's pays by straight commission I was told, and commission only jobs were not allowed. I think I would have grossed more than $360/week there, no doubt.

    I was pretty happy at Hecht's except when I had to wait on one of my ex-patients.

Every time I encountered one, I relived the pain of not being able to be an eye doctor anymore and all I have lost.

The first time it happened was the worst. My first "patient encounter" was my ex-hair-stylist. Beautiful. She was so shocked to see me behind the handbag counter wearing a badge, at first she just stared, mouth gaping. I also needed a haircut, desperately.

I'm feeling totally humiliated in front of my chatterbox ex-hairdressser in Potomac. I wanted to melt into the floor like the "Wicked Witch of the West". "Hello, how are you?" I ask, but don't wait for an answer. I add, "I'm doing research for a book." Smiling, but in need of a sprint away from her before she could start asking questions, I inform my coworker, "I'm going to the ladies' room." I walk away swiftly, but still hear her comment, "So *here's* where you are working now." I wave without turning. Oh, shit! She's going to tell everyone. Why the hell did they have to put me in handbags today?!

I have many, many humiliating moments as a check-out girl, after all Lenny and Pat's preaching "no-way-you-are-gonna-do-that-check-out-girl-Mary Ann" talks, having to wait on my old patients. Those patients used to let me operate on their eyes and trusted me implicitly with their sight, and now I'm telling them about the best buys in the store. *They believed me*.

My wealthy patients often spent more on purchases in one hour of shopping than I earned ringing out hundreds of people in 80-120 hours, gross salary, all on my feet.

Then when I thought I was getting over my chagrin at seeing a patient, Judy bought some lingerie from me. I didn't recognize her, but she knew me right away.

"Hi, Mary Ann." Pause. There's only "Mary Duke" on my badge. This person knows me. Who is she? I think she was surprised I didn't recognize her. Probably was. She worked for me over five years, and it's only a year since we split.

"It's Judy!"

"Oh…hi. I didn't recognize you." Her hair was totally different, much longer. Truthfully, I thought she looked much older with it. I always liked her short hair. Whatever.

"You're working here now?"

"Yes." What else to say?

"Thank you," she says as I hand her her purchases.

"You're welcome." She smiles a little and leaves. I stand still and watch her walk away. When she is out of sight, I tell the girl next to me, "I'll be right back." I run after Judy. She doesn't turn, and I see everything. Judy must have flipped open her cell phone as soon as she got around the corner, as she was already laughing with someone into her phone. I sense she was laughing at me. I am angry. All I say is, "I have four children to support. The Board gave me five years. Do you think that's fair? Thanks for all of your support." By the look on her face, I'm convinced she is laughing about me.

I got humiliation down as a feeling, absofuckinglutely.

Chapter 31

WILD AND CRAZY

Less than a month from my courtroom sentencing and handcuffing, I'm feeling more than a wee bit "wild and crazy". I'm allowed, right? My relatives are from Slovakia, like Steve Martin's character from *Saturday Night Live*. It's in my genes, not my fault. I can't hold back any longer and speak my mind, like my parents always said I could do, if I know I am right. Remember, the "Oh, Jesus, I can't be submissive and hold back" from the first chapter? Here goes: I's just gots myself so sicks and so's tireds of the bad talkin's goin's on. With all the I's is's, and yous is's and the we be's and they's be's and we all be's a doin' dis and a doin' dat, I just can't take it anymore. One morning after breakfast I verbally assault one particularly horrendous male offender of the English language.

I scream at him: "To Be! It is the derivative of the verb: To Be! It is, I *am,*...you *are,*...he, she, it, *is*...We are! You are! They are! It's English 101! My three year old speaks better than you do! How do you expect to get *any respect* in the real world when you don't even know how to say: I *am?* It's not *I's is!*"

Silence. ...Oh Jesus Christ, Blessed Mary and Joseph.....whooooa is me... I realize I overstepped my bounds by the dead silence in the entire cafeteria.

The man I addressed jumped up, sprang towards me and screamed back, "I's goin' to be's a talkins just like I's is! You's ain'st goin's to be a tellins *me* hows to be's a talkin! Who's do yous thinks yous be's a talkin to?"

Time to go, Mary Ann! Where's a damned guard when I need one? I grab my unfinished tray, hand in my silverware in a blur, and trot back to Unit 1. Something made me turn as I was running. There was the head cook in her glass office smiling and bowing her head, chuckling away.

I avoided the man and I liked that guy. We used to work out together in the shitty little "gym" area that stunk of sweat and had a few rusty free weights and an ancient stationary bike. (I was the only woman who worked out. After a few weeks at the gym, a guard walked by, saw me and yelled "Women are only allowed to work out on Wednesday mornings from ten 'til noon! Get out of the gym, Duke"! Guess I should have read the Guidebook, huh? At least, I didn't get written up for that broken rule.) But from the few times I did work out at the same time as the man whose grammar I corrected, I knew he was strong and loved to box! Brilliant move, Dr. Duke, publicly embarrass and anger one of the strongest and most aggressive men in the whole jail. (Along with most of the people who heard me correct him whose grammar is just as bad.) So I ate at unusual times, missed laughing with Lenny and Pat, and ate fast to scurry to safety in my room.

Two days later he came up to me in the hallway. I was a little afraid. If I was publicly humiliated like him, I certainly may still be royally pissed off and want to slap him up side the head. He stopped short of me, but was in my walking path, so I had to stop and face him.

He spoke first, "I *am,* (not I's is), glad you pointed that out to me. I *am* trying to say those words better. Thank you".

I smiled at him both in surprise and relief, and believe it or not, was speechless.

I reached out and shook his hand and smiled broader. He smiled back at me and squeezed my hand back. Oh my God, I got through to one person, actually the one person I was the toughest on... Wow, there is hope.

*   *   *

Public transportation, buses, nausea. I haven't used public transportation since before Popsi died, *25 years ago*, and I inherited his 1972 V-8 forest green Dodge Dart Swinger. I was "IT" in that car. No pollution control whatsoever, great AC, very light weight, that car had wings, and I was no longer bus sick back and forth to medical school. I was the only student at Albany Medical College with an American made fifteen-year-old shit mobile. I would drag race any other students' daddy's old Porsche or Mercedes in a heartbeat with Popsi's light V8, though, and usually won.

But damn it, I have to take a nauseating bus to Silver Spring to get a new I.D. No cab allowed. A copy of "Mapquest" is left for me. I hate computers, maps, and many other such usable commodities. Unless there is an XY (male) specimen driving me with directions, since I'd rather be a music listening passenger, whose only duty is to change CD's, I need GPS. God, I do miss my BMW.

My spirits are the highest they've been, however, in a very long time. It's a sunny, crisp December day, and I have a brief "Get out of Jail Free" pass, except for the cheap bus fare. Surviving the bus ride better than anticipated, I walk across Georgia Avenue leisurely. It's a busy thoroughfare and I can be run over if not careful. But I am walking slowly, enjoying my brief minutes of freedom and the beautiful day.

I've never been to this Motor Vehicles' Bureau. It is a small office and packed with people speaking many languages. Finally, it's my turn. I sit at a very pleasant looking three-hundred-pound-plus woman's window. (I'm really not an anti-obese person. I just think people are overweight for simple reasons. First, they love to eat. Second, their gene pool is full of overweight people. Third and last, but certainly not least, it is 1,110% more acceptable in America to overeat and be obese than it is to binge drink. And obesity does not impair one's ability to drive until one can't fit behind the steering wheel.)

"Hello, how are you today?" she politely asks.

"I'm doing just fine, thank you. How are you?"

She rolls her eyes and says, "Busy."

"I see you are, very busy." And I smile pleasantly at her.

"What's your name?"

"Mary Ann Duke."

A few moments pass before she looks up. I'm thinking, oh shit, don't look me up *too* much, Ma'am. I just want an ID, not a driver's license, so don't worry about all of the nasty charges you see on my record.

She's finally looks up and asks, "Would you like your driver's license?"

I don't respond. I think I must have heard her incorrectly. Is she offering *me* a driver's license? I briefly dart my eyes to the right and left, as if someone had approached from behind, whom she must be addressing. She looks at me questioningly.

I respond flatly, as I definitely think she must be mistaken, "I just need an ID for my job, please."

Her response will forever make me smile. "Honey, you have a valid driver's license. Do you want a new one?"

She's kidding me, right, trying to make a little joke out of my pages of charges? I smile a little at her kidding; I'm a good sport. "No, thank you, I just need an ID for a job."

"Oh", she responds. "Why don't you want your driver's license?"

Now, I think she must be a little slow, or just plain dumb as dirt and can't read, because she remains serious with her question.

Now I'm blunt with her, "Because I don't have one."

"My computer screen says you do."

"I'm sorry, Ma'am, but I'm confident that I do *not* have a valid driver's license."

I let go, as always, lean forward and admit, "Ma'am, I am incarcerated right now for DUI. I am confident that I do *not* have a valid driver's license whatsoever. I am *in jail*. There is *no way* I am still legal to drive."

"My computer screen says you are."

Pause. She peers into her computer screen again and says, "It says on my monitor I can issue you a valid driver's license." I am in shock at her words, smile, maintain my patience, and politely ask, "Ma'am, could you please get your supervisor?"

I sit back in my uncomfortable chair and wait for the supervisor. I'm in jail for three drunk driving charges with three wrecks, I think, and I can't believe this lady is offering me a driver's license. I'm incredulous that she asked me such a stupid question. *If only my medical license lost twenty days after my first DUI was so simple to get back.*

The supervisor arrives. Now there is another three-hundred-pound-plus woman in front at me, and I am double-teamed, if not out-weighed. But I do not want to get into any trouble and obtain a license I'm *not* supposed to have.

The supervisor speaks clearly as she looks up at me, "We can issue you a valid driver's license."

I'm astounded.

I readmit leaning in to the supervisor, "I am incarcerated for DUI, Ma'am. I am *in jail*. I *can't possibly* have a valid license. I am just here for an ID for a job. I don't even have a car."

Pause, not much of one, because there is a big line waiting. The supervisor, I made sure to check her badge, speaks softly to me, "Listen, Honey, you have a valid license. They are twenty dollars. An ID is fifteen. I would greatly suggest you get your driver's license, as you never know. You may be in an emergency and need it."

I smile for the camera.

I get a shiny new driver's license without even an alcohol restriction.

I can drive a car after three DUI's with three wrecks while serving time, but lost my entire life's work, my only means of livelihood, after my first. I never harmed a patient, but sideswiped other people in cars.

*   *   *

What a wacky, wacky world we *do live in!!!*

*   *   *

I feel the most carefree I've felt in years leaving that MVA. I can't wait to show my smiling new license to Lenny and Pat. We'll be hysterical!

As I bask in the sun at the bus stop, I think, "Maybe your luck has finally turned, Dr. Duke. Or,…this damned license proves how twisted and unjust the systems can be".

I smile wryly. The way things are going today, though, maybe I should get a law degree and run for President after menopause is over. Ha, Mr. Kapp thought I was a "leader", even if I did hate his English class.

At least, I'd be doing it for the right reasons. I've lived on both sides of the fence, barb-wired and gated, and know what stress, desperation and addiction can do to people. It wouldn't be to get back at the good ole' boys or for power. It would just be the biggest house-cleaning project Baba and my parents prepared me for. I would do it just to be fair and not greedy, and I'd wear a bulletproof body suit and a Kevlar helmet. I smile imagining how that would look. Good luck, Mrs. Clinton. You've got a long row to hoe.

But conservative Chile elected its first female President, Dr. Michelle Bachelet. She's a single mom, a doctor and has been tortured and incarcerated, too! Yeah, I'll skip law school. I'm going to my children's soccer games instead. One doesn't need a law degree to run this country properly. One just needs an excellent, trustworthy staff, insurmountable integrity, intelligence and chutzpah. I've been blessed with bunches of each. What a dream. "Presi*d*ent Duke"; it works. Sounds just as good as "Dr.".

Nah, Baba didn't want me to be President. Baba wanted me to be a doctor, and so did I, or I wouldn't have been able to achieve it. I want my noble profession back, and I deserve to be an eye doctor again. I want to help people see better, and help people any way I can. When profits, God willing, come from this book, I will devote my life first, of course, to my children, but I also want to help the poor, underprivileged, and suffering. Guess that's my new calling. I will be good at it, if at least understanding.

The light turns green and a shiny BMW goes by with a handsome male driver. I beam at both the driver and the beautiful car, and ponder...hmmm, some day I'm going to drive at least one of those again.

The bus arrives, and I'm still grinning in my reverie as I drop in my fare. The bus driver grins back.

EPILOGUE

I found out I was the only M.D. in the joint after all. I couldn't believe that Doc *really* was a plastic surgeon with those hideously meager hair plugs, so I innocently asked his wife one night, "Hi, I'm Dr. Mary Ann Duke. I know your husband. Where is his plastic surgery office"? She blushed crimson, then angrily turned and flounced away from me, but not before she spit out over her shoulder, "He's *not* a doctor"! I told Lenny and Pat, and they grilled Doc (who knows, maybe they held him down, probably!) until he caved and finally admitted to stealing doctors' prescription pads. He then fraudulently signed their names for Oxycontin, Viagra, you name it and sold drugs, albeit "prescription" drugs. Doc thought he was far superior to all of the other drug dealers, because he sold "real medications" and impersonated a physician. What a weirdo; no wonder he gave me the creeps.

Pat, my pony-tailed bisexual friend, restarted his hair salon business and is so busy, "It's like I never left"! I can imagine his patented hand flop over the phone line.

Lenny is still stocking shelves at Giant. He thinks his parole officer is going to make him do it for his full five years on parole, but maintains his calm aura.

I lost touch with everyone else except my buddies from Father Martin Ashley's, Kristin and Tony. Kristin and Tony dated for two years after leaving rehab. Tony went to jail for only *one* month for his first three DUIs (not six months like I did), while still having two more DUIs pending court date. Kristin and Tony continued to drink excessively. Kristin called me every day and was helping me write as we talked on our unlimited cell phones for hours a day.

Kristin was arrested for two DUIs *after* rehab. Tony dodged court and skipped to California and lived on credit cards to avoid court for his last two arrests (DUIs). Kristin was devastated when he told her he was going so far away to avoid more jail time. Kristin never saw Tony again. Tony died coughing up blood in California, leaving behind a six-year-old daughter. Tony was thirty-six-years-old. Less than one year later, a sober Kristin committed suicide from carbon monoxide poisoning in her garage. She always said, "Duke, Tony was the love of my life". I really miss speaking to her every day; we had become best friends. What a tragedy and waste of young lives. Gees, I pray Peggy had her breast cancer treated, my friend from Seven Locks Jail.

I was incarcerated two days before Thanksgiving, November 2005 and was released on April 3, 2006; however, I just got off of three years of probation in November 2008. If I accidentally break the law again, I will not have to make up the six months that were suspended, yet hanging over my head like a noose for the last three years. Remember, my original sentence was one full year with six months suspended/waived unless I violated my probation.

I bumped into Grandma by accident. God bless her; I didn't recognize her. She recognized me first; it had been a year-and-a-half since we shared a jail cell in Clarksburg. Grandma looked so much better with *all* long blonde hair, and not that one/third gray look. I saw her at Home Depot of all places, and I rarely go there. We hugged and kissed. I even shed a tear. Grandma really helped me in that claustrophobic jail cell. Davie informed me later, "She's probably violating her parole, being in the same damned store she stole from". No wonder she was in a flurry as she scribbled her number on the back of a crumpled receipt. Grandma gave me her ever *toothless*, winning smile and exclaimed, "I'm staying sober"! Yep, Grandma's sober, but still living on the edge.

*   *   *

Over four years have passed since I lost my medical license. My office is a turnkey operation. I just need to vacuum and turn the lights on. I thought I'd advertise using my cell phone number and save money hiring help and starting a business line. Send out postcards to all my old patients, put my sign out the Board made Dr. Jones take down, and elate to Colonial Opticians, "I'm baAack!" Then pray the phone rings, just like the good old days when I was so proud to open my own office.

I phoned Diz, my beloved roommate from medical school, on my 45th birthday (we hadn't talked in five years since she called me on my 40th, but you know how it is, good friends catch up with each other and just pick up where they left off even if it was a whole five years ago), and I gave her an earful about my tumultuous life. Diz is amazed at my story, then flatly states, "Duke, I quit being a pediatrician five years ago just after the last time we talked."

"You've got to be kidding! Why?!" Diz's words shocked the hell out of me.

"I just got too frustrated, Duke! I had to do a physical on an asthmatic in six-seven minutes, because the insurance reimbursements kept going lower and lower. I couldn't spend twenty minutes (which each parent deserved) to explain about the allergens their child should avoid. If I saw only three patients per hour; I wouldn't cover my overhead!"

Then she totally blew my mind with, "I really don't even miss it. Too frustrating!" I was speechless. Diz was *the most dedicated doctor and she QUIT!* I had my license stolen from me, but I am still so emotionally wiped out my dear roommate quit in total disgust and outrage. Diz was so fearful and traumatized that she purchased a $42,000 malpractice insurance "tail" which covers her from ever losing her savings and home from a *future* law suit. Screw that! I never bought one of those "tails" and it's too late to sue me now. (Three-year statute of limitation in Maryland.) Gees, Diz could have bought a Mercedes with that money. What a waste; she would never be sued.

Luckily, Diz has a husband who loves her and supports her and continues practicing pediatrics, so she can rest from the maddening mayhem the insurance companies and legal system have made of the noblest profession, medicine.

*   *   *

I call Mom and Dad and deadpan, "Mom and Dad, I just can't sell until I hear about the appeal."

"We're worried about you, Honey," Mom replies.

"I know. I know. Something's gotta give. For God's sake, isn't four years without my medical license and jail for six months enough suffering for the Board?"

"I hope so," Dad deadpans back. My parents don't have the financial means to help me. I can sense their coronary artery spasm (chest pain) over the phone line. I have enough of my own that would kill both of them, especially after the American Academy of Ophthalmology took away my board certification status on my birthday June 6, 2007, over two-and-one-half years *after* the Board took my medical license. Those ophthalmology boards were an enormous amount of studying, stress and time (not to mention money for plane fares, hotel rooms and board review courses). I was supposed to be "grandfathered" (they call it) for life. I am still shocked by that low blow.

* * *

Throughout it all, Edward continues to bring alcohol into my home, but, at least, I could see Eloise. He won't let me see Eloise unless he brings alcohol into my home in hopes of sex, also. Since getting out of jail in April, 2006 I have seen her less than one hour per month. In three years, I have seen my six-year-old daughter with Edward no more than 40 hours and have had $40,000 in attorneys' fees, child support and "supervising nannies'" fees while *un*employed.

To repeat, in early 2008, a pediatrician named Amy Castillo's story from Silver Spring, MD (same county and Circuit Court as me) made international news. She was even on the *Larry King Live* show May 1st. Dr. Amy Castillo fought for almost two years to keep her children away from her very mentally ill, suicidal and threateningly homicidal estranged husband. The Montgomery County Circuit Court repeatedly gave her husband "***unsupervised visitation***" while she got to pay alimony, despite her protestations that he was threatening to "kill the children but leave her alive to suffer". Dr. Amy Castillo's husband drowned their three small children in a hotel room near the inner Harbor of Baltimore, one by one. Her children were six, four and two years of age. The autopsy report revealed that the six-year-old boy put up a heroic struggle.

An unquestionably chilling statement for the judgment of the Montgomery County Judicial System.

A murderer or rapist is allowed a trial by jury that may last one to two weeks, but a large family of children can be purloined from their loving mother's care and given to an abusive father with an "ex-parte" hearing, when the defendant/the children's mother is not even able to be present, *by one single judge's ruling,* whether that judge is male or female.

This same court ruled against me on my medical license appeal in 2006, and against me on a restraining order I should have easily obtained on Edward in 2007 and (three strikes and you are out!), also ruled against my having more visitation with Eloise multiple times in 2007 and in 2008. *I am not even allowed to call her.*

Amy and I have become kindred spirits; she had brunch with me at my home on Christmas Day, 2008. She leaned into me and asked me after we chatted for four hours non-stop, *"Why didn't they (the judges) listen to me"?!* My simple response was blunt, "Because there is a double-standard. You are a woman. The men get away with it"! (I almost said, "The men get away with murder"; *thank God I didn't!!*) Instead I finished with my usual quotable quote. "The women get put down. A penis prevents problems". Amy leaned back in her chair and stared at me in stunned, sorrowful silence.

I'll never, *ever* forget that moment with her tortuously pained face and beautiful tear-filled eyes on Christmas Day.

*   *   *

My older three children I see every other weekend "supervised" for $20/hour. Yet again, I find the court system patriarchal, but continue to fight for more time. An unemployed mother should not have to pay $1,050/month in child support and $890/month in supervision fees (both post-tax dollars, plus at least $1,000/month in attorneys' fees) to see her children a total of forty hours a month, separately. Seventeen (17) hours every other weekend (no overnights) for my older three and two measly three-hour visits/month, Wednesday afternoons, to the tune of

$35/hour for a U.S. Marshall to supervise me with Eloise. *A father can rape his own daughter in the great state of Maryland, and Maryland law does not preclude the father from visitation prior to the daughter's emancipated age of eighteen. The law says <u>nothing</u> regarding that the visitation be supervised. <u>It does not have to be supervised even in the case of rape!</u>* But I need a U.S. Marshall. (What a filthy double standard, absolutely disgusting!) Eloise keeps asking to see her siblings, but the judges won't even allow her to come to Mommy's home. I have to meet her in "the community". I pay almost $40,000/year, post-tax dollars, to see my children separately, no more than forty (40) hours/month while unemployed. Does this sound crazy? Welcome to my world, a female doctor's world. At least my children are alive and not murdered.

*   *   *

I lost both of my appeals for my medical license on the state level in the Court of Appeals and the Court of Special Appeals in Maryland. The only higher court is the Supreme Court of the United States of America. I think the Supreme Court has bigger fish to fry than Mary Ann Duke, M.D. from Johnson City, New York, and I know there is a wait list of several years. I just can't sit at the bar and have a couple of drinks waiting for a few tables to clear. I'm hungry right now! Anyway, the Supreme Court has only one woman, so what the fuck good is that?!

I need to get my life back; I deserve to be a doctor again after my decades of hard work and dedication; I must know the facts about medical license revocations. Public Citizen News' headline from November/December, 2006: <u>Public Citizen Study Finds that Doctors Committing Serious Crimes Allowed to Practice Medicine.</u> The lead author was Dr. Paul Jung from the University of Maryland. I obtained the whole study and spoke to Dr. Jung. It was an exhaustingly arduous countrywide study of ten years from 1990-2000. I am only citing the facts regarding revocations.

1. 29 doctors committed murder or were convicted of manslaughter. Only 20 revocations. 2 doctors had absolutely no action taken; thusly, still practicing medicine after killing someone.

2. 171 convictions of rape, sexual assault, public indecency, or any sex-related conviction. Only 69 revocations. 11 got nothing.

3. 835 drug dealing or prescribing violations. 161 revocations. 301 no action taken, over 1/3rd! (Drug dealing, aka like "Doc" or worse, a real doctor should have served some jail time for multiple felonies.)

4. 850 Medicare, Medicaid or insurance frauds. 94 revocations. 571 not a damned thing was done. (Wow, guess insurance fraud is the way to go, huh? Small pun.)

5. 5 practiced without a license. (My dubious Botox move, which I was immediately put on track for revocation with a "Cease and Desist" order.) <u>Zero, (the big **0**), revocations!</u> 1 suspension, 2 probations and 2 got nothing. Do *you* think I was singled out?

6. 85 Income tax evasions. 14 revocations. 20, almost ¼ again got nothing.

7. 144 theft, bribery, unspecified frauds. 40 revocations. 31, over 1/5th nothing.

8. 242 Criminal conduct related to the practice of medicine. 26 revocations. 110 nothing. (That doesn't sound right either, no way!)

9. 475 "Unspecified convictions". 127 revocations. 12<u>9</u> nothing done yet again.
10. This one is most important to me: 67 public drunkenness or "driving under the influence." Ten, 10 revocations. 15% revoked and 8 doctors got no reprimand whatsoever.

Out of a total of 2,903 convictions, only 561 doctors had their license revoked and almost double that, 1,185 doctors got no reprimand whatsoever. The filler numbers are probations, restrictions on licenses, suspensions, but my point is the low numbers of doctors revoked and *how very many got nothing*.

I bet a million dollars not one of those 15% revoked "drunks" were only twenty days after their *first* drunk driving arrest that they hadn't even gone to court for yet. Actually, I'd bet ten trillion dollars I am the only one ever!

I am confident I have been singled out to hold that painful crown on my own head.

Two doctors out of twenty-nine have literally gotten away with murder and can still treat patients.

And only 15% of the drunks got revoked. No one ever said life was fair, though. Now did they? Nope. Dr. Jung could not give me any specific numbers for Maryland only. This was a countrywide study. He also had no facts from 2000-present.

I asked him, "What percentage of the revocations and what percentage of the doctors who received no punishment whatsoever were men or women?"

"We didn't keep records of that."

They should have. I bet those statistics would have been *very* interesting.

* * *

But, it's the new millennium, and high time for everyone to go from the general to the specific and learn the truth. I want to know what is going on right now, right here at home, in Maryland. "It's a matter of public record", I was told by the Department of Health and Human Services in Baltimore, and I "should request it from the Maryland Medical Board directly". So I did. I faxed, e-mailed, and sent certified return-receipt-requested letters to the Board requesting how many medical licenses in Maryland were taken away in the past ten years (before mine was in 2004). After my third attempt in six weeks and offering to pay, I received the information.

For the *fifteen years* before my license was revoked, only one doctor received a harsher sentence than mine. He was a male psychiatrist. He was given a "permanent revocation" for terrible record keeping, lack there of, including no medication changes, mental status of patient, response to treatment, etc… He also slept with his patient. That's all. (sarcasm)

I reapplied for my Maryland medical license in 2008 and was very complete with my application. (See Appendix B.) Six weeks later a polite "Fuck you" letter arrived from the Board stating I cannot reapply until September 28, 2010. (Appendix C) I will have to file bankruptcy before then and/or lose my hard-earned home office, run on a die-hard battery and not eat; stop seeing my children and paying child support and go to jail for not paying child support/contempt of court. But then again, jail would be preferable to being on the street. At least in jail one can get "two hots and a cot" and my "abs" would get back into their six-pack shape from my sit-up/push-up Janie fuckin' Fonda workouts! Good golly gee! *WHAT A BLOODY NIGHTMARE.*

* * *

Persevering, as Baba would want me to, I wrote and/or called the Governor of Maryland at least six times in the past year. I thought a Governor's pardon was just the ticket I needed to get my life back and start earning a living again. He chooses the members of the Maryland Medical Board, remember? Thus logic would dictate, climb up the totem pole to meet the dicktator, right? My first letter to the Governor (written by a patient/friend) went without response. (Appendix D) Six weeks later I wrote my own letter. (Appendix E)

The P.S. in my letter to the Governor was exactly this: "As offered in my original letter, here are twenty exceedingly egregious cases. A point that I did not make before is that the time between the 'crime of moral turpitude' and the suspension/revocation by the Maryland Board of Physicians, when the doctors' actual prescription pads, DEA (Drug Enforcement Administration) and CDS (Controlled Dangerous Substance) numbers are confiscated is usually *years*. If a physician is capable of rape, murder, home ecstasy labs, child pornography, falsifying records and prescription drug fraud; logic would dictate these physicians would be capable of continued prescription drug fraud to make ends meet; exacerbating our country's gross drug problem until their DEA and CDS numbers are terminated".

Please, Google www.mbp.state.md.us, then click on "Practitioner Profile" and then enter in these physicians' license numbers: D33271, D40524, D08462, D24580, D17735, D32654, D02524, D14605, D22212, D16665, D17933, D62991, D44550, D08283, D46921, D32043, D58918, D39793, D12748 and D42002.

I have a top twenty list unlike David Letterman's top ten. My list includes a doctor who treats mononucleosis with 80 mg. of Oxycontin, overdosing two teenagers and killing them; however, his license was not taken until a lengthy "investigation" found *nine more patients* who were "mistreated", but luckily didn't die! (High dose narcotics, like Oxycontin are definitely *NOT* the correct treatment for mono, med school 101.) There is a doctor who raped his mute, retarded patient (the nurse who accompanied the patient heard grunting and discovered the mute, retarded patient's sweats at her ankles and the grunter was the doctor); another who raped his girlfriend's 14-year-old daughter repeatedly over a year (and I believe never spent a day in jail) or simply the psychiatrist who sleeps with his patient and continues to treat her husband. Truly tragic is the obstetrician who performs abortions and kills the mother, too, or causes massive brain damage in another patient, both patients within a four-month-period. No problem, he can be reinstated to then perforate a patient's uterus, colon, rectum and bladder. It took two-and-one-half *years* for the Board to "voluntarily suspend" his license from the time of the first two women. (One dead and the other brain dead, not much difference, ya think? Did Sarra have a life? No.) Why the Board allowed him to practice again *ever* is beyond me. It also took almost *two years* for the Board to finally revoke his license after yet another two women almost died from his abortions. One of my favorites is the pediatrician who blamed his red eyes on a "flare-up" of his glaucoma. What did he blame his staggering and swaying on? Eye drops don't cause intoxicated imbalance. His first patient complaint was in 1989 and his license wasn't suspended until 2000; thus, (being a member of the "penis prevents problems club") he got to continue earning a living seeing infants and children pleasantly inebriated for over a decade until he had enough money to retire on, anyway.

      There are doctors who murder their wives, get convicted of second-degree manslaughter and are probably out of jail before I can even begin to reapply for my medical license, and *I never once hurt an eye nor any patient's eyesight.* Reading any of these Maryland Board public records will either curl your hair or grow it back blonde, and just think! I only researched the little ole' state of Maryland.

* * *

Within ten days of my second letter to the Governor, I received a letter from the State of Maryland Commission on Human Relations stamped (not signed) by Henry B. Ford. (Hmm, thought he was long dead after inventing the automobile.) (Appendix F) Before I had a chance to call, a woman from the Commission called *me*, and I put her on speakerphone so that two other women I was with, could hear. She said, "We can only help you if you are a secretary or receptionist for the Board."

"Excuse me?" I ask. I thought I didn't hear her correctly.

"We can only help you if you actually worked for the Board."

I politely ask, "May I, please, speak to Mr. Henry Ford?"

"No, he's not here."

"May I, please, speak to your supervisor?"

Pause. "Okay, I'll try to reach her."

Unknowingly, I hadn't put the phone on pause while I bitched at my two witnesses. "Can you believe this shit? The amount I paid in taxes to the State of Maryland probably paid her salary and Mr. Ford's for years! Why can't they help me? I was self-employed and paying their salaries!!!"

The supervisor apparently had already gotten on the line during my mini-rant and heard every word. She said, "I heard what you said", in a threatening tone.

I replied, "Great! Then I don't have to repeat myself!"

She reinforced everything the first woman said. "You can only be helped by the Commission if you actually worked at the Board's office in Baltimore. I reasked to speak to Mr. Ford. She said, "He's not here."

I had the nerve to ask, *"Does he even exist?"*

She answered, "He asked me to take care of this for him." My deduction: maybe he *is* long dead, like I previously thought. I was pissed off that I wasn't even allowed to speak to the man who "stamped" the letter and logarithmically more pissed off that the Governor referred me to some bullshit "Commission on Human Relations" that can only help me if I was a paid employee for the Board. Is the hand not connected to the wrist not connected to the elbow not connected to the shoulder not connected to the clavicle not connected to the neck not connected to the brain in this great state?...Obviously not. Or the Governor just sent me on a wild goose chase to get rid of me. Within a few weeks, I received a follow-up letter from the supervisor. (Appendix G) Thanks for nothing.

*   *   *

A couple of months later I made my last call to the Governor. Hmm. I finally got a prompt response after I told his receptionist that I was going to "slap the Governor's office with a law suit and slap hard if I didn't get a telephone call from him within 48 hours"!!

It had truly been a rough morning on the phone. I usually give good phone but that morning I spent almost two hours on the phone with credit card companies asking for a lower interest rate. I was repeatedly told, "You can't get a lower interest rate unless you are collecting unemployment". How does one collect unemployment if one was/is self-employed? If any reader knows, please, contact me at author@thegoodthebadandthecrazy.com.

The following hour was spent on the phone with my mortgage company asking for the same thing, a lower interest rate. My mortgage company said, "You can't get a lower interest rate unless you *are* employed". I told them I was self-employed as an author and they told me "that didn't count". Notwithstanding, I was in a pretty foul mood when I called the Governor. The Governor's Chief Legal Counsel wrote me and the letter was in my mailbox within 48 hours, believe it or not. She stated that they couldn't help me with my "situation". (Appropriately, this is Appendix "H", because I think I *am* in hell.)

The truth remains the truth and I'd like to know it! *What **indeed** is my "situation"*?! I need some clarification. I am a true American with the truest of American spirit and grit. I am an American-born, American educated board-certified eye surgeon and physician who wants to contribute to society not only through her God-given talent to be an outstanding ophthalmologist and help people see better, but also to contribute to the American system by being a productive tax-paying member of society. My tax dollars can help the less fortunate and I want to pay them and do just that: help people!

If the State of Maryland's government system does not help a medical doctor, a healer, who has devoted her life to helping people, *who do they help?!* Does the "system" help the poor, homeless alcoholic or drug addict or disabled veteran on the street who doesn't have the potential to earn much more than minimum wage? I think most definitely *not!* If an educated doctor who wants to pay taxes and help society see better, who has dedicated her youth to becoming educated enough to try to make a difference in this world is just beaten down by the system; I sincerely doubt the State of Maryland/Governor's office/beaurocratic bullshit gives a damn about anyone nor anything except their own pocketbook and their next election.

Did anyone help Dr. Amy Castillo *before* she had three dead babies? I pray that God gives her strength to carry on without her children and for all the abused women and men in this world. Please, God, help little Eloise persevere until I can get her back along with more time with James, Marika and Nadia. *Children need to be with their mothers* more than this vindictive, patriarchal judicial system allows. It has been over twenty years now since the tide has changed and the men are winning custody more often than the women, especially the *ABUSIVE* fathers.

Ever since child support really became an issue in the 80's; that is when men started to win more and more physical and legal custody. I now know there is more corruption and despicable deceit in America than I could have ever dreamed of as a child. I understand why my kindergarten teacher friend has trouble saying the Pledge of Allegiance every day in school after she lost custody of her three daughters to her physically abusive husband, who is now physically abusing her daughters. She doesn't believe in the last words anymore, "with liberty and justice for all". I also understand now why those women were happy to see each other in jail. It sure beats being cold and hungry and homeless and feeling the need to use drugs to escape, or sell them to survive.

*   *   *

In closing, try to even *imagine* how I felt when the police came and took my children? My despair was overwhelming. I have *no idea* how I got out of bed and saw patients. I don't know how I functioned at all. Going to jail was a piece of cake, *and jail was a walk through hell,* compared to my life, trying to do everything for everyone but myself, and then killing all of my emotional pain with alcohol. I just woke up mildly hung-over and did it all over again.

I'm sorry, "Board", but I know you screwed up and screwed me and my family over. What, were the "good ole' boys" simply envious that the little Czechoslovakian girl from nowhere and nothing except a family filled with strength and stamina and excellent morals was doing better than most of the doctors in town? Because I had the foresight to save money and commuting time with a home-office? Or does it stem way back to 1988 when I could have saved Sarra Umstadter's life if her asthma was worked up by the Vice Chairman like I asked him to; and that is why New York revoked my license while I was in rehab *and* almost eight weeks *before* Maryland revoked me? Maryland is my home state of practice. The "sister" states revoke *after* the "mother" state does. Who the fuck loses their license twenty days after their first drunk driving arrest for the "unforeseeable future", who has never been sued and never harmed a patient? No one, unless they have been targeted by some networking good ole' boys! Bingo!

All I needed was six months off (not six years revoked) with the first three in rehab. (Many people commit suicide; even kill their entire family along with themselves when they lose their livelihood. Add on top of that losing custody of one's beloved children. I certainly thought about it. I would never hurt my children in a gazillion years, but taking the *giant nap* did seem like the easy way out on more than one occasion, because suicide *is* the seductive option.) But, now, I'm glad you did what you did. What you did to me was total discrimination, sleazy, contemptible and sick, but now I'm glad you did it.

Otherwise I would never have finished this book project...
Intense thought.

And life goes on. Go on your merry way, just remember the old saying: "What goes around comes around". And remember, too, all that gold bullion you are collecting can't be melted down and poured into your urn with you and your ashes. The bullion also weigh down the casket and make it crack easier, so the bugs can get in sooner. And gold doesn't buy you a seat next to God. Let's move on; I'm tired of writing about the wretched, ya think? Abso(you got it)lutely!

*   *   *

I have no choice. In order to see any of my children more, I have to go back to my home away from home, court. Shit. But I'll be okay...No matter what, Baba taught me to persevere.

*   *   *

May 2, 2007 was the last time all of my children and I were together as a family in the community, not at Mommy's home. That fact is insane, especially since I still have to be supervised with my older three children. Eloise's father insists that Eloise cannot come to my home nor can she come over on days when I have her half-siblings with me. We have not been together as a family even on a holiday since Christmas, *2006*. I can't even speak to her on her birthday. Do you think her father and the judicial system is battering me? What harm can I do on a speakerphone? I love my baby girl. I fought with her father nightly to keep her, remember he wanted me to abort her, and now all I get is to pay $610/month in child support, including in the $35/hour in supervision fees to a United States Marshall, while unemployed, unable to even get a waitressing job in this economy or a spot at Starbuck's. For God's sake, I *should have* named this book *INSANE*, ha, maybe the sequel. *Mothers need their children as much as children need their mothers.* I often cry just *thinking* about Dr. Amy Castillo's pain. I can't begin to imagine *enduring it daily,* every second of every minute, of every single day.

*   *   *

I'll always treasure my last birthday night's visit, however brief and without Eloise. James sat on my lap and hugged me for a long time. He was almost twelve on that day and much bigger than I. But that June day he sat on my lap and hugged me like a baby. James asked, while holding me, head on my shoulder, "Did we ever throw up on your neck"? I laughed. "All the time, James. If you live near me when you have babies, I'll babysit them any time you want and let them throw up on me, too"! Everyone laughed.

What an evening!! We watered the flower seeds we planted and watered the dahlias and gladiolas already growing. Soon we'll have beautiful flowers and maybe even a watermelon from the one seed Nadia carefully planted. Baba would be proud of our nurturing. (We *did get* that watermelon!)

James' sitting on my lap and hugging me like a baby, Marika's never ending smile and wave; their hand made cards and gifts, and dear Nadia's comment made my day. Nadia rarely refers to her father's new wife as "Mom". It still hurts when she says it, though, but I forgive her, of course I do. She did break my heart once when she yelled, "I never got to see you and Daddy happy together like James and Marika"! She turned and ran and locked herself in the bathroom. She finally came out, after much urging, and I could tell she had been crying. "I love you, Nadia. I never wanted to hurt you. I'm sorry you were so little that you do not remember". I wanted to cry, too. I understood her resentment, her sense of loss, and pain.

So I cling to the words Nadia said to me on my birthday. They were simple and beautiful: "Mommy, I want you to buy four houses in a row. Then we can live next door to each other and run over and see each other and not even have to call"! Those words say it all. My children love me and miss me. She even said "four" and remembered Eloise. I was so happy.

"Okay, Nadia, I'll do that. I promise. Thank you for saying that. I would like that very much, too". Please, God, help me persevere and afford, at least, a couple condos together some day.

*   *   *

I'm balling my eyes out thinking about her kind words as I walk into my quiet, empty home…with pictures of my children everywhere.

"Keep going, Honey", my Baba would always say. "Never give up and ask God for guidance. He'll help you if you pray". "But Baba", I think, "I *do* pray. And I am *so tired* of always having to fight for myself. I'm a really good person; I should not have to fight for my rights all of the time". Then I decide to do what Baba always told me.

"Dear God, please, grant me the serenity," and I get on my knees and bow my head in my family room, "to accept the things I cannot change, courage to change the things I can, and the wisdom to know the difference. And, please, God, may some people be helped by reading my book. Thank you for the strength to finish it. Thank you for my angels from heaven, and thank you for giving me such a great Baba, who really taught me how to persevere."

APPENDIX A

"It is the best kept, dirty little secret of our Family Court System: Fathers who batter their spouses are TWICE as likely to go for full or joint legal custody. And studies show that over 2/3rd's of the time the *fathers' win*." According to the Honorable Susan B. Carbon, a New Hampshire Family Court Judge: "What the public has to acknowledge is that the Judges need to be accountable for their actions and now they are not."

THIS IS NOTHING SHORT OF A NATIONAL SCANDAL.

Ever since child custody and support became an issue over twenty years ago, up to 70% of men have been winning contested child custody cases, even IN CASES OF SEXUAL ABUSE OF THEIR OWN CHILDREN (GIRLS *AND* BOYS).

Please Google: www.batteredmotherscustodyconference.org

Please Google: www.smalljustice.org

These are two excellent sites, even with video footage, about the complete injustice in the Family Court Systems all across America. Women are getting beaten down and our *children are suffering the most*. Don't the fathers and the judges *SEEEEE THAT*? ARE THEY *BOTH BLIND*?!!

What adds insult to injury is that the "Guardian ad Litems" or the children's attorneys are allowing these rapes and sodomies to happen. Mothers and their children have about as much rights today as they did in the days of slavery. The Women's Liberation Movement did _nothing_ for women except make women have to _pay their abusers to have custody of their children so that they can continue to abuse their children whether it be physically or emotionally or both!_

Breaking the Silence is a PBS digital presentation that is truly heart wrenching. It was underwritten by the Mary Kay Ash Charitable Foundation in 2005. It is no longer available to the public. PBS took it off the market after being threatened with lawsuits. The first sentence out of the narrator's mouth is: "All over America battered mother's are losing custody of their children when they file for divorce." A poor mother's comment: "I naively thought that if someone molests their kid, that they would just go to jail!"

Then the narrator continues, "Even with a proven record, abusers are winning joint and _sole legal custody._"

"To win custody of the kids, over and against the mother's will, is the ultimate victory short of killing the kids" said Joan Maier, Professor of Clinical Law, George Washington University. "It is the best way to hurt her and kick her down is to get custody of the kids."

The narrator continues, "One third of the women in the United States will be victims of domestic violence. It will have devastating effects on their children."

Walter Anderson, Chairman and C.E.O. of Parade Magazine admits to being very abused as the youngest child of three. Joe Torre, manager of the New York Yankees and President of the Safe at Home Foundation admits to horrible child abuse. Friends told him to go to the police and his response was, "My Dad was the police."

A young man thinks back and says, "I was just snatched up from my normal life and all anyone would tell me was: Your Mom is crazy, and she is going to a mental hospital."

Lundy Bancroft, a child advocate, stated, "It is very wide-spread amongst abusers to use custody and visitation litigation as a continuation of the abuse."... "There is a societal misconception that mothers are heavily favored over fathers in custody litigation."... "The maternal preference went out over twenty years ago and the studies now show that *fathers* have preference for custody."...

I called Counselor Joan Maier, Clinical Professor of Law at the George Washington University School of Law. Look at her website: dvleap.org which "dv" stands for domestic violence. She told me about another web site called: The Leadership Council. She stated again: "Short of killing the children, the best way to keep a mother down is to take away her children and the battering of a wife does not stop after a divorce. It often gets worse."

Dear God, look what happened to me and to dear Dr. Amy Castillo, the pediatrician from Silver Spring, just down the road from me twenty minutes. Her sick estranged husband murdered their three small children, only six, four and two years of age, two boys and the littlest a baby girl. Please, God, give her strength to go on. Even I don't know what I would do having to live her daily tortuous pain. How does she even get out of bed in her now quiet home, all alone? Dr. Amy Castillo cannot bear to practice medicine as a pediatrician. It is too hard for her to endure seeing children all day, and she can't have any more on her own. I offered to carry her baby.

Mothers need their children as much as children need their mothers. (Please see last few pages of "Documentation" section at end of book.)

The American legal system knows that mothers will never stop fighting for their children. And many fathers won't either. The <u>*attorneys are the only winners and custody battles keep the Circuit Court Systems very busy.*</u> There is only one possible solution for the many, many parents, both mothers and fathers, who pay child support but don't get enough visitation or even phone contact with their children.

Pick a day. Call it "A" day, for No More "Abuse" Day. Let's make it my Baba's birthday, April 1st. On April 1st, 2010, every parent, again, mother *or* father, who is not seeing their children enough, yet paying child support, just not go to work. Take a vacation day, and go to their local courthouse and file *pro se or for oneself* (obviously without an attorney and just costs a filing fee which is still around $100.00) for increased visitation and contact with their children.

There are standard forms available online and in the courthouse. Just fill out the forms for more "Custody and Visitation" and file a short piece of paper that you are now representing yourself or *pro se*. If you have an attorney, make sure they file what is called "a line" withdrawing their appearance as your attorney of record. Okay, easy. No sweat. If the lines aren't too long, maybe everyone will have time to hit a few golf or tennis balls before dinner. Here's the hard part, but critical, abso-you-got-it-lutely VITAL that everyone continues to play ball. Always remember, there is POWER IN NUMBERS, GREAT POWER. The

HARD PART is that everyone that filed, every last parent, mother or father, every last frustrated, pained, lonely, depressed suffering parent who is being kept from their children, STOP PAYING CHILD SUPPORT. Don't pay April's, May's, June's, July's or August's; DON'T PAY ONE DIME UNTIL *AFTER* YOUR COURT DATE EVEN IF YOU ARE THROWN RIGHT IN JAIL!!!

Jail is horrible, but remember: THERE IS POWER IN NUMBERS! GREAT POWER!! They can throw us all in jail, but they can't keep us there too long, because there are too damned many of us!! My bet is every one of the parents, fathers or mothers, who is denied access to their children are tax-paying members of our great society! The judicial system can't keep us locked up for long, just think what would happen to our nation's economy then; they will let us out to go to work and to MAKE ROOM IN THE JAILS FOR THE *REAL CRIMINALS.*

WE ARE JUST MOTHERS AND FATHERS TRYING TO SEE OUR CHILDREN!!!

(I almost killed myself after the Christmas holidays just to stop feeling the pain in my life without my children, my career, debt beyond debt, losing my home, *just everything!!*)

Appendices B-H

Maryland Board of Physicians
C. Irving Pinder, Executive Director
4201 Patterson Ave., 3rd floor
Baltimore, MD 21215

March 5, 2008

Dear Maryland Board of Physicians:

Marching to my own beat as always, my "Babas" (grandmothers) and parents taught me no other way, I shall start and finish this letter with a joke for levity, because the middle is very serious. Do you remember Gary Larson's books in the early 80's of "The Far Side"? If not, he was a brilliant cartoonist with extremely funny captions apparently stemming from his childhood. One of my favorites is a sketch of a young boy with glasses (presumably the author). The young boy is peering down at one little goldfish in a classic round clear glass fish bowl. The boy's cheeks are puffed out because he is sucking the water out of the fishbowl. The single goldfish is wide eyed looking up at the boy, now swimming in only a couple of inches of water. The dot-dot-dot to circled thought from the little boy's head as he stares back at his captive goldfish is "Do you want to talk *now*?"

Please consider my reinstatement application open as per the above date for which 120 days are allowed to complete. I spoke to Ms. Gage Blair and she told me that indeed a "reinstatement" packet is required, not an entire "new" application. For the record also Mr. Melvin Bergman left me a telephone message a few weeks ago which I saved which stated he has not heard from the Board in writing "in probably a year and they (the Board) has not called me in probably six months." I e-mailed the Board regarding requests for patient files as Mr. Bergman informed me that "he did not have a list for patient files at all", and I have not received a patient list for requested files from the Board. If any of my patients request their files, please send me a written certified return-receipt request with all of their names. I will be most happy to furnish patient files for any patients for whom I can locate their files. Please note that Dr. Reginald Barnes worked in my office for several months (also Dr. Shelly Belson for a few days) and very unfortunately my patient files are not 100% complete like they were when I was in solo private practice.

I am aware that the current board knows my case and also is in receipt from early January, 2008 of a certified copy of my entire file from the Montgomery County Circuit Courthouse. Please defer to it as I did when completing the reinstatement application.

A very reputable person from Physician's Rehab. in MD I quote: "You should wait Dr. Duke. It is the same Board, hasn't changed." A computer wizard MIT PhD said I need to be "nicey nice" in this letter to you and "wait to include any grievances for an appeal". Well, this "computer wizard" crashed my son's Dell XPS 600 recently while installing a simple Kodak printer.

B

Truthfully, I no longer have time to wait for yet another appeal. (This would be the fourth.) On top of everything, logic warrants since the Board currently knows my case, that fact should save everyone's time.

*   *   *

I need and deserve to get my Maryland medical license back as soon as possible to feed my four children and help my patients who still ask about me and my licensure status when I see them in the grocery store.

In the end, I decided to write my own heartfelt letter, and I don't know how to be anything *but* nice, and direct.

I attended an AA meeting at Our Lady of Mercy on March 9, 2008, necessitating me to rewrite this letter which I began on the 5th. A young woman led the meeting and spoke about killing a man in a drunk driving accident. She stated that she had "very much trouble trying to stay sober after it happened. How could I not drink?", she went on, "All I was doing was opening horrendous amounts of mail about law suits and the rest were bills, and I didn't even have enough money to pay for my cell phone." She attended a different AA meeting during this period of her life, (to clarify, post DUI/involuntary manslaughter, however, before she stopped drinking, even admitting to smelling of alcohol at AA meetings) and she was awestruck. A man led the meeting and spoke of the exact same grievous event, *his own* DUI and involuntary manslaughter charge. She went up to him after he presented and asked him "Why did you keep on drinking?" The man simply said, "How could I *not?!*"

That story is not anyone's rational for relapsing. It is only a factual story about two humans who had the same traumatic experience.

The young woman stated that she did not go to court until two years after her arrest. She was sentenced to only *one* year in jail and had only one year on probation. At her trial the family of the man whose life was taken in her DUI said, "Just keep helping other alcoholics."

For my drunk driving offences I was told by Officer Bond that no one was hurt or went to the hospital and after reading the court transcript, there was no mention whatsoever by any of the victims from the accident that they needed medical care. I do know that only I went to the hospital. I am very grateful that no one was hurt and extremely grateful no one was killed. I served six months in jail, had six months suspended, three years of probation, four years of breathalyzer on ignition,("interlock" it is called at 65$/ month on my minivan which goes off every 5-6 minutes (not just upon starting the car) in city traffic and out on the highway. Even when I am sitting idle in my driveway it goes off. Until they can make those battery draining devices DNA sensitive, basically anyone can be blowing for the driver and the driver could be drinking. My son asked me if he could try it once and I said "NO!" I am sure my ex-husband would have had a field day with me if I allowed our son to do it and heaven forbid if my son just had an eclipse gum or used mouthwash which would trigger a positive alcohol reading. NO ONE uses my finicky breathalyzer, consequently making a trip to see my 75 year old parents six hours drive away too difficult even for a long distance runner. My 2003 Dodge Grand Caravan is on its third Sears Diehard top of the line battery, and currently is in the shop for the third time in just over a year, because the owner of the company says it is my battery or electrical system, and when I take it in to check the electrical system, after putting in a new battery, the Dodge dealer confirms it is the battery or ignition interlock. I'm also on my 4th or 5th ignition interlock unit. My probation continues to cost $46/mth even though I am not required to report anymore. I also was not required to go to AA by the judge who incarcerated me for DUI. The difficult part about not driving to Silver Spring to see my probation officer is that she does not return my phone calls until the fourth or fifth one. I have the phone records. She does, however, allow me to leave the state to see my elderly parents (Thanksgiving, 2006) or go to an ophthalmology conference.

Adding $111 ($65 plus $46) plus $650/month child support plus $780/month for nannies fees plus $212 times two/month for county visitation ($212 paid by taxpayers, not included below) with my youngest child for which I have almost $30,000 in attorney's fees for...that makes 4,200/month to see my children for 40/hours *per month post tax dollars*. That comes to over $50,000/year before taxes before I have fed them, ate myself, stayed warm and sheltered, bought health insurance and bought gas and new batteries for my minivan. Clearly, one can see I need to get back to the only profession I devoted my life to.

I need more attorney fee money too. My children need to be around their strong, funny Mommy more. Does the Board know an excellent family law attorney in Montgomery County?

*   *   *

I truly wish I had been given a second chance at rehab like the Board promised me in November, 2004. Instead of coming over to talk to me about rehab (like Ms. Cromer said they were going to do on the phone), in half an hour I lost every piece of paper, every hard earned license, CDS, DEA...every last prescription pad. I lost my whole life's work, almost 30 *years, (well over half my entire life),* because I started working very hard in high school at age 14 to be the valedictorian again after I surprisingly was the valedictorian of my junior high.

In just *30 minutes,* I lost 30 years of laborious study and labor to be flippantly told "cancel your patients for the unforeseeable future."

I was *never once* sued in over 14 years of solo private practice. The average doctor is sued once every seven years. In over 14 years, just outside our nation's capital where the concentration of attorneys is probably highest in the world, one would think I should have at least been hinted at a law suit twice (to keep up with the national average), if not double that. 25 days after being incarcerated for six months for DUI, (again, no one was physically hurt to my best knowledge), I am granted a valid *un*restricted driver's license.

But 20 days after my first drunk driving arrest (1st), that I hadn't even gone to court for yet, the Maryland Medical Board of Physicians sends Ms. Cromer with 14 pages of public humiliation and degradation, egregiously including my personal life on a Saturday night. In all of the 107 revocations that Ms. Wulff sent to me (since they are a matter of public record), dating from 1990 through September, 2005, only one male psychiatrist who slept with his patient got a harsher penalty than mine. The first real evidence that the Board had on me was my blood work in December, 2003 after a chemical peel on my face. That was the second time in my life that I ever had an Oxycontin. The first time was in early 2001 after an abdominal hernia repair and chemical peel.

After December 8, 2003, I lost my medical license *within* 1 year.

Why then does the Board reinstate doctors who write fraudulent prescriptions and admit to recreational use for him and his wife for over 15 years who have two *felony* counts, D40524? Why does the Board take almost 11 years to revoke a pediatrician who drank D08862 during office hours in 2000 whose first patient complaint was in 1989, D0462? Why does the Board wait for a doctor's sixth (6th) drunk driving arrest and urination of cocaine times 3 or 4 to revoke, D17735? Why does it take the Board 3 and ½ years to revoke a physician who treated two teenagers with mononucleosis with 80mg of Oxycontin such that they died of "anoxic encephalopathy" or an overdose in layman's terms, the first patient on January 12, 2003 with a total of nine patients in between who were "over prescribed for" and luckily didn't over dose, D33271? Why does it take 2 and ½ years to just "suspend" a gynecologist's license who murdered his wife with a hammering to her head at 9:00 in the morning after she had been visiting relatives for two weeks until the night before in Germany, D24580...(obviously not premeditated)...I remember driving by the crime scene on August 15, 2001. That murder was all over the news, even front page of the Potomac Almanac. My point is, maybe some of his relatives were not capable of murder, but this doctor had a valid DEA and CDS until the Board suspended him on December 17, 2003 and didn't revoke him until May 27, 2005, and those relatives could have been selling Oxycontin prescriptions, et.al. affording homes in the Caribbean and private planes to get there. Oh, well, he'll probably be out of jail for second degree manslaughter of his *wife* before my 5 year and ten month revocation is over...*and I never once even hurt an EYE.*

Please refer to the "SUMMARY SUSPENSION" of November 30, 2004.
Page 1: INVESTIGATIVE FINDINGS

#1. "The Respondent also holds *inactive* licenses in Virginia, the District of Columbia and New York State.

That statement is either an error on your part or that of the State of New York. If I was indeed inactive in the State of New York, then why did New York State revoke me on August 8, 2005 fifty (50) full days *before* the Maryland Board revoked me on September 28, 2005. If they were doing it with reciprocity, does not the home state need to revoke the physician first?
For the record I was told by Attorney Robert Bogan's secretary April that there is no such thing as a "permanent revocation" in the State of New York. A maximum revocation is three years. I was sent a cover letter with the medical licensure application for New York informing me that I could reapply on August 8, 2008.

Footnote 1: The statements regarding the Respondent's conduct are intended to provide the Respondent with notice of the basis of the suspension and the charges. They are not intended as, and *do not necessarily represent a complete description of the evidence, either documentary or testimonial*, to be offered against the Respondent in connection with this matter.

2. "As of October 2003, the Respondent was granted privileges at the Johns Hopkins Wilmer Eye Institue at Green Spring."
I was granted privileges at Johns Hopkins Wilmer Eye Institue at Green Spring in September, 1998 for refractive surgery procedures. On October 16, 2003 "Her appointment as Active Staff by Johns Hopkins Hospital has been approved for the period of October 16, 2003 through May 31, 2005 with full requested privileges at any Johns Hopkins Hospital site." Please see letter from Carolyn H. Dunn, Credentials Coordinator.

Please also note letters of recommendation from Julia A. Haller, M.D. and Terrence P. O'Brien, M.D dated January 27, 2004 and February 13, 2004, respectively.

3, 4 & 5. "On November 16, 2004, Board staff received an anonymous complaint that, *inter alia*, the Respondent had recently treated patients after consuming alcohol."...

On September 9, 2002, the Respondent was reported by a Suburban Hospital staff member to have arrived...The Respondent's colleagues also reported that the Respondent smelled of alcohol. The Respondent completed the surgeries without incident. As a result of this incident, the Respondent was referred by hospital authorities to the Physician Rehabilitation Committee ("PRC") of the Medical and Chirurgical Faculty of Maryland ("Med-Chi").

I'm tired of typing, so will end here and not go through every page. (Good news, eh?)

Lastly, there was no mention of "rehab" whatsoever on November 30, 2004 which is exactly what I needed. After a horrendously costly divorce after only 7 years, both emotionally and financially, (I understand "cheaper to keep her" now.), four full term plus babies in under 7 years, one week (7 days) of vacation/year, 15 different medications by the Board recommended psychiatrist, $250,000 robbery on August 30, 2004, necessary termination of pregnancy followed by blackout DUI on November 10, 2004, ex-husband suing me in court for more October 26, 2004, breast biopsy 2004, and most horrific of all, losing custody of my precious children and again in an appeal 2004, if I could handle 2004, I can handle anything.

But those simple words Ms. Cromer tossed over her shoulder on her way out, carrying my Maryland medical license in it's beautiful lacquer frame, which she didn't even take the time to give back to me..."Remember to cancel your patients for the unforeseeable future."

My parents are 75, I'll soon be 47, and the future goes by us every single minute.

The grandfather of my five year old daughter read the 14 pages and barked, "This is absolutely Draconian". With his thick British accent, I thought he said "Dra*cu*lian" meaning like Dracula, blood sucking. I didn't know he actually said "draconian" until a few years later and that the meaning was, like Draco, the Athenian ruler known for his overly harsh punishments. Oh well, ...what's the difference?

On page 6 of the "UNREPORTED IN THE COURT OF SPECIAL APPEALS OF MARYLAND No. 324" filed April 16, 2007 there is a footnote 1 which states: "Although the Board has the authority to entertain an "early" petition"...

It has been almost 3 and ½ years since my license was "Summary Suspended" by the Board on November 30, 2004. I mailed to you copies of all of my urines to date. I forgot to include a letter from my then psychiatrist which allows for the presence of amphetamines and benzodiazepines in my urines as he prescribed them for me. It is the first document enclosed after this cover letter.

I currently have a different psychiatrist and the correct diagnosis, *post traumatic stress* disorder. I am pleased to report being fully recuperated from my brief period of alcohol dependency and as such prepared to take on the duties and responsibilities of a board-certified ophthalmologist.

I humbly request that my reinstatement application be affirmed as soon as possible without retaking any medical school/internship boards or boards of the American Academy of Ophthalmology. Humbly also I request the Maryland Board write to the American Academy of Ophthalmology and ask that my board certificate be "re-grandfathered" which is exactly what I deserve. In advance, I thank you sincerely for your time.

If there is anything else you request, please do not hesitate to contact me.

I e-mailed this letter to the e-mails from the Board that I have. Unfortunately, I was never given Mr. Pinder's exact e-mail so please forward this to him, Ms. Porter and Ms. Wulff. I also sent it on to my family and concerned friends.

Thank you everyone for your assistance.

To end with levity as promised.

My other favorite Gary Larson is one of a woman looking under the cushions of a sleep sofa to see only her husband's head, no arms or legs, just his head and withered face poking out. It is obvious that he was stuck in the sofa for some time, (quite impossible and incongruous, additionally humorous). There next to his squished head, found simultaneously, is the woman's hairbrush. The wife quips: "So *that's* where you've been hiding! ... Oh, ...thank God I found my hairbrush!"

Truthfully I feel like the man stuck in the coach, and no one cares about him unless he stands tall. And speaks out. My last question to the Board is: How can you *not*...want such a strong and persevering doctor like myself as part of the medical community of Maryland who fights so hard for medicine and America?

Sincerely,

Mary Ann Duke, M.D.
10220 Democracy Boulevard
Potomac, Maryland 20854

H) 301-983-0030
Cell) 301 674-3696
madukemd@yahoo.com

STATE OF MARYLAND

DHMH   Board of Physicians

Maryland Department of Health and Mental Hygiene
4201 Patterson Avenue • Baltimore, Maryland 21215-2299

Martin O'Malley, Governor – Anthony G. Brown, Lt. Governor – John M. Colmers, Secretary

April 15, 2008

CERTIFIED AND REGULAR MAIL
Mary Ann Duke, M.D.
10220 Democracy Boulevard
Potomac, MD 20854

Dear Dr. Duke:

The Maryland Board of Physicians (Board) is returning to you the enclosed documents. The Board received a packet of materials and a fee in the amount of $629.00 on or about March 28, 2008. On or about April 1, 2008, the Board received a reinstatement application, and on or about April 2, 2008, the Board received an addendum to your reinstatement application.

Under the Maryland Board of Physician's Final Decision and Order of September 28, 2005, which revoked your license for a minimum of five (5) years, it was ordered that:

> ...the Board will not entertain an application for reinstatement from Dr. Duke of her medical license any earlier than five (5) years from the date of this Final Decision and Order;

This means that the Board will not accept an application for reinstatement from you any earlier than September 28, 2010.

Therefore, the Board is returning the documents that you submitted. Also the Board will return the fee that you paid. A refund of $629.00 will be sent to you in several weeks.

Prior to the date of September 28, 2010, please do not send the Maryland Board of Physicians any documents related to reinstatement or a reinstatement application or any fees.

Yours sincerely,

C. Irving Pinder
Executive Director

C: Barbara Vona, Chief, Compliance Administration

Toll Free 1-800-492-6836 • 410-764-4777 • Fax 410-358-2252
Web Site: www.mbp.state.md.us

The Honorable Governor Martin O'Malley
Maryland State House
100 State Circle
Annapolis, Maryland 21401
410-974-3901

Dear Governor O'Malley,   February 1, 2008

My name is Mary Ann Duke, M.D. Until recent I was a Board Certified Ophthalmologist and Ophthalmic Eye Surgeon with a thriving private practice in Potomac, Maryland. Though initially licensed in New York I also became licensed in Virginia and Washington, DC. Upon moving to Maryland I obtained a medical license in 1989. While in private practice I performed cataract and oculoplastic procedures along with state of the art refractive eye surgeries using YAG, Argon and Excimer lasers (Lasik and PRK) when treating diabetic retinopathy and retinal tears in addition to applying therapies when resolving complications associated with advanced glaucoma and macular degeneration. Being a practicing surgeon in good standing I applied and am proud to have been selected for surgical privileges at the prestigious Wilmer Ophthalmological Institute of the Johns Hopkins University School of Medicine in addition to five hospitals.
Unfortunately, due to a brief but horrific circumstance, I have experienced a difficulty in which your intervention is requested. Before discussing this issue please allow me to provide additional pertinent background information.
I received my medical degree at age 23 from Albany Medical College in Albany, New York. I received high honors in all of my Ophthalmology courses while also assisting in the writing of advanced research papers. While in medical school I received the Honored Senior Research Award for Outstanding Research Accomplishment and was also the sole recipient of the prestigious Sandoz Award in Ophthalmology. At age thirty I was Board Certified by the American Academy of Ophthalmology in addition to being an active member in good standing of five professional Ophthalmological Associations. In 1991 I was elected for four years as a legislative representative of the Medical and Chirurgical Faculty of Maryland to the Maryland State Legislature.
Unfortunately, due to a series of horrific life circumstance I lost my medical licenses. This occurred in November of 2004 and resulted from over two years of an exceedingly difficult and stressful divorce. As a result of having become depressed resulting in great anxiety I began for the first time in my life to abuse alcohol. The Maryland Medical Board investigated a complaint alleging alcohol consumption which was confirmed. I was directed by the Board to obtain psychiatric counseling from a doctor of their choosing, Carol Kleinman, M.D. During the eight months I received at least weekly counseling and treatment from Dr. Kleinman she subjected me to many prescription medications with grievous results. In an effort to personally confront my alcohol abuse I discontinued seeing Dr. Kleinman and on August 15, 2004 proceeded to admit myself to a 28 day treatment program at Father Martin's Ashley rehabilitation center. I remained at the center until September 11, 2004 at which time I was voluntarily discharged. Unfortunately, upon returning home my depression and anxiety were again triggered when learning that while away my home had been burglarized.

D

On September 30, 2004 my Maryland medical license was renewed for two years without restrictions. Six weeks later while continuing to experience severe depression and as a result relapsing, I was charged with and later pleaded guilty to a DUI. Having investigated various complaints the Board compelled me on May 24, 2005 to sign a five year voluntary suspension under threat of licensure revocation. Suffering utter despair resulting in severe depression triggered by the Board's decision to suspend my medical license for five years I shortly afterwards relapsed into renewed alcohol abuse resulting in two additional DWI's that did not result in any injuries (I was later sentenced to one year and served six months in jail with six months suspended). In an effort to again confront my demons I voluntarily admitted myself on July 18, 2005 to the Talbot Recovery Campus in Atlanta, Georgia where I remained for fourteen weeks.

After having spent in excess of $50,000.00 on alcohol abuse treatment programs over a one year period and despite Dr. Carol Kleinman's ineffective, inappropriate and very costly treatment combined with unnecessary psychotropic medications I am pleased to report that since my completion of the fourteen week alcohol recovery program at Talbot's on November 5, 2005 that I have effectively confronted my demons. Unfortunately, the Maryland Medical Board revoked my medical license due to having failed to fully comply with the suspension agreement. I have been advised by the Board that only after a period of five years can I then apply to have my medical license reinstated. I appealed the Board's revocation decision. Unfortunately, due in large part to ineffective counsel, I did not prevail.

I am a mother of four children whom I dearly love. I am pleased to report being fully recuperated from my brief period of alcohol dependency and as such prepared to take on the duties and responsibilities of again being an ophthalmologist. I am forever grateful to the Talbot Recovery treatment center. They truly saved my life.

During the past few months I have obtained from the Maryland Medical Board copies of many case files involving far more serious offenses than mine where in each only brief suspensions or revocations were imposed. Each involves far more egregious conduct when compared to my minor alcohol driven driving offenses.

I invite you to visit me day or evening at my home in Potomac. I will gladly provide you with copies of twenty exceedingly egregious cases as cited above. In reviewing them I feel certain you will come to the same conclusion as have I regarding my suspension and subsequent revocation. In reviewing the investigative findings within each of these cases I feel certain you will conclude that I have been discriminated against and not treated either fairly or equally under the law. I respectfully ask that you review this matter.

Sincerely,

Mary Ann Duke, M.D.
10220 Democracy Boulevard
Potomac, Maryland 20854

H) 301-983-0030

Cell: 301-674-3696

The Honorable Governor Martin O'Malley
Maryland State House
100 State Circle
Annapolis, Maryland 21401
(410) 974-3901

Dear Governor O'Malley,   March 23, 2008

The enclosed letter was signed/stamped for by the "Governor's Office" the first week of February.

I completely understand not receiving a response yet as your office must be extremely busy, and I know exactly what "busy" feels like. However, when I called last week to see if you indeed received it, the pleasant woman on the phone said, "Was it signed?"

If I didn't sign my letter and it wasn't acknowledged for that reason, the following letter has my signature.

Lastly, I understand that inviting you to my home is probably way too much to ask.

I will be happy to meet you at your office at your earliest convenience.

Sincerely,

Mary Ann Duke, M.D.
H (301) 982-0030
Cell: (301) 674-3696
madukemd@yahoo.com

P.S. As offered in my original letter, here are twenty exceedingly egregious cases. A point that I did not make before is that the time between the "crime of moral turpitude" and the suspension/revocation by the Maryland Board of Physicians when the doctor's actual prescription pads, DEA and CDS numbers are confiscated is usually *years*. If a physician is capable of rape, murder, home ecstasy labs, child pornography, falsifying records and prescription drug fraud, logic would dictate these physicians would be capable of continued prescription drug fraud to make ends meet, (exacerbating our country's gross drug problem), until their DEA and CDS numbers are terminated. License numbers: D33271, D40524, D08462, D24580, D17735, D32654, D02524, D14605, D22212, D16665, D17933, D62991, D44550, D08283, D46921, D32043, D58918, D39793, D12748, D42002.

I have many, many more which I can send you on a memory stick to save taxpayers' dollars if you would like Governor O'Malley. Thank you sincerely for your time and effort.

E

State of Maryland
Commission on Human Relations

OFFICERS
Henry B. Ford, Executive Director
J. Neil Bell, Deputy Director
Benny F. Short, Assistant Director
Glendora C. Hughes, General Counsel

Governor
Martin O'Malley
Chairperson
Norman J. Gelman
Vice-Chairperson
John W. Hermina, Esq.
Commissioners
Rabbi Elan Adler
Sambhu N. Banik, Ph.D.
JoAnn Fisher
Thomas E. Owen
Shawn M. Wright, Esq.

April 3, 2008

Ms. Mary Ann Duke, MD
10220 Democracy Boulevard
Potomac, MD 20854

Dear Dr. Duke:

Thank you for your correspondence to Governor Martin O'Malley in which you express concerns of alleged discrimination by the Maryland Medical Board. The Governor received your letter and asked me, as Executive Director of the Maryland Commission on Human Relations, to respond on his behalf.

The Maryland Commission on Human Relations is the State agency responsible for enforcing Maryland's anti-discrimination laws. These laws are in the areas of employment, housing and access to places of public accommodations on the basis of race, gender, national origin, religion, age, disability, sexual orientation, color, marital status or genetic information.

Your correspondence is being forwarded to our Intake Unit for review. An official from that Unit will be in contact with you to conduct an interview to determine whether this is a discrimination complaint which falls within our jurisdiction.

Thank you, again, for your letter. The Governor appreciates hearing from you, and on his behalf, I thank you for your interest in this matter. Should you have any additional questions or concerns, you may contact Ms. Joann Cole at 410-767-8600 or toll-free at 800-637-6247 or via email at jcole@mail.mchr.state.md.us.

Sincerely,

Henry B. Ford

Executive Director

cc: Joann Cole, Supervisor, Case Control, Commission on Human Relations

HBF/jw

[ ] **MAIN OFFICE**
William Donald Schaefer Tower
6 Saint Paul Street, 9th Floor
Baltimore, Maryland 21202-1631
410-767-8600 • 1-800-637-6247
TTY 410-333-1841 • TTY 410-333-1737

[ ] **EASTERN SHORE OFFICE**
Salisbury District Court Multi-Purpose Ctr.
201 Baptist Street, Suite 33
Salisbury, Maryland 21801
410-713-3611
410-713-3614 Fax

[ ] **SOUTHERN MARYLAND OFFICE**
Joseph D. Carter Center
23110 Leonard Hall Drive
P.O. Box 653
Leonardtown, Maryland 20650
301-880-2740 • 301-880-2741 Fax

[ ] **WESTERN MARYLAND OFFICE**
Potomac Plaza
44 N. Potomac St., Suite 202
Hagerstown, Maryland 21740
301-797-8521
301-791-3060 Fax

Home Page Address:
http://www.mchr.state.md.us

E-Mail Address:
mchr@mail.mchr.state.md.us

State of Maryland
Commission on Human Relations

OFFICERS
Henry B. Ford, Executive Director
J. Neil Bell, Deputy Director
Benny F. Short, Assistant Director
Glendora C. Hughes, General Counsel

Governor
Martin O'Malley
Chairperson
Norman I. Gelman
Vice-Chairperson
John W. Hermina, Esq.
Commissioners
Rabbi Elan Adler
Sambhu N. Banik, Ph.D.
JoAnn Fisher
Thomas E. Owen
Shawn M. Wright, Esq.

April 22, 2008

Ms. Mary Ann Duke
10220 Democracy Boulevard
Potomac MD 20854

Dear Ms. Duke:

Receipt of your correspondence concerning the Maryland Medical Board is acknowledged.

Unfortunately, the circumstances surrounding your situation do not meet the meaning of "Discrimination in Employment or Public Accommodations" as defined by Article 49B of the Annotated Code of Maryland. Therefore, after carefully considering all of the information that you have provided, it has been determined that a complaint cannot be authorized for investigation, as the Maryland Commission on Human Relations (MCHR) does not have jurisdiction to handle these types of inquiries.

We regret that we could not be of further assistance. If we may assist you with another matter in the future, please do not hesitate to contact us.

Sincerely,

Joann Cole
Intake Supervisor

Cc: Cynthia Johnson, Intake Officer

[✓] MAIN OFFICE
William Donald Schaefer Tower
6 Saint Paul Street, 9th Floor
Baltimore, Maryland 21202-1631
410-767-8600 • 1-800-637-6247
Fax 410-333-1841 • TTY 410-333-1737

[ ] EASTERN SHORE OFFICE
Salisbury District Court Multi-Purpose Ctr.
201 Baptist Street, Suite 33
Salisbury, Maryland 21801
410-713-3611
410-713-3614 Fax

[ ] SOUTHERN MARYLAND OFFICE
Joseph D. Carter Center
23110 Leonard Hall Drive
P.O. Box 653
Leonardtown, Maryland 20650
301-880-2740 • 301-880-2741 Fax

[ ] WESTERN MARYLAND OFFICE
Potomac Plaza
44 N. Potomac St., Suite 202
Hagerstown, Maryland 21740
301-797-8521
301-791-3060 Fax

Home Page Address:
http://www.mchr.state.md.us

E-Mail Address:
mchr@mail.mchr.state.md.us

MARTIN O'MALLEY
GOVERNOR

Office of Legal Counsel
Shaw House, Room 201
21 State Circle
Annapolis, Maryland 21401

STATE OF MARYLAND
OFFICE OF THE GOVERNOR

Elizabeth F. Harris, Chief Counsel
Catherine J. Motz, Deputy Counsel
Christine Wellons, Deputy Counsel
Tele: 410-974-3005   Fax: 410-974-2077

October 22, 2008

Mary Ann Duke, M.D.
10220 Democracy Boulevard
Potomac, Maryland 20854

Dear Dr. Duke:

It is my understanding that you have again contacted the Governor's office regarding your concerns about the disciplinary actions taken against you. As we previously stated to you in a letter dated May 20, 2007, the Governor has no authority over these disciplinary actions, and there is nothing that the Governor's office can do to help you with your situation.

Sincerely,

Elizabeth F. Harris
Chief Legal Counsel to the Governor

Documentation

Dec. 5, 1990   Potomac Gazette   Page A-59

BUSINESS

Eye doctor opens new office

Opthalmologist's facility is in Potomac

by Jo Beck
Special to the Gazette

Photo by Dan Gross

Dr. Mary Ann Duke recently opened an opthamology office in Potomac.

Deciding where to open her new opthalmology practice was easy for Dr. Mary Ann Duke. "I wanted somewhere that was close to the city," she explained.

"But since I grew up in the country, I wanted some open spaces. In Potomac I still feel like I'm in the country," she said.

Duke is a native of upstate New York. She graduated from Rensselaer Polytechnic Institute in Troy, N.Y., and then went on to medical school at Albany Medical College in Albany. Because Duke chose a six-year accelerated program, she graduated from medical school at age 23.

At graduation, she received the coveted Sandoz Award for excellence in opthalmology, and she was also awarded the Dean's Senior Research Award for her research, which focused on herpes infections of the eye.

New Business

Dr. Mary Ann Duke
New opthalmology practice

Sovran Bank Building
Potomac
298-7107

Duke served her four year opthalmology residency at Albany Medical Center Hospital.

Duke is a member of Sigma Xi, a scientific research society. She regularly attends seminars and conferences in her field. "I'm keeping my skills right up to date," said Duke.

Duke has a special interest in cataract surgery, eyelid surgery, and laser surgery to the retina. Some surgery is done in Duke's office, and some procedures require a hospital setting.

She is certified at Shady Grove Adventist, Washington Adventist, and Holy Cross Hospital, and she is now seeking privileges at Suburban Hospital.

FOCUS ON YOUR FUTURE

Blocking ultraviolet light from the eyes is essential to well being

Rays are not part of visible spectrum

by Kamran Ali Memon
Staff writer

At any age, sight is vitally important to the well-being and fullness of life sought by individuals. With the years, the need for sight becomes even more important—not just for the richness of life that it insures, but as a practical way to stay connected to the world.

The care given to preserving vision is of great importance. Potomac eye physician and surgeon Mary Ann Duke says it is essential to block ultraviolet light out of the eyes.

Ultraviolet light is not part of the visible spectrum because it has a shorter wavelength than visible light does. Ultraviolet rays can not be used by the retina, Duke said.

When ultraviolet light enters the eye, it damages the lens behind the pupil and contributes to cataract formation, she said.

It also leads to waste deposits under the retina, Duke said. Such deposits are among the early signs of Macular Degeneration, the leading cause of blindness in this country for people over 65. "It affects your reading or central vision first," she said.

Duke said there are several ways to block out ultraviolet light.

One option is UV-blocking sunglasses. Lenses, treated in a chemical bath, block 97 percent of ultraviolet rays, Duke said. Many optical shops provide this service, she said. Optical shops can also use a spectrometer to measure the amount of ultraviolet filter already in a pair of sunglasses, Duke said.

A compound called silver halide can be incorporated into glass lenses when they are first made, Duke said. "This ultraviolet blocking substance undergoes a photochromic change when outside, causing the lenses to darken. The lenses return to their natural lighter state when inside," she said. When the lenses are dark, they block out 99 percent of ultraviolet light. When the lenses are light, they block out 30 percent of ultraviolet rays, she said. These darkening lenses can only be made with glass.

Polarized lenses can block out 100 percent of ultraviolet rays, Duke said. They are especially good around water where there are many reflected rays, she said. The lenses can be made with plastic or glass, she said.

In addition, "There are some gas permeable contact lenses on the market with UV filtering capability," Duke said.

Everyday plastic glasses can be treated with an ultraviolet blocking chemical bath to produce a transparent barrier to 97 percent of ultraviolet rays, Duke said. This is very helpful to people who use computers for several hours a day, she said. "This is important because we do not know the full, damaging effect of UV rays emitted from video display terminals. It is known that a significant amount of UV light is emitted," she said.

"Along with your No. 15 sunblock, one should wear UV blocking sunglasses this summer," Duke said.

Duke graduated from Medical College and did her ophthalmology residency in A Her Potomac office is at Falls Road, Suite 208. F ther information, call 299-

Mary Ann Duke

Johnson City Senior High School

566 REYNOLDS ROAD O JOHNSON CITY, NEW YORK 13790
TELEPHONE (607) 729-9211

February 27th, 1979

TO WHOM IT MAY CONCERN:

With no reservations whatsoever do I write this letter of recommendation for Mary Ann Duke. Her character is exemplary of what every American parent, teacher, school or citizen might wish.

Mary Ann's scholastic achievements and attitude illustrate not only her scholarship but also her character. Since she was a freshman, she has selected the most challenging and replete course of study throughout her high school career. She is always prepared and actively contributes to the success of every class session. But more importantly, she initiates additional opportunities for greater learning experiences. She is indeed a responsible learner, for she is capable of extending herself with projects that involve independent study and sustained effort. She seeks constructive criticism and welcomes any additional suggestions an instructor might offer. In this her senior year, she has pursued a level of course work that will afford her an opportunity to obtain advanced standing and even college credit for her work in high school. She is currently involved in the Advanced Placement Program of the College Testing Admissions Program.

Mary Ann possesses the leadership qualities that America needs. She has been actively involved with her fellow classmates since she entered school. Her peers not only admire her but also welcome her participation and leadership in both scholastic and extra-curricular programs. She is co-captain of the Girl's Varsity Basketball team, voted the Most Valuable Player of the Tennis Team, participated in track, not to mention that she was elected President of the National Honor Society, President of the Key Club and is a member of the Senior Class Steering Committee. Her leadership qualities are enhanced by her always pleasant, well-mannered persona and her immaculate appearance.

If any organization has an opportunity to extend itself to a deserving student, indeed Mary Ann Duke is the epitome of just such a student. Whichever college she might attend will certainly be proud to have Mary Ann and will benefit from her attending that university. I know she still has two sisters attending college and any assistance in helping her obtain her education would be greatly appreciated by her.

To be sure, Mary Ann Duke is the kind of student and person who personifies what every American should strive to become. It is with great pleasure that I write this letter of recommendation; for Mary Ann is a deserving student and will be a definite contribution to any college, but more importantly to America.

Very truly yours,
Paul Kapp
Paul Kapp, Coordinator of English

laer Polytechnic Institute
Name: Mary Ann Duke

Number: 660104397

4/3/2006
DEGREES AWARDED:
Bachelor of Science
Major: Biology

DATE:
May 1983

ial Transcript

Mary A. Duke
10220 Democracy Blvd.
Potomac, MD 20854

Advisor(s)/Type:

Undergraduate Academic Record

Fall 1979
Bachelor of Science
Biomedical Engineering

Course #	Course Title	Att	Grd	Ern	Qpts
2020	PRINCIPLES OF BIOLOGY II	4	S	4	0
ote:	Adv. Placement				
1100	CHEMISTRY I	4	A	4	16
1310	GERMAN I	3	A	3	12
1000	LITERATURE ELECTIVE	3	S	3	0
ote:	Adv. Placement				
1100	MATHEMATICS I	4	A	4	16
1100	PHYSICS I	4	B	4	12
1200	GENERAL PSYCHOLOGY	3	A	3	12
0110	PHYSICAL EDUCATION I	0	S	0	0
	ATT	ERN	QHR	QPTS	GPA
	25	25	18	68	3.77
tive	25	25	18	68	3.77
	Dean's List				

Spring 1980
Bachelor of Science
Biology

Course #	Course Title	Att	Grd	Ern	Qpts
1200	CHEMISTRY II	4	A	4	16
1320	GERMAN II	3	B	3	9
4220	JOYCE'S ULYSSES	3	A	3	12
1200	MATHEMATICS II	4	B	4	12
1200	PHYSICS II	4	B	4	12
0120	PHYSICAL EDUCATION II	0	S	0	0
	ATT	ERN	QHR	QPTS	GPA
	18	18	18	61	3.38
tive	43	43	36	129	3.58
	Dean's List				

Summer 1980

Course #	Course Title	Att	Grd	Ern	Qpts
BIOL 2010	PRIN-OF BIOLOGY I	4	A	4	16
CHEM 2230	ORGANIC CHEMISTRY LAB	1	B	1	3
CHEM 2240	ORGANIC CHEM II LAB	1	C	1	2
CHEM 2250	INTRO ORG CHEM I	3	B	3	9
CHEM 2260	INTRO ORG CHEM II	3	B	3	9
PSYC 4961	ALCOHOL AB & DRUG ABUS	3	B	3	9
	ATT	ERN	QHR	QPTS	GPA
Term	15	15	15	48	3.20
Cumulative	58	58	51	177	3.47
Status	Dean's List				

Fall 1980

Course #	Course Title	Att	Grd	Ern	Qpts
BIOL 2210	GENERAL PHYSIOLOGY	3	A	3	12
CHEM 2410	PHYSICAL CHEMISTRY I	3	B	3	9
PHYS 1300	PHYSICS III	4	B	4	12
PSYC 4320	PHYSIOLOGICAL PSYCH	3	P	3	0
PSYC 4424	ANALYSIS OF INT. RELATIONS	3	A	3	12
ZPHE 0220	ADV SWIMMING	0	S	0	0
	ATT	ERN	QHR	QPTS	GPA
Term	16	16	13	45	3.46
Cumulative	74	74	64	222	3.46
Status	Dean's List				

Spring 1981

Course #	Course Title	Att	Grd	Ern	Qpts
BIOL 2500	GENETICS & EVOLUTION	3	B	3	9
CHEM 2420	PHYSICAL CHEMISTRY II	3	C	3	6
LITR 4020	MODERN POETRY	3	P	3	0
MATH 1300	MATH III	3	B	3	9
ZCNS 0090	TECHNIQUES ON PAPER	3	A	3	12
ZPHE 1850	PROF TEST BADMINTON	0	S	0	0
	ATT	ERN	QHR	QPTS	GPA
Term	15	15	12	36	3.00
Cumulative	89	89	76	258	3.39
Status	Dean's List				

Albany, New York 12208

Name Duke, Mary Ann Sex F Soc. Sec. No. 093-50-8753 Birthdate 6/6/61
Address at Admittance 181 Albany Avenue, Johnson City, NY 13790 Birthplace Binghamton, NY
Matriculation Date 9/8/81 Class of 1985

Degree (s) Obtained From: Degree Date Rec'd

Rensselaer Polytechnic Institute B.S. 5/83

AMC Year I 9/10/81–5/14/82			AMC Year II 8/26/82–5/20/83			AMC Year III 9/7/83–6/17/84			AMC Year IV 6/18/84–5/18/85		
Course	Hours	Grade	Course	Hours	Grade	Course	Weeks	Grade	Elective	Weeks	Grade
Physiology	174	G	Microbiology &			Medicine	8	G	*Surgery	3	E
Biochemistry	174	G	Infectious Disease	148	G	Pediatrics	8	G	Clin. Ophthalmology	2	EH
Histology	92	G	Pharmacology	126	G	Surgery	8	G	Clin. Ophthalmology	2	EH
Epidemiology &			Systems Pathology	138	G	Psychiatry	8	G	Clin. Ophthalmology	4	EH
Biostatistics	30	G	Medicine 1:			Ob/Gyn	4	G	*Neurology	4	G
Neurosciences I	120	G	Clinical and			Ophthalmology	2	EH	Clin. Nuclear Med	4	G
Focal Problems in			Laboratory Dx.	183	G	*Anesthesiology	1	P	Clin. Lab. Cardiol.	4	G
Medicine	44	G	Medicine II: History			*Radiology	1	P	DX Radiology	2	G
Gross Anatomy	166	G	Taking & Phys. Dx.	70	G				Intro to Computers	2	G
Radiology	12*		Cellular Basis of						Intro Comp. in Med	2	G
General Pathology	45**		Cancer Medicine	45	G				*Er/Amb Medicine	4	G
			Scientific Basis of						DX Radiology	1	G
*See Gross Anatomy			Human Behavior	31	G				*Medicine	4	E
**See Systems Pathology			Hum. Reproduction								
(Year II)			& Genetics	100	G						
			Neuroscience II	86	G						
			Introduction to								
			Psychiatry	30	G	*GRADED ON A PASS/ FAIL BASIS			*REQUIRED COURSES		

National Board Examination – Part I National Board Examination – Part II Date of Graduation 5/23/85 Degree M.D.
Date Written: June 14–15, 1983 Date Written: September 25–26, 1984 Honors:

Definition of terms: Hours – total number of contact hours, weeks – number of weeks assigned to the rotation.
Grading System (effective 6/69): E=Excellent, G=Good, P=Pass, U=Unsatisfactory, Pass/Fail.
Honors(H) are awarded for superior academic achievement.

Albany Medical College

THE ONE HUNDRED FIFTY-FIFTH COMMENCEMENT

Thursday, May 23, 1985
2:00 P.M.

Saratoga Performing Arts Center
Saratoga Springs, New York

Academic Dress

Academic Dress in this country is derived from garments worn at medieval British universities, especially Oxford, which was founded in the twelfth century. Its early chancellors were representatives of the bishop. Because of this close university-church relationship, students and faculty wore clerical garb.

The cap, gown and hood enable one to distinguish the institution from which the wearer was graduated, the field of learning in which the degree was earned and the level of the degree — bachelor, master or doctorate.

The black mortarboard cap is standard at most colleges and universities throughout the United States. Its distinguishing feature is the color of the tassel, which is black for holders of bachelor's and master's degrees. It may be gold for doctor's degrees and the governing officers of an educational institution.

Although academic gowns for each level are traditionally black, many institutions permit doctoral recipients to wear gowns of characteristic institutional color. In recent years many colleges and universities have also adopted gowns of the institutional color for degrees other than the doctorate. Academic protocol allows trustees, presidents and marshals of higher institutions to wear gowns of special design and color.

The level of degree is indicated by the cut of the gown. The bachelor's gown is relatively simple and is characterized by its long pointed sleeves. The master's gown is somewhat fuller and its sleeves are square at the ends. The doctoral gown is cut rather full and velvet panels reach down the front and around its neck. The sleeves are bell shaped and are decorated with three horizontal velvet bars.

The hood is the most distinctive feature of academic attire. Used originally as a cowl, as a shoulder cape and as a container in which to collect alms, it is now worn at the back, suspended from the shoulders. The length and width of the velvet border indicate the level of the degree. That for the master's degree is three and one-half feet long with a three inch border. The doctor's hood is four feet long and the border is five inches wide. The inner lining is colored with the official color or colors of the institution conferring the degree. The color of the border indicates the field of learning in which the degree was earned — i.e. MEDICINE-green; PHILOSOPHY-dark blue; EDUCATION-light blue; LAW-purple; SCIENCE-golden yellow.

It might be noted that military uniforms and religious habits are appropriate apparel at academic convocations.

Albany Medical College

AWARDS DAY CITATION

The Sandoz Award in Ophthalmology

is awarded to

Mary Ann Duke

Class of
1985

_____
President and Dean

May 8, 1985
Date

Albany Medical College

SENIOR STUDENT RESEARCH

Award

In recognition of an outstanding research accomplishment while a student at the Albany Medical College.

This certificate is awarded to:

Mary Ann Duke

May 8, 19 85   by _____

Date   President and Dean

Class of 1985 Awards and Prizes

The Alumni Association Medal
"...shows promise of typifying the ideal alumnus..."
Anthony C. Campagna

The Ralph D. Alley Prize
"...clinical acumen, skills and knowledge in Thoracic Surgery..."
Mark P. Callery

The David J. Dickerman Alumni Prize
"...best clinical performance in Obstetrics and Gynecology..."
Rosalind A. Dickman

The Kenneth M. Archibold Prize
"...exemplary obstetrical skills and knowledge..."
Catherine A. McGovern

The C. R. Bard Urological Award
"...best performance in urological surgery..."
Michael L. Goldaber

The Richard T. Beebe Fellowship
"...outstanding performance in third year...enable to study in a laboratory of international distinction..."
Frances R. Wallach and Susan E. Ruane

The John Milton Bigelow Prize
"...best examination in diseases of the nose and throat..."
Floyd E. Seskin

The Mary E. Carroll Award
"...shows good academic and behavioral standing..."
Nancy C. Sapio

The Duggett Trust Prizes
"...most effective professional performance and conduct..."
Robert T. Morrison and Darrell J. Triulzi

The Dean's Senior Research Award
"...outstanding research endeavors..."
Mary Ann Duke, Thomas J. Kuettel and Robert E. Shangraw

The Charles Robert Award
"...outstanding academic achievement in surgery..."
Robert E. Shangraw

The Janet M. Glasgow Memorial Achievement Citation
"...outstanding scholarship achievement..."
Susan B. Yeon and Cindy J. Weinberg

The Neil Hellman Prize
"...outstanding sensitivity and commitment to humanistic values..."

The Lamb Foundation, Inc. Prizes
"...most nearly approached the ideal in doctor-patient relationship..."
Anthony C. Campagna, Joseph M. Delehanty and Karen D. Wood

The Allan Marsh Prize
"...greatest proficiency and aptitude for surgery..."
Mark A. Coppes

The Clifford K. Marsh Scholarship
"...sincere desire to become a family practice physician..."
Nancy C. Sapio

The Frederick McCandless Prize
"...best performance in psychiatry..."
Scott D. Rogge

The Kenneth B. Olson Prize
"...best potential for developing a career in clinical oncology..."
Melanie F. Kaye

The Anna Perkins Scholarship
"...dedication, skill and devotion to family practice..."
Thomas J. Kuettel

The Robert D. Reinecke Prize for Research in Ophthalmology
"...scientific or academic excellence in ophthalmology..."
Daniel S. Casper

The Sandoz Award in Ophthalmology
"...a willingness to share and teach..."
Mary Ann Duke

The Jack Spivaley Memorial Fellowship
"...special study or research..."
Susan B. Yeon

The Jack Spivaley Prize
"...excelled in pediatrics..."
Jayne A. Vianest

The Upjohn Achievement Award
"...for excellence in outpatient medicine..."
Christine M. Brown

The S. Oakley Vander-Poel Prize
"...the best clinical examination in general medicine..."
Susan B. Yeon

The R. J. Wharton Prize
"...greatest proficiency in pediatrics..."
Cindy J. Weinberg

The Harold G. Wiggers Award
"...in the opinion of classmates, exemplifies the qualities of an outstanding physician..."
Rebecca A. Preston

474

The Albany Medical College
of Union University
Albany, New York 12208

DEPARTMENT OF OPHTHALMOLOGY
(518) 445-5447

August 15, 1984

Gregory B. Krohel, M.D.
Department of Ophthalmology
Albany Medical College
Albany, N.Y. 12208

Dear Greg:

I am writing to recommend Mary Ann Duke, a third year medical student who is applying to your program. I have served as her student advisor for the past year and am very pleased to write this letter. Mary Ann is in the six year RPI-Albany Medical College biomedical program which is an extremely demanding course of study. She has performed at a good level during her time at Albany Medical College with an average to slightly above average record. One grade which I believe does not appear on her transcript is her recently completed rotation in surgery which ended during the first week of July. This is an extremely demanding and hard grading course at Albany for which she received a grade of excellent. The comments of her mentor on that rotation noted that she was a hard working student who was well regarded by both house officers and attendings. She was noted to be dedicated, interested and showed excellent relationships with her patients. I think this grade rather accurately reflects her current level of performance.

She has in addition this past year undertaken a number of research projects in the Department of Ophthalmology and has shown an outstanding degree of motivation and dedication to her work. Outstanding in this area has been a study involving immunoperoxidase, identification of herpes virus infections in clinical and laboratory cases. She was given this project as only a basic concept and has worked hard to develop a technique. This has resulted in a very well received poster at the 1984

ARVO Meeting and the related scientific paper has been submitted for publication to Investigative Ophthalmology. She has in addition been involved in a number of clinical projects related to external eye disease and has carried these out in an outstanding manner. The members of the Department including myself who have worked with her on these projects are highly enthusiastic about the quality of her work. I feel that she shows real potential for a career in academic ophthalmology and I would give her my highest recommendation for your consideration.

I hope you will consider her seriously for your program and would be very happy to talk with you by phone if you have any additional questions.

Sincerely,

Richard S. Smith, M.D.
Professor and Chairman

RSS:bja

Mrs. Meyer Herschenhorn
Apt. 5K 175 So. Swan St.
Albany, N.Y. 12202

March 19, 1987

Dr. Richard Smith
re. Dr. Mary Ann Duke

I felt compelled to let you know about the thorough eye examination I received from Dr. Mary Ann Duke! For many, many years I have gone to a well known opthamologist and I was in and out of his office in three minutes, always doubting that I had a complete exam. With

our

Dr. Luke there were no doubts.

I felt very comfortable with her — she explained everything to me during her examination. I would not hesitate to recommend her to friends & family and I wish her great success — we need good doctors in every field!

Respectfully
Sylvia Hirschenhorn

Oct. 13, 1987

Dear Dr. Smith,

    I would like to take a minute of your time to tell you about the inservice that Dr. Mary Ann Duke gave the Neg. staff at Childs in Sept.

    I know that I can say for my fellow staff members that we found her talk to be educational, informative, and kept the focus at our interests. Her slides and talk stimulated us to ask questions pertinent to learning more about the surgery which I feel in turn will enable us to deliver better neg. care.

    I do think that people should receive positive recognition for work well done, and so the reason for this note. I have been an R.N. at Childs for 8yrs. and never has an opthalmology resident taken the time to give us an interview. I just wanted you to know that the interview was appreciated and it would be nice to see more in the future.

Dr. Smith I do hope that you share this note with Dr. Duke so that she will know our feelings.

Thank you for your time.

Sincerely,
Mrs. Mary McCarthy RN

161 Washington Avenue
Albany, New York 12210

ph 518.427.4300
fx 518.449.3386

John J. Bach Jeffrey W. Cannell
PRESIDENT **DIRECTOR**

w.albanypubliclibrary.org

October 19, 2007

Mary Ann Duke
10220 Democracy Blvd
Potomac, MD 20854

Dear Mary Ann:

Sarra Umstadter had her disastrous eye operation on Thursday, January 7th, 1988. As far as I can determine, the story did not get to the newspapers until April 19th. The New York State Health Department charged Child's Hospital with malpractice on April 6th. I checked the Times Union newspaper for a week after January 7th and saw no mention of the incident.

Enclosed are several articles about the case. There will be a charge of $.80 for 8 photocopies. Payment should be made to the Albany Public Library. Thanks.

— She never sent me a bill.

Sincerely,

Ellen K. Gamache
Ellen K. Gamache
Local History Librarian

CHILD'S HOSPITAL FACES CHARGES FOR 5TH TIME GIRL BRAIN-DAMAGED AFTER EYE OPERATION

By Mary D'Ambrosio Staff writer

Section: LOCAL
Page: B1
Date: TUESDAY, April 19, 1988

Caption: MOTHER, DAUGHTER - Abbey Umstadter sits on the floor of her Schaghticoke home Monday with her daughter, Sarra.

For the fifth time in less than 18 months, the state Health Department has charged **Child's Hospital** with providing inadequate and unsafe medical care.

The latest incident involves a 19-month-old girl who was left with brain damage after ungoing minor eye surgery. Sarra

Umstadter of Schaghticoke was left unable to eat, talk or move on her own after her heart stopped during a January eye operation.

The Health Deparment charged April 6 that doctors failed to do their jobs properly in the case, according to department spokesman Vicki Zeldin.

Earlier, on Jan. 20, the Health Department had informed the hospital that it would begin enforcement proceedings for five previous incidents between October 1986 and June 1987, Zeldin said Monday. Those five incidents resulted in four citations against the hospital.

"When we move on enforcement, it is because there is a pattern of problems that are uncorrected," Zeldin said.

Enforcement proceedings often involve overhaul of medical departments, a review of staff medical credentials and fines, ranging from several thousand dollars for minor problems to about $70,000 for major ones, Zeldin said.

The hospital has until April 20 to respond to the latest citation.

Sarra, the youngest of William and Abbey Umstadter's three children, had surgery on at Child's for a "lazy eye" Jan. 7 upon the recommendation of her ophthamologist, Abbey Umstadter said Monday.

"I told her when she came out she'd have perfectly straight eyes," Umstadter said, recalling her last words to her child.

Instead, a courier came running into the hospital cafeteria to get Sarra's parents shortly after the procedure began, and they rushed to the operating room where the surgeon "was standing there practically in tears," Umstadter said.

The doctors were not identified by the Health Department and the hospital declined to reveal their names.

Abbey Umstadter said the surgeon told her Sarra had gone into cardiac arrest. The child was transferred to Albany Medical Center Hospital about a half mile away, where she lapsed into a coma. Doctors expected her to die, and the Umstadters made funeral arrangements.

The girl survived and went home March 22. Because of what her mother described as severe brain damage, the child cries loudly, but cannot eat, move on her own or talk. She is fed through a tube.

"You try to move her, and she screams," Abbey Umstadter said. "I don't know if she'll be with us for a year, two years or until she's 45."

During an interview Monday, Abbey Umstadter sometimes talked about her only daughter in the past tense. "They took her away from me," said the 25-year-old mother, who wants to be a nurse. "I have a totally absent baby."

The Health Department did not cite a direct cause for the incident. William Madden, hospital administrator, said doctors have no idea what went wrong in the operating room.

Madden said the hospital would not necessarily refute the Health Department criticisms, but that a separate hospital investigation showed that the doctors' actions did not cause the baby's heart to stop.

"To date, our investigation does not indicate anything we did or did not do that would cause this very unfortunate incident," Madden said Monday. "We have not been able to determine the cause of heart failure."

However, a Health Department "statement of deficiencies" charged, among other things, that:

*The ophthalmology surgeon failed to cancel the eye surgery after abnormal test results on the baby.

*An anesthesiologist failed to evaluate the effects of two drugs, proventil and isuprel, which the report said when combined can cause quickening of the heart.

*The surgeon and a resident failed to clear the surgery with Sarra's pediatrician.

[handwritten: Not me, I was a 2nd year resident]

The report also charged "failure to have adequate systems in place to prevent substantive violations of hospital policies and procedures" in the case.

In the past, the Health Department has cited the hospital for the following incidents:

*In June 1987, a 45-year-old female patient went to the hospital for a biopsy. After being taken to the recovery room, she had to be transferred to another hospital and undergo a hysterectomy for a puncture wound. A November 1987 Health Department report charged the hospital with medical staff deficiencies and failure to report the incident properly.

*Also in June 1987, a patient's bowel was punctured during a tubal cauterization. In the same November report, Child's also was cited for medical staff deficiencies and the mishandling of medical records.

*In April 1987, a patient hospitalized for a cornea transplant got "inadequate anesthesia due to an equipment malfunction," according to a May 1987 Health Department statement of deficiency.

The patient hemorrhaged, causing a "possible loss of patient sight," the report said. A machine that administered anesthesia had been used twice before it underwent a maintenance check, the report said, charging the hospital department of anesthesiology had "failed to assure the proper quality of medical treatment in a hospital."

*On March 11, 1987, a patient suffered "serious post-operative complications" from a surgical procedure. The Health Deparmtment charged that "physician response time was excessively delayed," that the patient's blood loss during surgery was not documented, her difficulty in breathing was not noted and that doctors called their instructions in over the phone rather than going to see the patient. The patient's current condition was not immediately available.

*On Oct 1986, a 44-year-old patient lost 3,000 centimeters of blood during an operation. Again, deficiencies in medical staff were cited.

Child's is a 35-bed not-for-profit hospital that has moved increasingly to outpatient and minor surgery functions in recent years, specializing in eye, ear, nose, throat and plastic surgery.

Umstadter has retained Farley Jones, attorney with the Troy firm of E. Stewart Jones, to review the medical records in her daughter's case. (518) 274-5820

Factbox:

All Times Union materials copyright 1996-2007, Capital Newspapers Division of The Hearst Corporation, Albany, N.Y.
HOME | CONTACT US | SUBSCRIBE TO NEWSPAPER | HOW TO ADVERTISE | PRIVACY RIGHTS | COPYRIGHT | CLASSROOM ENRICHMENT

Albany County Supreme Court.

STATE FAULTS HOSPITAL FOR CARE DEFICIENCY

By Mary D'Ambrosio and Kathleen Haddad Staff writers

More than three months after 19-month-old Sarra Umstadter of Schaghticoke underwent minor eye surgery at **Child's Hospital**, neither state Health Department nor hospital officials are spelling out why she went home severely brain damaged.

But the director of the health agency's Bureau of Hospital Services faulted the hospital for deficiencies in treating the girl, whose heart stopped on Jan. 7 in surgery to correct a "lazy eye."

"This was an incident that was precipitated by deficiencies in care provided to a patient," Wayne Osten said Tuesday.

Earlier, William Madden, the hospital's administrator, said physicians had no idea what went wrong in the operating room, and Abbey Umstadter, Sarra's 25-year-old mother, said doctors had repeatedly told her that the loss of her daughter's mental ability was "an act of God."

On April 6, the department issued a list of 22 medical violations in the Umstadter case. Among them were failure of the eye surgeon to cancel the operation after abnormal lab findings, failure of the anesthesiologist to evaluate the simultaneous use of two medicines that can speed up the heart rate, and the performance of a preoperative exam by a third-year ophthalmology resident rather than a pediatrician.

[handwritten: Not me, I was a 2nd year resident.]

It was the fifth time since November 1986 that the Health Department had cited Child's for deficient patient care. Osten said his agency's orders for corrective measures as well as plans to fine the hospital were in the works before the toddler - who had also suffered a mild case of cerebral palsy and chronic lung problems before being admitted for the eye surgery - became the latest known victim of deficient care at Child's.

The Health Department first noticed "a pattern or trend" there in 1987 after several accidents with patients, and thereafter "we started spending more and more time in the hospital," Osten said.

The incidents that contributed to the Health Department's decision to charge Child's with hospital code violations consistently involved surgical and anesthesiology services, a pattern that sets the hospital apart from others, where most incidents are medication errors, frequently minor ones.

In response to the question of whether the department's scrutiny was strong enough to protect patients, Osten said, "There is no way we at the state Health Department can be at a hospital every day." Instead, he said, hospitals must monitor themselves.

He characterized Child's chief problem as a lack of quality control at all levels, from its governing body to the administrators and medical staff.

When one hospital department did function properly, Osten said, that failure was not always investigated and remedied by another internal group.

"You don't identify an issue like that overnight," he said, referring to the hospital's inadequate internal monitoring.

Health Department and hospital officials will meet Tuesday to settle the state agency's "enforcement proceeding," which is likely to include a fine and set a schedule for improved systems. Under state public health law, fines of up to $1,000 are permitted for each documented deficiency.

Osten said he did not anticipate closing the hospital - which the department has ordered 10 times elsewhere in the past five years - because the 35-bed facility on Hackett Boulevard showed a willingness and a capacity to correct its "serious" deficiencies.

Two years ago, **Child's Hospital** and Albany Medical Center announced the formation of a joint ambulatory surgery center. AMC agreed to send its less complicated ambulatory cases - about 2,400 annually - to Child's and concentrate on more difficult cases. The two institutions exhcanged board members as part of the agreement.

The anesthesiology department at Albany Med recently began providing the anesthesiology at **Child's Hospital**.

The pact to provide Child's anesthesiology services took effect March 1, according to AMC spokesman Gregory McGarry. It was made for financial reasons and to provide quality care and was "in the best interest" of both hospitals, McGarry said.

Factbox:

All Times Union materials copyright 1996-2007, Capital Newspapers Division of The Hearst Corporation, Albany, N.Y.
HOME | CONTACT US | SUBSCRIBE TO NEWSPAPER | HOW TO ADVERTISE | PRIVACY RIGHTS | COPYRIGHT | CLASSROOM ENRICHMENT

Section: MAIN
Page: A1
Date: MONDAY, July 25, 1988

*ALBANY MED BLAMED FOR CHILD'S LAPSE

Kathleen Haddad Staff writer

State Health Commissioner David Axelrod said he holds Albany Medical Center partly responsible for deficiencies at affiliated **Child's Hospital** that left a Schaghticoke toddler brain-damaged.

"As far as I'm concerned, there was a heavy responsibility on the part of the medical center," Axelrod said last week in an interview on a wide range of topics.

But an Albany Medical Center official said **Child's Hospital** was responsible for its own quality assurance program.

The toddler, Sarra Umstadter, went into cardiac arrest in January prior to routine surgery to correct "lazy eye." The state Health Department said the child should not have been anesthetized and surgery should have been canceled because of the child's abnormal preoperative condition. Health officials also questioned the simultaneous use of two heart-quickening drugs that are not supposed to be used together.

The Umstadter incident was the sixth in two years at Child's that precipitated statements of deficiency by the Health Department.

Axelrod said he discussed the patient care problems a year ago in a meeting with Albany Medical Center officials, including chief executive officer Dr. J. Richard Gaintner and **Child's Hospital** officials, including Episcopal Diocese Bishop David Ball. The diocese owns the hospital.

Albany Medical Center Hospital in 1985 entered an agreement with **Child's Hospital** that sent the medical center's routine outpatient surgery to Child's. The pact was intended to alleviate Child's financial problems and the medical center's overcrowded operating rooms.

It called for three members of Albany Med's board to join Child's board and for Albany Medical Center to employ the medical director of Child's ambulatory surgery program, a position traditionally concerned with the quality of patient care.

The arrangement received Health Department support, which was needed because Child's eventually sought the department's approval to change its hospital-based outpatient surgery program to a free-standing ambulatory surgery center.

"Part of that relationship was predicated upon there being the availability of quality assurance activities from the medical center," Axelrod said. "And they supplied the medical director." He added that the responsibility for patient care "falls to the board. And the board (of Child's) included members of the medical center."

Those members were Gaintner, Albany Med board Chairman Richard Sonneborn and Dr.

Robert Whalen.

During the meeting Axelrod held last year, he expressed "concern for the extent of oversight by the medical center" and "the quality surveillance" at Child's, he said.

"I think that the assurances provided to me with respect to **Child's Hospital** were not fulfilled, and I don't take lightly to failures of that sort," he said.

"All the concerns that I had were not addressed because, if they were addressed, what happened would not have happened," Axelrod said of the Umstadter incident. "My distress was very much heightened by the fact that we had discussed effectively the very issues which resulted, I think, in a problem of quality at **Child's Hospital**."

Dr. Anthony Tartaglia, vice president for patient care at Albany Medical Center, responded to Axelrod's statement:

"Quality assurance at **Child's Hospital** has always remained the responsibility of Child's even under terms of the joint agreement between AMC and Child's for the ambulatory surgery program there. The medical center has never been given the authority or the responsibility for the management of Child's Hospital's quality assurance program. Although we have the opportunity to provide input into Child's quality assurance program, no one at any time asked us to develop or implement our institution's very stringent quality assurance program at Child's."

The agreement, on file at the state Health Department, says that the ambulatory surgery medical director "shall report administratively" to Albany Medical Center and "shall be resposible for the quality and integrity of the (ambulatory surgery program's) professional activities on a day-to-day basis." The medical director also was to report to the Child's board and the steering committee of the ambulatory surgery center, according to the agreement.

Axelrod said **Child's Hospital** would ultimately be permitted to continue its ambulatory surgery program. He said the hospital and the department have been working out a plan to correct its deficiencies.

Factbox:

All Times Union materials copyright 1996-2007, Capital Newspapers Division of The Hearst Corporation, Albany, N.Y.
HOME | CONTACT US | SUBSCRIBE TO NEWSPAPER | HOW TO ADVERTISE | PRIVACY RIGHTS | COPYRIGHT | CLASSROOM ENRICHMENT

The Board of Physician Quality Assurance
OF THE STATE OF MARYLAND

Be it known that MARY ANN DUKE on the 31st DAY OF JULY, 1989, having offered evidence of satisfactory completion of education, clinical training and examination is qualified and hereby licensed to practice Medicine and Surgery in the State of Maryland in accordance with the Maryland Medical Practice Act.

And in testimony whereof, the names of the Chairman and Secretary of the Board are inscribed and the seal of the Board is affixed hereto.

Witness:

_____
Chairman

_____
Secretary

RETINA CONSULTANTS, P.C.
SUITE 312
6410 ROCKLEDGE DRIVE
BETHESDA, MARYLAND 20817
(301) 530-5200
FAX: (301) 493-6577

STEPHEN S. PAPPAS, M.D., F.A.C.S.
LAWRENCE M. KING, JR., M.D., F.A.C.S.
ROBERT F. STEPHENS, M.D., F.A.C.S.

DISEASES AND SURGERY
OF THE
VITREOUS AND RETINA

June 11, 1991

Credentialing Committee
Medical Staff Office
Suburban Hospital
8600 Old Georgetown Road
Bethesda, MD 20814

Dear Sir:

I am writing to recommend Mary Ann Duke, M.D. for admission to the Staff of the Ophthalmology Department at Suburban Hospital in Bethesda, Maryland.

Dr. Duke received her Doctor of Medicine at Albany Medical College in 1985 and did her ophthalmology residency at the Albany Medical College from 1986-1988.

She was awarded the Dean's Senior Research Award in 1985 and the Sandoz Award for Excellence in Ophthalmology in 1985. She has several publications to her credit.

She is a member of the American Medical Association, the American Academy of Ophthalmology, and the Sigma Xi Scientific Research Foundation.

I have known Dr. Duke since she arrived in this area in September 1989. I have assisted her in the care of her patients and found the level of ophthalmology practice with these patients to be excellent. I have not seen her perform surgery but her patients who have had surgery, whom I have seen, have had excellent results.

The patients that I have seen of Dr. Duke's have loyalty and respect for her as an individual and her professional skills.

Dr. Mary Ann Duke is a well-trained ophthalmologist with excellent skills in both clinical and surgical ophthalmology.

On the basis of my knowledge of her and association with her, I would recommend her for admission to the staff of ophthalmology at Suburban Hospital without reservations.

Credentialing Committee
June 11, 1991
Page 2

If any further information is needed, I will be most happy to furnish the same.

Sincerely yours,

Lawrence M. King, Jr., M.D., F.A.C.S.

LMK:jad

RETINA CONSULTANTS, P.C.
SUITE 312
6410 ROCKLEDGE DRIVE
BETHESDA, MARYLAND 20817
(301) 530-5200
FAX: (301) 493-6377

STEPHEN S. PAPPAS, M.D., F.A.C.S.
LAWRENCE M. KING, JR., M.D., F.A.C.S.
ROBERT F. STEPHENS, M.D., F.A.C.S.

June 13, 1991

DISEASES AND SURGERY
OF THE
VITREOUS AND RETINA

Joel S. Gordon, M.D.
Chairman
Department of Ophthalmology
Suburban Hospital
8600 Old Georgetown Road
Bethesda, Maryland 20814

RE: MARY ANN DUKE, M.D.

Dear Dr. Gordon:

It has recently come to my attention that Dr. Mary Ann Duke is applying for privileges in ophthalmology at Suburban Hospital.

I first became acquainted with Dr. Duke when she moved into the area a year ago and after working for another ophthalmologist for a brief period of time decided to open up her own office in Potomac. Her CV indicates that she has had good medical training at the Albany Medical College from which she graduated in 1985. She completed her residency in ophthalmology also at the Albany Medical College in 1988. She has successfully passed the American Board of Ophthalmology examinations and is a member of the American Academy of Ophthalmology. She has received several honors in the past and has participated in at least seven publications, some of which she was the senior author and others of which she was a contributing author. It would appear, therefore, that academically she is well qualified to become a member of our staff.

I have not had an opportunity to observe her surgical ability but on the other hand I have not heard any adverse reports either. If there is any question regarding her surgical skills and ability, I would suggest that she be admitted on the staff on a probational status for a short period of time, during which period she may be observed by one or more of our members of the department who can then verify the extent of her surgical capabilities. Inasmuch as she is currently on the staff of Holy Cross and Shady Grove Adventist Hospital and is performing surgery there in a satisfactory fashion, perhaps this probational period by us would be unnecessary.

TO: Joel S. Gordon, M.D.
RE: Mary Ann Duke, M.D.
June 13, 1991

    I am impressed by her zeal and determination to succeed as a solo practitioner in this already over-crowded area.

    Unless the Credentialing Committee has some adverse information regarding this applicant of which I am not aware, I would recommend that she be given privileges in ophthalmology at Suburban Hospital.

Sincerely yours,

Stephen S. Pappas, M.D., F.A.C.S.

SSP/das

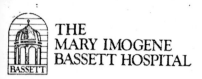

THE MARY IMOGENE BASSETT HOSPITAL

One Atwell Road
Cooperstown, New York
13326-1394

June 14, 1991

Credentialing Committee
Medical Staff Office
Suburban Hospital
8600 Old Georgetown Road
Bethesda, MD 20814

RE: MARY ANNE DUKE MD

To Whom It May Concern:

I received a telephone call from Dr. Duke indicating that she would like a letter of recommendation for staff privileges at your hospital and indicated that you had received a less than flattering letter from the Acting Chairman of the Department of Ophthalmology in Albany.

Dr. Duke spent three months with us in 1989; I am making an exception to my general rule by enclosing for your perusal a copy of my final evaluation on her. I would like to direct your attention to the last paragraph; I was the resident in question 15 years ago. I am well acquainted with all members of the department at Albany, both past and present, as I trained three of the full-time attendings in that department. From my vantage point, I think a lot of the comments that are being generated in regard to Dr. Duke are related to a significant amount of unpleasantness between a previous member of the department in Albany and the current attendings. Because of a personal relationship between Dr. Duke and that attending, a great deal of hostility was projected onto her. That, combined with her tendency not to be a "cookie cutter" resident with strong personal opinions of what was right and wrong combined to create what I considered to be a significant witch hunt. This feeling has been confirmed with my conversations with other members of her residency group. The events which caused her to be placed on probation were, in my opinion, procedural rather than substantive, and would not have been cause for probation within this department. If Dr. Duke wishes to share any of that information with you, she certainly has the option.

I do know that Dr. Duke has worked assiduously to provide good care for her patients since leaving this program and suggest that you look most carefully

AFFILIATED WITH COLUMBIA UNIVERSITY

Credentialing Committee
June 14, 1991
Page 2

at the letters from those with whom she has been associated for the past two years.

Sincerely,

Charles B. Deichman, M.D.
Ophthalmologist-in-Chief
Clinical Professor of Ophthalmology
Albany Medical College
(607) 547-3960

CBD/dan
enc.

Dict: 06/14/91
RIT: 06/17/91
Trans: 06/17/91

C O P Y

The Mary Imogene Bassett Hospital
Cooperstown, N. Y. 13326

April 27, 1989

Richard S. Smith, M.D.
Professor & Chairman
Department of Ophthalmology
Albany Medical College
Albany, NY 12208

RE: FINAL EVALUATION - MARY ANN DUKE, M.D.

Dear Dr. Smith:

This letter will serve as the final evaluation for Mary Ann Duke during her three month senior resident rotation at this hospital. At the outset, let me state that Mary Ann's performance during her three months was generally creditable with no delinquencies in the patient care arena. What problems occurred were more in the area of interpersonal relationships which I will discuss later in this letter. This is most notably in the check-off evaluation provided by Dr. Ludwig when compared with the check-off evaluation provided by the other two attendings.

When Mary Ann arrived I explained that I was aware of the fact that she had been "under the gun" during the previous six months and that her performance here would be evaluated strictly on how she performed during her rotation at this institution. As a result, I think she was far less defensive and more able to concentrate on the job at hand without carrying a lot of emotional baggage from her previous experiences.

In the area of patient care, Mary Ann certainly has an extensive area of ophthalmic knowledge. In addition to her daily readings I am aware of the fact that she spent a great deal of time studying for the OKAP examinations. Her patient evaluations were at least average in regard to completeness and accuracy. Indeed, I had very little to criticize as far as her notes were concerned. Her clinical application of that knowledge was also at least average although, at times, there was a little bit of a tendency on her part to trust a little bit more in her judgment than in that of the attendings. I don't necessarily think that that was a bad approach but it is one that will stick in the craw of those who are totally convinced that "chiefs are chiefs and indians are indians."

In the surgical arena Mary Ann's surgical skills were pretty much undeveloped when she arrived as her intraocular experience had been virtually nonexistent with the exception of trauma cases while she was chief resident. She took

COPY

Richard S. Smith, M.D.
April 27, 1989
Page 2

The Mary Imogene Bassett Hospital
Cooperstown, N.Y. 13326

direction well and progressed significantly during the course of her three months. She was interested in enhancing her skills and developed a quite meticulous approach to her surgery.

I would judge her overall performance at Bassett to be on an average with residents as a whole.

Having said that I must comment on the resident evaluation form filled out by Dr. Ludwig which I do not believe accurately reflects Mary Ann's performance, but is related to her interpersonal relationships and points up what I think is the crux of some of the difficulties that Mary Ann has had in the past. It is clear that Dr. Ludwig and Dr. Duke did not hit it off and as a result I think Mary Ann "tuned out" Dr. Ludwig with the end result being the evaluation that you see. Clearly, Mary Ann tends to polarize peoples reactions to her. She is clearly somewhat head strong and has a tendency not to listen if her mind is made up or if her priorities are elsewhere. This can certainly be very aggravating to some people but both Dr. Beer and I found that gentle persistence would tend to surmount these obstacles.

I must say that some of Mary Ann's nonprofessional priorities outside the hospital would tend at times to impinge on her on call responsibilities, although not to the detriment of patient care. This occasional tendency bothered Dr. Ludwig considerably more than the rest of us and is something which will, I am sure, resolve itself when Mary Ann is out in private practice.

All in all, I think Mary Ann has the potential for being a good ophthalmologist in a private practice setting. She will work best in an independent setting rather than in a group as she tends to march to the beat of a somewhat different drummer. I don't think that that tendency is all bad as I am sure you can remember a resident approximately 15 years ago who had that same tendency and still managed to survive. Mary Ann is still young, with her desire to perform well tempered by more maturity and a touch of wisdom should stand her in good stead.

Sincerely,

Charles B. Deichman, M.D.
Ophthalmologist-in-Chief
Department of Ophthalmology
(607) 547-3960

CBD/dan/d2
encs.

Dict: 4/27/89
RIT: 4/28/89
Trans: 4/28/89

July 9, 1991

Suburban Hospital
The Credentialling Committee
Medical Staff Office
8600 Old Georgetown Road
Bethesda, MD 20814

RE: Mary Ann Duke, MD

Dear Dr. Gordon:

I am pleased to support the candidacy of Dr. Mary Ann Duke for admission to the medical staff at Suburban Hospital. In my capacity as Director of the Retina Service at Albany Medical College I worked with Dr. Duke during the second two years of her residency in ophthalmology which she completed in 1988. During this time, she demonstrated competence in all areas of general ophthalmology, both medical and surgical.

She is a conscientious and hard working young physician, devoted to her patients and possessed of high professional ethical standards. She is, I know, committed to her ongoing professional growth and has attended a number of postgraduate courses and seminars since completing her formal training. She has completed the requirements to stand before the American Board of Ophthalmology for certification and has already successfully completed the written portion of the Board examinations.

Dr. Duke carries my unqualified recommendation for admission to your staff. I believe she will be an asset to the ophthalmology department at Suburban Hospital.

If you have any questions or require any additional information, please feel free to write or call.

Sincerely,

Shalom J. Kieval, MD

SJK/sd

American Board of Ophthalmology

Founded in 1916
Please address all communications to
William H. Spencer, M.D., Executive Director
AMERICAN BOARD OF OPHTHALMOLOGY
111 PRESIDENTIAL BOULEVARD
SUITE 241
BALA CYNWYD, PENNSYLVANIA 19004
(215) 664-1175

...ld M. Burde, M.D., Chairman
Bronx, NY

William Tasman, M.D., Vice-Chairman
Philadelphia, PA

December 11, 1991

Mary Ann Duke, M.D.
10,000 Falls Road
Suite 208
Potomac, MD 20854

Dear Doctor Duke:

The members of the American Board of Ophthalmology take great pleasure in informing you that you have successfully passed the certifying examination of the Board. Please accept our congratulations.

A copy of this letter may be used if it is necessary to inform hospitals and various agencies that you are a Diplomate of the American Board of Ophthalmology.

Please fill out the enclosed form telling us how you want your certificate inscribed and where it should be sent. The certificate will be sent to you within the next six to eight weeks depending on a prompt return of this form.

Sincerely yours,

William H. Spencer, M.D.

WHS:cw

Enclosure

...glas R. Anderson, M.D., Miami, FL
Banks Anderson, Jr., M.D., Durham, NC
...rge R. Beauchamp, M.D., Cleveland, OH
Brooks Crawford, M.D., San Francisco, CA
...ert C. Drews, M.D., Clayton, MO
...n T. Flynn, M.D., Miami, FL
...rge Edw. Garcia, M.D., Boston, MA
...Thomas Hutchinson, M.D., Boston, MA

John L. Keltner, M.D., Davis, CA
Malcolm N. Luxenberg, M.D., Augusta, GA
Denis M. O'Day, M.D., Nashville, TN
Dennis M. Robertson, M.D., Rochester, MN
Ronald E. Smith, M.D., Los Angeles, CA
H. Stanley Thompson, M.D., Iowa City, IA

Mary R. Ladden, Administrator

MICHAEL ANCHORS, M.D., PH.D.

INTERNAL MEDICINE AND FAMILY HEALTH CARE

9711 MEDICAL CENTER DRIVE, SUITE 107
ROCKVILLE, MARYLAND 20850
TELEPHONE 738-8840

January 3, 1992

Suburban Hospital
Credentials Committee and any other
  concerned individuals

Dear Sirs,

    This letter is in support of the application of Dr. Mary Ann Duke to become a member of the medical staff of Suburban Hospital in ophthalmology. I have known Dr. Duke for approximately one year and have increasingly directed all my ophthalmology referrals to her. I have done so because I find her work to be of the highest quality. The feedback I have received from patients I have referred to her has been uniformly positive.
    She is highly motivated and evinces the highest personal standards for herself and her work. Her conduct is professional and appropriate. Her office is well-run: waiting times are short and appointments conveniently made. She has Saturday hours and visits nursing homes. Needless to say, as a result, her practice is growing rapidly.
    I can't see any reason why she should not be included in the Suburban staff, especially since Suburban Hospital is located in the middle of her catchment area. Indeed, if she is not included, ophthalmologic surgery on my patients will have to be performed, less conveniently, at another hospital.

Yours truly,

Michael Anchors M.D.

Michael Anchors, M.D., Ph.D.
(from Harvard)

Orkan George Stasior, M.D., F.A.C.S., F.C. Ophth.
23 Hackett Boulevard ○ Albany, New York 12208
(518) 449-1210 ○ FAX (518) 449-1297

Wed. Jan. 8/92

Dear Mary Ann -

Great to talk to you yesterday. Enclosed are copies of letters that were sent to-day to Drs. Stundon & Caldwell. Please keep walking tall?

All the best for 1992.

Best,
I got
(His son was in my medical school class and became an ophthalmologist too. Orkan Stasior optometrist)

EYE SURGERY ○ PLASTIC AND RECONSTRUCTIVE SURGERY ○ EYELIDS AND TEAR DUCTS ○ COSMETIC SURGERY

ALBANY EYE PHYSICIANS & SURGEONS, P.C.
Orkan George Stasior, M.D., F.A.C.S., F.C. Ophth.

January 8, 1992

Fred Caldwell, M.D., Chairman
Credentials Committee - Medical Staff Office
Suburban Hospital
8600 Old Georgetown Road
Bethesda, Maryland 20814

RE: Mary Ann Duke, M.D.

Dear Dr. Caldwell:

Dr. Mary Ann Duke informed me that she is applying for staff privileges at the Suburban Hospital.

I have known Mary Ann Duke since she was a medical student at Albany Medical College. On graduation she was awarded the Sandoz Ophthalmology Prize for outstanding eye research. She decided to specialize in ophthalmology and was happily accepted in our eye residency program. When she was the Chief Resident at the Albany Medical Center, she received high praise from the other residents and various attendings.

Dr. Duke has developed sound clinical and surgical skills. I heard a positive report about her from Dr. Charles Deichman, Chief of the Eye Department at Mary Imogene Bassett Hospital in Cooperstown, New York, where our residents obtain their intensive cataract surgical training. Based on her rotation with him, he remarked that she was "very solicitous of her patients, her work-ups were good, and she developed fine surgical skills". At the Albany Medical Center, after her retinal rotation, Dr. Shalom Kieval, the Director of the Retinal Service, complimented Dr. Duke, stating that she was "conscientious, hard working, well prepared and had good surgical skills". At The Child's Hospital, where the residents are exposed to a high volume of private eye surgery, she received high marks for her diligence and surgical skill. I was the Chief of the Eye Department at that time and received numerous comments about the eye residents. I received only excellent feedback about her.

In summary, from my personal observations and knowledge of Mary Ann Duke, M.D., I can recommend her highly for staff privileges at your hospital.

Sincerely,

Orkan George Stasior, M.D., F.A.C.S.
Clinical Professor of Ophthalmology
Albany Medical College

OGS:da

(handwritten note: Dr. Stasior was very disappointed his son did not get the ophthalmology award, but was happy, also, that I did.)

The Child's Hospital Professional Building ○ 23 Hackett Boulevard ○ Albany, New York 12208

DEPARTMENT OF THE AIR FORCE
USAF MEDICAL CENTER, WRIGHT-PATTERSON (AFLC)
WRIGHT-PATTERSON AIR FORCE BASE, OHIO 45433 - 5300

January 12, 1992

To Whom It May Concern.

I am writing on behalf of Dr Mary Ann Duke with whom I worked as a fellow ophthalmology resident from July 1986 to June 1988 at the Albany Medical Center, Albany, New York. I was one year senior to Dr Duke and had the opportunity to work with her on numerous occasions, both in the operating room and in the clinic. I found Dr Duke to be an excellent physician in all respects. Her clinical acumen, surgical skills, and compassion allowed patients the very best of ophthalmologic care. I would not hesitate to recommend Dr Duke for privileges at any hospital.

Dr Duke has asked me to comment on her probation while at the Albany Medical Center. I strongly feel that probation was an unduly harsh reaction under the circumstances. One case involved a patient with sub-acute bacterial endocarditis who developed a visual field deficit due to an occipital lobe embolic infarct. Dr Duke was the "on call" resident when an ophthalmology consultation was requested by the internal medicine resident early in the morning. Dr Duke initiated her evaluation then, because it was the beginning of the day, appropriately transferred care to the daytime "consult" resident. There was no harm to the patient due to this. As the patient was fully heparinized, treatment would not have been changed. Dr Duke was put on probation for six months for not putting a complete note in the patient's chart. The note was completed by the "consult" resident within one hour.

A second case involved the discharge of a patient with a micro-hyphema due to blunt trauma seen as a consultation through the emergency room. It is a common and accepted practice to discharge these patients and follow them as outpatients. The patient in question subsequently developed a layered hyphema that was interpreted as a rebleed. The hyphema eventually cleared with no residual visual deficit. Dr Duke was put on indefinite probation for sending the patient home instead of admitting him to the hospital after the initial evaluation. Again, it is common practice to follow micro-hyphemas as outpatients. The care of this patient was totally appropriate.

A review of events is appropriate in any case where an adverse occurrence is involved. However, placing a resident-in-training on probation is a decision that can have future ramifications which were not fully considered in this case. Such punishment should be based on trends in behavior, not isolated events. I and Dr Duke's fellow residents felt that the probationary periods were unwarranted and unfair. Dr Duke is an excellent physician and surgeon whom I would recommend without hesitation.

STEPHEN J. BOGAN, M.D.
Chief, Ophthalmology Services

JOHN LODGE, M.D.
8132 OLD GEORGETOWN ROAD
BETHESDA, MARYLAND 20014

January 13, 1992

Joel R. Schulman, M.D., Chairman
 Credentials Committee
Medical Staff Office
Suburban Hospital
8600 Old Georgetown Road
Bethesda, Maryland 20814

Dear Doctor Schulman,

This is a letter of recommendation for Mary Ann Duke, M.D. who is applying for privileges at Suburban Hospital.

Dr. Duke graduated from Albany Medical College where she also completed a three year residency in ophthalmology at that institution. At the end of her training the Department of Ophthalmology of the Albany Medical College recommended to the American Board of Ophthalmology that Dr. Duke had successfully completed her course of study in their department and that she be permitted to stand for their examination.

Dr. Duke took the examination, was successful, and has been certified by that licensing body as a Diplomate of the American Board of Ophthalmology. After becoming board certified, Dr. Duke has been invited to become a Fellow of the American Academy of Ophthalmology.

Since coming to Washington she has applied for privileges at Holy Cross, Shady Grove and Washington Adventist Hospitals. Her credentials were reviewed by each of the respective departments of ophthalmology, she was found qualified and was granted privileges at these institutions.

Since beginning practice in Washington, Dr. Duke has taken call for me on numerous occasions. I have found that her treatment of my patients was appropriate and her personality warm and caring. I have taken calls for her and have also found that her patients had been properly cared for and that they were pleased that she was their ophthalmologist.

(Graduated from Johns Hopkins)

I have been an Attending Ophthalmologist at Suburban Hospital for many years and was Chairman of the Department for five of them. Based on my experience at Suburban, and my associations with Dr. Duke, it is my belief she is a worthy and competent ophthalmologist and that she be granted privileges at our hospital.

Sincerely,

John Lodge, M.D.

JL/es

Anne Caesar, M.D.
4464 Forest Glen Court
Annandale, VA 22003

January 24, 1992

Dr. Joel Schulman
Chairman, Credentialing Committee
Medical Staff Office
Suburban Hospital
8600 Old Georgetown Road
Bethesda, MD 20814

Dear Dr. Schulman:

I am a physician writing to you on behalf of Dr. Mary Ann Duke. I understand that there is some concern with respect to Dr. Duke's having considered bilateral cataract extraction for my father, Peter F. Caesar.

My 85 year-old father has had worsening cataracts for many years, that had progressively limited his ability to see, read, and conduct his daily activities. His prior ophthalmologist in Maine had repeatedly urged him to have his cataracts surgically removed, but my father preferred to have as little contact with physicians as possible. He consistently downplayed his limitations and stubbornly refused surgery.

In the spring of 1991 when my parents moved to the Washington area, I was struck by how much my father's vision had deteriorated. He found it increasingly difficult to navigate his surroundings without assistance; for shaving and cutting his food he had come to rely upon my mother, who is in frail health after several CVA's and a recent MI. I was concerned that my father would be unable to get to the telephone or see to dial 911 in the event that my mother had another anginal attack. My father was referred to Dr. Duke, who thoroughly explained the pros and cons of cataract surgery, including the potential for improvement in my father's vision and the risks of intraocular hemorrhage, postoperative infection, retinal detachment, and the risks associated with anesthesia. Much to the surprise of my mother and myself, my father finally agreed to have surgery performed.

My mother was greatly relieved at my father's change of heart, given his prior reluctance to have surgery. She was determined to seize the moment, and repeatedly urged Dr. Duke to repair both eyes at once, hoping to avert the possibility of my father's changing his mind and refusing a subsequent operation to repair the second eye.

Dr. Duke in no way recommended or encouraged this course of action. Instead, she tried to discourage my parents from this approach, explaining the risk of infection to both eyes if bilateral surgery were performed. By this time, however, both my parents were eager to have the surgery performed, and they continued to press for a bilateral procedure, having decided that the benefits were worth the risks.

Dr. Duke meticulously managed my father's peri- and postoperative care and achieved excellent results with the surgery on my father's left eye; his vision has markedly improved to the point that he does not need glasses to see. While my parents were disappointed that bilateral surgery could not be performed, after the impressive results on his left eye, they are eager to proceed with surgery for the right cataract within the next month.

If I can be of any further assistance in this matter, please do not hesitate to contact me at (703) 354-6887.

Sincerely,

Anne Caesar MD

Anne Caesar, M.D.

(Shady Grove Hospital put me in front of the firing squad, because I attempted to acquiesce to my patient's demand for bilateral surgery. They made me be proctored. It was so difficult to schedule a surgery. No ophthal— wants to sit and WATCH! That's the RESIDENT)

Montgomery Medical Group, P. A.

Locations
Shady Grove Road
2 & Suite 105 & Suite 204
, MD 20850
-8500
1/330-4394

19530 Doctors Drive
Germantown, MD 20874
301/540-4432
FAX 301/916-0470

One North Main Street
Mt. Airy, MD 21771
301/831-5656
FAX: 301/831-0129

Administrative/Business Office
15235 Shady Grove Road
Suite 103
Rockville, MD 20850
301/926-8500
FAX: 301/948-1765

APR. 1 3 1992

April 10, 1992

Murray Hammerman, M.D.
Chairman, Department of Ophthalmology
Shady Grove Adventist Hospital
9901 Medical Center Drive
Rockville, Maryland 20850

Dear Dr. Hammerman:

I have known Mary Ann Duke, M.D., ever since she opened her office for the practice of ophthalmology in this area.

I have referred patients to her on a number of occasions. These patients have had medical and/or surgical problems. She has been well-liked by her patients in every respect. Each case has been handled in a most professional manner with prompt diagnosis and treatment.

Her professional relationship with her colleagues has been exemplary. Communications have been excellent.

I am most pleased with Dr. Duke in every aspect and will continue to refer patients for consultation and/or consultation with treatment.

If there is any further information you desire, please do not hesitate to contact me.

Very truly yours,

Steven Dolinsky, M.D.

SD:acw

APR. 23 1992

9220 Farnsworth Drive
Potomac,,Md.
April 15, 1992

Dr. Mary Ann Duke, M.D.
10000 Falls Road
Suite 208
Potomac, Md., 20854

Dear Dr. Duke:

I am writing this letter to acknowledge and to express my appreciation for the skilled professional care and concerned personal support you have afforded me over the past year.

Upon the swift development of cataracts in both eyes, I became deeply concerned about obtaining skilled qualified care convenient to my residence. It was increasingly difficult (and dangerous) for me to drive to the office of the competent Silver Spring opthamologist who had originally diagnosed the cataracts. I consider myself fortunate to have discovered your name in the yellow pages of the POTOMAC COMMUNITY DIRECTORY. Aft calling your newly-opened office and confirming your impressive professional credentials, I was greatly relieved. Your clear and thorough explanation of the risks and benefits further assured me. Also, another reason for switching doctors was to assure that the surgery could be performed at Shady Grove Adventist Hospital.

Following the right eye cataract surgery in August, 1991, the left eye surgery in October, 1991, and the retina treatment in November, 1991, I was restored to my former eyesight - 20/20 for the right eye and 20/30 for the left eye. Also, I was not disappointed in the wonderful care received from the nurses and staff members of Shady Grove Hospital.

You have proved yourself a welcome and valued addition to the Potomac Community.

Sincerely,

Elizabeth D. Crandall

MICHAEL ANCHORS, M.D., PH.D.
INTERNAL MEDICINE AND FAMILY HEALTH CARE

9711 MEDICAL CENTER DRIVE, SUITE 107
ROCKVILLE, MARYLAND 20850
TELEPHONE 738-8840

April 15, 1992

Murray Hammerman, M.D.
Medical Staff Office
Shady Grove Hospital
9901 Medical Center Dr.
Rockville, MD 20850

Dear Dr. Hammerman,

    This letter is in support of the application of Dr. Mary Ann Duke to join the associate staff of Shady Grove Hospital in ophthalmology. I have known Dr. Duke for approximately one year and have increasingly directed ophthalmology referrals to her.
    I have done so because I find her work to be of the highest quality. The feedback I have received from patients referred to her has been uniformly positive. She excels in rapport with patients and follow-up of their problems. I have never had difficulty in reaching her, and she has taken care of my patients with emergency problems expeditiously.
    She is highly motivated and evinces the highest personal standards for herself and her work. Her conduct is professional and appropriate. Her office is well-run: waiting times are short and appointments conveniently made. She has Saturday hours and visits nursing homes. You can see why her practice is expanding rapidly.
    I see no reason why she should not be quickly granted associate status. In fact, we need more certified surgeons on the staff. Her permanent presence will surely enhance the reputation of your department.

Yours truly,

Michael Anchors, MD

Michael Anchors, M.D., Ph.D.

(Harvard)

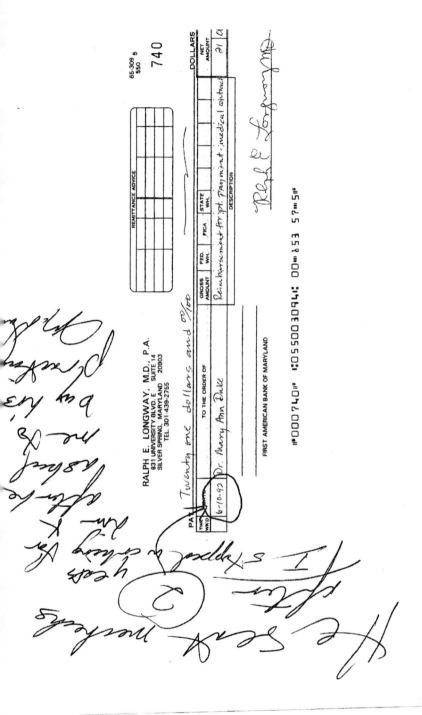

CROSS CURRENTS

Summer/Fall 1992 — A Publication of Holy Cross Hospital

Eye Center Opens

It took coordination, cooperation, timing and teamwork to make it work but according to Carol Morris, RN, "The eye center opened on time and everything is running favorably." The eye center, located on the first floor within the minor surgery department, offers a full range of ophthalmological services. While the services offered through the eye center are not new to Holy Cross, now laser and surgical procedures can be performed in a cohesive, specialized environment.

"Having everything in a coordinated environment will make things much simpler for patients, physicians and staff," said John Anderschat, MD, chief of ophthalmology. "Patients frequently got lost trying to find the laser labs on the fourth floor. Now, they can walk in the front door and have a nice, relaxing wait in a new, comfortable waiting room. Keeping the surgical services out of the *main* operating room also makes the procedures more efficient and requires less waiting time for the patients and nurses."

The new laser suites offer services utilizing Yttrium-Aluminum-Garnet (YAG) or Argon laser capabilities. YAG can be used after cataract surgery to remove posterior capsule opacification, which usually forms within six-months after cataract surgery and causes clouding of the eye. YAG is also used to place an opening in the iris for treating narrow angle glaucoma. The Argon laser is used to close holes in the retina, to treat diabetic retinal blood vessel disease and some forms of retinal degeneration, and to treat chronic open angle glaucoma. More than 90 percent of all laser procedures are performed on an outpatient basis and don't require anesthesia.

The eye center's ophthalmic operating room is fully monitored

Eye Center (cont'd on page 2)

Mary Ann Duke, MD, performs cataract surgery on Mr. Joseph Langdon of Silver Spring in the new eye center. "This type of an environment for outpatient procedures really helps to relax my patients," said Dr. Duke.

What's Inside

- *President's Column...*
- *Community Health Seminars...*
- *A Giving Community...*
- *Classes, Resources and Support Groups...*

Cross Currents

John Anderschat, MD, uses YAG to treat Ms. Hazel Pasco of Washington, DC, who was diagnosed with narrow angle glaucoma. Maryann Abbott, RN, assisted with the procedure.

Eye Center (cont'd from page 1)

and equipped with general anesthesia capabilities, allowing almost any type of ophthalmic procedure. Some of the surgical procedures include cataract surgery, retinal detachment repair, corneal operations and transplants, all eyelid procedures – cosmetic or otherwise, and a variety of glaucoma treatments.

Mary Ann Duke, MD, an ophthalmologist on staff at Holy Cross, said, "This new setup exudes a more relaxed environment which makes for a more relaxed patient. Everyone at Holy Cross really caters to you and I like that. The whole process has been well organized and professional. It really seems like everyone is trying to do whatever they can to make things run smoothly. Holy Cross is a great place for me to d my work."

The move into the new suite required coordination and a tota team effort from many hospital departments according to Ms. Morris, the nurse manager responsible for the eye center. "Th process didn't just affect the nurses and medical staff. All of the hospital's patient support services have played a significar role. Without any of these depa: ments, something could have been missed."

According to John O'Donnel director, biomedical engineering "We spent about three months planning the move and less thar day with the actual move. Ther was so much coordinating neces sary, where the anesthesia gas needed to be, retro-fitting the cases for the gas, plumbing and electrical requirements and then the many site investigations. W worked with the manufacturer c the microscope to ensure everything necessary for the move was

Eye Center (cont'd on page

CROSS CURRENTS is a quarterly newsletter published for the community by Holy Cross Hospital of Silver Spring. Your comments are welcome. Please write to: Holy Cross Hospital, Publications Office, 1500 Forest Glen Road, Silver Spring, Maryland, 20910. For general referral information on programs and services offered by Holy Cross Hospital, you may call 301/905-0100.

Holy Cross Hospital is the largest acute care facility in Montgomery County with 442 beds. Serving the area since 1963, the hospital offers medical, surgical, obstetric, newborn, pediatric, gynecologic, psychiatric, critical care, emergency, diagnostic, rehabilitative, home care/hospice, and adult day care services. A teaching institution through its affiliations with The George Washington University School of Medicine and Children's National Medical Center, Holy Cross Hospital hosts the largest medical staff in the county.

Holy Cross Hospital is a member of the Holy Cross Health System Corporation, a nationwide system of hospitals and healthcare facilities and services sponsored by the Congregation of the Sisters of the Holy Cross with headquarters in South Bend, Indiana.

BOARD OF TRUSTEES

Officers
E. Burns McLindon
Chairman
Sister Joan Carusillo, C.S.C.
Vice Chairman
Charles R. Bailey, Jr.
Secretary/Treasurer
James P. Hamill
President and Chief Executive Officer

Trustees
James Bentley, Ph.D.
Joseph E. Culver
Sister Jeanette Pettig, C.S.C.
Louis G. Gaidieri, M.D.
Thomas C. Gaspard
Bernard Heckman, M.D.
Sister Mary Jane Honan, C.S.C.
Sister Gladys Marie Martin, C.S.C.
Sister Patricia Mulvaney, C.S.C.

Holy Cross Hospital is accredited by the Joint Commission on Accreditation of Healthcare Organizations and is a member of the American Hospital Association, the Maryland Hospital Association, the Catholic Health Association, and the Council of Teaching Hospitals of the Association of American Medical Colleges.

Our Mission

Faithful to the spirit of the Congregation of the Sisters of the Holy Cross, the Holy Cross Health System exists to witness Christ's love through excellence in the delivery of health services motivated by respect for those we serve.

We foster a climate that empowers those who serve with us, while stewarding our human and financial resources.

Holy Cross Hospital, Silver Spring, embodies this mission in an environment of mutual respect, productive teamwork, effective communication, and warm hospitality. A special focus of our ministry is a sensitive response to the needs of the poor.

Summer/Fall 1992

Cross Currents

Eye Center (cont'd from page 2)

in place, in order to limit the downtime for the scope."

"Staffing the new area was also an adventure," Ms. Morris said. "Everyone pitched in to train the staff."

"Maintaining proficiency in a center such as this requires a team of individuals working together," said James Loreto, MD, an ophthalmologist on staff at Holy Cross. "It takes individuals who are very interested in the procedures and very good at what they do. Usually, the patients coming through the eye center are elderly individuals who aren't sick. They are coming in for elective treatment which requires special care. The staff at Holy Cross is aware of that and they know how to treat the patients."

In The News...

Bob Grossman, director, adult day care center, has been appointed to serve on a task force of the National Institute of Adult Day Care. The task force, which is comprised of nine individuals from across the country, is producing a national guide for the training of day care employees. Mr. Grossman is a member of the Alzheimer's Association speakers bureau and recently presented a lecture on "Psychosocial Effects of Strokes" to the Montgomery County Stroke Club.

Edward Soma, MD, was one of five recipients of the prestigious John Carroll medal for 1992, which is presented annually by the John Carroll Society. Dr. Soma was recognized, along with his medical practice, Clinical Radiologists, P.A., for their gratis work with the Archdiocesean Healthcare Network last year. Dr. Soma is a staff radiologist at Holy Cross Hospital and also has an office in Silver Spring.

Mark Your Calendars...

Community Health Seminars Include Women's Body Image, Back Pain and Colon Cancer

Body Image: Looking Good and Feeling Bad

Holy Cross Hospital's semi-annual women's health seminar will take place Wednesday, November 19, 7:00 to 9:30 p.m. The seminar will feature Dr. Barbara Morris, psychotherapist/faculty member, Georgetown University Medical Center, and Dr. Carolyn Carr, deputy curator of the National Portrait Gallery, Smithsonian Institution. Dr. Pamela Parker, a pediatrician on staff at Holy Cross, will be the introductory speaker.

Dr. Morris will discuss how body image profoundly influences the way women feel about themselves, and the negative feelings that can diminish a woman's sense of self.

Dr. Carr will discuss how art and media influences a woman's perception of body image.

Back Pain Seminar Offered

"Ouch! My Aching Back," a seminar on back pain, will be presented Tuesday, October 27, 7:00 to 9:30 p.m. at Holy Cross Hospital. The program will discuss factors associated with back pain, describe medical and surgical treatment options and identify preventive measures to reduce the risk of back injuries.

Philip Schneider, MD, an orthopedist, and Paolo Venier, a physical therapist, will present the program.

Colon Cancer: Are You At Risk?

Dr. Milton Koch, a gastroenterologist on staff at Holy Cross, will be one of the featured speakers for this important discussion in November, 1992. The seminar will focus on the warning signs, diagnosis, treatment and prevention of colon cancer. Three exhibits will also be on display relating to nutrition, digestive diseases and the National Cancer Institute.

Call the consumer education office at 301/905-1215 for more information about any of these seminars or other consumer education events.

Summer/Fall 1992

HOLY CROSS
HOSPITAL

August 27, 1992

Mary Ann Duke, M.D.
10000 Falls Road
Suite 208
Potomac, MD 20854

Dear Dr. Duke.

    I wanted to drop you a note and thank you for taking the time to speak with me about the new Eye Center at Holy Cross Hospital and for allowing me to photograph the cataract surgery in August. As you can see by the enclosed publication, the article and one of the less graphic photos were used in *Inside Scene* and I have received quite a bit of positive feedback. The article and photo will also appear in the summer issue of *Cross Currents*, our community newsletter, which is scheduled to reach homes in mid-September. I am enclosing a copy of the publication for your personal use or to display in your office and I have sent several copies to Mr. Langdon. As soon as *Cross Currents* is published, I will forward several copies as well. I will also try to send you some of the other photographs.

    It was a pleasure working with you on this article. If I can be of any additional assistance, please let me know. Again, thank you very much for your cooperation and assistance. I would love to hear what you think of the article.

Sincerely,

Ken Frager
Publication Specialist

PATRICIA R. SHER
STATE SENATOR
8TH LEGISLATIVE DISTRICT
MONTGOMERY COUNTY

FINANCE COMMITTEE

STATE EMPLOYEES HEALTH
INSURANCE ADVISORY COUNCIL

JT. ADVISORY COMMITTEE
ON LEGISLATIVE DATA
SYSTEMS

SENATE OF MARYLAND
ANNAPOLIS, MARYLAND 21401-1991

OFFICE ADDRESS:
PRESIDENTIAL WING
SENATE OFFICE BUILDING
(301) 858-3137 (WASHINGTON AREA)
(410) 841-3137 (BALTIMORE AREA)

HOME ADDRESS:
2905 BARKER ST.
SILVER SPRING, MARYLAND 20910-1004
(301) 589-1555

May 19, 1993

Mary Ann Duke, M.D.
10,000 Falls Road, Suite 208
Potomac, Maryland 20854

Dear Mary Ann:

It was a real pleasure meeting you last night. I hope that I didn't terrify you when I asked you to marry my son - I was only joking!

You were lots of fun and I thoroughly enjoyed being with you. I hope that you will take the time to talk with some of the legislators to help them understand some of the problems doctors are facing and I would be happy to assist you in setting us these dialogues.

Please stay in touch.

Sincerely,

Patty Sher

Patricia R. Sher

PRS/jkd

MONTGOMERY COUNTY MEDICAL SOCIETY

June 10, 1993

Mary Ann Duke, M.D.
10000 Falls Road, #208
Potomac, Maryland 20854

Dear Dr. Duke:

On behalf of all of the physicians in the Montgomery County Medical Society, I wanted to take this opportunity to thank you for your participation in the Society's Speakers Bureau this past year. The Speakers Bureau is an invaluable program to the community, as it enables physicians to share their knowledge and experience with the public in a positive, educational forum.

This year you and your Society colleagues spoke to over 600 people in and around the county, from local area high schools to employees of the Nuclear Regulatory Commission. We have received numerous letters of thanks and appreciation for your volunteer efforts, as well as requests for repeat performances in the coming year. As a Speakers Bureau participant, you should take pride in the fact that our community is better educated on health-related issues as a result of your efforts.

Again, we appreciate and thank you for your willingness to participate in the Speakers Bureau this past year and we look forward to working with you on more projects in the coming year.

Sincerely,

Arthur W. Sagoskin, M.D.
Chairman
Community Affairs Committee

SPRING 1994
VOL. 4 NO. 2

FOR THE MEMBERS OF THE MARYLAND, DC, AND VIRGINIA MEDICAL SOCIETIES

PHYSICIAN'S PRACTICE DIGEST

NETWORK

OR NO WORK

THE PERILS OF SELECTION AND DESELECTION

SPRING 1994, VOL. 4 NO. 2

PPD
PHYSICIAN'S PRACTICE DIGEST
THE PHYSICIAN'S GUIDE TO PRACTICE MANAGEMENT

Climbing the Corporate Ladder — 22

How To Fire Employees — 28

Professional Courtesy — 34

COVER STORY

NETWORK OR NO WORK:
THE PERILS OF SELECTION AND DESELECTION
by Bruce Goldfarb 12

FEATURES

On the Line: Important Elements of Physician Recruiting
by Daniel Alan Lindenfeld 18

Climbing the Corporate Ladder
by Sarah Peterson 22

The Physician of the Future
by Phil Douglas 26

Conflicts in Patient Relations
by Kelley A. McDonald 31

Something For Nothing
by Carol Sorgen 34

Can This (Two-Physician) Marriage Be Saved?
by Rebecca A. Clay 38

COVER STORY

NETWORK OR NO WORK

The Perils of Selection and Deselection

By Bruce Goldfarb

MARY ANN DUKE, MD, IS A WELL-TRAINED, CARING, DEDICATED PHYSICIAN WITH IMPECCABLE CREDENTIALS. WHY IS SHE EXCLUDED FROM THE REGION'S LARGEST MANAGED CARE NETWORKS?

Physicians once held almost God-like stature, omnipotent in the struggle against infirmity and death. Today, practicing medicine is to live with the sword of Damocles over one's head. Physicians have been reduced to relying on the kindness of strangers — for authorization, for reimbursement, for admission to provider networks that have access to increasingly larger blocks of patients.

Nearly 44 million Americans, or one-fifth the U.S. population, are enrolled in health maintenance organizations, according to industry data. Their ranks swell almost 9% per year.

In most cities, HMOs and other managed care companies control hundreds of thousands of lives, leaving a shrinking pool of fee-for-service patients available. According to Chicago-based SMG Marketing Group, about 1.3 million Marylanders, 500,000 Virginians and 400,000 D.C. residents are enrolled in HMOs.

NETWORK OR NO WORK

The American Medical Association reports that 350,000 of the nation's physicians, or about two-thirds, are involved in some type of managed care system. This number is expected to rise under health reform and the growth in managed care.

For an increasing number of physicians, it is a matter of "network or no work" — either join provider panels, or watch as patient after patient apologetically explains that there's a new health plan at work and you aren't in it.

Out of the Loop

Mary Ann Duke, MD, a 32-year-old board certified ophthalmologist, is struggling to survive during the time in her career when a physician's income should be peaking. Three years ago she launched a solo practice in Potomac, MD, an affluent suburb of the District of Columbia.

Dr. Duke's medical career began with promise. She completed an six-year accelerated B.S.-M.D. program at Rensselaer Polytechnic Institute, which accepts only 1% of 2,000 applicants. She received the Sandoz ophthalmology award and the senior research award upon graduation from Albany Medical College.

After residency, Dr. Duke moved to the Washington area in 1989 to be near her sister and commence what should have been a cozy and well-planned life. She worked briefly with two other physicians before venturing on her own in November of 1990.

Despite a $120,000 gross, Dr. Duke's practice generates little real income. After overhead and payroll for a staff of one, taxes and FICA, insurance premiums and other assorted costs of business, Dr. Duke says she brings home around $20,000 a year.

What she needs is patients. But the patients are locked up in managed care plans. "People don't go to the phone book for their doctor anymore, they go to their participating provider directory because they don't want to go out of the plan and pay out-of-pockets," she says.

The over-supply of physicians has created a buyer's market that permits insurers and managed care companies to be choosy about who they want to include in a provider network. In terse, one-sentence form letters, payor after payor has told Dr. Duke that they don't want any more ophthalmologists in Potomac, MD.

To date, Dr. Duke has been denied admission to provider networks operated by Aetna, Cigna, Met Life, Capitol Care, and Health Plus. "I'm cut out of all of the big ones," she says. "PruCare has had me on hold for a year and a half. I haven't applied to Blue Cross-Blue Shield but I'd probably be rejected from their PPO also."

Unlike a credit report, where you are entitled to find out what marks are against you when rejected, managed care companies are not obliged to explain their reason for exclusion.

"They never tell you anything," Dr.

WHEN IS A TOWNHOUSE NOT A TOWNHOUSE? WHEN IT'S BUILT BY GOSNELL.

RIVER FALLS
Potomac's Family Community

Almost four years in the planning, River Falls' Town Estates represent a new concept in luxury living. Here, residents can enjoy the elegance, space and comfort of the finest custom homes while enjoying the ultimate luxury of freedom.

These homes are unlike anything you have ever seen before. Starting from the generous 36 foot widths and attached two-car garages to NINE foot ceilings on first floor. Add the extensive architectural detailing from the interior three-piece moldings to the exterior molded bricks. And floor plans designed to make living easy and built with pride and quality that goes into every Gosnell home.

Town Estates offer homeowners the best of all worlds. A new standard of convenient living ... the secluded natural charm and active community life of River Falls ... quick access to fine stores, entertainment, transportation and workplaces ... plus all the space and elegance of a luxury home. If you want to enjoy a new carefree lifestyle without sacrificing comfort and quality, River Falls' Town Estates were designed for you. Come see it now.

Take beltway Great Falls Exit 41 onto G.W. Pkwy. (Clara Barton) west to left at MacArthur Blvd. Go 2/10 m. to right at Brickyard Rd. Follow to model home on corner at 10400 Stable Lane.

HOURS: 12-5 daily.
PHONE: 301-299-3700.
Brokers welcome.

Why River Falls is today's best buy
- Well-established local builder since 1925
- Custom designs without the custom price
- Homes designed for family living
- Neighborhood with old-fashioned values
- Community-owned amenities
- Highly regarded public and private schools

GOSNELL INC.
Clarence W. Gosnell, Incorporated

"My grandfather taught my father and my father taught me."

...ke says. "It's like pulling teeth getting ...etter from them.

...e Black Box

If joining a panel of providers is a ...unting task, remaining in a network ...fraught with uncertainty. Most net...orks have contracts that allow the ...yor to cancel without cause with a ...day notice. With physician profiling, ...yors have the means to review prac... patterns and weed out providers ...o don't meet their yardstick — what...er it may be.

Blue Cross and Blue Shield of the ...tional Capital Area (BCBSNCA) is the ...strict of Columbia's largest health ...n, with 28% of the health insurance ...rket or nearly 1 million people. The ...ues dominates the DC market, with ...nost 500,000 federal employees ...cluding one-third of Congress) and ...ut 40% of employees at the region's ...gest employers.

In 1993, the Blues employed a physi...n profiling system called Pro/file to ...aluate the practice patterns of more ...n 5,600 physicians. The company used Pro/file to eliminate one-third of the providers in its network for Select Preferred Provider Plan, the largest PPO in the region.

BCBSNCA medical director Gregory K. Morris, MD, says Pro/file shows the cost and resource utilization of physicians compared to the distribution of practice patterns as they exist in the community. "The system we used is designed around the fact that every physician is different, and the patient mix is different," he says.

The Blues invited 66% of the providers to join Select PPP based on their "rankings relative to their peers," according to Dr. Morris. Virtually every

> "PEOPLE DON'T GO TO THE PHONE BOOK FOR THEIR DOCTOR ANYMORE, THEY GO TO THEIR PARTICIPATING PROVIDER DIRECTORY BECAUSE THEY DON'T WANT TO GO OUT OF THE PLAN AND PAY OUT-OF-POCKETS."

physician to whom an invitation was extended accepted the offer.

Exactly how Pro/file evaluates physicians is a closely held trade secret. Critics charge that the software simply identifies physicians who practice expensive medicine and fail to provide a complete picture of how a provider manages care.

"They did a scatter plot of doctors and fired those who they said were at the high end," says John Lossing, MD, a District neurologist. "It's the leading edge of irrational, unfair managed care."

Critics say that physicians who charge less are not necessarily those producing lower costs. According to BCBSNCA data, the costs for lumpectomy were compared for two sur-

---

Physicians and their immediate family members can receive preferential treatment in mortgage financing!

The AMA-Sponsored Home Mortgage Program is provided exclusively by Prudential Home Mortgage and offers Physicians special features such as:

- ☐ **Free estimate of your affordable loan amount with no obligation**
- ☐ **Low down payment programs**
- ☐ **Reduced loan origination fee**
- ☐ **Refunded appraisal cost after closing ($360 or more)**
- ☐ **Competitive rates on a wide variety of mortgage products**
- ☐ **Toll-free application process**

Just call... 1-800-443-8877
Mortgage counselors are available to assist you from 8 a.m. to midnight (Eastern time) Monday through Friday.

Prudential Home Mortgage

NETWORK OR NO WORK

> "PHYSICIANS OUGHT TO KNOW WHERE THE INFORMATION COMES FROM AND BE GIVEN A CHANCE TO RESPOND. IT OUGHT TO BE OPEN, EXPLICIT, AND SUBJECT TO REVIEW."

geons with practices at the same D.C. hospital. Surgeon "A" charged $442 for the professional fee and produced total costs of $1,908 per case, including hospital charges. Surgeon "Y" earned more, $645, but resulted in a total of $1,796 per case.

"Profiling itself doesn't tell you much about the quality of the physician, their demeanor or how they practice," says Dr. Morris. "But we decided to move ahead and use it for a number of things," including laying the groundwork for next-generation provider networks.

"What I want to do is use the same information we have regarding physician practice patterns to identify doctors for whom I would strike a deal," he explains. Physicians who accept the proposed deal would be freed from utilization review in return for continual notification to the Blues and an agreement to use case management.

"This frees the physician up to practice as they will, but allows us to track and monitor," Dr. Morris says. "As long as they continue to practice as they have in the past, it frees up my resources and gets them out from under the thumb."

The problem is that physicians have only sketchy information about what sort of patterns are acceptable. "It's totally black box. There's no clue," says Dr. Lossing. "They don't give any guidelines. They say, 'You figure it out. If you do too much, you're fired.'"

The most serious flaw to Pro/file, Dr. Lossing says, is that the methodology used in the analysis has not been publicly reviewed by peers and independently validated.

Physician profiling is "a deterrent to optimal quality of care," says Dr. Lossing. "It's the reverse of defensive medicine. In defensive medicine, doctors tend to order more scans and consults to be covered in case of a suit. The reverse of that is the fear of being fired or deselected by these managed care entities."

But Dr. Morris contends that Pro/file doesn't need to be independently validated. "WordPerfect has not been publicly validated, and they don't publicly disclose how it works. That code is proprietary, but the fact is that it works," he says. "The comments focused at the Pro/file system are in my opinion misguided because the real issue is the output, the data of the system, what kind of judgements we can make based on the data we get. There is a tremendous amount of meaningful information that comes out of this."

The Vagaries of Profiling

The use of "black box" profiling methods for network selection is inappropriate, says H. Gilbert Welch, M.D., director of the Center of Evaluative Clinical Sciences at Dartmouth Medical School.

In the March 3, 1994, issue of the New England Journal of Medicine, Dr. Welch and two co-authors described the vagaries of physician profiling in a study of more than 15,000 physicians in two states.

Dr. Welch and colleagues performed profiles of 12,720 attending physicians in Florida and 2,589 in Oregon, and found up to three-fold difference in the utilization of services in those states. Further, there were wide discrepancies in profiles within individual hospitals and within specialty groups.

Unlike "black box" analyses, Dr. Welch publicly disclosed how the profiling was conducted in the NEJM paper. "Everything is spelled out, it's in the literature," he says. "We tell them exactly what's going on."

The veil of secrecy shrouding profiling prevents physicians from appreciating, — and criticizing — the methodology used.

"Physicians ought to know where the information comes from and be given a chance to respond. It ought to be open, explicit, and subject to review. It's no fair to be judged on a report card you don't understand," Dr. Gilbert says.

"Of everything I've read about

physician profiling going on in the community, there's never been any publication describing exactly what methods are being used," he says. "It's not appearing in a place where physicians can scrutinize it."

Any Willing Provider

Relief from arbitrary and capricious provider network selection may be furnished by "any willing provider" legislation that removes barriers to physician selection.

Generally, "any willing provider" laws contain language requiring that an insurer or managed care company accept into a provider network any hospital or physician willing to accept the terms and conditions being offered.

"Any willing provider" laws are on the books in 16 states, with more expected to address this controversial issue. Proposals along these lines are invariably backed by physicians and hospitals, and hotly contested by insurers and business.

An "any willing provider" law doesn't guarantee membership on a provider panel, but it eliminates the use of "black box" statistics for selection and deselection.

The insurer or managed care company could include physician profiling as a term of its contract, giving providers the option of accepting or rejecting the condition. But theoretically, all information is above-board and in the open.

Legislation introduced in the District of Columbia last July by council member John Ray (D), the "Health Care Provider Availability Act," has been stalled in committee for months but may be acted upon in the near future.

"Any willing provider" legislation has also been proposed by Virginia lawmakers. Observers give the bill uncertain prospects during the current legislative session.

The Maryland General Assembly is considering HB 691, known as the "Health care Patient Access Act," which would allow patients to continue seeing their provider even if the

employer who sponsors the health benefit switches to a non-participating network.

"I can't even see and get paid for following up someone for whom I've lasered a hole in the retina," explains Dr. Duke. If signed into law, HB 691 would require payors to reimburse non-participating providers at the usual and customary rate paid to network physicians.

"We're willing to accept the reduced HMO or PPO fee as long as we can keep the continuity of care with our patients," Dr. Duke says. "Continuity of care is the hallmark of good medicine." **PPD**

Bruce Goldfarb is editor of Physician's Practice Digest.

The Albany Medical College
of Union University

OFFICE OF THE ASSOCIATE DEAN
THE NEIL HELLMAN MEDICAL RESEARCH BUILDING

July 30, 1984

Gregory B. Kroehl, M.D.
Department of Ophthalmology
Albany Medical College
Albany, NY 12208

RE: MARY ANN DUKE
Class of 1985

Dear Doctor Kroehl:

Mary Ann Duke is a determined, highly disciplined person. She has a clear sense of goals and purposes and a drive to achieve them. She approaches new problems forcefully, directly, and with clarity. She has great enthusiasm and high spirits.

She has her sights set on a career in Ophthalmology. She has already been involved in several research projects with members of the Department of Ophthalmology and is to be a co-author of at least one paper in the indexed literature. Her academic work in Ophthalmology has been of "Honors" caliber.

She clearly has the capacity to achieve her goals and will work very hard to that end. I am pleased to recommend her to you.

Sincerely yours,

Alan D. Miller, M.D.
Associate Dean

ADM/mvc

"Contents of this recommendation are nontransferable and cannot be released to another institution without the written consent of Ms. Duke. She has not waived right of access to this recommendation."

Professional Misconduct and Physician Discipline

Physician Information

Physician Name:	Anna Majerovics, MD
Address:	4 Old English Road Slingerlands, New York 12159
License Number:	161263
License Type:	MD
Year of Birth:	1955
Effective Date:	06/15/2002
Action:	license suspension for no less than four months and until proven fit to practice. The suspension was stayed June 15, 2002 and the physician was placed on probation for five years.
Misconduct Description:	This is a modification of the December 31, 1999 order where the physician did not contest the charge of fraudulently practicing medicine. This order stays the suspension and places the physician on probation for five years.
License Restrictions:	During the period of probation the physician may only practice medicine when her practice is supervised by an independent physician who is on-site and in a position to oversee and assess her practice on a daily basis. The physician's practice of medicine during the first six months is limited to 4-5 hours per week after which the physician's practice may be increased to 8-10 hours per week. The physician is also prohibited from prescribing any medications for herself or for family members and during the first year of probation the physician may not prescribe any controlled substances. During the period of probation the physician must refrain from the use of drugs and alcohol and must have a designated individual who oversees her compliance. The physician must also engage in mental health therapy and have a therapist who evaluates her progress and compliance with therapeutic recommendations.
Board Order:	lc161263.pdf lc161263.pdf

Return to Professional Misconduct and Professional Discipline
Return to Welcome Page

Send questions or comments to:
opmc@health.state.ny.us

Home Page / From the Commissioner / Directory Services / Vital Records /
Info for Consumers / Info for Providers / Info for Researchers /
Public Health Forum / What's New / HELP! / Search our Web Site

(I liked these two doctors when I trained under them during my ophthalmology residency.)

Physician Search
By Physician
By License Number
By License Type
By Effective Date

Professional Misconduct and Physician Discipline

Physician Information

Physician Name: Howard Leon Tanenbaum, MD
Address: Center For Sight
349 Northern Boulevard
Albany, New York 12204
License Number: 158307
License Type: MD
Year of Birth: 1935
Effective Date: 06/29/2000
Action: License limited precluding the physician from prescribing medications to family members and $5,000 fine.
Misconduct Description: The physician admitted to the charge of failing to maintain accurate patient records.
License Restrictions: The physician's license is permanently limited prohibiting the physician from prescribing medications for family members.
Board Order:

lc158307.pdf

Return to Professional Misconduct and Professional Discipline
Return to Welcome Page

Send questions or comments to:
opmc@health.state.ny.us

Home Page / From the Commissioner / Directory Services / Vital Records /
Info for Consumers / Info for Providers / Info for Researchers /
Public Health Forum / What's New / HELP! / Search our Web Site

Sept. 2, 2002.

My dearest,

I am so sorry for my obscene/distraught behavior the other night—my heart is heavy for all those things I shouted at you, which I did not mean. I know that gave you so much hurt and anguish.

Thank you for talking to me---I had no idea that you were taking any medications from your internist, and that when mixed, would have such an adverse effect on you--I could not understand what had happened. However, it does not atone for my appalling behaviour where I was yelling and accusing you of all sorts of things. I was very distraught and did not understand that you were having a drug reaction, especially in your weakened post-part condition. I know that I threatened many things, but believe, in my heart, I did and do not mean them. I was trying to shock you to gain some sense of perspective. Believe me, no one was more shocked than I to see the police at the door, as I still cannot believe that somehow I (must be me?) dialed them! I feel so badly of falsely accusing you of anything when you were actually very ill.

I know that you are an excellent, wonderful and caring mother—I have known and watched you for more that 14 months and you are the mother of our precious baby daughter, Isabelle. I have also watched you take incredible care of your other three children, more so with the terrible stress and pain you have all been through—I should have remembered that the other night! Your professionalism and caring did not deserve the disrespect that I gave you the other night. It will never happen again.

I love you dearly and pray that we can move forward—please forgive me.

All my love,

[signature]
xm

(Eloise's father)

WASHINGTON PSYCHIATRIC CENTER
Alen J. Salerian, M.D.
Medical Director

MEDICAL REPORT

PATIENT NAME: DUKE, MARY N.
HOSPITAL NUMBER: 0
PSYCHIATRIST: Alen J. Salerian, M.D.
UNIT:
DATE OF ADMISSION:

Mary N. Duke is a 41-year-old mother of four children, ophthalmologist, who is currently a patient under my care.

On August 31, 2002, Dr. Duke had an unusual drug reaction to Ambien, Flexeril, Klonopin, and Celexa prescribed by her primary care physician, Michael Anchors, M.D. All of those medications were prescribed for her mild mood disorder, which she experienced after the birth of her daughter.

I carefully reviewed Dr. Duke's medications, obtained all the relevant details from her, and came to the conclusion that the particular combination of her medications caused her to experience a period of amnesia, agitation, and irritability on August 31, 2002.

As of today, September 16, 2002, Dr. Duke is free of any adverse affects of any medications, medically and psychologically stable, and able to perform her duties as a physician. Her judgment and mood and cognitive functions are excellent. There is no impairment in her abilities as a mother. I will continue to see Dr. Duke for follow-up treatment to ensure that she fully recovers from her drug reaction.

If there are any questions regarding her medical status, do not hesitate to call me at 202-885-5634.

Alen J. Salerian, M.D.
PSYCHIATRIST
Diplomate of The American Board of Forensic Medicine

DATE: Sep 17 '02

406/OTI:P10/079/4045
D: 09/16/02
T: 09/16/02

1228 Wisconsin Ave., N.W. - Washington, DC 20016 - Phone:202-885-5634 - Fax: 202-885-5643

Washington Psychiatric Center

Alen J. Salerian, M.D., P.C.
Medical Director

October 8, 2002

Phoebe Shih
Child Protective Services
1301 Piccard Drive
Rockville, MD 20850
Fax: 240-777-3557

Dear Ms. Shih:

Per our conversation today, I am writing to provide follow-up information on Mrs. Marianne Duke.

Once again, I want to confirm that I have been following her psychiatrically and I am confident that she is psychologically stable and compliant with our treatment guidelines.

Her drug urines done at Shady Grove Hospital were essentially negative for foreign substances including amphetamines, cocaine, LSD, PCP and so on.

It is my opinion that whatever reaction she had medically a couple of weeks ago which resulted in some confusion and disorientation, resolved itself. She continues to have problems with occasional insomnia, which is most likely a complication of her postpartum period. I am treating her mood instability and insomnia problem with Ambien and Lorazepam.

Overall, I am very pleased with her compliance with treatment guidelines and the fact that all her symptoms are fully resolved without any residual effects of emotional or cognitive impairment. From a medical/psychiatric perspective, I do not see any need or justification for any supervision of her duties as a mother. Therefore, I am most comfortable with the recommendation that she does not need any administrative supervision. If there are any questions regarding her medical or psychiatric care, please do not hesitate to call me at 202-244-9000.

Sincerely yours,

Alen J. Salerian M.D.
Diplomat, Forensic Medical Examiners
Medical Director, Washington Psychiatric Center

Cc: MaryAnn Duke, M.D

Dr. William F. Minogue
Senior Vice President,
Medical Affairs
Suburban Hospital
8600 Old Georgetown Rd.,
Bethesda, MD 20814

Oct. 30, '02

Dear Dr. Minogue:

I am writing to you concerning cataract surgery on my left eye performed by Dr. Mary Ann Duke on Sept. 9, '02 at Suburban Hospital.

From conversations that I have had with Dr. Duke, I understand that there has been some criticism of how she conducted the operation. As the principal party involved, I wish to say that those are not my feelings on the matter. As far as I am concerned, the operation was carried out in a thoroughly professional manner. I experienced minimal pain and discomfort and received maximal care from Dr. Duke, both at the hospital and in post-operative treatment. I have made a complete recovery.

If you need further testimony, please feel free to contact me.

Sincerely,

Lawrence S. House
706 Midland Rd.
Silver Spring, MD
20904

cc: Dr. Mary Ann Duke

8600 Old Georgetown Road
Bethesda, Maryland 20814
(301) 896-3100

December 23, 2002

Mary A. Duke, MD
10220 Democracy Blvd
Potomac, MD 20854

Dear Dr. Duke:

It is a pleasure to inform you that the Board of Trustees has approved your reappointment to the Medical Staff of Suburban Hospital for the 2003- 2004 term. Your current status is Active in Ophthalmology.

Your delineation of privileges was approved with the changes noted.

I look forward to your continued association with Suburban Hospital.

Sincerely,

Brian A. Gragnolati
President and CEO

BAG/ecc
Enclosure: Copy of approved delineation of privileges

NAME: DUKE, MARY
ACCT # 028713824   MR # 1558740
AGE: 41
EXAM DATE: 05/04/2003
LOCATION: ER   STATUS: REG ER
DOCTOR: RANDOLPH, FREDERICK W
SUBURBAN HOSPITAL DEPT OF RADIOLOGY

RE: 000590474 WRIST 3 VIEWS (L)

CLINICAL HISTORY: The patient is a 41-year-old female with a history of left wrist injury.

FINDINGS: The bones of the left wrist appear mildly osteopenic. No acute fracture or subluxation is seen. Mild degenerative changes are noted in the carpometacarpal articulations.

INTERPRETATION: MILD DEGENERATIVE CHANGE AND MINIMAL DIFFUSE OSTEOPENIA. NO EVIDENCE OF ACUTE FRACTURE OR SUBLUXATION IN THE LEFT WRIST.

(My missed broken wrist.)

05/04/03

** REPORT SIGNITURE ON FILE 05/04/2003 **
REPORTED BY: H.HANNAH KIM, M.D. (ES)
SIGNED BY: KIM, H HANNA

05/04/2003
MDI/DB   BATCH NO:

Phone 301-294-1122   Fax 301-294-2239
14915 Broschart Road • Suite 104 • Rockville, Maryland 20850
www.imagimed.com

DUKE, Mary
DOB: 06/06/61
Referred by: William Wolf, M.D.

05/20/03: MRI EXAMINATION OF THE LEFT WRIST:

A high resolution magnetic resonance imaging examination of the left wrist was performed. Images were acquired in the sagittal, axial, and coronal planes. Both spin-echo and inversion recovery sequences were employed.

Examination of the left wrist reveals a nondisplaced fracture of the radial styloid. There is edema in the distal radius and within the radial styloid fragment, as well as within the surrounding soft tissues. There is probably some bony resorption that has occurred about the fracture fragments. There is no evidence of an accompanying intracarpal or dorsal or volar radiocarpal ligamentous injury. The triangular fibrocartilage complex does appear to be intact. There is no evidence of tendinopathy.

IMPRESSION:

1. There is a <u>subacute nondisplaced fracture</u> of the radial styloid. Please see comments. *(Positive for fract)*
2. There is no evidence of ligamentous injury.
3. The triangular fibrocartilage complex is intact.

Timothy J. Greenan, M.D./tl/052103

The Health Information contained in this FAX/Report is **Highly Confidential**. It is intended for the exclusive use of the addressee. It is to be used only to aid in providing specific healthcare services to this patient. Any other use is a violation of **Federal Law (HIPAA)** and will be reported as such.

TIMOTHY J. GREENAN, M.D., MEDICAL DIRECTOR

ACCREDITED BY AMERICAN COLLEGE OF RADIOLOGY

MARY ANN DUKE, M.D.
EYE PHYSICIAN & SURGEON

299-7107

10220 DEMOCRACY BLVD.
POTOMAC, MD 20854

June 24, 2003

Luz Sandoval-Shewell, LGSW
Child Welfare Services
7300 Calhoun Pl., Suite 400
Derwood, MD 20855

Dear Ms. Sandoval-Shewell:

I was baffled by the tone and the nature of your phone call earlier today. I was particularly puzzled by your verbal threats of "I will take you to court and you will lose everything; your children, your home and your practice".

As a loving mother and dedicated physician, I am deeply concerned whether your statements actually represent the views of the Child Welfare Services.

My point, however, is to reassure you that I am a caring and loving and competent mother. In fact, I am grateful that the state is so carefully taking measures to provide a safe and healthy environment for every child.

I spoke with my attorney and my physician. They were both troubled by your comments, yet Dr. Salerian is most anxious to provide a detailed psychological/medical report about my mental state, but he is kindly requesting that you fax him at 202-244-6610 an appropriate request clarifying the relevant questions. I have the greatest trust and confidence in Dr. Salerian's professionalism, as he has been the former Chief Psychiatric Consultant to the FBI, is a faculty member at George Washington University, and is the Medical Director of a highly respected psychiatric center in Washington, D.C., specializing in the treatment of psychiatric and substance abuse disorders.

Also, a final and absolute demand is that you not speak with my ex-husband about any of my alleged problems. Doing so would be a serious violation of my privacy.

Sincerely,

Mary Ann Duke, M.D.

Cc Alen J. Salerian, M.D.
    Melvin G. Bergman, Esq.

DEPARTMENT OF HEALTH AND HUMAN SERVICES

Douglas M. Duncan
County Executive

June 27, 2003

Charles L. Short
Director

Dr. Alen J. Salerian
Washington Center for Psychiatry
Washington, DC 20015
Phone: 202-244-9000
Fax: 202-244-6610

Dr. Alen Salerian:

I am a social worker with Child Protective Services in Montgomery County, Maryland.

Dr. Duke, as I understand, is your client. For the purposes of my investigation, Dr. Duke has given me authorization to contact you and obtain information related to her treatment. Her letter of authorization will accompany this fax.

As you are aware, I am under ethical and professional responsibility to assess and determine whether children have been harmed or are at risk of harm while in the care of their parents and or caregivers.

Dr. Duke has indicated that you are treating her for psychiatric as well as substance abuse issues. The Department is requesting the following information:

- What is Dr. Duke in treatment for?
- Does Dr. Duke receive treatment for substance abuse through you? If so, what is the treatment plan?
- How long has she been in treatment?
- With what frequency does she get drug/alcohol tested? What have been the results of the tests?
- What is Dr. Duke's level of compliance with the treatment plan or program?
- What is her diagnosis?
- Is she attending group therapy? If so, whom with and how often?

I would like to thank you in advance for your time and prompt attention to this matter. If you have any questions, please do not hesitate to call me. My number is 240-777-1032. My office fax number is 240-777-3409.

Respectfully,

Luz A. Sandoval, LGSW
Child Protective Services
Child Welfare Services

Children, Youth and Family Services • Child Welfare Services
1301 Piccard Drive, Fourth Floor • Rockville, Maryland 20850 • 240/777-3500, TTY 240/777-3556, FAX 240/777-3534

Medical and Chirurgical Faculty of Maryland

**PHYSICIAN REHABILITATION PROGRAM\\
PROGRESS NOTE - First meeting**

Mary Ann Duke, M.D.
August 18, 2003

This was an initial meeting with this 42-year-old, Caucasian female ophthalmologist who was originally referred to the PRP in October of 2002 following reports of her smelling of alcohol in the OR of Suburban hospital. At that time, there was no concrete evidence present to support the notion that the physician had a pervasive substance abuse problem. The case was closed in December 2002 barring no further problems. In June, 2003, a caller from a governmental agency called to anonymously report that this physician had been investigated by this agency due to being found "passed out drunk" with her nine month old child. The agency worker also reported that the physician had been taken to Suburban's ER by police "drunk out of her mind," but that colleagues covered up for her. A Montgomery County police officer, Officer Todd Bond, also called the PRP to report that he had been to the physician's home on five occasions in the last two years. He said that Child Protective Services had been called three times. He reports to have seen the physician "drunk" and believes she has a real problem. The PRP sent two concern letters via registered mail to the physician during the months of June and July but she did not respond until the last week of July. At the time of her call, she was in her psychiatrist's office and became increasingly angered as we discussed the situation. She finally agreed to meet but delayed the meeting for several days.

This physician arrived on time accompanied by her boyfriend's father whom she referred to as her "mentor." The physician met with this writer and Dr. Stanley Platman. The physician wanted to see her chart and what records were received by the PRP before she shared her story. She denied having a substance abuse problem but did admit to "drinking too much" the day in May that the police were called to her home. She reported that she had been outside weeding her yard earlier in the day and had too much to drink without eating anything. She said she and her boyfriend had just had a horrendous fight. She had gotten out of the shower and realized her boyfriend was not home. She apparently called the police who handcuffed her while she was nude and took her to the emergency room. She stated that her arm was broken during this episode but was released without ex-ray or treatment. She could not recall how much she actually had to drink that day.

The physician reported that she has recently been under the care of a psychiatrist, Dr. Alen Salerian, in Washington, D.C. She said she has known him and his wife for some time and trusts him. She stated that she has been prescribed Topamax, 25 mg and Klonopin, prn. She was not clear what the Topomax was prescribed for but thought it was to help her with stress and to relax. She also repeatedly referred to the day of the interview as Friday when in fact it was on a Monday. She states that she had an old prescription of valium from her internist which she has been taking and therefore had not yet filled the prescription for the klonopin. She denies having a drug or alcohol problem.

Mary Ann Duke, M.D.
Page 2

She and her mentor discussed the problems she has faced with her ex-husband. She stated that she also has been going through various conflicts with her current boyfriend who is the father of her youngest daughter. She reported that while married to her ex-husband, he regularly assaulted her by spitting at her and shoving her. She stated that the police never did anything about her reports. She indicated that her ex-husband had a drinking problem. Currently, she says that she is getting treatment for stress and depression due to the divorce and child support payment battles. She said that her ex-husband instructed her seven year old son to call 911 if he ever found his mother asleep on the couch. This explains why the police were called and she was found asleep with her nine month daughter. The physician indicated that she had fallen asleep on the couch after drinking a glass of wine but denied that her nine month old was in danger due to the fact that her home is "baby proofed" and that by appearance alone, she is doing very well. Overall, her explanation was that her children were fine, she is a good mother and that she is working very hard to raise them in spite of her ex-husband who "only wanted her for a green card."

The physician agreed to sign a contract but balked several times at the length of the contract and the urine screen protocol. She refused to submit one at the time of the interview because she was suffering from diarrhea. It was agreed that further information would be collected, including a possible separate evaluation and information from her treating psychiatrist. She would sign the monitor agreement once that information was collected.

Elaine Gisriel, MS
Physician Rehabilitation Advocate

Medical and Chirurgical Faculty of Maryland

Physician Rehabilitation Committee

September 3, 2003

Mary Ann Duke, M.D.
10220 Democracy Blvd.
Potomac, MD 20854

PERSONAL AND CONFIDENTIAL
Via Certified Mail

Dear Dr. Duke:

This letter is to confirm your appointment with Dr. Ellen McDaniel on September 18, 2003. Dr. McDaniel has not received any historical information regarding your case. Enclosed, please find a release of information so that once your initial interview is complete, Dr. McDaniel may receive additional information to complete her evaluation. Please be advised that if there is information provided after your initial interview that requires a follow-up visit, you will be expected to meet with her again and cover the cost of any additional meetings. Please sign the release and return to my attention. *(I have to pay for and see the psychiatrist of their choosing.)*

If you have any questions or concerns pertaining to this matter, please feel free to call Dr. Stanley Platman at his office, 410-554-6601 or at his home number, 410-889-2758. I look forward to meeting with you again once the evaluation process is complete.

Sincerely,

Elaine Gisriel

Elaine Gisriel, MS
Physician Rehabilitation Advocate

enclosure

CC: Dr. Stanley Platman
     Dr. Ellen McDaniel

The Physician Rehabilitation Committee of The Maryland State Medical Society
1202 Maryland Avenue, Second Floor, Baltimore, Maryland 21201
(410) 962-5580 TOLL FREE 1-800-992-7010 FAX (410) 962-5583

Medical and Chirurgical Faculty of Maryland

Physician Rehabilitation Committee

September 16, 2003

Ellen McDaniel, M.D.
P.O. Box 100
13032 Highland Road
Highland, MD 20777

PRIVILEGED AND CONFIDENTIAL
Re: Mary Ann Duke, M.D.

Dear Dr. McDaniel:

Dr. Mary Ann Duke is seeking the support and advocacy of the Physician Rehabilitation Program (PRP) of MedChi, the Maryland State Medical Society. To assist us in this endeavor, we are referring her to you for an evaluation.

Dr. Duke has been referred to the PRP on two occasions. The first was last October (2002) when she was referred by Suburban Hospital's Vice President of Medical Affairs due to complaints that she smelled of alcohol in the Operating Room. Dr. Duke is an Ophthalmologist and has privileges at Suburban Hospital. These complaints were filed by OR staff, however, no BAL testing was completed. Dr. William Minogue reported during the original referral call that he had interviewed the Ophthalmology and Anesthesia departments at the hospital following the complaint that she smelled of alcohol in the OR. He stated that he learned of chronic problems with this physician including reports of impaired speech, tremor, irritability and rumors that she was involved in a divorce due to drinking. However, Dr. Duke stated that none of these concerns were shared with her when she met with Dr. Minogue and was in fact reassured by him that the issue was resolved. The PRP sent Dr. Duke a letter of concern, to which she responded and was interviewed by PRP Director, Michael Llufrio. Collateral information was collected by her boyfriend. At that time, there was no concrete evidence present to support the notion that she had a pervasive substance abuse problem Therefore, the case was closed pending further reports or problems.

In June, 2003, an anonymous caller reported that this physician had been investigated for reports of drinking abusively and having the police called to her house. The caller also reported that the physician had been taken to Suburban's ER by police but, "colleagues covered up for her." Montgomery County Police also confirmed that they had been called this physician's home. The PRP sent two concern letters via registered mail to the physician during the months of June and July but she did not respond until the last week of July. She contacted the PRP from her psychiatrist's office and sounded increasingly angry as we discussed the situation. She finally agreed to meet with PRP staff but was unable to clear her schedule for almost three weeks.

Mary Ann Duke, Page 2

Dr. Duke arrived on time accompanied by her boyfriend's father whom she referred to as her "mentor." She initially appeared nervous during the interview and reported to be suffering from an intestinal problem. The physician wanted to see her chart and what records were received by the PRP before she shared her story. She denied having a substance abuse problem but did admit to "drinking too much" the day in May that the police were called to her home. She reported that she had been outside weeding her yard earlier in the day and had too much to drink without eating anything. She said she and her boyfriend had just had a horrendous fight. She had gotten out of the shower and realized her boyfriend was not home. She stated that she called the police who handcuffed her while she was nude and took her to the emergency room. She stated that her arm was broken during this episode but was released without ex-ray or treatment. She could not recall how much she actually had to drink before this incident.

The physician reported that she has recently been under the care of a psychiatrist, Dr. Alen Salerian, in Washington, D.C. She said she has known him and his wife for some time and trusts him. She stated that she has been prescribed Topamax, 25 mg and Klonopin, prn. She was not clear what the Topomax was prescribed for but thought it was to help her with her stress and to relax. She states that she had an old prescription of valium from her internist which she has been taking and therefore had not yet filled the prescription for the klonopin. She denies having a drug or alcohol problem.

With the support of her mentor, also her baby's grandfather, she focused on the problems she has faced with her ex-husband. However, she also admits to having various conflicts with her current boyfriend who is the father of her youngest daughter. She reported that while married to her ex-husband, he regularly assaulted her by spitting at her and shoving her. She stated that the police never did anything about her reports. She indicated that her ex-husband had a drinking problem. During her interview with Mr. Llufrio in October 2002, she reported her marriage ended due to his infidelity.

Currently, Dr. Duke is receiving treatment for stress and depression due to the divorce and child support payment battles. She said that her ex-husband has instructed her seven-year-old son to call 911 if he ever found his mother asleep on the couch. The physician indicated that when the Department of Social Services visited her home, she had fallen asleep on the couch after drinking a glass of wine but denied that her nine month old was in danger due to the fact that her home is "baby proofed." Overall, her explanation was that her children were fine, she is a good mother and that she is working very hard to raise them in spite of her ex-husband who "only wanted her for a green card." She believes the Social Services worker is over zealous and she has been treated unfairly.

The physician agreed to sign an Advocacy Contract with the PRP but balked several times at the length of the contract and the urine screen protocol. She refused to submit a urine test at the time of the interview because she was suffering from diarrhea.

At this time, we are referring Dr. Duke to you for an evaluation. Typical concerns for your consideration in evaluating this individual should include:

- *Does there exist and/or what is the extent of any psychiatric, chemical dependence or organic problem?*
- *Does any additional (overt or underlying) pathology exist, significant or relevant to this case?*
- *What additional assessments might be needed for clarification of diagnostic issues (neuropsych or psychological testing, personality batteries, a physical exam, etc.)?*
- *What are your treatment or referral recommendations?*

Mary Ann Duke - Page 3

- If a problem is identified, what may be the impact of the problem on the physician/participant's judgement and ability to perform as a physician?

Dr. Duke has given me his permission to relay this information to you for the purposes of the evaluation. A copy of the release to disclose confidential information is enclosed. If you have any questions or concerns, please contact me at 1-800-992-7010. Thank you for your assistance in this matter. Please send your bill along with a copy of your evaluation to the Physician Rehabilitation Program.

Sincerely,

Elaine Gisriel, M.S.
Physician Rehabilitation Advocate

MARY ANN DUKE, M.D.
EYE PHYSICIAN & SURGEON

10220 DEMOCRACY BLVD.
POTOMAC, MD 20854

September 16, 2003

Elaine. M. Gisriel, M.S.
1202 Maryland Avenue, 2nd floor
Baltimore, MD 21201

Dear Ms. Gisriel,

    I am trying so hard to be cooperative. Please believe that I want to do whatever it is that you and Dr. Platman want me to do to get this resolved. I believe that Dr. Platman and I must just have had a little miscommunication on the phone last week. I simply asked to see my file before it was sent anywhere else. Dr. McDaniel was absolutely fine with meeting with me before she saw my file. Like a patient requests a file from me, may I please have a copy of my file from your office. I am very aware that there may be a small fee for it just like there is in my office. To make life a little simpler on you, Ms. Gisriel, I changed the name on the form that you sent to me yesterday and faxed it back to you. I can give to you a credit card number if you would like. Please let me know. I am meeting with Dr. McDaniel on Thursday.

Sincerely,

Mary Ann Duke, M.D.

MARY ANN DUKE, M.D.
EYE PHYSICIAN & SURGEON

01-299-7107

10220 DEMOCRACY BLVD.
POTOMAC, MD 20854

September 22, 2003

Elaine M. Gisriel, M.S.
Physician Rehabilitation Advocate
1202 Maryland Avenue, 2nd floor
Baltimore, MD 21201

RECEIVED
SEP 26 2003

Dear Ms. Gisriel,

Dr. Ellen McDaniel and I met on Thursday, September 18th, as scheduled. That evening we all lost power. I spent the last four days " camping out ". You probably did too. I just got power back yesterday. I was going to call you today, but thought that it would be easier for you and I and Dr. Platman if I just put the facts in writing. Please believe me that it is definitely my wish to resolve this issue in everyone's best interest as soon as possible.

In all fairness to your letter writing and to mine and to what is ultimately sent fairly to Dr. McDaniel, I am responding to your letter to her as I have some grave concerns as to the truthfulness of its content. I am not criticizing you negatively, Ms. Gisriel, because you barely know me; however, this entire situation has an impact on me that I feel is not fair, so I must be fair to myself and my family and respond in detail.

Dr. William Minogue met with Mr. Desmond ffrench-Mullen and myself last October, 2002 and all he did was apologize for what Suburban Hospital had done to me. He had a two sentence complaint signed by some of the O.R. staff whose names were whited out, that read, " Dr. Duke arrived in the O.R. Her breath smelled like alcohol". There was nothing written of I quote your letter, " impaired speech, tremor, irritability, and rumors that she was involved in a divorce due to drinking". What is your basis for writing this to Dr. McDaniel? I find this description by you in gross error and in fact deformation of my character. It is false. I have enclosed a copy of my first patient's letter to Dr. Minogue. You already have this letter, but I just wanted to reiterate that I kissed Mr. House on the cheek before I started his cataract surgery. I am quite sure that Mr. House would <u>never</u> have let me operate on him if he smelled alcohol on my breath, and I did <u>not</u> have a mask on when I kissed him.

Of great import also is Suburban should have sent me immediately to the E.R. for a blood alcohol level which I would have happily agreed to. How to they have concerns that a Physician is impaired and let them operate two cases in a row? They owed me an apology and that is exactly what DR. Minogue did in front of Mr. ffrench-Mullen and on tape. This PRP referral should never be sent to DR. McDaniel as it was an error by Suburban Hospital. I have enclosed numerous pages which will not make a whole lot of sense to you as they are in Norwegian, but they prove that my ex-husband had a tremendous amount of debt to the Bank of Norway when I married him. He did not tell me about this debt. It was the equivalent of 155,000.00$ U.S. I found out about it on my honeymoon. Not that you really care, but I am a good old, little religious girl from a small town in upstate New York and my parents would have guilt-tripped me to death if I got a divorce 3 months after I got married, so I bailed him out. I took on his debt on top of the debt that I had of my own,(approx. 70,000.00$), and worked my a__ off starting a practice on my own. I told all of this to DR. McDaniel. For the record, <u>I am divorced</u>,because I no longer could be sugar momma to a lying,cheating no good husband who went out with my best friend. He also asked for me back. He said quote, " This isn't what I want." I replied, " You asked for it. You got it. Toyota." I will send to you a copy of the P.I. investigations if you need proof that he cheated on me.

Please refer to Mr. Llufrio's letter dated October 4, 2002. I quote, " Her question as to why she was suspected of drinking prior to surgery and no one intervened is a good one. However, there are certain aspects of her personality that would easily be seen as arrogance. This could make her a target, or at least unpopular with some." He summed me up pretty well. God blessed me with a lot of strong attributes for which I am thankful, and for which many people are very jealous.

May 3, 2003 was an isolated, horrendous day. As you wrote, I had not eaten, worked all day in the yard, (my older children were at their Father's), and I had a horrendous argument with my boyfriend. Nobody " covered up " for me. I called 911 myself. It was a Saturday night. The police did not allow me the dignity to put a robe on. They completely humiliated me and denegrated me. Why do not we ask Officer Todd Bond how rough he was with me that he indeed broke my radius and calcaneus bones? Please stand corrected in paragraph four. My left arm was in severe pain in the emergency room at Suburban Hospital. I insisted on an X-ray. I was crying I was in so much pain. They finally did an X-ray at approximately 3;30 a.m. I have a copy of it which I showed to Dr. McDaniel. She saw the break in the radius. <u>Suburban Hospital sent me home with an untreated fracture</u>. I was in a great deal of pain over the next six weeks. At the three week point I had an M.R.I. and obtained a cast. I took so much Motrin that I developed purpura all over my body and had to see my Internist. He said I can no longer take Motrin. My platelet count was down a little.

In the midst of all this, the social worker comes to my house and interviews my boyfriend and I and says everything is all right. Then she goes back to her office and calls me on June 24, 2003 and threatens to ruin my life. Please see her enclosed letter.

Of final note, I do not know any woman who works harder than I. I do not have live-in help. My Nanny likes to leave on time. Literally, I run in the house after office hours, pick up the baby, and start my evening job of being a single Mom. If I have to say so myself, I am doing a very wonderful job. My divorce has definitely been a living hell. I do not wish it on anyone. I wonder how many times Officer Bond was here when I called him when my husband spit at me? My attorney's fees are abyssmal. I have no time to myself. Now you want me to pay at least 65.00$ per/week for four years to find nothing, to punish me more for May third. I have never been sued. I have <u>never</u>, <u>ever</u> <u>compromised</u> any patient in any way whatsoever.

I do not have a substance abuse problem. As previously stated, I would like to resolve this issue as soon as possible. You wrote in your third paragraph, Ms. Gisriel, that I did not respond until your third letter. That is true. My office manager was on vacation for two weeks in June/July and I do not think that I opened mail for two weeks. You did not seem to believe me on the phone but that happens a lot. Then I take a day off from work and open it all at once. If I recall, it was not only my schedule that allowed us not to meet for three weeks. I believe it was a combination of your's, Dr. Platman's, and mine that allowed us not to meet. I am not trying to give you a hard time, Ms. Gisriel, I just want to be treated fairly. Obviously, I do not think I have been given a fair shake.

Sincerely,

Mary Ann Duke, M.D.

cc. Dr. Stanley R. Platman

MARY ANN DUKE, M.D.

EYE PHYSICIAN & SURGEON

299-7107

10220 DEMOCRACY BLVD.
POTOMAC, MD 20854

Stanley R. Platman, M.D.
1202 Maryland Avenue, Second Floor
Baltimore, MD 21201

OCT - 6

October 3, 2003

Dear Doctor Platman:

I am in receipt today of Ms. Elaine Gisriel's letter dated September 18, 2003. I am astonished that you are allowing her to send a letter that does not tell the truth. Please re-read the letter I sent to you last week. In all fairness to everyone involved, I cannot sign a release to Dr. McDaniel that does not portray the truth.

Not only does Ms. Gisriel's letter liabilize me but it also includes hearsay which deformates my character. I find her statements legally and personally very damaging and insulting, and most importantly not truthful.

The entire first page of her letter dealing with Suburban Hospital in October of 2002 should be completely omitted as I have, on tape from Dr. Minogue, a complete and total apology of their wrongdoing. Mr. ffrench-Mullen was present when I met with Dr. Minogue, as he was present when I met with Mr. Llufrio, you and Ms. Gisriel. The liabilizing and false statements in Ms. Gisriel's letter also gravely concerned Mr. Desmond ffrench-Mullen. Suburban Hospital had no business sending me to you in October of 2002 since they had absolutely no proof and were simply on a witch-hunt. To reiterate my point, Dr. Minogue, who was the Medical Director at the time, profusely apologized to me in front of Mr. ffrench-Mullen on tape.

I am confident, Dr. Platman, that if you were in my shoes you would feel exactly as I do.

Ms. Gisriel also writes that my divorce occurred because of "drinking". If she had been in court with me all day yesterday, she would completely understand why I am no longer married to my lying, cheating spouse. I find her hearsay basically in deformation of my fine character. Ms. Gisriel writes, "that I may want to send Dr. McDaniel a letter of rebuttal". What is most pertinent here, is that Ms. Gisriel send her the written truth in the first place. I refuse to allow her to liabilize me.

Indeed, both Mr. ffrench-Mullen and I remember telling you and Ms. Gisriel that I insisted on an x-ray at Suburban Hospital. I had an x-ray there that night of which I have a copy. Suburban Hospital sent me home with an untreated broken arm in two places. I later received treatment and an MRI as I was in so much pain. Please refer to my previous letter.

I will be most happy to sign the release to Dr. McDaniel by the deadline of October 13, 2003, after Ms. Gisriel writes the truth and sends me a corrected letter.

Sincerely,

Mary Ann Duke, M.D.

Cc Elaine Gisriel, MS

Phone 301-294-1122 Fax 301-294-2239
14915 Broschart Road • Suite 104 • Rockville, Maryland 20850
www.imagimed.com

DUKE, Mary Ann
DOB: 06/06/61
Referred by: Anchors, M.D., Michael

10/24/03: MRI EXAMINATION OF THE LUMBAR SPINE:

A magnetic resonance imaging examination of the lumbosacral spine was performed. Images were acquired in the sagittal and transaxial planes.

There is a prominent S1-S2 segment. At L5-S1, there is discogenic disease, a diffuse posterior disc bulge and a central subligamentous HNP impressing on the ventral aspect of the thecal sac without definite lateralization. The remaining disc spaces of the lumbosacral spine are otherwise unremarkable. There is no central canal spinal stenosis. There is no neural foraminal stenosis. The conus medullaris appears unremarkable.

IMPRESSION:

NOTE: There is a prominent S1-S2 disc space.

1. There is discogenic disease, a diffuse posterior disc bulge and a central subligamentous HNP at L5-S1, impressing on the ventral aspect of the thecal sac without definite lateralization.

Timothy J. Greenan, M.D./cm/102703

The Health Information contained in this FAX/Report is **Highly Confidential**. It is intended for the exclusive use of the addressee. It is to be used only to aid in providing specific healthcare services to this patient. Any other use is a violation of Federal Law (HIPAA) and will be reported as such.

TIMOTHY J. GREENAN, M.D., MEDICAL DIRECTOR

ACCREDITED BY AMERICAN COLLEGE OF RADIOLOGY

MARY ANN DUKE, M.D.
EYE PHYSICIAN & SURGEON

301-299-7107

10220 DEMOCRACY BLVD
POTOMAC, MD 20854

October 28, 2003

Estelita Dimaculangan has been my nanny for almost 5 years. She works 8am to 6pm, Monday through Friday. Her sister, a trained nurse, named Juliet Gueverra, is willing to be my live-in nanny after her sister leaves, and on weekends. She can start immediately,

Sincerely,

Mary Ann Duke

Witness:
Estelita B. Dimaculangan
Juliet B. Guevarra

THE WILMER OPHTHALMOLOGICAL INSTITUTE
THE JOHNS HOPKINS UNIVERSITY SCHOOL OF MEDICINE
THE JOHNS HOPKINS HOSPITAL

Carolyn H. Dunn
Credentials Coordinator
Administrative Project Coordinator

Wilmer Bldg 1st Floor
600 North Wolfe St.
Baltimore, Maryland 21287
(410) 955-2830
FAX (410) 502-3229

October 31, 2003

To Whom It May Concern:

Re: Mary Ann Duke

Mary Ann Duke was appointed as Active Staff by Johns Hopkins Health Care LLC in September 1998 to enable her to treat patients an the Wilmer Eye Institute at Green Spring Station, an ambulatory surgery center. Her practice was limited to refractive surgery procedures.

Her appointment as Active Staff at Johns Hopkins Hospital has been approved for the period of October 16, 2003 through May 31, 2005 with full requested privileges at any Johns Hopkins Hospital site.

Carolyn H. Dunn
Credentials Coordinator

DEA # AS8929535

BERNARD STOPAK, M.D., P.A.
NEUROLOGICAL SURGERY
5454 WISCONSIN AVENUE • SUITE 840
CHEVY CHASE, MD 20815
301-652-6621

NAME: MARY DUKE MD

ADDRESS: _____ DATE: 11/11/03

℞ (Please Print)

a 60 yr pt harboring a ruptured disc at the L5 S1 level is appropriately taking Vicoprofen for pain & Ambien for sleep. These medications are appropriate for her care at this time.

REFILL _____ TIMES   PRN   NR

_____ M.D.

TO INSURE BRAND NAME DISPENSING, PRESCRIBER MUST WRITE 'BRAND NECESSARY' OR 'BRAND MEDICALLY NECESSARY' ON THE PRESCRIPTION.

Carol C. Kleinman, M.D.
PM/2 for Windows
Prescription record: Duke, Mary Ann

Date	Drug	Form	Strength	Quantity	Route	Frequency	Refills	Generic OK?
1/17/2003	Ambien	tab	10 mg	#20	PO	i q hs	0	No
1/23/2003	Xanax	tab	0.5 mg	#20	PO	i bid	0	No
2/15/2003	Trazadone	tab	75 mg	#30	PO	i q hs prn	0	No
2/17/2003	Ambien	tab	10 mg	#30	PO	i q hs	0	No
2/29/2003	Ambien	tab	10 mg	#60	PO	i-ii qhs prn	0	No
2/29/2003	Lithium Carbonate	tab	300 mg	#90	PO	ii-iii q hs	3	No
1/12/2004	Antabuse	tab	250 mg	#100	PO	ii q hs x 1	0	No
1/12/2004	Lexapro	tab	10 mg	#50	PO	i q am	0	No
2/19/2004	Zyprexa	tab	10 mg	#14	PO	i q hs	0	No
4/01/2004	Zyprexa	tab	10 mg	#90	PO	iqd	0	No
4/01/2004	Lexapro	tab	10 mg	#360	PO	i q am	0	No
4/01/2004	Lexapro	tab	10 mg	#120	PO	i q am	0	No
4/01/2004	Zyprexa	tab	10 mg	#270	PO	iqd	0	No
5/06/2004	Ambien	tab	10 mg	#10	PO	i q hs	0	No
5/13/2004	Ambien	tab	10 mg	#20	PO	i q hs	0	No
5/20/2004	Ambien	tab	10 mg	#10	PO	i q hs	0	No
5/20/2004	Geodon	tab	80 mg	#100	PO	i po bid	0	No
6/10/2004	Ambien	tab	10 mg	#7	PO	i q hs	0	No
6/10/2004	Zyprexa	tab	10 mg	#10	PO	iqd	0	No
6/10/2004	Lexapro	tab	10 mg	#7	PO	i q am	0	No
6/28/2004	Librium	tab	25 mg	#10	PO	i bid prn	0	No
7/01/2004	Librium	tab	25 mg	#60	PO	i bid prn	0	No
7/01/2004	Lexapro	tab	10 mg	#21	PO	i q am	0	No
7/01/2004	Zyprexa	tab	10 mg	#45	PO	1 1/2 po q d	0	No
7/01/2004	Ambien	tab	10 mg	#30	PO	i q hs	0	No
7/29/2004	Lexapro	tab	10 mg	#160	PO	i q am	0	No
7/29/2004	Ambien	tab	10 mg	#20	PO	i q hs	0	No

(handwritten, quantity column circled: "INSANE AMOUNT OF CHANGING MEDICATIONS. My brain was beyond fried.")

8/24/2004

DATE: 01/15/08 WELLCARE PHARMRX 5530 WISCONSIN AVE CHEVY CHASE, MD 20815
TIME: 17:44:36 << FREEDOM DATA SYSTEMS - PRO/RX - PATIENT TRANSACTION REPORT FOR : MARY A DUKE >>

PATIENT ADDRESS ==> 10220 DEMOCRACY BLVD POTOMAC MD 20852

FOR THE TIME PERIOD 01/01/2000 TO 12/31/2007

DATE	RX #	QTY	DRUG NAME	NDC NUMBER	REF#	DOCTOR NAME	RPH	PRICE	ORIG DATE	DAYS SUPPLY	DAW
/03/03	254844	28	ALPRAZOLAM 0.5MG TAB	00378 4003 01		KLEINMAN	AW	$5.56	12/03/03	14	0
/29/03	256648	60	AMBIEN 10MG TAB	00024 5421 31		KLEINMAN	AW	$162.72	12/29/03	30	0
/29/03	256650	90	LITHIUM CARB. 300MG	00054 4527 25		KLEINMAN	AW	$19.35	12/29/03	30	0
/12/04	257548	100	ANTABUSE 250MG	65347 0706 01		KLEINMAN	AW	$119.76	01/12/04	60	0
/04/04	259352	30	PROPRANOLOL 20MG TAB	00591 5555 01		KLEINMAN	AW	$4.30	02/04/04	10	0
/04/04	259254	60	CHLORDIAZOPOXID+10MG	00555 0033 02		KLEINMAN	AW	$8.40	02/04/04	30	0
/11/04	259777	80	VICOPROFEN	00074 2274 14		STOPAK	AW	$38.31	02/11/04	12	0
/06/04	266483	10	AMBIEN 10MG TAB	00024 5421 31		KLEINMAN	AW	$29.20	05/06/04	10	0
/20/04	267672	10	AMBIEN 10MG TAB	00024 5421 31		KLEINMAN	AW	$29.20	05/20/04	10	0
/03/04	268780	80	VICOPROFEN	00074 2274 14		STOPAK	AW	$38.31	06/03/04	12	0
/10/04	269334	7	AMBIEN 10MG TAB	00024 5421 31		KLEINMAN	AW	$22.03	06/10/04	7	0
/10/04	269335	50	CHLORDIAZOPOXIDE 5MG	00555 0158 02		KLEINMAN	AW	$7.99	06/10/04	5	0
/17/04	269842	14	AMBIEN 10MG TAB	00024 5421 31		KLEINMAN	AW	$41.57	06/17/04	14	0
/01/04	271015	30	AMBIEN 10MG TAB	00024 5421 31		KLEINMAN	AW	$86.22	07/01/04	30	0
/01/04	271016	30	TOPAMAX 50MG TABS	00045 0640 65		KLEINMAN	AW	$94.50	07/01/04	30	0
/01/04	271021	23	ZYPREXA 10MG	00002 4117 60		KLEINMAN	AW	$210.42	07/01/04	15	0
/01/04	271022	100	CHLORDIAZOPOXIDE 5MG	00555 0158 02		KLEINMAN	AW	$13.94	07/01/04	29	0
/19/04	272228	30	TOPAMAX 100MG	00045 0641 65		ANCHORS	AW	$121.28	07/19/04	30	0
/19/04	272229	27	SMZ-TMP DOUBLE STR.	00093 0089 05		ANCHORS	AW	$7.32	07/19/04	9	0
/21/04	271022	200	CHLORDIAZOPOXIDE 5MG	00555 0158 02	1	KLEINMAN	AW	$25.39	07/01/04	29	0
/26/04	271022	300	CHLORDIAZOPOXIDE 5MG	00555 0158 02	2	KLEINMAN	AW	$36.83	07/01/04	29	0
/29/04	273241	20	AMBIEN 10MG TAB	00024 5421 31		KLEINMAN	AW	$58.31	07/29/04	20	0

TOTAL PRESCRIPTIONS 22 TOTAL EXPENSES $1,180.91

SIGNATURE _____
EARL MCLAREN, R.PH.

EARL MCLAREN
Comm. Expires 3/1/10 EMP
Prince Georges County

(List of medications from
only one pharmacy.
I frequented three or four.)

Medical and Chirurgical Faculty of Maryland

Physician Rehabilitation Committee

24 January 2003

William F. Minogue, M.D.
Senior Vice President, Medical Affairs
Suburban Hospital Healthcare System
8600 Old Georgetown Road
Bethesda, MD 20814-1497

PRIVILEGED and CONFIDENTIAL
RE: Mary Ann Duke, M.D.

Dear Dr. Minogue:

I hope you are well and living life to the fullest. This missive is dispatched in regard to my meeting with Dr. Duke and contact with her family and colleagues.

Dr. Duke is a forty-one-year-old, separated, white, female, ophthalmologist, who was referred by her hospital. Her referral was the result of a complaint of her smelling of alcohol in the OR. An investigation revealed several complaints about her, including the charge that she was involved in a "nasty divorce" that was catalyzed by her drinking. Dr. Duke has been at her hospital since 1990. She reported that she has developed a successful practice. She denies drinking prior to doing any surgery. She questioned why no one said anything to her on the day in question. "Why did they let me do two cases if they thought I had been drinking?" She also described her relationship with one of the OR nurses as rather difficult. "I am a young, attractive, vivacious, successful woman. Some nurses hate me for it." The referenced nurse reportedly once wrote her up for being late to a procedure and has complained about the type of music (Rock and Roll) she plays during procedures. Dr. Duke further put forth that she had just given birth in August and was breast feeding, therefore not consuming alcohol at that time. She also proffered that she has begun to wonder about her hospital's support for cataract surgery. She related that she is the only ophthalmologist at the hospital still doing cataracts and wondered if maybe they didn't want them done there anymore. She said that another hospital where she practices told the department to transfer cataract procedures to surgi-centers.

As to the reports of abusive drinking, Dr. Duke described her drinking, when she drinks, as light. She stated she will have a glass or two of wine once or twice a week. Her heaviest drinking, she reported, was in medical school when, "everybody went out to celebrate on Friday nights." Even then she claimed to have drunk moderately. She did validate the report that she is in a difficult divorce, but denied drinking has anything to do with it. Rather, it was a matter of infidelity on the part of her estranged husband. She has three children by her marriage and a fourth from her current relationship.

The Physician Rehabilitation Committee of The Maryland State Medical Society
1202 Maryland Avenue, Second Floor, Baltimore, Maryland 21201
(410) 962-5580 TOLL FREE 1-800-992-7010 FAX (410) 962-5583

William F. Minogue, M.D.
RE: Mary Ann Duke, M.D.
24 January 2003
Page 2

Accompanying her to our appointment was her new baby's grandfather. He spoke highly of Dr. Duke and said he had never observed her to drink abusively. He added that he thought she was an excellent mother, and felt that she was also a good physician. As I needed more information, I asked Dr. Duke to sign releases allowing contact with the hospital, her current paramour, and colleagues. I spoke with this Dr. Duke's paramour this afternoon. He spoke highly of their relationship and her dedication as a mother and physician. He reported that he has never been concerned about her in any way, drinking or otherwise. He described her as someone who, "hardly drinks at all." There were no concerns about Dr. Duke as a person or as a physician, reported by her colleagues.

On the surface this physician does not present any information that would suggest a drinking problem. Her question as to why she was suspected of drinking prior to surgery and no one intervened is a good one. However, there are certain aspects of her personality that would easily be seen as arrogance. This could make her a target, or at least unpopular with some. She reported that she planned to moderate her tone with staff at the hospital and be more aware as to how she is presenting to others. If this is the problem, then hopefully there would be no further concerns raised. If there is some pathological process at work that is not immediately evident then problems will likely continue and even worsen. Our plan was to allow Dr. Duke to self-moderate. Since then I have received no reports that Dr. Duke has continued to be problematic or have difficulties. If there are concerns in the future please call me.

Thank you for your assistance in this matter and for referring Dr. Duke.

Sincerely,

Michael C. Llufrio, NCAC II
Director

CAROL C. KLEINMAN, M.D., J.D., F.A.P.A.
5480 Wisconsin Avenue Suite 1006
Chevy Chase, Maryland 20815

(301) 654-1810
FAX (301) 656-2137
E-mail: cckleinman@aol.com

November 14, 2003

Colm Gage, LCSW-C
FAX 240 777 9546

RE: Mary Ann Duke, M.D.

Dear Mr. Gage:

    Dr. Mary Ann Duke has made all of her appointments and has been very cooperative and involved in treatment. Her diagnosis is Bipolar II Disorder. She is taking lithium carbonate 900 mg daily. Her blood level a few days ago was 0.6 (0.6-1.2) within the therapeutic range. She has not misused alcohol recently, and her alcohol blood level was negative. A complete tox screen was negative. There is NO evidence of poly substance abuse.

    I am very comfortable treating Dr. Duke as an outpatient with random and frequent alcohol and drug screens. She does not need inpatient treatment. There is no evidence that a 28 day inpatient drug program has better results than outpatient treatment.

    With continuation of lithium, antidepressant and outpatient therapy, Dr. Duke's prognosis is excellent.

Sincerely,

Carol C. Kleinman, M.D., J.D.

Contemporary Insurance Services

Israel Teitelbaum
Insurance Broker
Attorney at Law (D.C., MD)

Aton Teitelbaum
Insurance Broker

11301 Amherst Avenue • Suite 202 • Silver Spring, Maryland 20902
Telephone (301) 933-3373
Toll Free 1-800-658-8943
Fax (301) 933-3651
E-mail: sales@cisinsurance.com
www.cisinsurance.com

December 16, 2003

Mary Ann Duke, M.D.
10220 Democracy Blvd.
Potomac, MD 20854-4438

Dear Mary Ann:

Your malpractice insurance policy through The Medical Protective Company has been renewed effective February 25, 2004 and the renewal policy will follow shortly. Certificates of Insurance have been issued and copies are enclosed for your files.

Last year's premium was $2,340, Medical Protective's renewal premium and comparisons to other Maryland insurers are shown below.

Year	*Medical Protective*	Medical Mutual	*The Doctors Company
2	*$5,022*	$ 7,853	$ 9,992
3	*$6,781*	$11,615	$13,323
4	*$7,534*	$14,560	$15,322
5+	*$8,370*	$16,359	$16,654

*We anticipate a rate increase of approximately 20% for The Doctors Company for February 1st. That increase is included in the projection shown above. This is an estimate only.
All applications and premium indications are subject to underwriting approval, and assume claims free status, with no claims paid or reported within the last five years.

Premiums for Claims Made policies are shown above. If a Claims Made policy is cancelled for any reason other than death, qualifying retirement or disability, an Extended Reporting Period Endorsement ("tail") would need to be purchased to complete the policy, or "Prior Acts" coverage may be obtained from the new carrier. The Claims Made premium indications shown above include prior acts coverage so **a tail need not be purchased from your current insurer to make a switch. If you are considering retirement within the next five years or before age 55, please call us to discuss those plans to assure that a free tail is available at retirement.**

Your premium is higher than last year because Medical Protective has taken a rate increase for your specialty. Significant rate increases or premium adjustments have been taken by other Maryland insurers, reflecting a nationwide trend. Medical Protective remains competitive for your specialty and we recommend that you renew your current policy.

If you would like to pay in full, please remit a check to us for $5,022, **made payable to The Medical Protective Company**, with a copy of the enclosed invoice.

[handwritten: Very low malpractice for an eye surgeon, Inc had me law suit on of made against on]

In California our Agency name is IT Insurance Services

MARY ANN DUKE, M.D.
EYE PHYSICIAN & SURGEON

10220 DEMOCRACY BLVD.
POTOMAC, MD 20854

December 22, 2003

Dear Dr. Passamani,

    I would greatly like to accept your offer for Medical leave from Suburban Hospital. I wish to rescind my resignation. Had you informed me of the conquences of resigning, I most certainly would have accepted your offer of Medical leave.

    Please, Dr. Passamani, allow me to accept the Board's offer to take Medical leave from Suburban Hospital that they granted me on December 10, 2003 for as long a time period as the Hospital deems necessary.

Sincerely yours,

Mary Ann Duke

Mary Ann Duke, M.D.

National Practitioner Data Bank
Healthcare Integrity and Protection Data Bank
P.O. Box 10832
Chantilly, VA 20153-0832

http://www.npdb-hipdb.hrsa.gov

DCN: 5500000031965581
Process Date: 12/22/2003

ADVERSE ACTION REPORT
TITLE IV CLINICAL PRIVILEGES ACTION

Report Number 5500000031965581

This report is maintained in: [X] The National Practitioner Data Bank

[ ] The Healthcare Integrity and Protection Data Bank

The information contained in this report is maintained by the National Practitioner Data Bank for restricted use under the provisions of Title of Public Law 99-660, as amended; and 45 CFR Part 60. All information is confidential and may be used only for the purpose for which it was disclosed. Disclosure or use of confidential information for other purposes is a violation of Federal law. For additional information or clarification, contact the reporting entity identified in Section A.

A. REPORTING ENTITY

Entity Name: SUBURBAN HOSPITAL HEALTHCARE SYSTEM
Address: 8600 OLD GEORGETOWN ROAD

City, State, ZIP: BETHESDA, MD 20814

Entity Internal Report Reference (e.g., claim number):

Name or Office: EUGENE PASSAMANI, MD
Title or Department: SENIOR VP MEDICAL AFFAIRS
Telephone: (301) 896-2578

Type of Report: INITIAL REPORT

B. SUBJECT IDENTIFICATION INFORMATION (INDIVIDUAL)

Subject Name: DUKE, MARY ANN

Other Name(s) Used:

Gender: FEMALE
Date of Birth: 06/06/1961

Organization Name:
Work Address: 10220 DEMOCRACY BLVD

City, State, ZIP: POTOMAC, MD 20854
Country:

Home Address: 10220 DEMOCRACY BLVD

City, State, ZIP: POTOMAC, MD 20854
Country:

Deceased: NO
Date of Death:

Social Security Numbers (SSN): 093-50-8753

Professional School(s) & Year(s) of Graduation: ALBANY MEDICAL COLLEGE, ALBANY NY 1985

Occupation/Field of Licensure (Code): PHYSICIAN (MD) (010)
State License Number, State of Licensure: D38796, MD
Other, as Specified:

CONFIDENTIAL DOCUMENT - FOR AUTHORIZED USE ONLY

al Practitioner Data Bank
care Integrity and Protection Data Bank
ox 10832
lly, VA 20153-0832

www.npdb-hipdb.hrsa.gov

DCN: 5500000031965581
Process Date: 12/22/2003
Page: 2 of 2

Drug Enforcement Administration (DEA) Numbers: BD1945724

FORMATION REPORTED

Type of Adverse Action: TITLE IV CLINICAL PRIVILEGES

Adverse Action Classification Code(s): VOLUNTARY SURRENDER OF CLINICAL PRIVILEGE(S), WHILE UNDER, OR TO AVOID, INVESTIGATION RELATING TO PROFESSIONAL COMPETENCE OR CONDUCT (1635)

Other, as Specified:
Date Action Was Taken: 12/09/2003
Date Action Became Effective: 12/09/2003
Length of Action: PERMANENT
Years:
Months:
Days:
Description of Act(s) or Omission(s) or Other Reasons for Action Taken: "DR. DUKE RESIGNED HER MEDICAL STAFF MEMBERSHIP AND CLINICAL PRIVILEGES WHILE UNDER INVESTIGATION FOR POSSIBLE IMPAIRMENT."

Basis for Action: SURRENDERED CLINICAL PRIVILEGES (AD)
Other, as Specified:

SUBJECT STATEMENT

If the subject identified in Section B of this report has submitted a statement, it appears in this section.

REPORT STATUS

Unless one or more boxes below are checked, the subject of this report identified in Section B has not contested this report.

[ ] If box is checked, this report has been disputed by the subject identified in Section B.

[ ] If box is checked, at the request of the subject identified in Section B, this report is being reviewed by the Secretary of the U.S. Department of Health and Human Services to determine its accuracy and/or whether it complies with reporting requirements. No decision has been reached.

[ ] If box is checked, at the request of the subject identified in Section B, this report was reviewed by the Secretary of the U.S. Department of Health and Human Services. The Secretary's decision is shown below:

Date of Original Submission: 12/22/2003
Date of Most Recent Change: 12/22/2003

(Same day entered right in front of me.)

END OF REPORT

CONFIDENTIAL DOCUMENT – FOR AUTHORIZED USE ONLY

National Practitioner Data Bank
Healthcare Integrity and Protection Data Bank
P.O. Box 10832
Chantilly, VA 20153-0832

http://www.npdb-hipdb.com

DCN: 5500000031965581
Process Date: 12/22/2003
Page: 1 of 1

REPORT RESPONSE SERVICE LOGIN INSTRUCTIONS

To access the on-line Report Response Service, go to http://www.npdb-hipdb.com and click Respond to a Report. The Welcome to the Report Response Service screen displays. Click the Respond to a Report icon on this page to proceed to the Report Response Log In screen.

As the subject of a report, you are assigned a unique Report Password. This Report Password applies to all reports on file with the Data Bank(s) for which you are the subject.

If you have more than one report for which you wish to dispute report information (add, modify, or remove a Subject Statement, initiate or withdraw a dispute or request for Secretarial Review, or modify your address as maintained by the Data Bank(s)), you must enter one Report Number in the appropriate field on the Report Response Login screen, along with your Report Password. Once you have completed your transaction for that report, return to the Report Response Login screen and enter the next Report Number for which you wish to dispute report information. Use the same Report Password for all Report Numbers.

Report Number: Found on the first page of the report, which follows the Notification of a Report in the Data Bank(s) sent to inform you of a report submitted to the Data Bank(s), or in your self-query results.

Report Password: K6shzNY9eu

NOTE: Enter the Report Password exactly as it appears here. The Report Password is case-sensitive. File this information in a secure place for future access to the on-line Report Response Service.

CONFIDENTIAL DOCUMENT – FOR AUTHORIZED USE ONLY

ROBERT F. STEPHENS, M.D., F.A.C.S.

ALAN G. PALESTINE, M.D.

LEONARD M. PARVER, M.D.

FADI P. NASRALLAH, M.D.

January 08, 2004

Re: DR. MARY ANN DUKE

To Whom It May Concern:

This is to certify that I have known Dr. Mary Ann Duke professionally since she first began to practice in the Washington area in 1990.

I have shared many patients with her over the years, and have noted that she is an excellent and meticulous surgeon. Furthermore, she has shown excellent clinical judgment.

I hope that this information is of benefit to you, and please do not hesitate to contact me if I can be of further service.

Sincerely,

ROBERT F. STEPHENS, M.D. F.A.C.S

DISEASES & SURGERY OF THE VITREOUS & RETINA AND UVEITIS
6410 ROCKLEDGE DRIVE, SUITE #400, BETHESDA, MD 20817 • (301) 530-5200 • FAX (301) 493-6577
1145 NINETEENTH STREET, SUITE #500, WASHINGTON, D.C. 20036 • (202) 833-1668 • FAX (202) 833-4698

January 19, 2004

Mary Ann Duke, M.D.
10220 Democracy Blvd.
Potomac, MD 20854

Dear Doctor Duke:

On December 22, 2003 you performed cataract surgery on my left eye. I want to tell you what a positive experience it was.

The procedure was done at the Silver Spring Ophthalmology Group. Because of the arrangements you and Diane made with the facility, everything went very smoothly and there were essentially no forms for me to complete. All of the staff were friendly, helpful, courteous and informative. The preparation prior to surgery, the surgery itself and the post-surgery "recovery" were uneventful.

Upon removal of the patch covering my eye the day after surgery, it was immediately obvious to me how much my left eye vision had improved. Without any corrective eyeglass lens, my distance vision was 20/20. In addition, when driving at night, there were no longer any visual problems.

I want to thank you for all that you did regarding the setting-up for this procedure, as well as for your professional ophthalmic expertise. I am very pleased with the entire experience.

Sincerely,

Alan C. Levy

Alan C. Levy

ROSALIE L. BAIR, M.D., P.A.
Surgery of the eyelids, orbit, and lacrimal system

1612 Shields Drive
Bethesda, MD 20817

19211 Montgomery Village Ave., Suite B-21
Gaithersburg, MD 20879

Telephone (301) 571-4334
Facsimile (301) 571-4313

January 24, 2004

Re: Mary Ann Duke, M.D.

To Whom It May Concern:

I have known Mary Ann Duke, M.D. in a professional capacity for approximately nine years. During this time I have referred many patients to her, all of whom she handles with the utmost capability in a professional manner. I have also had the opportunity of working with her in the operating room and I find her to be an outstanding surgeon as well as a caring physician.

If I can be of any further assistance, please don't hesitate to call.

Sincerely,

Rosalie L. Bair, M.D.

RLB:bjz

THE WILMER OPHTHALMOLOGICAL INSTITUTE
THE JOHNS HOPKINS UNIVERSITY SCHOOL OF MEDICINE
THE JOHNS HOPKINS HOSPITAL

Julia A. Haller, M.D.
Katharine Graham Professor of Ophthalmology

Maumenee 740
600 North Wolfe Street
Baltimore, MD 21287-9275

Office: 410-955-4714
Appointments: 410-955-2159
FAX: 410-614-7632
Email: jhaller@jhmi.edu

January 27, 2004

Re: Mary Ann Duke, M.D.

To Whom It May Concern:

It is my great pleasure to write a strong letter of recommendation for Dr. Mary Ann Duke. I have known Dr. Duke for almost twenty years during her training and since as a professional colleague. We have collaborated in patient care over the years, and I have had the opportunity to personally see her surgical results and observe her clinical care.

Dr. Duke is a highly competent, extremely ethical, and exceptionally caring physician. Her patients are quite devoted to her. She provides superb medical and ophthalmological care for them.

Please do not hesitate to contact me if you require any further information.

Sincerely,

Julia A. Haller, M.D.

JAH:cdk

Current Chairwoman of the entire Department of Ophthalmology at Wills Eye and Ear, Phili., PA. I believe, but am not sure, that Dr. Julia Haller is the first female head of an ophthalmology department in the United States

THE WILMER OPHTHALMOLOGICAL INSTITUTE
THE JOHNS HOPKINS UNIVERSITY SCHOOL OF MEDICINE
THE JOHNS HOPKINS HOSPITAL

Terrence P. O'Brien, M.D.
Associate Professor of Ophthalmology
External Diseases and Cornea
Director, Ocular Microbiology Laboratory
Director, Refractive Eye Surgery

The Eye Surgery Center at
Green Spring Station
10753 Falls Road, Suite 455
Lutherville, MD 21093-4535
410-847-3508/FAX 410-847-3519
Email: tobrien@jhmi.edu

February 13, 2004

Re: Mary Ann Duke, MD

To Whom It May Concern:

    It is my pleasure to write in support of Dr. Mary Ann Duke, an ophthalmologist in good standing with privileges at The Wilmer Laser Vision Center of The Wilmer Eye Institute at Green Spring Station, a facility of the Johns Hopkins Medical Institutions. I have known Dr. Duke for the last 12 years and I am confident in my assessment of her capabilities based upon my personal observation of her professional development. I have known Dr. Duke as a colleague for the last ten years. I have also been her supervisor in refractive eye surgery in my capacity as Medical Director of The Wilmer Laser Vision Center. I have directly observed her to not only provide competent care, but to also perform in a compassionate manner as a practitioner. I feel confident to endorse her competent training in ophthalmic surgery as well as her clinical professional abilities.

    I enthusiastically and objectively recommend Dr. Mary Ann Duke without reservation as a competent, well trained and ethical ophthalmic surgeon within Johns Hopkins Medicine.

With thanks for your kind attention,

Sincerely,

Terrence P. O'Brien, MD
Director, Refractive Eye Surgery

(Head of Refractive Surgery at Bascom Palmer Eye Institute in Miami, FL now.)

www.wilmereyeinstitute.net

Medical and Chirurgical Faculty of Maryland

25 March 2004

Pamela Cromer, Compliance Analyst
Maryland Board of Physicians
4201 Patterson Avenue, P. O. Box 2491
Baltimore, MD 21215-0095

Physician
Rehabilitatio
Committe

PRIVILEGED and CONFIDENTIAL
RE: Mary Ann Duke, M.D.

Dear Ms. Cromer:

I hope you are well and living life to the fullest. This missive is dispatched in regard to our involvement with Dr. Mary Ann Duke. This information is protected by state and federal confidentiality regulations and is released with her knowledge and permission, via a signed release.

Our first encounter with Dr. Duke, then a forty-one-year-old, separated, white, female, ophthalmologist, who was referred by her hospital, took place in the fall of 2002. Her referral was the result of a complaint about her allegedly smelling of alcohol at her hospital. An investigation, by the hospital, revealed several complaints about her, included was a report that she was involved in a "nasty divorce" that was catalyzed by her drinking. Dr. Duke had been at her hospital since 1990. She reported that she had a successful practice. She denied drinking prior to doing any surgery. She questioned why no one said anything to her on the day in question. "Why did they let me do two cases if they thought I had been drinking?" She also described her relationship with one of the OR nurses as rather difficult, stating, "I am a young, attractive, vivacious, successful woman. Some nurses hate me for it." The referenced nurse reportedly once wrote her up for being late to a procedure and had complained about her music choice (Rock and Roll)in the OR. Dr. Duke further put forth that she had just given birth in August (2002) and was breast feeding, therefore not consuming alcohol at that time.

As to the reports of abusive drinking, Dr. Duke described her drinking, when she drank, as "light." She stated she would have a glass or two of wine once or twice a week. Her heaviest drinking, she reported, was in medical school when, "everybody went out to celebrate on Friday nights." Even then she claimed to have drunk moderately. She did validate the report that she was in a difficult divorce, but denied drinking had anything to do with it. Rather, it was a matter of infidelity on the part of her estranged husband. She has three children by her marriage and a fourth from her current relationship.

Accompanying her to that first appointment was her new baby's grandfather. He spoke highly of Dr. Duke and said he had never observed her to drink abusively. He added that he thought she was an excellent mother, and felt that she was also a good physician. As I needed more information, I asked Dr. Duke to sign releases allowing contact with the hospital, her current paramour, and colleagues. I spoke with Dr. Duke's paramour that afternoon. He spoke highly of their relationship and her dedication as a mother and physician. He reported that he has never been concerned about her in any way, drinking or otherwise. He described her as someone who, "hardly drinks at all." There were no concerns about Dr. Duke as a person or as a physician, reported by her colleagues.

The Physician Rehabilitation Committee of The Maryland State Medical Society
1202 Maryland Avenue, Second Floor, Baltimore, Maryland 21201
(410) 962-5580 TOLL FREE 1-800-992-7010 FAX (410) 962-5583

Pamela Cromer
RE: Mary Ann Duke, M.D.
25 March 2004
Page 2

On the surface Dr. Duke did not present any information that would suggest a drinking problem. Her question as to why she was suspected of drinking prior to surgery and no one intervened was a good one. However, there were certain aspects of her personality that could be seen as arrogance and generally off-putting. This could have made her a target, or at least unpopular with some. She reported that she planned to moderate her tone with staff at the hospital and be more aware as to how she was presenting to others. We recommended to the hospital that if this were the problem, then hopefully there would be no further concerns raised. We further suggested that if there were a pathological process at work, which was not immediately evident, then problems will likely continue and even worsen. The hospital was going to monitor and let us know if there were additional problems.

We received no additional reports about Dr. Duke until June 2003 when an anonymous report claimed that Dr. Duke had a serious drinking problem and needed help. There was a report that the police were called to her house, as well. It took several attempts to get Dr. Duke to respond to our request for a meeting. In August she came in. Again, she was accompanied by her paramour's father, one M. Desmond ffrench-Mullen, C.B.E., whom she described as her "mentor." She admitted that there was an episode in May of 2003, when the police came to her house. She reported that she had a "horrendous argument" with her boyfriend and "drank too much" that day. She had been working in her yard and claimed that she did not eat enough and became drunk because of it. After completing her yard work she showered and learned that her boyfriend had left the house. She called police. She reported that when they came they handcuffed her, not allowing her to dress and transported her to the emergency room. She also said that the police broke her arm during this event, but she related that she received no treatment at the hospital. She steadfastly denied that she had a substance abuse problem, but did tell us that she was seeing a Dr. Salerian for stress related issues. She said she was on Topamax and Klonapin. She and Mr. ffrench-Mullen espoused that she had been having trouble with her boyfriend and still was dealing with the aftermath of her divorce. There were ongoing battles over child custody and she claimed that her ex-husband, "only wanted me for a green card." Child protective services also became involved, possibly from a report by her ex-husband. Dr. Duke also believed he called the police several times. Montgomery County Police confirmed that there had been five calls to her residence.

We sought to engage Dr. Duke and enrol her in the program. She initially agreed to sign a contract, but balked at the length of time for monitoring and the toxicology screening protocol. We also sought her permission to get information from Dr. Salerian and refer her for an independent evaluation. We requested information from Dr. Salerian, but never received any directly form him. Dr. Duke, however, provided us with several pages of handwritten notes and a copy of a letter he wrote to child protective services in June of 2003. They are enclosed for your perusal. As to an independent evaluation, Dr. Duke resisted this but finally agreed to see Ellen McDaniel, M.D. Dr. McDaniel performed her assessment in September 2003, but could not send us a report as Dr. Duke refused to sign a release. She maintained that we misrepresented the facts about her case, as reflected in letters to Elaine Gisriel (Ms. Gisriel was assigned to Dr. Duke's case until 31 October 2003) and Dr. Platman, which are also herewith. She eventually relented and we received a report from Dr. McDaniel in early November. Dr. McDaniel diagnoses were, Bipolar II with hypomania, r/o Bipolar I, r/o antidepressant-induced mania, alcohol abuse. She referred Dr. Duke to Carol Kleinman, M.D. for treatment.

Pamela J. Cromer
RE: Mary Ann Duke
25 March 2004
Page 3

On 8 December 2003, there was an incident at Suburban Hospital. Dr. Duke was perceived to be impaired and was asked to "stand down." She was asked to submit to toxicology testing and relented to the request. She had positive results for alcohol, benzodiazepine and a pending opiate level at that time. Copies of the reports are enclosed. I met with Dr. Duke the next day. She was distraught and appeared burned on her face. She reported she had given herself a "chemical peel" and left the solution on too long resulting in the burns. She related that she had taken a vicoprofen for the pain. She stated that she was in treatment with Dr. Kleinman and admitted that she had not been adhering to her medication regimen. However, now she was. She also related that Dr. Kleinman was having her undergo urine toxicology screens. Dr. Kleinman was on vacation and unavailable at that time. Dr. Duke had an appointment to see her on the 15th. I recommended that she not see patients until she saw Dr. Kleinman and asked her to sign a release. A copy of a note from Dr. Kleinman's 15 December appointment, as well as copies of toxicology screens and an initial evaluation are enclosed. I discussed with Dr. Duke the option of entering an inpatient facility for an intensive evaluation or possibly even treatment. She resisted this suggestion stating that she would need to discuss this with Dr. Kleinman. I met with her again on 31 December 2003. She had learned that Suburban Hospital was going to report her the Board of Physicians. I again advised her to undergo an inpatient evaluation. I recommended that she enter the Professional Renewal Center in Lawrence, Kansas. She again resisted, but did accept their phone number. Mr. ffrench-Mullen who, as always, accompanied her to her appointment, stated that he though the recommendation for an intensive evaluation was a good one that could be helpful to her.

During this time we received a contact from Mr. Charles Cichon of the Board of Physicians. He indicated that the Board had opened an investigation and would be requesting information. Dr. Duke did not follow up and did not return calls, during February and March, but did sign and return a release of information that I sent her earlier this month, after your phone call indicating that you would be sending a request for information.

Dr. Duke never signed a contract with the PRP, however, we remain available and would be happy to work with her and will continue to reach out to her.

Sincerely,

Michael C. Llufrio
Director

enclosures

CAROL C. KLEINMAN, M.D., F.A.P.A.
5480 Wisconsin Avenue Suite 1006
Chevy Chase, Maryland 20815

TEL (301) 654-1810
FAX (301) 656-2137

May 18, 2004

Mr. Colm Gage
Child Welfare Services
3rd Floor
1301 Piccard Drive
Rockville, MD 20850

RE: Mary Ann Duke, M.D.

Dear Mr. Gage:

I am writing to update you on Dr. Duke's progress since my last letter of April 22, 2004. Dr. Duke continues to make progress toward her goals. Aside from the one positive blood alcohol level ["BAL"] of March, 10, 2004, all of her BAL's have been negative. She is taking Zyprexa, a mood-stabilizer, and antipsychotic medication approved for the treatment of bipolar disorder, and it has been very helpful to her in controlling her moods and her behavior. The only negative has been weight gain. She has gained 14 pounds since she started Zyprexa, and is getting very uncomfortable with the increase in her weight. She is taking phentermine, a weight loss drug prescribed by her primary care doctor, to help her control her weight. I am following her blood tests carefully to be sure that she does not develop diabetes. Nevertheless, she and I are beginning to discuss the possibility of changing from Zyprexa to another medication in that same group, that is weight neutral.

Dr. Duke did have some positive benzodiazepam levels in her urine tox screen several months ago. She was taking Librium for detoxification from alcohol. Since she has been taking the Zyprexa, the benzodiazepam levels have been negative. She continues to require Ambien 10 mg for sleep.

Recently we have decided to taper off the Lexapro [an antidepressant medication]. Dr. Duke told me that she thought that the Lexapro might be making her manic.

Dr. Duke continues to attend sessions regularly, and is engaged in treatment and compliant with medication regimens and tox screens and BAL screens. She is progressing toward our goals. Her diagnosis continues to be Bipolar II Disorder and Alcohol Dependence in Remission. It is my opinion that her prognosis is excellent.

If you need further information, please don't hesitate to contact me.

Sincerely,

Carol C. Kleinman

Carol C. Kleinman, M.D.

STATE OF MARYLAND
DHMH Board of Physicians

Maryland Department of Health and Mental Hygiene
4201 Patterson Avenue • Baltimore, Maryland 21215-2299
Robert L. Ehrlich, Jr., Governor – Michael S. Steele, Lt. Governor – Nelson J. Sabatini, Secretary

May 19, 2004

Mary Ann Duke, M.D.
10220 Democracy Blvd.
Potomac Maryland 20854

Re: License # D38796
Case # 2004-0390

Dear Dr. Duke:

Attached is a typed narrative from the interview on April 20, 2004. Please initial each page, sign the last page and the attached Interview Statement and return all papers to me at the Board.

In addition, as agreed during the interview, the Board is requesting clarification of additional questions. The questions are as follows:

1. Could you provide written details surrounding the incidents that took place at Suburban Hospital (the "Hospital") on March 1, 2001, January 16, 2002, September 9, 2002 and December 8, 2003; what if any action taken by the Hospital?
2. Could you provide written details surrounding the following Montgomery County Police Reports:
   a. R01-234213 – September 24, 2001; and
   b. R03100296 – May 3, 2003.
3. How and when did Child Protective Services in Montgomery County become involved with your family?
4. What is the status of the involvement with Child Protective Services?
5. Is there a formal agreement regarding the custody of your four children? If so, what are the terms of that agreement?

Thank you for your cooperation in this matter.

Are male doctors' personal lives delved into this extreme? I thought one doctor's blamed everything on his wife!

410-764-4777 • Fax 410-358-2252 • Toll Free 1-800-492-6836
Web Site: www.mbp.state.md.us

Mary Ann Duke, M.D.
May 19, 2004
Page Two

In the meantime, should you have any questions, please do not hesitate to contact me at 410-764-3786.

Sincerely,

Pamela J. Cromer
Compliance Analyst

PJC

Attachments

C: Kenneth Armstrong, Esquire
Dr. Yemisi Koya, Esquire, Manger, Compliance Investigations
Lisa Watts, Esquire, Compliance Analyst, Probation

Why is my life personal plastered on the Internet?

STATE OF MARYLAND

DHMH Board of Physicians

Maryland Department of Health and Mental Hygiene
4201 Patterson Avenue • Baltimore, Maryland 21215-2299

Robert L. Ehrlich, Jr., Governor – Michael S. Steele, Lt. Governor – Nelson J. Sabatini, Secretary

August 12, 2004

Kenneth Armstrong, Esquire
Armstrong, Donohue, Ceppos & Vaughan
204 Monroe Street, Suite 101
Rockville Maryland 20850

Re: Mary Ann Duke, M.D.
License # D38796
Case # 2004-0390

Dear Mr. Armstrong:

I apologize for the delay in responding to your letter dated June 21, 2004. As discussed during our telephone conversation on June 24, 2004, I am not able to disclose the police reports September 24, 2001 or May 3, 2003.

In response to your request for additional information on the specific events at Suburban Hospital on March 1, 2001 and January 16, 2002, attached is a letter dated February 28, 2002 from William F. Minogue, M.D. to Dr. Duke outlining the events of March 1, 2001. The details of January 16, 2002 are as follows:

Dr. Duke had 2 cases scheduled today, 1/16/02, to begin at 910AM. Dr. Duke late. Multiple pages by the O.R. charge nurse to inquire about her arrival time. Dr. Duke did not answer pages. Office called to see if she could be located but to no avail. Dr. Duke arrived to the O.R. for 910 case at 1020 with out explanation.

In addition, please provide the Board a signed written statement from Dr. Duke's Office Manager verifying that she has no recollection of terminating her employment with Dr. Duke.

Thank you for your cooperation and if you have any further questions, please feel free to contact me at 410-764-3786.

Sincerely,

Pamela J. Cromer
Compliance Analyst

PJC
Cc: Mary Ann Duke, M.D.
Dr. Yemisi Koya, Esquire, Manager, Compliance Investigations

I'm in rehab (14 weeks) and the BOARD is STILL HOUNDING ME.

8/17/04

LAW OFFICES
ARMSTRONG, DONOHUE, CEPPOS & VAUGHAN
CHARTERED
204 MONROE STREET, SUITE 101
ROCKVILLE, MARYLAND 20850

(301) 251-0440
FAX (301) 279-5929
www.adclawfirm.com

LARRY A. CEPPOS (Md., D.C.)
H. PATRICK DONOHUE (Md., D.C.)
H. KENNETH ARMSTRONG (Md., D.C.)
BENJAMIN S. VAUGHAN (Md., D.C.)
EDWARD S. HOROWITZ (Md., D.C.)
J. ERIC RHOADES (Md., D.C.)
SUSAN B. BOYCE (Md., D.C.)
ANDREW J. MARTER (Md., D.C.)

OF COUNSEL:
EDWARD A. GONSALVES (Md., D.C., Va.)

ROBERT C. MAYNARD (Md., Pa., Ohio, D.C.)
PENNY KAHN (Md., D.C.)
KAREN A. FERRETTI (Md., D.C.)
JAMES S. KNERR (Md., D.C.)
JEREMY R. KRUM (Md)

EDWARD C. DONAHUE
(1923-1993)

August 24, 2004

Pamela J. Cromer
Compliance Analyst
Board of Physicians
Maryland Department of Health and Mental Hygiene
4201 Patterson Street
Baltimore, MD 21215-2299

Re: **Mary Ann Duke, M.D.**
Case No. 2004-0390
License No. D38796

Dear Pam:

Thanks for your letter of August 19, 2004. I have asked Dr. Duke to make execution of the Authorization one of her first priorities on her return from Father Martin's Ashley. I will also endeavor to review with her the February, 2002 letter from Dr. Minogue and respond to you promptly.

As a separate issue, I was somewhat concerned about your response and reaction to the news that Dr. Duke had entered Father Martin's Ashley. In our previous meeting with you, Dr. Duke had expressed directly to you her concern about being away from her children and being away from her practice for 28 days as the primary reason why she was objecting to such a condition in any contract with the Physician Rehabilitation Program. As you know, such a 28-day program was a fairly normal routine in the contract. Dr. Duke had had conversations with Mr. Llufrio to determine if she could participate in the rehabilitation program without entering a 28-day in-patient treatment program. Mr. Llufrio left her the distinct impression that such a situation was possible, but would be an exception and not the rule. No final decision was made because of the change in Mr. Llufrio's status with the Physician Rehabilitation Committee and the Board of Physicians.

My understanding has always been that the Physician Rehabilitation Committee and the Board preferred in-patient treatment as a cornerstone to the full rehabilitation of all physicians with potential substance abuse issues. Dr. Duke has voluntarily taken

Pamela J. Cromer
August 24, 2004
Page 2

that step. Dr. Duke took this step knowing full well that her voluntary admission to Father Martin's Ashley would be reported to you, and that you would probably request or require production of records from that facility. She is also aware that you would continue to require records from Dr. Kleinman.

    Considering the context, I do not see how or why her decision should be a mark against her. Rather, I would think you would encourage physicians to take the steps Dr. Duke has taken to address any potential problem and increase the likelihood of success both for her and for the welfare of the patients of her practice.

    I look forward to working with you when she returns.

                           Very truly yours,

                           Kenneth Armstrong

KA:jmf

cc: Mary Ann Duke, M.D.

(When I picked up my file from Mr. Armstrong he said to me, "If you had given me $200,000, you were still going down.")

LAW OFFICES
ARMSTRONG, DONOHUE, CEPPOS & VAUGHAN
CHARTERED
204 MONROE STREET, SUITE 101
ROCKVILLE, MARYLAND 20850

(301) 251-0440
FAX (301) 279-5929
www.adclawfirm.com

LARRY A. CEPPOS (Md., D.C.)
H. PATRICK DONOHUE (Md., D.C.)
H. KENNETH ARMSTRONG (Md., D.C.)
BENJAMIN S. VAUGHAN (Md., D.C.)
EDWARD S. HOROWITZ (Md., D.C.)
J. ERIC RHOADES (Md., D.C.)
SUSAN B. BOYCE (Md., D.C.)
ANDREW J. MARTER (Md., D.C.)

OF COUNSEL:
EDWARD A. GONSALVES (Md., D.C., Va.)

ROBERT C. MAYNARD (Md., Pa., Ohio, D.C.)
PENNY KAHN (Md., D.C.)
KAREN A. FERRETTI (Md., D.C.)
JAMES S. KNERR (Md., D.C.)
JEREMY R. KRUM (Md.)

EDWARD C. DONAHUE
(1923-1993)

August 24, 2004

Personal and Confidential

Mary Ann Duke, M.D.
10220 Democracy Blvd.
Potomac, MD 20854

Re: **Suburban Hospital/BPQA**

Dear Mary Ann:

On your return, please make the execution of the enclosed Authorization as one of your first items of business and return it to Ms. Cromer.

A priority matter, although less important than the Authorization is the February 28, 2002 letter from Dr. Minogue, a copy of which we have received. You and I need to review this together so we can respond appropriately to Ms. Cromer.

Very truly yours,

Kenneth Armstrong

[handwritten: What absolute bullshit two and a half YEARS LATER. Witch hunt or what?]

KA:jmf

Father Martin's ASHLEY

A Treatment Center for Alcoholism and Chemical Addiction
JCAHO Accredited
All contributions are tax deductible, to the extent allowed by law.

Father Joseph C. Martin
Lora Mae Abraham
Co-Founders, Emeritus

Leonard Angus Dahl
President and Chief Executive Officer

September 10, 2004

Ms. Cassandra Hicks
Attorney at Law
600 Jefferson Plaza, Suite 203
Rockville, Maryland 20852-1150

RE: DUKE, MARY # 19609

Dear Ms. Hicks:

This letter is to inform you that the above person is a patient at Ashley, Inc. Ashley is an impatient program for the treatment of alcoholism and other chemical dependence. Dr. Duke was admitted to Ashley on August 15, 2004 for treatment of alcoholism and will be discharged on September 11, 2004 after successfully completing treatment. A psychiatric assessment was done and her history was consistent with depression, but not bipolar disorder. Her mood was stable during treatment.

If I can be of further assistance, please let me know.

Sincerely,

Bernadette Solounias, M.D.
Medical Director

BS: pmn

CONFIDENTIAL

FEDERAL LAW FORBIDS FUTURE DISCLOSURE OF THIS INFORMATION FROM CONFIDENTIAL ALCOHOL AND DRUG ABUSE PATIENTS RECORDS WITHOUT SPECIFIC WRITTEN CONSENT OF THE PATIENT.

MARYLAND BOARD OF PHYSICIANS
THIRD FLOOR
4201 PATTERSON AVENUE
BALTIMORE, MARYLAND 21215-0095
410-764-4777

SUBPOENA DUCES TECUM

CERTIFIED MAIL
RETURN RECEIPT REQUESTED

DIRECTED TO: Mary Ann Duke, M.D.
10220 Democracy Blvd.
Potomac Maryland 20854

Pursuant to Sections 14-206 (a) and 14-401 (g) of the Health Occupations Article of the Annotated Code of Maryland, YOU ARE HEREBY SUMMONED and COMMANDED by the MARYLAND BOARD OF PHYSICIANS to deliver IMMEDIATELY UPON SERVICE OF PROCESS a copy of any and all police reports regarding you, driving infractions committed by you or citations issued by the police to you, for driving infractions in your possession or your constructive possession and control; whether generated by you or any other individual or facility; which materials are in your custody, possession, or control.

And by virtue of the authority of the said BOARD OF PHYSICIANS, such information is thereby **immediately upon service** to an agent of:

Pamela J. Cromer, Compliance Analyst
Board of Physicians
4201 Patterson Avenue
Baltimore, Maryland 21215-0095
Telephone #: (410) 764-3786

The Health Insurance Portability and Accountability Act (HIPAA) does not preclude you from disclosing information required by this to the Board. HIPAA also specifically permits compliance with this subpoena without notification of the patient or the patient's concern.

FOR FAILURE TO OBEY this summons on petition of the Board a court of competent jurisdiction may punish the person as for contempt of court, pursuant to the provisions of the Health Occupations Article of the Annotated Code of Maryland Section 14-206 (b).

Given under my hand this 16th day of November, 2004.

Margaret T. Anzalone, Deputy Director
Board of Physicians
2004-0390

(Handwritten note: I was deluged with paperwork in 2004. I have no inkling how I kept it straight. Truthfully, I don't think it was possible. I was mourning the loss of my children, going to rehab, getting sober. On top of which, I was a nightmare medication roller coaster ride.)

National Practitioner Data Bank
Healthcare Integrity and Protection Data Bank
Box 10832
Chilly, VA 20153-0832

www.npdb-hipdb.com

DCN: 5500000035737645
Process Date: 12/01/2004
Page: 1 of 2

ADVERSE ACTION REPORT
TITLE IV CLINICAL PRIVILEGES ACTION

Report Number 5500000035737645

This report is maintained in: [X] The National Practitioner Data Bank

[ ] The Healthcare Integrity and Protection Data Bank

Information contained in this report is maintained by the National Practitioner Data Bank for restricted use under the provisions of Title IV Public Law 99-660, as amended, and 45 CFR Part 60. All information is confidential and may be used only for the purpose for which it is disclosed. For additional information or clarification, contact the reporting entity identified in Section A.

REPORTING ENTITY

Entity Name: JOHNS HOPKINS HOSPITAL
Address: MEDICAL STAFF ADMINISTRATION
600 NORTH WOLFE ST, BILLINGS ADMIN 326
City, State, ZIP: BALTIMORE, MD 21287-1824

Entity Internal Report Reference (e.g., claim number):

Name or Office: JEAN RUSSELL
Title or Department: CREDENTIALS MANAGER
Telephone: (410)614-4560

Type of Report: INITIAL REPORT

SUBJECT IDENTIFICATION INFORMATION (INDIVIDUAL)

Subject Name: DUKE, MARY ANN
Other Name(s) Used:
Gender: FEMALE
Date of Birth: 06/06/1961

Home Address:
City, State, ZIP:
Country:

Organization Name: THE JOHNS HOPKINS HOSPITAL
Work Address: WILMER EYE INSTITUTE
10753 FALLS ROAD SUITE 455
City, State, ZIP: LUTHERVILLE, MD 21093
Country:

Deceased: NO
Date of Death:

Social Security Numbers (SSN): 093-50-8753

Professional School(s) & Year(s) of Graduation: ALBANY MEDICAL COLLEGE 1985

Occupation/Field of Licensure (Code): PHYSICIAN (MD) (010)
State License Number, State of Licensure: D38796, MD
Other, as Specified:

CONFIDENTIAL DOCUMENT – FOR AUTHORIZED USE ONLY

National Practitioner Data Bank
Healthcare Integrity and Protection Data Bank
P.O. Box 10832
Chantilly, VA 20153-0832

DCN: 5500000035737645
Process Date: 12/01/2004

http://www.npdb-hipdb.com

Drug Enforcement Administration (DEA) Numbers: BD1945724

C. INFORMATION REPORTED

Type of Adverse Action: TITLE IV CLINICAL PRIVILEGES

Adverse Action Classification Code(s): SUMMARY OR EMERGENCY SUSPENSION OF CLINICAL PRIVILEG
Other, as Specified: (1632)

Date Action Was Taken: 11/30/2004
Date Action Became Effective: 11/30/2004
Length of Action: INDEFINITE
Years:
Months:
Days:
Description of Act(s) or Omission(s) or Other Reasons for Action Taken: SUMMARY SUSPENSION OF PRIVILEGES

Basis for Action: UNABLE TO PRACTICE SAFELY BY REASON OF ALCOHOL OR OT
SUBSTANCE ABUSE (F2)
Other, as Specified:

D. SUBJECT STATEMENT

If the subject identified in Section B of this report has submitted a statement, it appears in this section.

E. REPORT STATUS

An "X" indicates that the information in this report has been:

☐ Disputed by the Subject identified in Section B.

☐ Elevated for decision by the Secretary of the U.S. Department of Health and Human Services -- Pending.

☐ Reviewed by the Secretary of the U.S. Department of Health and Human Services, who has made the following comment concerning the report:

Date of Original Submission: 12/01/2004
Date of Most Recent Change: 12/01/2004

Even The Wilmer Eye Institute of Johns Hopkins waited until the next day to enter my suspended privileges

END OF REPORT

CONFIDENTIAL DOCUMENT – FOR AUTHORIZED USE ONLY

MEMORANDUM

TO: LAC; BSV

FROM: HKA

RE: Duke v. BPQA

DATE: December 6, 2004

I think it is virtually a certainty that I will still be in trial on December 15, 2004. Thus, I cannot cover this Hearing for Mary Ann Duke. Can one of the two of you handle this? We are charging her $250.00 an hour and she needs to get a retainer in for the Board Hearing.

Thanks.

End of Memo
KA:jmf

(I was dropped by my attorney two days before the BOARD hearing. See following page.)

LAW OFFICES
ARMSTRONG, DONOHUE, CEPPOS & VAUGHAN
CHARTERED
204 MONROE STREET, SUITE 101
ROCKVILLE, MARYLAND 20850

(301) 251-0440
FAX (301) 279-5929
www.adclawfirm.com

LARRY A. CEPPOS (Md., D.C.)
H. PATRICK DONOHUE (Md., D.C.)
H. KENNETH ARMSTRONG (Md., D.C.)
BENJAMIN S. VAUGHAN (Md., D.C.)
EDWARD S. HOROWITZ (Md., D.C.)
J. ERIC RHOADES (Md., D.C.)
SUSAN B. BOYCE (Md., D.C.)
ANDREW J. MARTER (Md., D.C.)

OF COUNSEL:
EDWARD A. GONSALVES (Md., D.C., Va.)

ROBERT C. MAYNARD (Md., Pa., Ohio, D.C.)
PENNY KAHN (Md., D.C.)
KAREN A. FERRETTI (Md., D.C.)
JAMES S. KNERR (Md., D.C.)
JEREMY R. KRUM (Md., D.C.)

EDWARD C. DONAHUE
(1923-1993)

December 13, 2004

Personal and Confidential

Mary Ann Duke, M.D.
10220 Democracy Blvd.
Potomac, MD 20854

Re: **Suburban Hospital/BPQA**

Dear Mary Ann:

This will confirm that you spoke with my Administrative Assistant, Jackie Foti, on December 13, 2004 advising that you are going to retain Mr. Bergman to represent you at the Hearing before the Maryland Board of Physicians on Wednesday, December 15, 2004. I will notify Ms. Cromer that I am no longer representing you in this matter.

Good luck to you.

Very truly yours,

Kenneth Armstrong

KA:jmf

cc: Pamela J. Cromer

STATE OF MARYLAND
DHMH Board of Physicians

Maryland Department of Health and Mental Hygiene
4201 Patterson Avenue • Baltimore, Maryland 21215-2299

Robert L. Ehrlich, Jr., Governor – Michael S. Steele, Lt. Governor – S. Anthony McCann, Secretary

December 20, 2004

Mary Ann Duke, M.D.
10220 Democracy Blvd.
Potomac Maryland 20854

Re: License # D38796
Case # 2004-0390

Dear Dr. Duke:

On November 30, 2004, the Maryland State Board of Physicians issued an Order summarily suspending your license to practice medicine in this State. A hearing was scheduled for December 15, 2004 to allow you to show cause why that Order should be vacated. The Administrative Prosecutor appeared before the Board at that time, but neither you nor your counsel appeared. The Board declined to grant a postponement request for your new counsel who simultaneously entered appearance and requested a postponement on the afternoon of December 14, 2004. No good cause having been shown at the hearing, the Board voted to continue your summary suspension. That summary suspension remains in effect, and you continue to have no authority to practice medicine in this State.

You are entitled to request a full evidentiary hearing before an Administrative Law Judge under COMAR 10.32.02.05. You must request this hearing in writing within ten days of the date of this letter if you wish to proceed in this manner. If you request such a hearing within ten days, a hearing will be scheduled within thirty days of your request.

Sincerely,

C. Irving Pinder, Jr.
Executive Director

C: Melvin G. Bergman, Esquire
Victoria H. Pepper, Assistant Attorney General, Administrative Prosecutor
Barbara K. Vona, Esquire, Chief, Compliance Administration
Dr. Yemisi Koya, Esquire, Manager, Compliance Investigations

410-764-4777 • Fax 410-358-2252 • Toll Free 1-800-492-6836
Web Site: www.mbp.state.md.us

(The BOARD would not extend my hearing date, despite needing new counsel at the last minute.)

STATE OF MARYLAND

DHMH Board of Physicians

Maryland Department of Health and Mental Hygiene
4201 Patterson Avenue • Baltimore, Maryland 21215-2299

Robert L. Ehrlich, Jr., Governor – Michael S. Steele, Lt. Governor – S. Anthony McCann, Secretary

January 27, 2005

Mary Ann Duke, M.D.
10220 Democracy Boulevard
Potomac, Maryland 20854

Re: Notice of Intent to Revoke Maryland Medical License and
Charges Under Maryland Medical Practice Act
MBP Case Number: 2004-0390

Dear Dr. Duke:

By the enclosed Notice of Intent to Revoke Maryland Medical License and Charges Under Maryland Medical Practice Act, the Maryland Board of Physicians (the "Board") notifies you of its intent to revoke your Maryland medical license pursuant to the Maryland Practice Act, Md. Health Occ. Code Ann. §14-101 *et seq.* Pursuant to §14-411 (g) of the Act, the enclosed Notice is a PUBLIC document.

The Board will sign the attached Order to Revoke Mary Ann Duke's Maryland Medical License unless you request a hearing, in writing, within ten (10) days from your receipt of this letter. The request should be addressed to:

> Barbara K. Vona
> Chief, Compliance Administration
> Maryland Board of Physicians
> Metro Executive Building, Third Floor
> 4201 Patterson Avenue
> Baltimore, Maryland 21215
> (410) 764-4780

If you request a hearing in this matter, an Administrative Law Judge will conduct the hearing in accordance with the Administrative Procedure Act, Md. State Gov't Code Ann. §10-201 *et seq.* The Administrative Law Judge will

(For the Botox)

410-764-4777 • Fax 410-358-2252 • Toll Free 1-800-492-6836
Web Site: www.mbp.state.md.us

submit proposed findings of fact and conclusions of law to the Board for the Board's consideration. If the proposed findings are adverse to you, you will be given an opportunity to file exceptions and present argument to the Board before the Board reaches a final decision.

Because your license to practice medicine in the State of Maryland is at issue, you are strongly urged to retain and be represented by an attorney at all stages of the procedure. If you choose to retain counsel, please be advised that in order to represent you at any proceeding in this case, your attorney must either be admitted to the Maryland Bar or specially admitted to practice law in Maryland under Rule 14 of the Rules Governing Admission to the Bar found in Volume II of the Maryland Rules of Procedure.

If you or your attorney has any questions regarding this matter, please contact Victoria H. Pepper, Assistant Attorney General, at (410) 767-1873.

Sincerely,

C. Irving Pinder, Jr.
Executive Director
Maryland Board of Physicians

Enclosures – Notice of Intent to Revoke Maryland Medical License and Charges Under Maryland Medical Practice Act

(Proposed) Order to Revoke Mary Ann Duke's Maryland Medical License

cc: Timothy J. Paulus, Deputy Counsel
Thomas W. Keech, Board Counsel
Victoria H. Pepper, Assistant Attorney General
Barbara K. Vona, Chief, Compliance Administration
Pamela Cromer, Compliance Analyst

Shelly G. Belson, M.D.
P.O. Box 2223
Rockville, MD 20847-2223

January 31, 2005

SENT BY CERTIFIED AND REGULAR MAIL

Mary Ann Duke, M.D.
10220 Democracy Blvd
Potomac, MD 20854

Dear Dr. Duke,

I was contacted today by the Maryland Board of Physicians in connection with the services that I provided to your patients at your office on December 6 and 8, 2004.

The Board informed me that your medical license had been suspended and that therefore your office should not bill or accept payment for any services rendered during the suspension period, including the two dates mentioned above.

The Board requested that I write you this letter and suggested I indicate to you that you are not authorized to use my provider numbers in the billing from your office and to please inform me if you have already done so.

Yours truly,

Shelly G. Belson

Shelly G. Belson, M.D.

I sign this Consent Order after having an opportunity to consult with counsel, voluntarily and without reservation, and I fully understand and comprehend the language, meaning and terms of the Consent Order.

_5/24/05_
Date

Mary Ann Duke
Mary Ann Duke, M.D.
Respondent

STATE OF MARYLAND
CITY/COUNTY OF Prince Georges

I HEREBY CERTIFY that on this _24th_ day of May 2005, before me, a Notary Public of the foregoing State and City/County personally appeared Mary Ann Duke, M.D., License Number D38796, and made oath in due form of law that signing the foregoing Consent Order was her <u>voluntary act</u> and deed.

AS WITNESSETH my hand and notarial seal.

Joanne C. Lilly
Notary Public

[Notary Seal: JOANNE CHRISTINE LILLY, NOTARY PUBLIC, PRINCE GEORGE'S CO., MD]
Comm. exp. Dec. 23, 2007

("Voluntary" — my eye!! I was railroaded!!!)

STATE OF MARYLAND

DHMH Board of Physicians

Maryland Department of Health and Mental Hygiene
4201 Patterson Avenue • Baltimore, Maryland 21215-2222

Robert L. Ehrlich, Jr., Governor – Michael S. Steele, Lt. Governor – S. Anthony McCann, Secretary

August 4, 2005

Mary Ann Duke, M.D.
10220 Democracy Boulevard
Potomac, Maryland 20854

Serve on:
Melvin Bergman, Esquire
Maryland Trade Center I
7500 Greenway Center
Suite 600
Greenbelt, Maryland 20770

(I'm being crucified while in a 14 week rehab.)

Re: License # D38796
Case Number: 2004-0390

Dear Dr. Duke:

    Enclosed is a Show Cause Order. The Board orders you to appear before the Board on **Wednesday, August 24, 2005 at 4:00 p.m. at 4201 Patterson Ave., Baltimore, Maryland 21215**, to show cause why the Board should not impose other disciplinary sanctions that it deems appropriate, including the permanent revocation of your license under the Board's May 25, 2005 Consent Order. The enclosed Show Cause Order also requires you to bring certain documents to the Show Cause Hearing.

    Because your right to practice medicine in the State of Maryland is at issue, you may retain and be represented by an attorney at the Show Cause hearing. If you choose to retain counsel, please be advised that in order to represent you before the Board, your attorney must be either admitted to the Maryland bar or specially admitted to practice law under Rule 14 of the rules governing admission to the bar found in Volume II of the Maryland Rules of Procedure.

    At the show cause hearing scheduled for August 24, 2005, an Assistant Attorney General will present the State's argument in support of the Show Cause Order. Following the State's presentation, you will have the opportunity to address the Board before its final deliberations on the matter. Each side will have twenty (20) minutes to address the Board. Neither you nor your attorney are required to appear at the Board on August 24, 2005. Be advised, however, that the Board intends to make a decision on that day whether further discipline should be imposed on your medical license.

410-764-4777 • Fax 410-358-2252 • Toll Free 1-800-492-6836
Web Site: www.mbp.state.md.us

Mary Ann Duke, M.D.
Re: License Number: D38796; Case Number: 2004-0390
Page 2

If you appear at the Board on August 24, 2005, bring with you any of the following in your possession:

1. all controlled dangerous substances in your possession;

2. all prescribed substances in your possession other than substances which have been prescribed for you by a licensed physician;

3. all Medical Assistance prescription forms in your possession;

4. all prescription forms and pads in your possession;

5. any and all prescription pads in your possession and on which his name and DEA number are imprinted.

The administrative prosecutor in this case against you is Victoria H. Pepper, Assistant Attorney General. If you have any questions about the Show Cause Hearing scheduled before the Board on August 24, 2005, please contact Ms. Pepper at (410) 767-1873.

Sincerely yours,

C. Irving Pinder, Jr., Executive Director
Maryland Board of Physicians

cc: Victoria H. Pepper, Assistant Attorney General, Administrative Prosecutor
Thomas W. Keech, Assistant Attorney General, Counsel to the Board

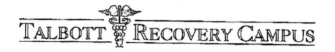

March 1, 2007

Mary Ann Duke, M.D.
Fax # 301-983-0030

Dear Dr. Duke:

Below is the information you requested extracted from the letter dated November 8, 2005:

"Dr. Duke had a total of 22 urine drug screens obtained randomly throughout her stay at Talbott Recovery Campus, including initial chain of custody urine drug screen. Her initial two urine drug screens were positive for Oxazepam, which is a medication metabolite used while at Anchor Hospital for detox and this was expected result. All remaining urine drug screens were negative for all substances tested. Dr. Duke had a struggle with observed urine drug screens which are a part of requirement at Talbott Recovery Campus. She was sent to a nephrologist and it was determined that she had Shy Bladder. She was able to successfully catheterize herself while being observed and her urine drug screens were negative for all substances tested. She did use prophylaxis Bactrim DS following each self cath. She was fully cooperative with this requirement though it was certainly stressful for her. There were no indications of any urinary tract infections secondary to this process."

Sincerely,

George M. MacNabb, M.D.
Diplomate, American Board of Internal Medicine
Certified, American Society of Addiction Medicine

GMM:sr

CONFIDENTIAL

800.445.4232 toll free   770.994.0185 phone   770.994.2024 fax
5448 Yorktowne Drive   Atlanta, Georgia 30349
www.talbottcampus.com

<u>Driver's license</u> granted 12/15/2005 while incarcerated for drunk driving arrest<u>s</u>, an <u>un</u>restricted driver's license

No malpractice suits in over 14 years of solo private practice in Potomac, yet <u>medical license</u> suspended 20 days after <u>1</u> DUI arrest 11/30/04.

Dear Mr. Pinder,

I am e-mailing you via the e-mail address of your secretary as per your request. I am also faxing this to you and sending it certified mail. In our modern days of technology, aren't you sometimes amazed that people say they still never received anything? I am...so just want to be sure you get this message.

As it is a matter of public record, and I was told by the Dept. Of Health and Mental Hygiene to contact you directly, and you will honor my request, I will be succinct and number my requests. Please send your respose to me at your earliest convenience via my e-mail, or however is easiest for you. This is a matter of the highest importance to me and my four childrens' lives.

I need the total number of revocations, (suspensions, voluntary resignations, etc... are not vital to me at this time), in the decade of 1990-2000 in the State of Maryland of Medical Licenses only. Please include the number of men and the number of women and why the licenses were revoked.

Please specify exactly the number of revocations also that did not allow the doctor to reapply for <u>five years,</u> including how many of those five year revocations were for men and for women and for what reason(s).

Lastly, please send to me the number of revocations from 2000-present. Please again specify how many were for women and how many were for men and for what reason(s). Please include the number of revocations from 2000-present that also had a five year time period on them before allowing reapplication.

Thank you so very much for your timely response. I am happy to pay whatever copying/research/mailing fees the acquisition of this information incurs.

Thank you again, sincerely yours,

Mary Ann Duke, M.D.

STATE OF MARYLAND

DHMH   Board of Physicians

Maryland Department of Health and Mental Hygiene
4201 Patterson Avenue • Baltimore, Maryland 21215-2299

Martin O'Malley, Governor – Anthony G. Brown, Lt. Governor – John M. Colmers, Secretary

February 22, 2007

Mary Ann Duke, M.D.
10220 Democracy Boulevard
Potomac, MD 20854

    Pursuant to the Maryland Public Information Act (PIA), Md. Code Ann., State Government ("SG"), §10-611 et.seq., I am responding to your emails to Mr. Pinder regarding actions taken by the Board revoking licenses of physicians.

    Attached please find a listing of all physicians whose licenses were revoked at any time since 1990. The physician license number and date of the order are also included. I have verified that all of the orders are available online at www.mbp.state.md.us. However, if you prefer, we can make copies of all of the orders and ship them to you. The current charge for copies is 50¢ per page plus $25 per hour of employee time beyond 2 hours. The regulations governing these changes can be found at Code of Maryland Regulations 10.01.08.04.

    All public information related to these revocation actions is included in the order. The Board does not keep information about the gender of its licensees; however, you may be able to determine gender from the names. By reviewing each order, you will be able to determine which meet the various other specifications included in your original email.

    I can be reached at 410-764-5930 if you have any questions about this response. If you wish to receive paper copies of the orders, please let me know so that I can notify you of the total estimated cost.

Sincerely,

Karen R. Wulff
Public Policy Analyst

[handwritten notes:] Practitioner profile — search by license number at bottom of profile → open the order & print.

Toll Free 1-800-492-6836 • 410-764-4777 • Fax 410-358-2252
Web Site: www.mbp.state.md.us

American Board of Ophthalmology

Founded in 1916

Edward G. Buckley, M.D., Chair
Durham, NC

Please address all communications to
John G. Clarkson, M.D., Executive Director
AMERICAN BOARD OF OPHTHALMOLOGY
111 PRESIDENTIAL BOULEVARD, SUITE 241
BALA CYNWYD, PENNSYLVANIA 19004-1075
(610) 664-1175   FAX (610) 664-6503   www.abop.org

James S. Tiedeman, M.D., Vice-Chair
Charlottesville, VA

June 6, 2007

PERSONAL AND CONFIDENTIAL

Mary Ann Duke, M.D.
10220 Democracy Blvd.
Potomac, MD 20854

Dear Doctor Duke:

Pursuant to prior notice to you, the Hearing Committee of the American Board of Ophthalmology held a hearing on May 24, 2007. This hearing was in accordance with Rule 9.2 of the Board's Rules and Regulations, regarding the revocations of your licenses to practice medicine in the states of New York and Maryland. Based on all of the evidence in this matter, the Hearing Committee made the following finding and recommendation:

"1. The Hearing Committee found, based on the evidence before it, that the licenses of Dr. Duke, a Diplomate of the American Board of Ophthalmology, ceased to be valid and unrestricted in the states of Maryland and New York and that, therefore, she is in violation of Rule 9.1.4."

"2. In view of the foregoing finding, the Hearing Committee recommended that, in accordance with Rule 9.3(a) of the Rules and Regulations of the American Board of Ophthalmology, the certificate issued by the American Board of Ophthalmology to Dr. Duke should be revoked."

Wallace L. M. Alward, M.D., Iowa City, IA
Suzanne T. Anderson, M.B.A., Issaquah, WA
Edward G. Buckley, M.D., Durham, NC
John G. Clarkson, M.D., Miami, FL
Janet L. Davis, M.D., Miami, FL
Martha J. Farber, M.D., Albany, NY
Mark J. Mannis, M.D., Sacramento, CA

David M. Meisler, M.D., Cleveland, OH
Marilyn B. Mets, M.D., Chicago, IL
James C. Orcutt, M.D., Seattle, WA
David W. Parke II, M.D., Oklahoma City, OK
Ivan R. Schwab, M.D., Sacramento, CA
Donald N. Schwartz, M.D., Long Beach, CA
Gregory L. Skuta, M.D., Oklahoma City, OK

James S. Tiedeman, M.D., Charlottesville, VA
David T. Tse, M.D., Miami, FL
Martin Wand, M.D., Farmington, CT
David J. Wilson, M.D., Portland, OR

Mary R. Ladden, Administrator

Founding Member Board of the American Board of Medical Specialties (ABMS)

SENDER: COMPLETE THIS SECTION

- Complete items 1, 2, and 3. Also complete item 4 if Restricted Delivery is desired.
- Print your name and address on the reverse so that we can return the card to you.
- Attach this card to the back of the mailpiece, or on the front if space permits.

1. Article Addressed to:

MARYLAND STATE BOARD OF PHYSICIANS
4201 PATTERSON AVENUE
BALTIMORE MD 21215

265760-V

2. Article Number (Transfer from service label): 7003 3110 0003 4401 5022

PS Form 3811, February 2004 — Domestic Return Receipt — 102595-02-M-1540

COMPLETE THIS SECTION ON DELIVERY

A. Signature: X /s/ ___ ☑ Agent ☐ Addressee
B. Received by (Printed Name): ___ C. Date of Delivery: 1-3-08
D. Is delivery address different from item 1? ☐ Yes ☐ No
If YES, enter delivery address below:

Service Type:
☐ Certified Mail ☐ Express Mail
☐ Registered ☑ Return Receipt for Merchandise
☐ Insured Mail ☐ C.O.D.

4. Restricted Delivery? (Extra Fee) ☐ Yes

Why did the BOARD want my file in January, 2008?

3/31/08

Dear Maryland Board of Physicians:
To M. Linny Pinder,

Enclosed is my completed reinstatement application, and another copy of the letter I mailed previously.

Ten remaining CME credits will be forwarded shortly.

If there is anything further requested by the Board, please do not hesitate to contact me.

Sincerely,
Mary Ann Dute

baltimoresun.com/news/local/bal-te.md.slayings01apr01,0,7738034.story

ltimoresun.com

her admits he drowned kids

k Castillo tells police he killed 3 children over divorce, custody battle

nnie Linskey and Nick Madigan

reporters

1, 2008

Castillo of Rockville walked with his three young
ren Saturday afternoon through Baltimore's Inner
or, where tourists congregate along the city's waterfront
enade.

t 5 p.m., he checked into the Marriott Hotel near
den Yards and took his children into Room 1060, a top-
room with two beds.

our later, one by one, Castillo drowned his children in
athtub, police said. When he was done, he laid their tiny,
d bodies on one bed: Anthony, 6, Austin, 4, and Athena,

he swallowed 100 Motrin pills and cut himself in the neck with a steak knife in an apparent
de attempt, police said. He woke up about 1 p.m. Sunday, after sleeping for hours - his dead
ren in the same room - and called the front desk, police said, to report what he had done.

l security alerted police and paramedics and, using a master key, opened the door.

ow what I did was bad," Castillo told the medics who arrived first, according to police charging
rs filed with the court. "I did it. I drown the kids last night around 6 p.m."

erday, police charged Castillo with three counts of first-degree murder and a dozen related
ges, including child abuse and assault. He was ordered held without bail and is scheduled to have
aring in District Court today.

e Saturday night, his estranged wife, Dr. Amy Castillo of Silver Spring, had been calling
tgomery County police, desperately trying to find her children while fearing that he had followed
ugh on his threats.

erday, Amy Castillo, a pediatrician with Kaiser Permanente's Mid-Atlantic region, was in her home on Waterford Road.

A family friend, Cheryl Wharton, read a brief statement to reporters: "Amy Castillo asks for your continued prayers during this unspeakably difficult time. She is surrounded by family and friends and is coping as well as can be expected. We ask that members of the press respect Amy's privacy as she bears this solitary cross."

Beginning at 10:30 Saturday night, she had called Montgomery County police to report that her husband, who according to court documents has a history of mental problems, was late dropping off the children. But police told her that they could not begin a search because Mark Castillo had the legal right to be with them and he had made no new specific threats.

"Statements like that that would have ramped this investigation up were not made to police," said Lt. Paul Sparks, a spokesman for the Montgomery County Police Department. He said Mark Castillo's tardiness would not constitute a criminal act until the children were missing for 48 hours.

Still, Sparks said, county police are reviewing how they handled Amy Castillo's calls.

"We are looking at our own response and what could have or should have been done that would have prevented this tragedy," Sparks said.

Baltimore police said yesterday in court papers that Mark Castillo had waived his right against self-incrimination and gave a taped confession to homicide detectives. He told them that the motive stemmed from a divorce and custody battle he was having with his wife, according to the charging document written by Detective Robert Ross of the homicide unit.

The mayor and the police commissioner called a news conference yesterday to discuss the killings.

"Cases like this one are difficult," said Police Commissioner Frederick H. Bealefeld III. "They have an incredible emotional impact on everyone involved."

Added Mayor Sheila Dixon: "This tragedy makes one wonder and question why someone would do such an act. We will be asking ourselves why, why could someone do this to three innocent young children?"

Mark Castillo, who had once lived in a van, recently rented a room from a Spanish-speaking family on Schuylkill Road in Rockville.

Yesterday, the owner, Maria Galvis, said she often saw the children when they visited with their father, whom she called "Mr. Mark."

"I can still see the children, and hear their voices," Galvis, a native of Colombia, said in Spanish. "Whatever Mr. Mark did, I still respect him. It's not up to us to judge him, because only God knows what went on in his heart at that moment."

Galvis described her tenant as "very educated, very proper and, above all, an excellent father." She said that whenever the children visited - usually twice a week - he made sure that they ate nutritious and that the floor on which they played was clean.

children were his eyes," Galvis said. "He adored them. It's extremely hard for me to believe what
ened."

Castillo rarely spoke about his problems with his wife, Galvis said, although he made clear to
hat he wanted to see the children more often and that the custody battle was arduous. Even then,
aid, he never spoke negatively about his wife.

said the police had been to her house twice, on Saturday and on Sunday, looking for Mark
illo and the children after they were reported missing. "Those children are three innocent angels,
ow we have to pray for strength for these parents," Galvis said.

family problems ran deep.

Amy Castillo's frequent objections during a long and bitter divorce and custody fight, Mark
illo had visitation rights with the children. On Saturday, he was permitted to be with them but was
osed to return them to her home by 8:30 p.m.

n he did not return, Amy Castillo began calling the Montgomery County police. She made her
call about 10:30 p.m., said Sparks, the police spokesman. A half-hour later, she called again and
e went to the Rockville home where Mark Castillo had rented a room.

re were people there," Sparks said. "Police talked to them and determined that he and the children
not there."

mother called police again at 9 a.m. Sunday and demanded to see an officer, who came and took a
rt. She tried reaching her husband on his cell phone but failed. Police also tried to call his cell
e, but calls went straight to voice mail, Sparks said.

e.linskey@baltsun.com nick.madigan@baltsun.com

yright © 2008, The Baltimore Sun

washingtonpost.com

3 Children Found Slain in Baltimore Hotel Room

Silver Spring Father Is in Police Custody; He Was Involved in Custody Dispute

By Daniel de Vise and Elissa Silverman
Washington Post Staff Writers
Monday, March 31, 2008; B01

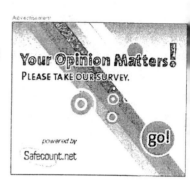

Three young children from Montgomery County were found slain in a hotel room in Baltimore yesterday, shortly after their father called the front desk to report that he had killed them, Baltimore police said.

The father, Mark Castillo, 41, of Silver Spring, was in police custody at a Baltimore hospital last night. Court records available online show that he was involved in divorce and child custody proceedings with the children's mother, Amy A. Castillo, 42, a pediatrician in suburban Maryland.

The children were identified as Anthony, 6; Austin, 4; and Athena, 2. They apparently lived in the 400 block of Waterford Road in Silver Spring with their mother.

The children, who had been seen playing at home Friday, were found in a top-floor room of a hotel near Camden Yards and the Inner Harbor.

Baltimore police spokesman Sterling Clifford said autopsies will be conducted to determine the cause of the deaths.

"We're looking at either suffocation or strangulation or possibly drowning," he said.

Police said the slayings might be linked to the custody dispute.

"It kind of looks that way," Clifford said, "but I'm just not sure." He said last night that the father had superficial cuts that "appeared to be self-inflicted."

"This is just a horrible tragedy," said Joe Vanderwalde, the mother's supervisor in the Kaiser Permanente system. "It is the worst thing I've ever heard of."

Police said the father and the children got a room Saturday in the Baltimore Marriott Inner Harbor at Camden Yards.

According to police, shortly after 1 p.m. yesterday, a call was received at the hotel's front desk from someone who said that he had killed his family and was about to kill himself.

Hotel security guards went to the Castillo family's 10th-floor room, according to police, and found the man and the bodies of the children.

erwalde, pediatrics service chief for the Mid-Atlantic Kaiser Permanente Medical Group, said hildren's mother had "tried so hard to do what she could for her children."

tried to "keep them away" from Mark Castillo, Vanderwalde said. But he said the father fought ustody.

06, according to court records, Amy Castillo was granted temporary sole custody on an gency motion, but Mark Castillo was granted visitation rights shortly afterward. At least twice ear, motions that would have withheld visitation rights were denied. At one point, according to ecords, Amy Castillo was fined for refusing visitation rights.

her time, according to the records, a court ordered a mental health examination for him.

couple had apparently moved to Waterford Road at least four years ago, a neighbor said, and they ed happy at first.

a Habesch, one neighbor, said she had attended parties at their home. She said Castillo spoke nly of his wife and told of the couple's plans to expand their family, which then included two ren.

last two years, I haven't seen him around," Habesch said.

esch said she had seen police come to the home.

h Lamirande, another neighbor, said he had seen the police called "at least a half-dozen times," ding once within the past week.

urrent address for the father was available. An effort to reach a lawyer who represented him in the rce proceedings was unsuccessful.

children's mother worked for several years as a pediatrician at the Kaiser Permanente facility on necticut Avenue in Kensington. Recently, she shifted her practice to a Kaiser facility in Largo, derwalde said.

has been a valued member of our department, and the whole department is mourning her edy," he said. "We will try to support her for whatever she needs."

aid he understood that the physician and Mark Castillo had not lived together for several years.

tgomery police are assisting in the investigation.

researcher Rena Kirsch contributed to this report.

all comments that have been posted about this article.

st a Comment

w all comments that have been posted about this article.

washingtonpost.com

Man Is Denied Bail in Deaths Of 3 Children
Judge Orders Suicide Evaluation After Father's Behavior Detailed

By Raymond McCaffrey and Dan Morse
Washington Post Staff Writers
Wednesday, April 2, 2008; B06

BALTIMORE, April 1 -- The Montgomery County man accused of drowning his three young children in the bathtub of a Baltimore hotel room was denied bail Tuesday and remained at a jail hospital after a court hearing during which officials said he was a suicide risk.

District Court Judge Nathan Braverman granted the prosecution's request that Mark Castillo, 41, be evaluated as a potential suicide risk and advised his public defender that Castillo could face the death penalty for charges that include three counts of first-degree murder in the deaths of Anthony, 6, Austin, 4, and Athena, 3.

An agent from the Maryland corrections system told the judge about suicidal behavior by Castillo in 2006, last year and again Saturday night after he allegedly killed his children in the hotel.

Castillo was not in the courtroom, having waived his right to appear at the bail hearing at the Baltimore Central Booking and Intake Center.

Braverman scheduled an April 29 preliminary hearing for the case, which resulted from the type of custody battle that experts say is becoming far too familiar.

Public defender Natasha Dartigue Moody argued that bail should be set because Castillo had no criminal convictions and no intention of avoiding prosecution. Moody portrayed a man who was a loving stay-at-home father before his separation from his wife.

But prosecutors said Castillo represented "a significant risk to public safety," said Margaret Burns, a spokeswoman for the Baltimore state's attorney's office. Burns said prosecutors had not decided whether to seek the death penalty against Castillo.

Baltimore Police Detective Donny Moses said an autopsy was pending on the bodies of the children, although police have ruled their deaths a result of drowning, based on statements from Castillo and evidence at the scene.

Police say Castillo told them that he submerged the bodies of his sons and daughter in the tub one by one, then placed them, naked, in a bed. He said he then swallowed 100 Motrin tablets and stabbed himself in the neck repeatedly with a steak knife before drifting into unconsciousness, police said. Castillo awoke 19 hours later and realized that he had botched his suicide, police said Tuesday. He nvestigators that he killed the children 2 1/2 hours before the deadline to return them to his ged wife's Silver Spring home.

Castillo, 42, a pediatrician, had fought in court to limit her children's contact with their father, has a history of mental problems. The legal fight between the couple stretched to July 2006. Amy llo was granted a limited divorce, according to a Feb. 19 docket entry. But that occurred after Castillo filed for a limited divorce, in which a couple can still call themselves husband and wife re living apart.

ustody hearing last summer in Montgomery County Circuit Court, Mark Castillo frustrated Michael Mason, who said he thought Castillo was having trouble controlling his anger during earing.

have limited ability to control yourself," Mason told Castillo. "You're very excited. You talk fast. You get very, very upset. Your therapist even talks about it. You have difficulties in olling your anger. . . . I'm trying to decide whether or not it is in the best interest of the children, is what my concern is. Not you, not her. . . . But you are just totally blind to that; you can't see

Mason also said a therapist had been working with Mark Castillo for six months. At the hearing, n told Amy Castillo that the therapist "suggests that he has difficulties for which he is still ng treatment and they do impact on some areas of his life." But, Mason said, "the difficulties do ose any threat or danger to the children."

xpert in killings of children, Richard J. Gelles, said he is sympathetic to the challenges faced by s and psychologists involved in such cases.

chiatrists can't predict the ones who do this without making a lot of false positives," said Gelles, of the University of Pennsylvania School of Social Policy and Practice, whose books include Book of David: How Preserving Families Can Cost Children's Lives."

trouble is that hindsight is perfect," Gelles said. He added that a lot of child custody fights ng before judges turn nasty, with futures difficult to predict.

Castillos had lived together in a brick split-level house from 2001. On Tuesday, cars packed the way of the home. A sign posted on the door asked for respect for Amy Castillo's privacy.

writer Daniel de Vise contributed to this report. Morse and de Vise reported from Montgomery ty.

all comments that have been posted about this article.

t a Comment

all comments that have been posted about this article.

ments that include profanity or personal attacks or other inappropriate comments or material will be removed from the site. Additionally, entries that unsigned or contain "signatures" by someone other than the actual author will be removed. Finally, we will take steps to block users who violate any r posting standards, terms of use or privacy policies or any other policies governing this site. Please review the full rules governing commentaries

You must be logged in to leave a comment. Login | Register

and discussions. You are fully responsible for the content that you post.

© 2008 The Washington Post Company

Ads by Google

10 Rules to Cut Belly Fat
Lose 9 lbs every 11 Days with these 10 Idiot Proof Secrets of Fat Loss.
www.FatLoss4Idiots.com

Spyware Removal Download
Free Spyware & Trojan scan. Winner of Best Anti-Spyware. Rated 5 Stars
www.pctools.com

①   June, 15/1989

Dr. Richard S. Smith

This short letter I am writing is a Commendation and a Recommendation for Dr. Mary Ann Duke.

I will give you a short synopsis of myself. I am an out-patient of the V.A. and have been since - Dec-1981 when I had my larynx removed (cancer) I am sixty seven (67) and have been wearing glasses sixty (60) of my sixty seven (67) years. In the past year, - I developed cataracts in my left eye. - because my right eye is highly near-sighted three (3) previous residents (which I can name if I had to) cancelled my cataract surgery.

In the past sixty years (60) when I awoke in the morning I would reach for my glasses, now thanks to Dr. Duke, I reach for my slippers instead.

Dr. Smith - thank you for someone special like - Dr. Duke

2

Please think of all the people she (Dr. Duke) can help the way she has helped me.
Thanking you in advance for taking the time to read this letter.

Raymond P. Couillahan
15 Wilson Ave
Town of Colonie
Albany, N.Y. -12205

FAMILY LAW § 9-101

TITLE 9.

CHILD CUSTODY AND VISITATION.

Subtitle 1. In General.

Sec.
9-101. Denial of custody or visitation on basis of likely abuse or neglect.
9-101.1. Abuse against certain individuals.
9-101.2. Parent convicted of murder of certain persons.
9-102. Petition by grandparents for visitation.
9-103. Petition by child to change custody.
9-104. Access to medical, dental, and educational records by noncustodial parent.
9-105. Unjustifiable denial or interference with visitation granted by order.
9-106. Notification prior to relocation of child.

Subtitle 2. Maryland Uniform Child Custody Jurisdiction Act.

9-201 to 9-224. [Repealed].

Subtitle 3. Removal of Child From State; Child Abduction.

9-301. Definitions.

Sec.
(a) In general.
(b) Lawful custodian.
(c) Relative.
9-302. Jurisdiction over custody and visitation.
9-303. Conflict as to lawful custodian.
9-304. Prohibited acts — In this State.
9-305. Prohibited acts — Outside of this State.
9-306. Clear and present danger to child.
9-307. Penalties.

Subtitle 4. Missing Children.

9-401. Definitions.
(a) In general.
(b) Law enforcement agency.
(c) Missing child.
9-402. Determinations of law enforcement agency upon receipt of report.
9-403. Clearinghouse for Missing Children; voluntary fingerprinting programs; advisory council.

Subtitle 1. In General.

§ 9-101. Denial of custody or visitation on basis of likely abuse or neglect.

(a) *Determination by court.* — In any custody or visitation proceeding, if the court has reasonable grounds to believe that a child has been abused or neglected by a party to the proceeding, the court shall determine whether abuse or neglect is likely to occur if custody or visitation rights are granted to the party.

(b) *Specific finding required.* — Unless the court specifically finds that there is no likelihood of further child abuse or neglect by the party, the court shall deny custody or visitation rights to that party, except that the court may approve a supervised visitation arrangement that assures the safety and the physiological, psychological, and emotional well-being of the child. (1984, ch. 529, § 2; 1985, ch. 659; 2006, ch. 112.)

Effect of amendments. — Chapter 112, Acts 2006, effective October 1, 2006, re-enacted this section without change.

Maryland Law Review. — For article, "Survey of Developments in Maryland Law, 1984-85," see 45 Md. L. Rev. 782 (1986).

University of Baltimore Law Review. — For article concerning the hearsay exception for child abuse victims, see 17 U. Balt. L. Rev. 1 (1987).

University of Baltimore Law Forum. — Child Custody and Visitation in Maryland: In the Best Interests of the Child, see 26 U. Balt. Law Forum 3 (1995).

Visitation rights not precluded by finding of sexual abuse. — A finding that noncustodial parent sexually abused child does not preclude all visitation rights to that parent. Arnold v. Naughton, 61 Md. App. 427, 486 A.2d 1204, cert. denied, 303 Md. 295, 493 A.2d 349 (1985).

Denial of visitation rights to natural parents. — Where the rights of natural parents have been terminated and a child has been

451

Creative Writing

M aster

O utstading

T errific

H appy

E xcellent

R ight

My Mom's the greatest because....
she took me to St. Ith-
ams 7 times.

(Oh, my dear baby boy,
I think it was 3 or 4, not 7.
I hope to take my angels from
heaven back there some day soon.